VIRGINIA WOOLF

Agatha Christie: The Woman and Her Mysteries, 1990

Mary Baker Eddy, 1998

*Nightingales: The Extraordinary Upbringing and
Curious Life of Miss Florence Nightingale*, 2004

We Two: Victoria and Albert: Rulers, Partners, Rivals, 2009

Becoming Colette (novel-biography), 2014

VIRGINIA WOOLF

AND
THE WOMEN
WHO SHAPED
HER WORLD

&

Gillian Gill

Houghton Mifflin Harcourt

Boston   New York   2019

For information about permission to reproduce selections from this book,
write to trade.permissions@hmhco.com or to Permissions,
Houghton Mifflin Harcourt Publishing Company,
3 Park Avenue, 19th Floor, New York, New York 10016.

hmhbooks.com

Library of Congress Cataloging-in-Publication Data
Names: Gill, Gillian, author.
Title: Virginia Woolf : and the women who shaped her world / Gillian Gill.
Description: Boston : Houghton Mifflin Harcourt, 2019.
Identifiers: LCCN 2019012511 (print) | LCCN 2019019205 (ebook) |
ISBN 9781328694485 (ebook) | ISBN 9781328683953 (hardcover)
Subjects: LCSH: Woolf, Virginia, 1882–1941 — Friends and associates. |
Woolf, Virginia, 1882–1941 — Family.
Classification: LCC PR6045.072 (ebook) | LCC PR6045.072 Z6439 2019 (print) |
DDC 823/.912 [B] — dc23
LC record available at https://lccn.loc.gov/2019012511

Book design by Greta Sibley

Printed in the United States of America
DOC 10 9 8 7 6 5 4 3 2 1

For Stuart

Women alone stir my imagination.

— *Virginia Woolf*

CONTENTS

Introduction   xi

PART I

The Pattle Legacy

1. Virginia Woolf's Indian Ancestresses —
   Thérèse de l'Etang and Adeline Pattle   3
2. Pattledom   18
3. High Society   40

PART II

*Virginia Woolf and the Thackerays — A Legacy of Literature,
Money, and Madness*

4. Finders Keepers   55
5. William and Isabella   66
6. Anny and Minny   80
7. Virginia Woolf's Mad, Bad Sister   104

PART III

The Angels of Hyde Park Gate

8. Julia Prinsep Jackson Duckworth Stephen   127
9. Stella Duckworth Hills   161
10. A Close Conspiracy   188

PART IV

Old Bloomsbury

11. From Cambridge to Bloomsbury   207
12. The Landmark Year   230
13. The Great Betrayal   245

PART V

A Tale of Two Sisters

14. Vanessa's Way, Part 1   263
15. Virginia's Way, Part 1   286
16. Vanessa's Way, Part 2   300
17. Virginia's Way, Part 2   330

Epilogue: The Bell Children and Their Aunt   348

Acknowledgments   353

Selected Bibliography   356

Notes   360

Photo Credits   398

Index   399

INTRODUCTION

VIRGINIA WOOLF matters to us. She speaks to our lives, inspires our polemic, lodges in our collective memory, and shapes our prose. For an English man who lived, as Woolf did, before most of us in today's world were born, that would be no small trick. For an early-twentieth-century English woman it is perhaps unique.

Woolf had an original mind, lived at an important point in history, read everything she could put her hand on, and labored every day, well or ill, mad or sane, to write novels, meet her book review deadlines, scrawl a pile of letters, work up bits of dialogue and thumbnail sketches, and record in her diary the things her mind was busy with. You learn to forge by hammering, goes the old French saying, and as she scribbled and typed, Woolf was forging a style. Elegantly personal. Unpretentiously authoritative. Chattily erudite. Eminently readable. Today, the name Virginia Woolf is a meme, and she is even more read, more quoted, and more influential than she was in her lifetime.

A writer by profession, she published a great deal of what she wrote and kept even more. Her family had long had a sense of history and understood that what was not written down might almost not have existed. The Stephens and Pattles, among Woolf's paternal and maternal ancestors, understood the value of old pieces of paper covered in handwriting. By keeping letters and diaries, they knew they stood a chance of becoming part of English social history.

In today's America you can become famous just by working hard at being famous, and girls and women can compete in the new fame game with boys and men, but this is all very new. Before the twentieth century, the handful of women whose names entered the historical record were empresses, queens, or aristocrats — Catherine the Great, Elizabeth I, Sarah, Duchess of Marlborough — or else the wives, mothers, sisters, daughters, and mistresses of famous men. We know about Milton's daughter and Stalin's, the mistresses of Horatio Nelson and Charles Dickens, Wordsworth's sister and Freud's sister-in-law, Marcel Proust's mother, and the wives of James Joyce or D. H. Lawrence or Vladimir Nabokov or Winston Churchill or — well, the list goes on. Adeline Virginia Stephen Woolf, in contrast, was solidly middle-class; and her father, Leslie Stephen, and her husband, Leonard Woolf, both much published writers in their day, are now read because they were related to her.

Being born in the England of Queen Victoria was a key to Woolf's success as a writer. By 1882, the year of Woolf's birth, England had produced more professional women writers — novelists, poets, essayists, travel writers, biographers, and journalists — than any other country, and in the nineteenth century there was an explosion of female literary talent in the United Kingdom. Jane Austen, Charlotte Brontë, and George Eliot are now high on our list of top English writers of all time, and many of us would argue fiercely that Mary Wollstonecraft, Mary Shelley, Elizabeth Gaskell, Elizabeth Barrett Browning, Emily Brontë, Anne Brontë, Christina Rossetti — I could go on — should be on everyone's "must-read" list.

Rare in her generation, Virginia Woolf valued the contribution of women to the English literary tradition as much as we do today. From childhood she immersed herself in the work of women writers of the past, and as a prolific reviewer and essayist she liked to choose books that allowed women's voices to be heard. She saw herself as a link in a chain of women writers, and this pride in tradition was a spur to her authorial ambitions. At the same time, she knew better than most the enormous obstacles that even the greatest women writers of the past had faced, and saw with clear eyes the sadness, often amounting to tragedy, of their lives.

England from the late eighteenth century on was one of the very few countries (the young United States was another) that chose to teach a good percentage of its daughters to read and write. Among English speakers, a market quickly grew up for poetry, fiction, and journalism that would appeal to the female reader. Seeing that market, educated women of small means turned their hands to writing, less in the hope of eternal fame than of respectable independence and support for their families, and they were in a race against time to do it. In our American world today, women can expect to live into their eighties, but Victorian women tended to die young.

Isabella Beeton, who compiled the famous cookbook published under her name, was not atypical, dying in childbirth at the age of twenty-nine, a victim of puerperal fever complicated by the syphilis she had contracted from her husband. The three (surviving!) Brontë sisters, Charlotte, Emily, and Anne, had genius on their side, but they were no luckier than poor Isabella Beeton. In between peeling endless potatoes at home and struggling with rich people's recalcitrant children away, they wrote novels and sent them under male pseudonyms to a London publisher, betting, astutely, that they could make a better life for their family as novelists than as governesses. The galloping consumption that was epidemic in England carried off Anne and Emily before they turned thirty, but Charlotte at least lived long enough to write her masterpieces, earn a modest affluence for her father and husband, and get a tiny taste of what it might be like to be a literary lion like William Makepeace Thackeray or Charles Dickens. All the same, even as Great Britain was birthing an unprecedented number of Great Women Writers, nineteenth-century English society as a whole still agreed with the librettist W. S. Gilbert that, if a beneficent autocrat were to rid society of "that singular anomaly, the lady novelist," she never would be missed.

As the daughter of the first editor of the *Dictionary of National Biography,* its entries almost exclusively about men, Virginia Woolf knew quite pertinently that the flame of even the greatest women writers was quickly extinguished once they lay in the grave. Despite the best efforts of women reviewers like Woolf herself and her adoptive aunt Anne Thackeray Ritchie before her, it was men who wrote the history of English literature, and men quickly decided that George Eliot was tedious, the Brontës hysterical, Rossetti overly pious, and Mrs. Gaskell as far below Dickens or Trollope as Elizabeth Barrett Browning was below her husband, Robert.

Thus, despite the relatively high representation of women in English literature, despite her family's established place among English literati, and despite the apotheosis of Jane Austen as the woman novelist even men could admit to liking, Virginia Woolf faced an uphill battle when she determined to be a writer. In 1905, when Woolf began her campaign to establish herself in the world of English publishing, her situation was, in fact, not very different from that of a young middle-class Saudi woman today who wants to be a lawyer, or a young middle-class Guatemalan woman today who wants to have her own fashion company, or a young middle-class Sudanese woman today who wants to be a surgeon. And I specify middle-class women since to be born into a family of even modest means of course gives a boost to anyone, female as well as male. In our twenty-first century, many of the poorest human beings on our planet are women, many of them illiterate.

❧

Woolf's family was safely upper-middle-class. As a girl, she enjoyed three copious if starchy meals a day, wore shoes and warm clothes, and lived in a multistory house near a big park. She took long, lovely summer holidays by the sea. She did not have to cook a meal, empty her commode, or starch her collars. Her father did not lose his fortune and send her out to work as a seamstress, a governess, a mill girl, or a prostitute. Unlike so many girls above and below her social status, she was not fated to become the wife, mistress, or chattel of an old man she did not know. A highly articulate child in a literary family, she was taught to read and write as a small child and was early given the run of her father's large library. What she lacked was a university education, and in this she was an odd throwback to women writers fifty years earlier, like Elizabeth Barrett Browning, George Eliot, and Florence Nightingale, all of them autodidacts for whom higher education was not a possibility.

From early childhood, it was clear to everyone that Virginia Stephen was highly intelligent and learned easily. If she had been a boy her father would have dreamed of Eton and Trinity for her, and even as a girl she might have followed in the path of several of her Stephen and Fisher girl cousins and attended a good girls' school, with a view to being admitted to Newnham or Girton, the two women's colleges at Cambridge University, the Stephens' alma mater.

Left to himself, her father might even have been amenable to sending Virginia to school and university. Leslie Stephen was a proud disciple of the utilitarian philosopher John Stuart Mill, and on a theoretical level he accepted Mill's advanced views on gender equality and higher education for women. At one point during his courtship of Julia Jackson Duckworth — Virginia Woolf's mother — Leslie Stephen, while insisting that it mattered more to him that a woman be of "noble character than learn anything," advanced Mill's argument that some women might have to support themselves in life and thus needed the tools education offers. I do not want, Leslie wrote rashly to Julia, to see my daughter, Laura, or perhaps your daughter, Stella, become "a mere young lady." Julia reacted to her suitor's letter in cold fury, reminding Leslie that she herself had received no systematic education. Did that mean she was not worthy of his love and esteem? Lovesick Leslie at once capitulated, and thereafter, for the daughters he and Julia produced, there would be no question of going to school, preparing themselves for earning a living if need be, or moving into their father's professional world of journalism and essay writing.

All her life, Julia Stephen, Virginia's mother, was fiercely anti-feminist and inexorably opposed to formal education for girls. A woman's value, in Julia's view, lay in her beauty, her charm, her easy command of social situations. That value was certified by the caliber of the husband she attracted. If Julia could help it, no daughter of hers would be mocked as a bluestocking and thus handicapped in the marital stakes. Julia saw beautiful Vanessa and Virginia, her Stephen daughters, as successful wives and mothers like her, and her oldest daughter, Stella Duckworth, as a spinster who would tend to the needs of her parents as they grew infirm.

It was all too easy for Leslie Stephen, a neurotic, self-absorbed workaholic, to accept his adorable and deliciously conventional young wife's views on women's education and dismiss John Stuart Mill's "feminism" as the product of Mill's submission to his wife, Harriet Taylor. It suited Leslie's busy editorial and research schedule, as well as his sense of connubial fitness, to give his second wife complete jurisdiction over the upbringing of their girls, and, philosophy aside, where was he to find the money to send the girls to school? The Cheltenham Ladies' College certainly offered a first-class education at very reasonable rates, but fees were still fees and had to be paid out of pocket. Leslie Stephen was not a wealthy man and his first duty as paterfamilias, he and Julia agreed, must be to ensure that the two sons of their marriage, Thoby and Adrian, got the private school education that would allow them to maintain their place in society.

The Stephen family's educational priorities were those of most of their class. As Virginia Woolf would later point out in her famous essay *Three Guineas,* Mary Kingsley, the renowned Victorian explorer and naturalist, was given no formal education. "I don't know if I ever revealed to you," Kingsley once wrote with restrained bitterness to a friend, "the fact that being allowed to learn German was *all* the paid-for education I ever had. Two thousand pounds were spent on my brother's, I still hope not in vain." In an allusion to *Pendennis,* a novel by her sort-of-grandfather William Makepeace Thackeray, Woolf went on in the same essay to satirize the familial duty to educate its sons as "Arthur's Education Fund."

> It is a voracious receptacle. Where there were many sons to educate it required a great effort on the part of the family to keep it full. For your [that is, men's] education was not merely in book learning; games educated your body; friends taught you more than books or games . . . In the holidays you travelled, acquired a taste for art; a knowledge of foreign politics; and then, before you could earn your own living, your father made you an allowance . . . while you learnt the profession that now entitles you to put K.C. [King's Counsel] after your name. All this came out of Arthur's Education Fund. And to this your sisters . . . made their contributions.

To Leslie Stephen's dismay, educating two sons proved more difficult and expensive than he had expected. Thoby and Adrian Stephen grew to be huge, handsome, virile young men, fond of hunting, but neither proved especially bright or exceptionally diligent. Scholarships to mighty Eton, which both Leslie and his older brother, James, had won, were quite beyond Thoby and Adrian, and to attend Eton as fee-paying boarders like George and Gerald Duckworth, Julia's sons from her first marriage, was financially out of the question for the Stephens. Leslie was obliged to pay full fees for his sons at less prestigious schools, and even then, severe economy had to be practiced at home. Thus, while their four brothers went off to school to prepare for admission to Cambridge, Virginia, Vanessa, and their half-sister Stella were, apart from music and dance classes to prepare them for young ladyhood, educated at home in whatever hours their busy parents could spare.

Stella Duckworth, the middle child of her mother's first marriage, sandwiched between the two brothers their mother adored, and labeled incurably stupid early in her life, accepted this system unquestioningly. Vanessa Stephen, the next-oldest daughter, aspired to be a painter and, having been born with her mother's iron will, stood up for herself and got the classes and teachers she needed to pursue her artistic dreams. It was brilliant, verbal, intellectually curious Virginia who suffered most from her mother's educational philosophy, although she did not come to realize this until after her mother's death.

A case can be made that Virginia Woolf's education at home prepared her better for life as a writer than any school or college could have. William Thackeray — whose nose was broken twice in school fights at Charterhouse — said that all his education at an elite English boarding school taught him was to loathe classical literature and take the birch without sign of weakness. In her youth, Virginia Stephen had time and opportunity to read voraciously, she could listen to her father's learned conversations with his acolytes, and Henry James and John Ruskin were just two of the literary giants who came for dinner at her house. But Virginia Woolf herself emphatically did not see her lack of formal education as an asset. From the time her brother Thoby returned elated from Cambridge University she felt that she had been cheated of her educational birthright through the preference given to brothers. Even as a girl, she passionately wished that the mellow pleasures of life in an ancient Cambridge college, which she would later evoke in her novels *Jacob's Room* (1922) and *The Waves* (1931), had been hers. She saw it as unjust that, by virtue of sex, not ability or effort, all four of her brothers became members of the age-old fellowship of intellect and scholarship that Cambridge University represented.

Her letters show that, by the time Virginia Woolf was in her late teens, she was an isolated and largely silent autodidact, excluded from participation in the communal aspects of learning, thinking, and writing. She was at ease only within the circle of family and in the company of young women who, to a greater or lesser extent, suffered from the same limitations she did. At twenty-two, Virginia Stephen was intellectually primed to start on the career of a professional writer, but she could not. Her father — deaf, depressed, dependent, cancer-ridden — blocked her path.

Only after Leslie Stephen died, in 1904, and she had recovered from the double psychic shock of missing him terribly and remembering how she had wished him dead, could Virginia Stephen spread her wings and start to soar. Beginning with modest contributions to the women's section of a religious periodical, she quickly moved on to the *Times Literary Supplement,* a rare achievement for a woman of her generation. By 1910 her reviews and essays were earning her enough to pay off her doctor's bills and acquire not just a room but a vacation home of her own in the Sussex countryside.

Virginia Woolf was eager to compete in the literary marketplace of her time and ready to be judged by its standards. In this she was like her contemporaries Vita Sackville-West, Rebecca West, Agatha Christie, Dorothy L. Sayers, and Katherine Mansfield. These writers, whose names clearly marked them as female, nonetheless did not relish the label "feminist." What made Virginia Woolf different, what makes her relevant today, is that she not only saw but also pointed out, publicly, and in print, that whatever you did, it always mattered if you were marked as female or male. Gender was one part of life's grand equation, Woolf argued, and if there was no female Shakespeare or Dante or Goethe, this was because the literary game, like all of society's games, had been rigged. To use a contemporary metaphor, the rules had been set by Team M to ensure the victory of Team M, the referee and linesmen all sported the phallic insignia, so what wonder if Team W rarely scored a goal, much less a win?

From the beginning of her professional career, Virginia Woolf took that hackneyed phrase "Cherchez la femme" as a reading mantra in the review and essay assignments she accepted. This, not her encyclopedic knowledge of English literature and her familiarity with French and ancient Greek, set her apart from her fellow reviewers. To take one famous example from the first volume of *The Common Reader,* in her essay "The Pastons and Chaucer" Woolf singles out the letters written by the mother of the family, Margaret Paston. Yes, Woolf tells her readers, this woman's letters are tedious and repetitive, even more so, perhaps, than those of her husband and sons, but they matter because Margaret's is one of the rare instances of a woman's voice coming down to us from the fifteenth century. At that time, very few women could read, much less write; books were precious possessions to be locked away, and literary models for women were almost unknown.

In another essay, Woolf celebrated Jane Austen as that rare woman who had been accepted into the canon of English literature. By the age of fifteen, Woolf points out, Austen was already writing not for her family and schoolroom friends but "for everybody, for nobody, for our age, for her own, in other words, even at that early age, Jane Austen was writing." Woolf mourns Jane Austen, dead at forty-two when she was just becoming a literary presence, her letters ceremonially burned by her sister to preserve her respectability. In another essay, this time on George Eliot, simply by judicious quotation Woolf suggests how much the savagely rapid decline in that great woman novelist's reputation after her death was due not just to her sex but to her physical appearance. In the eyes of male critics, the woman Mary Ann Evans was too plain for "George Eliot," the pen name she chose, to be part of the Great Tradition of English fiction.

When Virginia Woolf wrote things like that, Leonard Woolf, her husband and partner at the Hogarth Press, published them without enthusiasm. Her intimate friend Vita Sackville-West and her sister Vanessa Bell, who agreed about little else but who both felt threatened in their precarious versions of unconventionality, thought she was losing her mind — again! When Woolf's feminist call to arms first appeared in the tense interim between two world wars, people were busy debating the rise of fascism and the appeal of Stalinist Russia, and Woolf's arguments fell largely on deaf ears. For some twenty-five years after her death, Virginia Woolf did not have a big voice in the cultural conversation.

But all that changed with the rise of the new feminism. In the 1960s, my generation rediscovered Virginia Woolf, and her two short polemical essays *A Room of One's Own* (1929) and *Three Guineas* (1931) became inspirational texts. Women teaching women's history and feminist theory in the new women's studies departments found in Virginia Woolf a writer who two generations earlier had analyzed, clearly and elegantly, what was confusing and unfair about our lives. We applied what she had said about the barriers facing an imagined English writer called Judith Shakespeare and saw how much greater the barriers were for would-be painters and sculptors and composers and dramatists and film directors born female.

As Woolf had shone light on Sappho, on Margaret Cavendish, and on Aphra Behn, we took Scheherezade as our founding mother, savored the writing of Lady Murasaki and the nameless woman author of *The Pillow Book,* and rediscovered the artists Artemisia Gentileschi, Elisabeth Vigée Le Brun, and Rosa Bonheur. The idea of a woman needing a room of her own became an article of faith, and today almost any issue of the *New York Times Book Review* — to name just one major publication — that touches on the question of women and writing contains some reference to or quotation from Virginia Woolf.

As Woolf's essays and novels entered the new feminist canon, superbly edited collections of Woolf's diaries and letters also started to appear, and we discovered the woman behind the text. We found that, in equal partnership with her husband, Woolf not only chose and edited books for her private publishing company, the Hogarth Press, but in the early years got her fingers inky from setting type and gluey from attaching book covers made of wallpaper. From Woolf's letters and diary, we were able to follow from day to day how she mixed work and fun, town and country, solitude and society, men and women. We could follow her as she chronicled, documented, analyzed, criticized, and shaped the famous Bloomsbury group in her dual capacity as founding member and permanent outsider. We could watch her painfully striving to define a core self that was both/and, not either/or, female and male, straight and queer, sensual and pure, proudly independent and happily partnered.

And then there was the fact that, in a diary she carefully designed to hone her craft and record her world, Woolf never says that each morning she woke up to see if she was sane or mad. Would this be the day when once again she dropped off the edge of reason and crashed into the suicidal abyss where loved ones became demons and death was the only escape?

Madness is knit into the fabric of Virginia Woolf's greatness. From the age of thirteen, she suffered from a severe mental illness that was misunderstood by her doctors and exacerbated by the medical treatments they offered. But, and this is the key point, Woolf refused to define herself as a patient, much less a victim. She worked, she produced, she had fun, she found happiness. "Gather ye rosebuds while ye may," urged the poet Robert Herrick, and Woolf did, and when they pricked her fingers, she licked off the blood and picked some more.

৵

Given the societal constraints she lived under and the chronic mental illness that afflicted her, how did Adeline Virginia Stephen become the great writer Virginia Woolf? Part of the answer, I shall argue in this book, is that Woolf from earliest childhood had known powerful women and had reason to believe she could have power in her turn. Such a belief, in her generation and in ours, has a power of its own.

A rare combination of hyper-receptivity and icy critique, Woolf got her sense of female greatness from her books and from her family. She descended from a line of affluent, ambitious, enterprising women, and stories about them were passed along the generations. Different female definitions of success came down to the young Virginia Stephen as she heard about women like Thérèse Blin de Grincourt de l'Etang, her Franco-Bengali great-great-grandmother, or Adeline de l'Etang Pattle, her Anglo-Indian great-grandmother, or her mother's cousin Lady Isabella Somerset. Most important of all, Woolf knew, or knew of, two women who, despite everything her mother taught her, had managed to succeed as professional artists as well as wives — Julia Margaret Cameron and Anne Thackeray Ritchie.

The acclaimed Victorian photographer Julia Margaret Cameron, née Pattle, was Julia Stephen's aunt and namesake, and the young Woolf could get a sense of her great-aunt's artistic achievement because some of Cameron's exquisite portraits of Woolf's mother as a young woman were hung in her Kensington home. That those photographs made their mark is attested by the fact that they would find a place of honor in the various houses Virginia and her sister Vanessa later occupied in Bloomsbury. Julia Cameron, unlike several of her sisters, died before her great-niece Virginia was born, but in 1926 the

Hogarth Press issued a volume of Cameron's photographs, with a brilliant and affectionate essay on Cameron herself by Virginia. And Cameron, in all her exuberant, eccentric creativity, was in a sense reincarnate for the young Virginia Stephen in the person of her adoptive aunt Anne Thackeray Ritchie.

Anne Thackeray Ritchie, a successful novelist, memoirist, and literary historian, was an occasional but important presence in Stephen family life. The older daughter of William Makepeace Thackeray, Anne was born into the upper reaches of the Anglo-Indian community that had resettled in the south of England in the mid-nineteenth century. As a young woman she became a denizen of what Woolf liked to call Pattledom — the company of writers, painters, scientists, politicians, and industrialists that the Pattle sisters (among them Julia Cameron and Woolf's maternal grandmother, Maria Pattle Jackson) gathered around them.

Into the damp, narrow house where Virginia Woolf grew up, Anne Thackeray Ritchie brought a breath of air scented with frangipani, sandalwood, and cardamom, the air of India once breathed by Julia Margaret Cameron and her Pattle sisters. Julia Stephen, Virginia's mother, had savored that scent as a girl, but by the time Virginia was born, Julia found it too painful to talk about her ancestral Eden, with its nabobs and its artists. This is where Aunt Anny stepped in.

Like Thackeray Ritchie, Virginia would be not only a writer but a loving and loyal wife, a trusted family member, and a gifted social connector at the heart of England's cultural world. Like Thackeray Ritchie, Woolf would write essays and reviews that delved deep into the work of women writers of the past, even as she connected to creative, unconventional women in the present, such as the writer Vita Sackville-West, the composer Ethel Smyth, and the theater director Edy Craig. Unlike Thackeray Ritchie, who lost her beloved sister, Minny, at age thirty, Virginia always had Vanessa, and as writer and painter the Stephen sisters cross-pollinated throughout their lives. And if Thackeray Ritchie was a mere echo of the Great Tradition of English fiction, Virginia Woolf, with her novels *Mrs. Dalloway* and *To the Lighthouse,* became part of it.

❧

Behind every great woman we can name is a long line of able, energetic, talented women for whom greatness was not an option. For most of history and still today in many parts of the world, the names and achievements of these outstanding women die with them. In this book we see Virginia Woolf as a gleaming link in "a chain of women who, whether willingly or not, had learnt certain traits, certain attitudes from one another through the years," as her niece Angelica Garnett put it. Because of her fame, because of her achievement, Woolf is that rare woman who allows the women who went before her and stood about her to enter the historical record.

Legacy and inheritance — the passing on of cultural and financial assets as well as physiological traits from one generation to another — will be a central theme in this book. As a student of the female condition living in the first half of the twentieth century, Woolf was aware that in traditional societies around the world, women had been able to pass to their daughters little more than their given names and their social traditions. It took centuries for Western civilization even to accept that the ovum played an equal role with the sperm, that the womb was more than an inert medium in which the sperm-generated homunculus could develop. Well into the nineteenth century, a woman's property, inherited and earned, became the property of her husband when she married. Even in Woolf's generation, women's earning power was still under severe legal and economic constraints. Given this grim financial reality, as Woolf famously proclaims in *A Room of One's Own,* even a small inheritance — say, five hundred pounds a year, in 1920s English pounds — could make the difference between success and failure, fulfillment and frustration. A small inheritance could buy a woman the independence, the freedom of movement, and the opportunities for personal development that free men of all classes have traditionally enjoyed.

As we shall see, the women in Woolf's family line, starting with Woolf's great-great-grandmother Thérèse de l'Etang, born in the eighteenth century, and on to her Garnett great-nieces, born in the twentieth, had the lucky combination of talent and money. These were unusually beautiful, stylish, energetic, enterprising women, and, almost despite their male partners, they reliably passed these traits down to their daughters and their nieces, along with their names — Julia, Adeline, Virginia. Woolf's women, like Woolf herself, were fortunate enough to inherit the financial resources that enabled them to thrive and make their mark in the cultural ledger.

Each of the women we will meet in this book is a window onto Virginia Woolf's landscape. Her ancestors Thérèse and Adeline are small windows thick with bull's-eyes. Her surrogate aunt Anny Thackeray Ritchie is a high casement opened wide to the winds. One half-sister, Stella Duckworth, has panes blurred with tears; the other half-sister, Laura Stephen, is a basement window largely bricked up. Her mother, Julia, and her sister, Vanessa, are tall French doors giving onto the garden and thence out to the Cornish sea and the South Downs of Sussex, where Woolf summered and pleasured, read and wrote. Each of these women bequeathed something to Virginia Woolf. To her abiding sorrow, Woolf had no children of the body, but she passed that legacy on to the children and grandchildren of her mind — to us.

By looking at Woolf's womenfolk I hope we will better see our own, biological or chosen. Some we have known. Some we seem to have forgotten. Some, out of the blue, emerge from a diary or a little packet of letters hidden in a suitcase. Some are encoded in our genome. All do something to make us what we are. Following in Woolf's footsteps, using all our modern sources of information, we can go looking for them.

PART I

The Pattle Legacy

FROM
CALCUTTA
TO KENSINGTON
TO DIMBOLA

Virginia Woolf's Maternal Lineage

Ambroise-Pierre-Antoine de l'Etang
1759–1840

m.

Thérèse Josephe Blin de Grincourt
1767–1866

?

?

Virginie de l'Etang

Julie-Antoinette-Adeline de l'Etang
1793–1845

m.

James Pattle
1775–1845

James Pattle
1812–1818

Adeline Pattle
1814–1838
m. Collin Mackenzie
2 daughters

Julia Pattle
1815–1879
m. Charles Hay Cameron
6 children

Sarah Pattle
1816–1887
m. Henry Thoby Prinsep
4 children

Maria Pattle
1818–1892
m. John Jackson

Louisa Pattle
1821–1873
m. Henry Bayley
1 daughter

Virginia Pattle
1827–1910
m. Charles Somers-Cocks
2 daughters

Sophia Pattle
1829–1911
m. John Dalrymple
1 son, 1 daughter

Adeline Jackson
1837–1881
m. Henry Halford Vaughan
5 children

Mary Jackson
1840–1916
m. Herbert Fisher
11 children

Julia Jackson
1846–1895
m. (1) Herbert Duckworth
(2) Leslie Stephen

George Duckworth
1868–1934
m. Margaret Herbert
3 sons

Stella Duckworth
1869–1897
m. John Waller Hills

Gerald Duckworth
1870–1937
m. Cecil Scott-Chad

Vanessa Stephen
1879–1961
m. Clive Bell
3 children

Julian Thoby Stephen
1880–1906

Adeline Virginia Stephen
1882–1941
m. Leonard Woolf

Adrian Stephen
1883–1948
m. Karen Costelloe
2 daughters

Five generations of women in the family of Virginia Woolf

I

Virginia Woolf's Indian Ancestresses — Thérèse de l'Etang and Adeline Pattle

A TRADITION in the family of Virginia Woolf had it that the aristocratic beauty of the women on her mother's side could be traced back to her great-great-grandmother Thérèse Blin de Grincourt. She was a late-eighteenth-century heiress who married the Chevalier Ambroise-Pierre-Antoine de l'Etang. That Virginia Woolf had a touch of the French aristocracy is one of the little themes that come up in her own letters and in those of her sister Vanessa Bell. To her composer friend Ethel Smyth, for example, Woolf wrote, "If you want to know where I get my (ahem!) charm, read Herbert Fisher's [her politician first cousin's] autobiography. Marie Antoinette loved my ancestor; hence he was exiled; hence the Pattles, the barrel that burst and finally Virginia." We shall be finding out about that barrel later in this chapter.

A few stories about her great-great-grandparents Thérèse and Antoine de l'Etang came down to Virginia Woolf, wrapped in gossamer and giving off a faint but intoxicating scent of palaces — the apple blossom and lavender of Marie Antoinette's Petit Trianon, the jasmine and frangipani of the Nawab of Oudh's palace at Lucknow. Thus, in her introductory essay to the Hogarth Press's volume of the photographs of her great-aunt Julia Margaret Cameron — one of Thérèse de l'Etang's granddaughters — Virginia Woolf wrote, "Antoine de l'Etang was one of Marie Antoinette's pages, who had been with the

Queen in prison till her death and was only saved by his own youth from the guillotine. With his wife, who had been one of the Queen's ladies, he was exiled to India and it is at Ghazipur, with the miniature that Marie Antoinette gave him laid upon his breast, that he lies buried."

Note how, in this version, perhaps recounted to Virginia by her mother, Julia Jackson Stephen, or her maternal grandmother, Maria Pattle Jackson, the beautiful ancestress is a French aristocrat whom misfortune brings to India.

In his groundbreaking 1972 biography of his aunt Virginia, Quentin Bell gives a different but equally colorful version of the family story about the Chevalier de l'Etang: "His person was pleasing, his manners courtly, his tastes extravagant, and his horsemanship admirable. He was attached to the household of Marie Antoinette, too much attached, it is said, and for this he was exiled to Pondicherry."

Both stories are delightful and full of novelistic flair. Neither, unfortunately, was quite accurate. Tristram Powell, who reedited the Hogarth Press book on Cameron in 1973 and had new research to go on, felt obliged to correct the record. "The Chevalier de l'Etang was banished by the King *before* the Revolution, when he was an officer of the King's bodyguard and superintendent of the Royal Stud, he had written a book on horse management for the French army. Mme. de l'Etang was *not* one of the Queen's ladies. She was born in Pondicherry, India, the daughter of the Captain of the Port, and she did not go to France until she took her granddaughter there to be educated, probably in the 1820s."

In Powell's new account, Thérèse is at least placed firmly on the subcontinent for her birth and formative years, but the tacit assumption remains that she was European on both sides. Thérèse's very names seemed gratifying proof that she had been a French aristocrat, and so her reputation as the original family beauty could be proudly passed down to Virginia Woolf and Thérèse's many other descendants. What Virginia Woolf apparently never knew, because the nineteenth century had chosen to forget it, was that Thérèse was part Bengali.

That fact was uncovered only around the year 2000 by one of Virginia Woolf's distant cousins, William Dalrymple, a prominent historian of the British in the Indian subcontinent. His book *White Mughals: Love and Be-*

trayal in Eighteenth-Century India documents how some Englishmen serving the East India Company became part of Indian society, speaking the local languages, dressing in the local clothes, and marrying the local women. This "early promiscuous mingling of races and ideas," Dalrymple realized, had escaped both nationalist historians and postcolonialist critics because it was "on no one's agenda and fitted nobody's version of events." In his introduction, Dalrymple writes,

> This was something I became increasingly sensitive to when . . . I discovered that I was myself the product of a similar inter-racial liaison of the period, and that I thus had Indian blood in my veins. No one in my family seemed to know about this, though it should not have been a surprise: we had all heard stories of how our beautiful, dark-eyed Calcutta-born great-great-grandmother [that is, Sophia Pattle Dalrymple] . . . used to speak Hindustani with her sisters and was painted by Watts with a *rakhi* — a Hindu sacred thread — tied around her wrist. But it was only when I poked around the archives that I discovered she was descended from a Hindu Bengali woman from Chandernagore who converted to Catholicism and married a French officer in the 1780s.

☙

Ambroise-Pierre-Antoine de l'Etang immigrated to Asia when France was barely clinging to its remaining possessions in the subcontinent, as England took over most of northern India. De l'Etang probably landed in the bustling Franco-Indian port of Pondicherry, and there he found the woman who would become his wife and the mother of his children, Thérèse Josephe Blin de Grincourt.

Given the beauty of Thérèse's female descendants, it seems plausible that family legend is accurate and that she was a great beauty, but the only portrait that came down in the family was a miniature that Vanessa Stephen Bell wore in a locket as a young woman and seems to have been lost. As we shall see, Thérèse de l'Etang lived well into the photographic era when most families, even those of modest means, had their images captured for posterity. This paucity of portraits or photographs of Thérèse is, I would suggest, not incidental.

Thérèse's beauty may well have caught de l'Etang's eye, but her father would still have needed to come up with a significant dowry in order to tempt the extravagant young French aristocrat Quentin Bell paints for us. As the *capitaine du port,* Thérèse's father was clearly a man of means as well as a prominent citizen, and the "de" in their name marked the Blin de Grincourts as part of the nobility. All the same, in Pondicherry, Mademoiselle de Grincourt would have had a lower status than the Chevalier de l'Etang, not because, or not just because, the young woman had Asian blood, but because the young man had been born in France. Those born in the homeland moved to the top of the social hierarchy in the French colonies, which was one reason why ambitious young men were drawn there. What part of Thérèse's dowry derived from her maternal family we shall probably never know, but given the legendary wealth of late-eighteenth-century Indian noble families, it could have been considerable. The Indian legacy in the maternal family of Virginia Woolf was very probably monetary as well as genetic.

Antoine de l'Etang had once run the royal stud farm for Louis XVI and written a book on horse management, and when he moved on from Pondicherry to Lucknow to enter the service of the Nawab of Oudh, he found a very lucrative niche. Oudh (now usually known as Awadh) was a fabulously ancient, extremely rich princely state in the heartland of Bengal that had already come under the hegemony of the British East India Company. Horses had come into India from Mongolia, Turkey, and Persia in the sixteenth century when the Mughal invaders triumphed over the native Hindu armies, thanks largely to their cavalry. For Muslim rulers like the Nawab of Oudh, sovereign power was inseparably linked to horses, horse breeding, and equestrian skills.

We will probably never know exactly why King Louis XVI exiled the handsome master of his royal stud to a regiment in India, but it was clearly not a promotion. *Tout compte fait,* however, exile turned out to be a stroke of luck for Antoine de l'Etang. When the French Revolution broke out, he was safe in the vastness of India, and thus missed out not only on the Terror and the guillotine but on that final blow to his noble class — the ascendency of an upstart Corsican runt called Buonaparte. As for the legend of the chevalier and the queen, I wonder if it was not the well-calculated invention of a man with his way to make in a new world, a piece of cut-rate Alexandre Dumas energetically passed down in the family and finally gussied up for publication by those talented fantasists Virginia Woolf and Quentin Bell. Historians now tell us that the list of poor Marie Antoinette's lissome lovers existed mainly in the sadistic imagination of her enemies, and it is an established fact that there was no devoted and delectable little page called Antoine de l'Etang to brighten the torture of the queen's final months in the dungeons of the Conciergerie. Maybe the gift for storytelling was part of Antoine de l'Etang's legacy.

ॐ

The documentation on Thérèse Blin de Grincourt de l'Etang is still sparse, but it is now established that she had some five children, including two sons who seem to have died young, and then a number of grandchildren. But then, for reasons that have never been made clear, Madame de l'Etang moved from the India of her birth to France. Her husband, Antoine, remained in India and continued an active and successful life as a soldier and manager of equestrian centers, dying in 1840 in his very late seventies.

The probability is that Madame de l'Etang came to France as early as 1817 or 1818 and that she was accompanied by her daughter Adeline de l'Etang Pattle and Adeline's children. Certainly, a miniature by a French artist of Mr. and Mrs. James Pattle and their children places Adeline in France in 1818, since the picture shows the three oldest Pattle daughters (Adeline, Julia, and Sarah) as little girls, plus baby Maria, who was born in 1818.

Adeline was courageous to accompany her mother, Thérèse, on the arduous voyage from India to France. Though only in her mid-twenties, Adeline had already given birth to four, possibly five, children over the previous eight years, losing two of them in infancy, including the precious baby boy, and she was already pregnant again with a child who turned out to be another girl — Maria. The voyage indicates that there was an exceptionally strong bond between Adeline and her mother, and this was to set a pattern for the generations to come. As we shall see throughout this book, the relationships among the women in Virginia Woolf's maternal family — not just sisters and mothers

The Pattle family, 1818

and daughters, but aunts and nieces — were strong and close. The fiercely loving and protective relationship Virginia Woolf had with her sister Vanessa and Vanessa's three children, which we will be examining in Part V, echoed a pattern of female relations that dated back at least to the early nineteenth century.

Leaving her homeland and her husband was a radical move for Thérèse de l'Etang. Perhaps, at the beginning, she planned only to pay a visit to a place she had heard so much about, found she liked the country and the climate, and decided to stay and provide a home away from home for her Pattle granddaughters. The education of the Pattle girls is one piece of information that came down loud and clear in the family lore, and it is important to note that both Thérèse and her daughter Adeline had lost their only sons and thus failed to continue the family name and provide male heirs. Persuaded that the future of the family depended on the granddaughters making advantageous marriages, the two women may have decided that the Pattle girls needed the social polish and purity of language that only Paris could supply. Whatever Thérèse's reasons for emigrating, however, it obviously took energy, determination, and significant financial resources for a woman in her fifties to pack everything up and start a new life on a new continent.

Madame de l'Etang set up her household on a small estate in the little provincial town of Versailles, not far from Paris. Looked at prospectively rather than in hindsight, this was a far from inevitable choice of residence, but from this point the name Versailles becomes embroidered into the family history. Once settled in France, Madame de l'Etang proved herself able enough to manage her household and business affairs without husband and sons, and seems to have exercised a measure of matriarchal authority over her far-flung family in India and England. Over the years — and they were many, as we shall see — she received visits from one or more of Adeline's seven daughters, and from at least one of her English great-granddaughters, Isabella Somers-Cocks, known as an adult as Lady Henry Somerset.

A poor little rich girl destined to inherit half of the fortune of her very rich papa, Charles Somers-Cocks, the 2nd Earl Somers, Isabella lived in awe and terror of her beautiful, worldly, and intensely ambitious mother, Virginia, Countess Somers, Adeline Pattle's sixth daughter. Isabella looked forward to her visits to Madame de l'Etang, finding with her a freedom that she never knew at Eastnor Castle or the magnificent Somers London townhouse at Prince's Gate. In the words of Lady Henry Somerset's biographer Ros Black, on the modest estate in Versailles, under the benevolent eye of her very old Franco-Bengali great-grandmother, "Isabel reveled in the freedom to explore the woods, to spend time talking with the old lady, and to laugh, without censure, at the French Punch-and-Judy show."

In the story of Thérèse Blin de Grincourt de L'Etang of Pondicherry, Awadh, and Versailles, these visits to Versailles by Lady Isabella Somers circa 1860 are of surprising importance. They anchor the fact that Thérèse de l'Etang was quite astonishingly long-lived. Her birth has been given as 1767, and her death was in 1866, which would have made her ninety-eight or ninety-nine when she died. This means that, if Isabella Somers could spend vacations with her great-grandmother, her first cousin, Julia Jackson (Virginia Woolf's mother), born in 1846, might easily have done so too. Julia Stephen's mother, Maria Pattle Jackson, was one of the Indian-born granddaughters sent back to Thérèse in Europe to be educated — Virginia Woolf refers to her grand-mother, whom she knew very well, as "Dr Jackson's half-French wife."

Given the continuing influence of Madame de l'Etang over three genera-tions and given that some of the Pattle women and even some of their children knew her personally, we can assume that her deep-rooted Indianness would have been clear to them — which perhaps is why there are no photographic im-ages of her. The fine detail afforded by a daguerreotype might have revealed things about her appearance — the darkness of her skin, the abundance of her hair, the flash of her dark eyes — that were more Indian than French. A portrait would have risked telling a story that her family, transplanted from India to Eu-rope and rising fast in the social hierarchy in England, did not wish to tell.

If the members of the de l'Etang–Pattle family chose to forget and con-ceal their mixed racial heritage, it was not just an example of individual family prejudice. It was the result of deeply rooted societal preference. As William Dalrymple points out in his book, "this [late-eighteenth-century] promiscu-ous mingling of races and ideas, modes of dress and ways of living, was some-thing that was on no one's agenda and suited no one's version of events." Only at the beginning of the twenty-first century was it possible for a descendant of Thérèse de l'Etang not only to uncover the facts of her biracial heritage but also to announce them happily to the world. In the times of Thérèse's daugh-ter Adeline de l'Etang Pattle, of her granddaughter Maria Pattle Jackson, of her great-granddaughter Julia Jackson Stephen, and even of her great-great-grand-daughter Virginia Stephen Woolf, what we call multiculturalism was called miscegenation.

Today many of us like to celebrate evidence of a mixed racial heritage as a source of richness, but all through the nineteenth century and much of the twentieth, a "black" Indian or Caribbean ancestress (it was usually a woman) was something that English people with strong connections to the empire — and there were many — consistently chose to bury. Lytton Strachey's as-tonished protest in 1912 when his friend Leonard Woolf chose a "black" Sri Lankan protagonist for his first novel, *The Village in the Jungle,* was typical. After seven years as a colonial administrator in what was then Ceylon, Leon-ard Woolf — an English Jew, not incidentally — had learned to see the "natives" as people and even tragic "heroes." His friend Lytton, in contrast, never made the "passage to India," even though service in India over at least three generations had brought the Strachey family to eminence and affluence. As his letters document, when encountering "blacks," be they jazz musicians or Indian diplomats, Lytton Strachey felt an instinctive revulsion, and he was far more typical of his generation of Englishmen than was Virginia Woolf's husband.

What Thérèse Blin de Grincourt's descendants chose to remember was that she had secured the handsome, dashing Chevalier Antoine de l'Etang as a husband, and for those set on rising to the top of society — Virginia, Countess Somers, Virginia Woolf's great-aunt, for example, or George Duckworth, Virginia Woolf's half-brother — the idea of aristocratic French ancestors was intoxicating. Madame de l'Etang and her residence in a dower (widow's) house at Versailles could be spun into a story of a nobleman who had loved the queen and married one of her ladies before taking exile in India, and the name de l'Etang had a decidedly pleasant ring to it, much nicer than Pattle.

Thus, it was not by chance that Virginia Woolf's mother called her second son Gerald de l'Etang Duckworth, and that that was how young Gerald liked to sign his name in his letters home to Mama from Eton College. When the older Duckworth son, George, and his noble wife, Lady Margaret Herbert, had a son, the child was christened, as Virginia Woolf sardonically noted in a letter, Henry Austen George Herbert de l'Etang Duckworth. Woolf, unlike her Eton- and Cambridge-educated brothers perhaps, had more than enough French to see that pairing the word *étang,* "pond," with "duck" was a tad ridiculous.

I find it fascinating to realize that so many people in Virginia Woolf's family knew firsthand that the family stories about the aristocratic French ancestors, the de l'Etangs, were at best partially true. On some level, they knew that Thérèse de Grincourt had, in her descendant William Dalrymple's phrase, "Indian blood." Maria Jackson certainly knew, which means that Julia Stephen — the daughter who was so close to her and who, like her sisters, was born in India — could easily have known too. And since Mrs. Maria Pattle Jackson lived with her daughter Julia's family at Hyde Park Gate for most of her last decade, curious, story-loving little Virginia Stephen herself could have known. She could have gone upstairs for a courtesy visit to her invalid grandmother and idly said one day: "Grandmamma, tell me about your grandmamma. I hear she was French and very beautiful and lived in India and that I look rather like her. What was she like?"

We can be reasonably sure that such a conversation never happened. If it had, Virginia would have locked it away in memory and perhaps one day fashioned it into a story to amuse her husband, who knew India and wrote about it. Judging by a letter Virginia Woolf (then Stephen) wrote to her close friend Violet Dickinson in 1904, the story passed down in the family was that Thérèse de l'Etang was French. Virginia wrote to Violet that her family had received a visit from her first cousin Florence Fisher Maitland: "[Florence] said that my diamond and ruby ring was supposed to be precious and originally belonged to our great-great-grandmother, the Frenchwoman whose portrait Nessa wears in her locket. She [Florence] has a sapphire brooch which belonged to her for which she was offered five hundred pounds. She [Thérèse] was a rich old Lady, and most of our [presumably the Stephens' and the Fishers'] things apparently descend from her and are old French."

Racism was largely (though not entirely) foreign to both Virginia and Leonard, and for Virginia herself and her nephew Quentin Bell after her, it was cultural snobbery rather than social ambition that made so irresistible the story of a male ancestor carrying a miniature of the queen Marie Antoinette into his grave. As she makes plain in her famous novel *Orlando,* Woolf often wished she could leap back past the late Victorian era she had been born into, with its antimacassars and aspidistras and dumpy little monarch. Her goal as a writer and *salonnière* was to recapture the elegance, wit, and sexual abandon of France under the ancien régime, and her elective affinities moved from Shakespeare, Sir Philip Sidney, and Sir Thomas Browne in England to Voltaire, Madame du Deffand, and Choderlos de Laclos in France.

It rejoiced Virginia Woolf's aesthetic soul to imagine that, before there had been Maria Pattle Jackson, a grandmother she had known only too well and who talked of dogs and digestion, not Pondicherry and Lucknow, there had been the Chevalier de l'Etang, galloping along the Grande Allée next to the queen's carriage, sweeping off his hat, and daring to kiss his gloved hand.

From the information we have, it seems that the child with whom Thérèse de l'Etang was most closely allied was her daughter Julie-Antoinette-Adeline, and it was the marriage of this daughter to James Pattle that would define the maternal ancestors of Virginia Woolf as quintessentially English, with only charming tinges of French. When, as we shall see in the next chapter, the Pattles decided to move their whole families out of the India where most of them had been born and brought up, they settled in Kensington and the Isle of Wight, not Versailles and Paris. The transformation of Julie-Antoinette-Adeline de l'Etang into Adeline Pattle, and of her sister Virginie de l'Etang into Virginia Beadle, illustrates the rapid Anglicization of a Franco-Indian family in the first decade of the nineteenth century. Julie, Antoinette, and Virginie are names deliciously redolent of the ancien régime, but Adeline could be said in a solidly English way and Virginie easily became Virginia, so these were the names passed down in the family to Virginia Woolf. She was born Adeline Virginia Stephen and, until her marriage to Leonard Woolf, she used the initials AVS to distinguish her from her older sister Vanessa, whose initials were VS.

A striking portrait of Adeline de l'Etang as a young woman has recently come to light. It shows an exceptionally beautiful woman, elegantly clothed and hatted, with a long, oval face, dark eyes, dark hair, and thick dark eyebrows she may well have inherited from her Bengali maternal ancestors. The portrait strongly supports the family tradition that, like her mother Thérèse de l'Etang, Adeline the first was very beautiful, and her beauty may well have attracted the attention of James Pattle. However, following the death of their two brothers, Adeline and her sister or sisters became joint heiresses to the estate of their wealthy parents, so the de l'Etang–Pattle marriage was as much an alliance as a love match. Two prominent colonialist families in India, the one equipped with the elegance and grandeur of the fading French aristocracy, the other solidly part of the rising English bourgeoisie, with serious money, were combining their assets. James's father, Thomas Pattle, had been with the East India Company in the glory days when the company was taking over one Indian kingdom after another, and not incidentally earning fabulous profits for its shareholders. Thomas Pattle made a very large fortune, which he was able to pass on to his eldest son, James.

Adeline de l'Etang Pattle

Virginia Woolf, in her introduction to *Victorian Photographs of Famous Men and Women by Julia Margaret Cameron,* states that James Pattle, Julia's father, was one of those thorough bad hats that Great Britain happily bequeathed to her colonies. Woolf got this salacious story from the father of her good friend Ethel Smyth, who had heard it years earlier back in India, but this is another piece of Pattle oral history that turns out to be wrong. A recent contribution to the Wikipedia article on Adeline Pattle by her direct descendant Deborah Spooner establishes that Ethel Smyth's father was confusing James Pattle with a rapscallion younger brother.

Far from being a drunken rascal, James Pattle was a highly respectable public servant and a pillar of the English administration in Bengal. He and Adeline were married in Murshidabad, where James was a presiding judge, but he had moved to Calcutta when he was promoted up the legal hierarchy. In Calcutta, the James Pattle family lived in the exclusive neighborhood of Chowringhee, in a house so magnificent that it subsequently became the episcopal palace. James also seems to have been quite the family man, since he and Adeline had eleven children, ten daughters and one son. Of these, seven survived to adulthood — Adeline Marie, Julia Margaret, Sarah (or Sara) Monkton, Maria Theodosa, Louisa Colbrooke, Virginia, and Sophia Rickett — all, it will be noted, girls.

The sex of the surviving Pattle children mattered. When it came to the inheritance of estates, English law endorsed male primogeniture, whereby the eldest or only son inherited all or most of his father's estate. If there was no son, however, and no entail on an heir male, the daughters of a marriage divided their father's estate equally among them. The Pattle daughters were thus heiresses, though just how large a fortune they jointly inherited is one of the hard facts about the Pattles yet to be established.

James Pattle died in 1845, and according to Deborah Spooner, his dying wish was to be buried in the family plot in Saint Giles' Church, Camberwell, alongside his mother. Adeline determined to honor her husband's wishes and take his body back to England. Her teenage daughters Virginia and Sophia would go with her. The passage to and from India in the early nineteenth century was long, arduous, and full of risk, but the Pattle women had set sail for Europe before, and Adeline de l'Etang Pattle was a woman made of strong stuff. Within months of her husband's death, she found a buyer for their magnificent house in Chowringhee, sold off most of its accoutrements, and supervised the packing of the rest, including James Pattle's corpse, sealed up and preserved in a barrel of rum, as was standard for families who could afford it. Adeline and her daughters then set off on the arduous thousand-mile overland journey to the port of Pondicherry, whence they took ship for the even more arduous passage to France.

But if Adeline de l'Etang Pattle, age fifty-two, set sail with hopes of reuniting with her mother and making a new life in a new country surrounded by her children and grandchildren, those hopes were quickly dashed. It seems that the bung stopping up the cask of rum bearing James Pattle was not properly driven home. Thus, according to one version of the story, one night at sea, the cask suddenly burst and disgorged its contents. Adeline emerged from her cabin and, faced with the ghastly sight of her husband's pickled remains, went mad and died. The sailors, who were not a fussy lot, scooped up as much of the rum as they could.

For many decades, variations on this story of Adeline Pattle and the barrel of rum made the rounds of Anglo-Indian society, and one was related, firsthand, to Virginia Woolf in 1918 by Lady Strachey, Lytton Strachey's elderly mother. Lady Strachey had spent most of her early life in India, and she knew the Pattle family well. In a casual chat with Mrs. Woolf, she reminisced about "beautiful dead Pattles and Dalrymples . . . how old Pattle shot out of his tank and thereby killed his wife who thought him come back to life again, how the sailors drank him dry on the voyage to England."

The story of James Pattle and the barrel of rum is so marvelous, you can see why his descendants told it, with embellishments, from one generation to another, but let us pause for a moment to consider the grievous plight of Virginia and Sophia Pattle in the middle of the Atlantic. These two teenagers now presumably had to find two empty, sound barrels for the bodies of both parents, plus, amid the wrath of the ship's crew, enough rum to fill both casks. Then, on their arrival in England, after visiting Grandma in Versailles, they had to have both corpses conveyed to Camberwell for a decent burial under a proper headstone — all this before turning to the important business of finding husbands.

Sophia and Virginia Pattle were very young, but they coped, though, alas, we do not know how — revealing themselves worthy of their maternal heritage. The Pattle women, if you ask me, were pretty cool customers, and the more I think about Adeline Pattle, the less I am inclined to believe that she was terrified into madness and death. Confronted with the shattered barrel, the pool of rum, and the decomposing corpse of her husband, Adeline was a woman to curse the servant back in Calcutta who had not driven the bung home and demand another barrel of rum from the ship's captain. Given the death of her husband and the hectic pace of her activities in the previous months, she may have taken sail in a state of mental and physical exhaustion and fallen victim to some stray infection — but that sort of run-of-the-mill death does not make a fun story. On my reading of the sparse evidence, Adeline the first passed on not only beauty but energy, determination, pragmatism, and managerial skills to her female descendants — among them the successful writer, real estate investor, and publisher Virginia Woolf.

2

Pattledom

VIRGINIA STEPHEN Woolf had always known that her mother was born in India, and a clutter of Indian carpets, tiger-skin rugs, brass thingamajigs, and elephants large and small formed a background to her childhood and would make an occasional appearance in her novels. Virginia's adoptive aunt Anny Thackeray Ritchie had been born into the colonial diaspora of British India, and she would occasionally delight her Stephen nieces with stories of "Pattledom," the vibrant little cultural center that their maternal great-aunts Sarah Pattle Prinsep and Julia Pattle Cameron had created in England after repatriating from Bengal. Having received a wealth of love and support from the Pattle sisters, Aunt Anny was eager to keep their legend alive for the new generation, and in the young Virginia Stephen she found an attentive listener. Yet the person who had known the Pattles best, the person who had most benefited from their cultural and social legacy, was someone much closer to Virginia — her mother, Julia Stephen. But of Pattledom, Julia never spoke.

Until she married Herbert Duckworth at the age of twenty-one, Julia Jackson had spent much of her year with her Pattle aunties — Sarah Pattle Prinsep, at Little Holland House in Kensington, and Julia Pattle Cameron, at Dimbola Lodge in Freshwater, Isle of Wight. These were the two main poles of Pattledom, and, shuttling between them, young Julia Jackson had been loved and petted and admired, and very, very happy.

But, as we shall see in a later chapter, Pattledom was an Eden from which Julia had found herself cruelly exiled when she was only twenty-four. By the time her daughter Virginia was growing up, memories of her youthful happiness were one of the many pleasures that Julia Stephen denied herself. The self-sacrificing mother to eight ill-assorted children, living in a tall, dark house draped in red plush and smelling of boiled cabbage, Mrs. Leslie Stephen kept the images of her golden youth sealed away tight. Pattledom was too precious and too sad to be put into words — certainly for her husband, who hated to be reminded that she had been happy before she married him, and even for her daughters.

But on one occasion, not too long before she died, Julia Stephen did let slip a memory of Pattledom, and Virginia Woolf stored it away for future use. "Once when we were children," Woolf recalls in "Sketch of the Past," which she began in late 1939, "my mother took us to Melbury Road: and when we came to the street that had been built on the old garden, she gave a little spring forward, clapped her hands, and exclaimed, 'That was where it was.'" Not until the early 1920s, when she began researching her mother's family for a book, could Virginia Woolf put a name to that "it" — Pattledom.

ॐ

As we saw in the previous chapter, the women of the Pattle family began to make their move from Bengal to southern England during the 1840s. Their husbands had been born in Great Britain and made their careers in India, but the women had all been born, lived their lives, and had their children in India. Once they found themselves settled in the new place they had been told to call home, it did not take them long to discover that there was a foreignness about them that did not please many of their monocultural, monolingual, stay-at-home compatriots; in fact, it set their teeth on edge.

For four or five generations, England had sent her surplus sons to India to head up the bureaucracy and standing army of the East India Company. Of course, ruling in India was no easy billet, as Leonard Woolf, Virginia Woolf's husband, was to discover for himself as late as 1903. There was the heat and the bugs and the incessant noise so alien to the taciturn English, and not a few of the men who shipped out to the subcontinent died from disease, loneliness, and despair. All the same, Mughal India in the early eighteenth century was perhaps the richest empire the world has ever known, and it was like a giant piggy bank for the company's private shareholders and the English government.

At first the young colonialists in India, which then included today's Pakistan, Bangladesh, and Sri Lanka, found mistresses and even wives among the local peoples. Monsieur Blin de Grincourt, as we have seen, was one of these, as was William Thackeray's father, Richmond Thackeray, of whom more later. By the 1820s, however, such interracial relationships had come under censure at home. English men in India could still satisfy their desires with local women or, in not a few cases, local boys, but they needed wives and, luckily for them, after the long wars with Napoleon, England was awash with women. By the 1820s, many a rebellious daughter and surplus sister found herself on a slow boat to Pondicherry, and a new caste of Anglo-Indian women, the memsahibs, made notorious by twentieth-century writers like Doris Lessing and Muriel Spark, came into being.

By 1858 the tide of imperialist fervor was running high. After the English army savagely put down a major insurrection of the "native" troops, the East India Company was dissolved, India came under the direct rule of the British government, and England's queen could cock a snook at her German relatives by signing herself Victoria RI — Regina Imperatrix. But when the men who had sweated in starched collars and pith helmets to fashion England's "jewel in the crown" returned to the British Isles with their wives, and were reunited with the children they had sent "home," they got little praise or credit. Like the elephant-foot inkwells and mass-produced Benares brassware that by the early twentieth century marked the dingy middle class for novelists like Agatha Christie, those who had served the empire as proud pukka sahibs, "true gentlemen," all too often found themselves treated as second-rate citizens, their tanned, lined faces signaling that they were no longer quite English. The families of old India army colonels and district officers who had not managed to siphon money from Indian villagers tended to flock together in places like Brighton, a town that had once been trendy, or Hampstead, which was still hoping to become so.

Virginia Woolf captures that sense of second-class-ness in a passage in her 1916 novel *Night and Day*. The protagonist, Katharine Hilbery, lives in a house full of Indian memorabilia and asks her aunt, Mrs. Milvain, why she always refers to one cousin as "poor John." Mrs. Milvain replies: "He was the fool of the family. The other boys were so brilliant and he could never pass his examinations, so they sent him out to India — a long voyage in those days, poor fellow. You had your own room and you did it up. But he will get his knighthood and a pension, I believe, only it is not England."

This was the social challenge facing the older Pattle sisters as they began to make a new life on a new continent for themselves and their families, especially for their younger sisters and their daughters. It would take vision, determination, hard work, and lashings of Indian cash to convince England's intellectual and political elite that the term "Anglo-Indian" had connotations of the exotic and sophisticated, the artistic and witty, the quirky and charming. The name Pattle was no help. With its plebeian echoes of "cattle" and "kettle," "rattle" and "wattle," or worse, the troublesome Indian homonym Patel, Pattle clearly signaled the mercantilist bourgeoisie. It was a name Dickens might have come up with for a comic supporting character, like Miss Flite in *Bleak House,* but certainly not for a heroine. It should not surprise us that, within one generation of returning to England, the name Pattle disappears, while the aristocratic French name de l'Etang is carried forward.

∂◆

The first to arrive in England to settle was the Prinsep family. In India, Thoby Prinsep had been a high official in the East India Company, but when he was appointed to the company's supreme council in London, he and his wife, Sarah Pattle Prinsep, and their four teenage children returned to London. After a Grand Tour of Europe, the Pattles took out a long-term lease on Little Holland House, the rambling dower house surrounded by cow pastures on the Holland estate in Kensington.

In 1845, following the death of Adeline de l'Etang Pattle, the youngest Pattle sisters, Virginia and Sophia, joined the Prinsep household in Kensington. In 1848, Charles Hay Cameron took an early retirement from the Indian judiciary, and he and his wife, Julia, and their daughter, also named Julia, came back to England, leaving their sons to manage the family's coffee plantations. After some years in the Home Counties around London, the Camerons settled at Freshwater on the Isle of Wight, and Julia Cameron rapidly transformed the modest house into a rambling group of buildings complete with tower, which they named Dimbola Lodge, after their Sri Lankan estate.

By the 1850s, Sarah Prinsep in Kensington and Julia Cameron on the Isle of Wight had created a little mid-Victorian haven of European culture mixed with Indian allure. In its heyday Pattledom was a meeting place for some of England's most distinguished men — Tennyson, Thackeray, and Browning; Charles Darwin, Josiah Wedgwood, and William Gladstone; Dante Gabriel Rossetti, John Everett Millais, and John Ruskin. As Virginia Woolf was to discover in the 1920s, Pattledom was in many ways an early avatar of Bloomsbury. Such complex pieces of cultural machinery tend to seem effortless in retrospect but, on top of a genius for social relations and a generous entertainment budget, they require a lot of hard work and they are usually the work of women. Pattledom was set in motion and kept purring by Sarah and Julia, whose abundant energy galvanized friends to the point of exhaustion.

So, what was Pattledom actually like? In some respects, it was an English version of the French salon of Madame de Lafayette in the seventeenth century, or of Madame du Deffand in the eighteenth, a place where artists, musicians, and writers, scientists, industrialists, and politicians could regularly come together and talk. But instead of sitting in a circle on spindly gilt chairs drinking tisanes of an evening, the Pattle guests walked about the house and gardens on summer Sundays and ate casual meals at odd hours — alfresco, if weather permitted.

Pattledom was a good place for clever men — too good for a shy neophyte journalist like Virginia Woolf's father, Leslie Stephen, as we shall see — and there was great talk centered around the husbands, Henry Thoby Prinsep and Charles Hay Cameron. The ailing Prinsep and the reclusive Cameron were large, quiet men who had traveled far and done much, and they had higher

*Maria Pattle Jackson, one of the beautiful Pattle sisters
and Virginia Woolf's maternal grandmother*

mathematics and Indian tribal law, Persian poetry and Italian art at their fingertips. In the eyes of their wives and their guests, they were the undisputed lords
of Pattledom, but they preferred to keep on the far edges of the busy social action. The magnet that drew so many distinguished men down to rural Kensington to see the Prinseps on a Sunday or across the choppy Solent for a weekend
near the Camerons was the Pattle women. As everyone who knew them agreed,
the Pattle sisters and their daughters were almost overwhelmingly beautiful and

possessed of a captivating mixture of Parisian chic and the colorful exuberance of their native India.

At Little Holland House, Josiah Wedgwood, the scion of a great intellectual family as well as heir to a great pottery fortune, was happy to run into his elusive kinsman Charles Darwin. The dueling prime ministers William Gladstone and Benjamin Disraeli could occasionally be seen chez Prinsep, exchanging a cheerful handshake and talking of Whitehall and the weather. Alfred Tennyson, the poet laureate, was notoriously antisocial, but he became the particular pet of Julia Pattle Cameron, his neighbor on the Isle of Wight. As for the writer and illustrator William Makepeace Thackeray, whose family fortunes were thickly intertwined with British India, he was quite a fixture on the Pattle landscape, coming with his daughters Anne and Harriet (known as Minny) Thackeray as soon as they were out of short skirts.

Casual, outdoorsy, and freeform, Pattledom was mainly upper-middle-class professional, with a scattering of aristocrats once Sophia and Virginia Pattle found husbands, and it had a thick patina of the respectability and sexual restraint so often assumed to be typically Victorian. If Pattledom had distinct echoes of the French salons of old, where upper-class women had been queens of society, it was sharply different from the late-nineteenth-century Parisian high society of Balzac or Zola. Noblemen, bankers, and artists did not gather chez Cameron at Freshwater to clink and cavort and copulate (to use a favorite word of Virginia Woolf) alongside Jewish opera singers and little street whores, as they do in novels like *Splendeurs et misères de courtisanes* and *Nana,* and as they did in real Parisian society circa 1870. Pattledom was the confident, complex, and chaste world of the novels (though not always the lives) of Dickens, Meredith, and Thackeray, one to which men brought their wives and daughters and sisters but not their mistresses.

It must be admitted that the Victorian women we know so much about today were not much in evidence in Pattledom. Elizabeth Gaskell probably put in an appearance at Little Holland House, but as she was then only a "lady novelist" with a small readership, the diarists don't say much about her. The Pre-Raphaelite painter Dante Gabriel Rossetti brought his brother, William, but not his poet sister Christina, about whom Virginia Woolf would write one of her great essays. As for the then new literary phenomenon Charlotte Brontë, only Thackeray managed to pry her out of Yorkshire for a dinner party. The poet Robert Browning came to Pattledom on his own, eager to invite people to come and entertain his wife, Elizabeth Barrett Browning, in Florence. The journalist and literary critic George Henry Lewes also came alone since Mary Ann Evans (alias George Eliot), his wife in all but name, was deemed an adulteress who could never be received in respectable English society. Barbara Leigh Smith Bodichon, artist and social reformer, was similarly not acceptable to Pattledom because she was born illegitimate. On the other hand, if Barbara's first cousin Florence Nightingale, the most famous woman of her day after the queen, did not actually go to Little Holland House, she certainly knew the people who did.

ॐ

If, on the Isle of Wight, Julia Cameron had an edge over her sister in literary men and scientific luminaries, Sarah Prinsep had a corner on painters. Her son Valentine brought home to Kensington his artist friends Rossetti, Millais, Burne-Jones, and Holman Hunt, who were making a name for themselves as the Pre-Raphaelite Brotherhood. John Everett Millais, best known perhaps today for his 1851 painting *Ophelia,* was a good friend of Val Prinsep's, as was the actor-writer George du Maurier, Daphne du Maurier's grandfather.

The personal lives of the Pre-Raphaelite brothers were not exactly a pattern of Victorian respectability, as the Pattle descendant Henrietta Garnett shows in *Wives and Stunners,* a book based in part on previously unexplored papers in her mother's family. But Rossetti and his artist and writer friends did not bring their stunning mistresses with them to Pattledom, and, for the sake of the younger sisters and the nieces still in need of husbands, Julia Cameron and Sarah Prinsep were careful to maintain what the author Graham Robb calls "the tactical hypocrisy of the Victorians." Of course, Val Prinsep's lusty young friends were not blind to the beauty of the Pattle women, but they found no willing conquests. Burne-Jones was, according to Sophia Pattle's descendant William Dalrymple, eager to marry her, and Holman Hunt proposed marriage to sixteen-year-old Julia Jackson, but neither man was successful in his suit.

Sexual desire seems to have hit women in the Pattle family line rather late, a pattern to be replicated in the early twentieth century by their descendants Vanessa and Virginia Stephen. Ever since the days of Thérèse de l'Etang, the strategy for social success pursued by the women in the family was to hold out for the right match (though not necessarily the right man) and, as we shall see in the next chapter, Virginia and Sophia Pattle took that strategy to a whole new level. As a result, the problem of sex came to the surface at Little Holland House not when a Pattle niece ran off with a struggling artist, but when the Prinseps' resident artist, George Frederick Watts, married the teenage actress Ellen Terry and brought her to live in Kensington.

Sarah and Thoby Prinsep met the painter Watts in Rome during the Grand Tour they embarked upon after leaving Calcutta. Watts was living in Rome under the patronage of Lord and Lady Holland, and it was Watts who suggested that the Prinseps take Little Holland House. Watts was an excellent painter and a hapless man, and he gladly moved from the noble patronage of Lady Holland to the hands-on management of Sarah Pattle Prinsep. She installed Watts upstairs at Little Holland House, apparently rent and board free, declared him a genius to the whole world, and referred to him grandly as "the Signior."

All this was deeply gratifying to the son of a Marylebone piano-tuner, and in return Watts, though a rather reluctant portrait painter, did portraits of the Pattle sisters and their daughters and even the daughters' husbands, many of which have, happily, come down to us. The portrait of Leslie Stephen by Watts had pride of place in the reception rooms of Virginia Woolf's childhood home, and Woolf remembered her father standing in front of his portrait when guests came and making mildly disparaging remarks about it — in the full expectation of being contradicted.

In her memoir, *The Story of My Life,* published in 1908, Ellen Terry gave a heavily edited account of her early life, which she knew the public dimly recalled as scandalous. Terry claimed in her book that, when she married Watts, she had no understanding of sex and believed that, when Watts kissed her, he had in effect made her his. Somehow I doubt if that statement should be taken as a true confession. Dame Ellen was in financial difficulties when she took to writing her memoirs late in life, and it was in her interest to claim she had been an innocent lamb when she strayed off the primrose path. Certainly, Terry was born into a family and an English theatrical world that were striving for respectability, and the days of Nell Gwyn and Aphra Behn were long gone. All the same, if a girl living in the world of traveling entertainers like Ellen Terry had cared to open her eyes, there was plenty of illicit sex to be seen. Nubile girls were still at risk of rape, extramarital relationships were common among actors (Terry herself would later have one with the actor-impresario Henry Irving), and ambitious young women often had to choose between the casting couch and the sugar daddy. Charles Dickens, my readers will recall, found Ellen Ternan, the woman who became his secret mistress, when she appeared with him on stage.

But whether or not, in the moment that George Watts kissed her and proposed marriage, Ellen Terry knew the facts of life is irrelevant. She was barely sixteen years old, she loved and obeyed her parents, and, in crude twenty-first-century terms, they sold her to a rich and famous man three times her age.

At first the Terrys resisted marrying Ellen to Watts, who was, to put it mildly, no Romeo. Michael Holroyd quotes an unnamed biographer who opines that Watts was "emotionally unstable, sexually frustrated, and probably sexually ignorant." After he looked over the Watts-Terry marriage many years later, Lytton Strachey opined that, like those other eminent Victorians John Ruskin, Matthew Arnold, and Benjamin Jowett, Watts was impotent. However, when George Watts came back some time later, with new and better terms, Ellen's parents were ready to listen. Watts offered to pay Ellen's father a monthly sum calculated to cover the loss of income he would suffer if Ellen retired from the stage. All the numerous Terry children had to earn their keep almost as soon as they could toddle. As each child came along, he — or more especially she, as cute little girls were more popular with theatrical audiences — became an actor. Ellen Terry went on stage when she was about six, as one of the little princes in the tower in Shakespeare's *Richard III*.

The regular payment offered by Watts would mean a lot to the Terrys, perhaps the difference between traveling penury and a little house in the London suburbs. It would be a kind of Arthur's Education Fund for their sons, whom they wanted to send to school. Moreover, by the time G. F. Watts appeared on the scene, the Terry family had decided that Ellen's older sister, Kate, was the girl to back. In her late teens, Kate was already getting juicy parts, decent fees, and good reviews in the national press. Ellen was prettier than Kate, but she was a dreamy, idle girl who showed none of the fierce determination needed for a woman to make a career in the theater. Ellen herself was eager to move into the magic world of Pattledom, where, as she recalled in her memoir, "only beautiful things were allowed to come. All the women were graceful and all the men were gifted."

The Terrys were not bad people or bad parents. An age gap of thirty years between a husband and a wife was not unusual, and Watts, on a second look, seemed a decent working-class bloke, earning a living as a painter as the Terrys did as actors, but with more success and possessed of powerful backers in the Hollands and Prinseps. So, in February 1847, dressed in a brown silk gown designed by the painter William Holman Hunt and a white Indian shawl presented by the Pattle sisters, Alice Ellen Terry was married to George Frederick Watts. The contrast between the blooming bride and the withered groom made a powerful impression on all present. Ellen cried a great deal during the ceremony and was told to stop by her new husband. "It makes your nose swell," said George to Ellen.

Watts cared more about his bride's nose than her feelings because he was far more eager to paint her than to sleep with her. His first marriage would prove a professional triumph for George Frederick Watts. It was Ellen's image — as Persephone, Francesca da Rimini, Ophelia, Joan of Arc — that Watts captured in some of his greatest paintings. Outside the studio, on the other hand, Watts had little use for Ellen or need for her society, and he entrusted the education of Ellen to his friend, patron, and landlady, Sarah Prinsep. This proved a recipe for disaster — for the girl.

Sarah was happy to tolerate the bohemian young men her son Val had befriended, but turning Ellen Watts into a conventional little wifey was too much for even the efficient Mrs. Prinsep. Ellen's family had not quite figured out yet how to be middle-class, and she was coltish and unruly, casual in her manners, careless with her tongue, unaccustomed to being exercised on a leash. She could not have been more different than Sarah's favorite niece, the lovely, obedient, graceful Julia Jackson, the girl who would one day give birth to Virginia Woolf. No one denied that Ellen was affectionate, kindhearted, eager to please, and far from ignorant — could Julia Jackson recite yards of poetry and Shakespeare? — but she discharged an electricity that today we would call sex appeal, and it threatened to upset the sexual equilibrium at Little Holland House.

Sarah Prinsep became increasingly harsh in her attempts to discipline Ellen and make her conform to the rules of respectable Victorian womanhood. Within months, to the distress of her family and friends, Ellen grew pale, listless, and depressed. Kensington was not the sunny paradise she had dreamed of, and at night her "signior" husband might try some feeble caress, but nothing more. Things between Sarah and Ellen came to a head when Ellen appeared at a dinner party costumed as Cupid and wearing pink tights. Since her young girlhood, Ellen had played "trouser roles" on stage — these had in fact become her sister Kate's theatrical stock-in-trade. Ellen knew just how practical it was not to be encumbered by skirts and petticoats, and she was rightly proud of her legs, but Mrs. Prinsep was aghast to see them appear in her dining room.

Thus, according to Michael Holroyd, citing the various biographers of G. F. Watts, it was Sarah Prinsep who convinced Watts after barely a year that he should send Ellen back to her father's house. Basically, Sarah told the signior that he must either leave Little Holland House or send Ellen away, and Watts chose his studio over his wife. A separation settlement was negotiated, by which Watts would pay the Terry family — not Ellen herself — three hundred pounds a year. Though Watts would quickly turn against his wife and spread vicious rumors about why he had sent her away, he continued to pay the Terrys this money until Ellen secured a divorce some twelve years later.

For Ellen, at seventeen, the separation from her husband was a disaster. That she probably left Little Holland House a *virgo intacta* did not matter. She was seen as spoiled goods, rejected by her famous husband and his wealthy friends, a burden and an embarrassment to her parents and her siblings, a social pariah. Respectable admirers of the Terry sisters kept away, now that Ellen was back, though Charles Dodgson (Lewis Carroll), a highly respectable Cambridge mathematician, did continue his visits. Ellen's given first name was Alice, and in *The Story of My Life* Dame Ellen Terry wrote in gratitude: "[Dodgson/Carroll] was as fond of me as he could be of anyone over the age of ten." This was one of Terry's apparently naive confessions that Virginia Woolf could not comment on in her published review of Terry's memoir, but that she, as the victim of child sexual abuse, surely picked up on.

The Terry family had been wrong about Ellen. Somehow she found the strength to recover not only from the debacle of her marriage to Watts but from a six-year extramarital relationship with the whimsical architect Edward William Godwin. When he left her, Terry had two children as well as herself to support, so she returned to the stage and was soon recognized as the greatest woman actor of her time. The theatrical Terry family would stretch well into the twentieth century, with Ellen's son, the influential designer Gordon Craig; her costumier-director daughter, Edy Craig; and her great-nephew (Kate's grandson) Sir John Gielgud.

Ellen Terry, born in 1847, fought against heavy odds all her life, and the success she enjoyed came not from legacy, or even from luck, but from talent. With her many amours, her difficult children, her unending struggles to make ends meet, and her fabulous career as an actor, she has every claim to be a Great Victorian. As Virginia Woolf learned from her lesbian network, Terry was known for her warmth of heart and generosity of spirit, and, unlike her famous lover and theatrical collaborator Sir Henry Irving, she was cared for devotedly in her last years, dying poor in pounds, shillings, and pence but rich in love and laughter and reverence. For the writer Virginia Woolf, Terry was an inspiration and a new window onto Victorian culture.

Would Pattledom have been more interesting had it included more women like Ellen Terry, if the working-class artist's model Lizzie Siddal had come with her lover, Dante Gabriel Rossetti, for example, or if brilliant George Eliot had been welcomed with her partner, George Henry Lewes? No doubt, but, as Virginia Woolf began to understand in her Bloomsbury years, Pattledom mattered because it was a place outside the individual home where educated middle-class English men and English women could laugh and chat, innocently flirt a little perhaps, and exchange ideas, memories, and dreams as one human being to another. As Woolf knew well from her extensive research into English social history, such places became increasingly rare during the reign of Queen Victoria, and her own parents' home in Kensington had not been one of them.

As the nineteenth century progressed, upper-class Englishmen from an early age were herded into single-sex institutions — the prep school, the public school, the university, the regiment, the law firm, the civil service, the London club, Parliament. Well into the twentieth century it was possible for an unmarried Englishman to know nothing of women beyond the mother who wept to see him leave home, the sister who inked his initials onto his underwear, the school matron who dosed him with castor oil, and the Piccadilly streetwalker who beckoned him to prove his manhood. In mid-Victorian England, any social institution that allowed men and women to meet and talk and prove a common humanity was important. Pattledom, thus, in its small way, was important. It was not just a fun family story — it was a countervailing force in social history, and in the 1920s Virginia Woolf seized upon it as such, even as her friend and rival Lytton Strachey was leading the repudiation of all things Victorian with the book he derisively titled *Eminent Victorians*.

In 1923 the Woolfs planned for their Hogarth Press to bring out a book of photographs by Virginia's great-aunt Julia Margaret Cameron. The book would open with a biographical introduction by the Hogarth Press's star writer, Virginia Woolf herself, and it would be based on her original research. Virginia Woolf loved reading old letters and memoirs and diaries, and so, while collecting odd bits of oral testimony from friends like Anne Thackeray Ritchie, Lady Strachey, and Ethel Smyth, she plunged with delight into her own family's papers. These were ready to hand since her father, Leslie Stephen, following the death of his wife, Julia, in 1895, had dug them out of old boxes and trunks, organized, reread, and set them aside in good order, as a trained biographer should. Woolf found herself transported back to the world her mother, Julia Stephen, had known — Pattledom. There, she discovered, windows opened wide onto meadow or seashore; walls were green and blue and crowded with paintings and photographs; music filled the air; and the talk played and sparkled like a fountain. It was, in fact, a world singularly like the one she herself now lived in, but one that had largely sat silent during her childhood. Pattledom and Bloomsbury, Woolf discovered to her surprise, had much in common!

From her mother's papers Woolf learned that, at a time when English women were slowed to a walk by widening crinolines and tightening stays, the Pattle women when at home darted about in cool, form-fitting garments that gestured toward the sari and suggested a dance. And if, chatting among themselves, the sisters lapsed into the Hindustani of their childhood and raised their arms in laughter — the bracelets on their wrists chinking, the precious paisley scarfs slipping off their shoulders — old East India Company hands were transported back to lazy, fragrant evenings in Mughal gardens, smoking hookahs on marble verandas to the steady rhythm of the punkahs.

The bracelets, the shawls, and the infectious laugh came down in the family from the Pattle sisters to their daughters and granddaughters. When Vanessa and Virginia Stephen as tiny girls watched in delight as their mother, then still young and vivacious, transformed herself for an evening party, they were, without knowing it, falling under the old Pattle magic. And when Vanessa Bell redecorated her home after her marriage, she draped the furniture in the Pattle paisley shawls.

ॐ

For Woolf, a writer who had always been interested in resurrecting famous women of the past and who by the 1920s had come to identify herself as a feminist, the story of Julia Pattle Cameron (1815–1879) was especially exciting. Julia was the second Pattle sister and, by all accounts, the ugly duckling of the original swanlike septet. In the portrait we have of her by Watts, we see a young woman with a long, oval face, dark hair and eyes, and the firm dark brows of the family women down the ages. For a woman known for her boundless energy and sudden enthusiasms, her expression in this painting is surprisingly melancholy and reflective. Hair color apart, she looks very much like Virginia Woolf at the same age.

Surrounded by sisters who were acclaimed beauties, Julia Pattle was self-conscious about her own looks, but she had an eye for beauty, and like Woolf's painter character Lily Briscoe in *To the Lighthouse,* an urge to create it. As she wrote in an 1874 autobiographical fragment, "I longed to arrest all beauty that came before me." Given a chance, Julia Cameron thought, she might become an artist, but that chance was slow to come. In mid-nineteenth-century England, upper-middle-class women dabbled a good deal in the plastic arts as they did in music, but there was no path for them to take into art as career or profession.

Julia Margaret Cameron

In her early twenties, Julia Pattle was sent, we are told to our surprise, to South Africa to find a husband, but when that did not work out she returned to the Calcutta of her birth and there fell in love with and married Charles Hay Cameron. He was a brilliant lawyer some twenty years her senior, with a long and distinguished career already behind him. In 1835, Charles Cameron was appointed fourth member to the Supreme Council of India, a prestigious new administrative position, and for some twenty years, in the oppressive heat of Calcutta, Julia had her hands full as wife to a prominent jurist and educational reformer, mother to five sons and a daughter, and a leader in her community.

Since the governor-general of the East India Company at that time was not married, Mrs. Cameron was the first lady of British India, but there was nothing of the social butterfly and little obviously of the snob about her. Fluent in Hindustani since childhood, she communicated easily with the local citizens and actively seconded in private life her husband's public labors to bring European education to India. Her sympathies were as wide as they were passionate, and her interest in liberal causes went far beyond India. In 1848, for example, she was busy raising money for victims of the Irish famine, not a popular cause in England at the time.

When the Camerons installed themselves on the Isle of Wight in the early 1850s, the flood of remarkable people that washed over Dimbola Lodge every summer was overwhelming for some visitors. Caroline Amelia Stephen, Leslie Stephen's sister, her niece Virginia Woolf reports, was once heard to ask plaintively "is there nobody commonplace?" after she watched four of Benjamin Jowett's Balliol men drinking brandy and water while Tennyson recited "Maud" and Mr. Cameron, "wearing a coned hat, a veil, and several coats paced the lawn which his wife in a fit of enthusiasm had created during the night."

After a few years in England, despite her growing collection of famous and fascinating friends, her eager involvement in every aspect of Pattledom, her massive correspondence, and her social activism, for the first time in twenty-five years, Mrs. Cameron, the former vicereine of India, had time on her hands. As Virginia Woolf puts it, having hitherto dissipated her overflowing energies "in poetry and fiction and doing up houses and concocting curries and entertaining her friends," Julia Cameron was given a camera — or a lens, as she put it — and became a photographer.

It was her daughter, also called Julia, not her husband or one of her sons who were back in Ceylon watching the coffee plants die, who thought to give forty-nine-year-old Julia Cameron a camera. Like the story of Madge Watts, Agatha Christie's older sister, daring young Agatha to write a murder mystery, this story of the gift of a camera to Julia Cameron is one of those legendary, apparently random moments when a woman's life veers and takes a bold new heading. Soon after the death of her daughter, in the 1874 autobiographical fragment called "Annals of My Glasshouse," Julia Cameron wrote, "The gift from those I loved so tenderly added more and more impulse to my deeply seated love of the beautiful and from the first moment I handled my lens with a tender ardour, and it has become to me as a living thing with voice and memory and creative vigour . . . I longed to arrest all beauty that came before me, and at length, the longing has been satisfied."

Of course, receiving a camera and using it are two very different things, as many of us even in this digital age have discovered. Collodion wet-plate photography circa 1865 was not a pursuit for the lazy or the dim. Fortunately, Julia Cameron was neither, so her friends were not entirely surprised when she began, after some trial and error, to produce successful images.

That, unlike so many early photographers, Mrs. Cameron kept excellent records of her photographs and preserved the plates with meticulous care in a converted glasshouse might also have been expected of an educated woman in the age of domestic gurus like Catharine Beecher and Isabella Beeton. What did surprise the friends of the Camerons was that their dear Julia, so busy, so restless, so scatty, proved to have both a vision of what she wanted to achieve with her lens and the talent to execute it. In the words of her niece Julia Stephen, photography in Julia Cameron's hands "became truly artistic, instead of possessing merely mechanical excellence." Cameron began to submit her pictures for international competitions and to win medals, and she achieved a certain fame. Magda Kearney, an Australian scholar, tells us in an important article that Cameron put together albums that she gave to her supporters and friends, had her images exhibited in the British Museum and the South Kensington Museum, and through the Colnaghi Gallery had her most popular images reproduced as carbon prints.

Given the wearisome seven to twelve minutes needed for the exposures at that time, landscapes and still lifes might have been an obvious direction to take for a neophyte photographer. Mountains do not fidget, after all, and an apple does not scratch its nose. But the beauty Julia Cameron was interested in was of the human body. She aimed to capture on collodion gel not just the outer appearance but the inner truth of the men and women who peopled her domestic landscape, and once she had chosen her subjects, she was inexorable. Illustrious friends like Charles Darwin and Alfred Tennyson sat rigid for interminable minutes in front of her artfully ill-focused lens, and the images she produced of Victorian Grand Old Men now grace our biographies and history books.

But the photographs for which Julia Cameron was most cherished in her lifetime and that are today most prized by the art world are of the beautiful young women she knew. Ellen Terry was one of these, captured just before she was abandoned by her disagreeable husband, G. F. Watts. Another was May Hillier, the daughter of an Irish beggar woman. Famously impulsive, generous, and indifferent to social boundaries, Julia Cameron took May into her home, educated her with her own children, and launched her into middle-class society and affluence. But Julia Cameron's favorite subjects were members of her family, including her niece and namesake Julia Jackson.

Anyone who has the chance to see an actual Cameron print up close will agree that no reproduction quite does justice to her art. When in a recent exhibition I found myself face-to-face with a portrait of the widowed Julia Jackson Duckworth, I could for the first time really appreciate Cameron's expert handling of light and shadow, the subtle gradation of tone, the exacting yet revealing choice of pose as the subject turns her long slender neck as if to evade our inquisitive gaze.

Around 1870 the hitherto thriving coffee plantations in (then) Ceylon were wiped out by *Hemileia vastatrix,* a fungus also known as coffee rust. Charles Cameron lost a great deal of money and decided that he could no longer afford to live in England, though he seems not to have sold the Freshwater property or the small house he also owned near London. In 1876, the Camerons moved back to Ceylon, where at least one of their sons had turned to planting tea.

Charles Cameron had never been quite happy in England. He felt the cold intensely, preferred books to people, and displayed an attitude of amused resignation toward the manic schedule of social activities and house improvements maintained by his wife. Charles was once heard to remark in reference to his beloved coffee plantation in Sri Lanka, "Julia is slicing up Ceylon." Thus, he was more elated than depressed to be forced by financial difficulties to go back to the original Dimbola. "There was peace, there was warmth, there were the monkeys and the elephants which he had once lived among as a friend and a brother," as Virginia Woolf puts it.

Julia's feelings were probably rather different from her husband's, as she had built such a vibrant personal and professional life for herself in England. But she was unfailingly loyal to Charles and, unlike her sister Maria Jackson, who lived apart from her husband for many years, seems never to have thought of leaving Charles. Julia and Charles kept their financial problems a secret from friends, announcing out of the blue that they were going to visit their son in Ceylon but not saying that they expected to settle there again.

Standing on board ship at Southampton, with an ivory staff in one hand and a pink rose in the other, every inch the venerable patriarch and, for once, inviting the camera, Charles watched as his wife, "grave and valiant," bustled around to ensure that all the huge piles of luggage were safely put on board. These included two coffins packed with glass and china, and, as Virginia Woolf intuited, those coffins tell us a lot about how Julia Cameron felt as she sailed away from England.

Julia Margaret Cameron apparently took many photographs in Ceylon, but it is unclear if any of them survive. In 1878, Charles and Julia returned to England for a visit, but they failed to get in touch with their old friends. Anne Thackeray Ritchie, who had her first child, Hester, in that year, was hurt and amazed that her beloved old friend Julia Cameron was back but never came to see her. Then, on the evening of the child's christening, the nurse told the Ritchies an odd story. "A rather strange-looking lady" had come to the house unannounced, asked to see the baby, and put a beautiful white shawl around her. Anne Thackeray Ritchie wrote in her diary, "When I saw the white shawl I knew it came from my dear Mrs. Cameron."

Soon after her return to Ceylon, Julia Cameron died, at the age of sixty-four. Charles Cameron, twenty years her senior, soldiered on for several more years, managing even to pay one more visit to England. Virginia Woolf imagines the dying Julia looking out a big open window, "birds fluttering in and out . . . photographs . . . tumbling over the tables," and dying peacefully, with the word "Beautiful" on her lips. For myself, I wonder if the death could really have been so easy and so aesthetic. Did some tropical disease lay low that bundle of energy and determination and talent, Julia Margaret Cameron, or did she finally give in to the melancholy we see in the portraits of her?

Back in England, Julia Stephen did what she could to keep her aunt's memory alive. In the eighth edition of the *Dictionary of National Biography*, we find the single-column entry "Julia Margaret Cameron, photographer," a tiny female atoll poking up in an ocean of frothy male fame and windy self-congratulation. Julia Cameron's entry is signed "J.P.S." and is based, we are informed by the dictionary's editor, on "personal knowledge." "J.P.S." was Julia Prinsep Stephen.

Virginia Woolf, in her introduction to *Victorian Photographs,* surprisingly does not cite or refer to the *DNB* entry her mother had written, but we know that the proof of Julia Cameron's creative spirit was from birth before her eyes, as a set of Cameron's portraits hung in a dim hall at 22 Hyde Park Gate in Kensington. To Julia Stephen herself the images were reminders of childhood happiness and early married loss. For the Duckworth and Stephen children, the Cameron pictures were silent testimony to the years before their mother's second marriage to Leslie Stephen, years of which Julia rarely spoke. They were also powerful evidence of the legendary Pattle beauty that had passed to their mother from her mother, Maria Pattle Jackson, and which Julia had passed on to all three of her daughters.

And just as the Pattle beauty was passed on, so was the Pattle-Cameron creative impulse. Vanessa, from early childhood, determined she would be a painter. Virginia, when even younger, decided she would be a writer.

ॐ

In the early 1920s, Woolf not only brought Julia Cameron's photographs out of the Victorian penumbra and memorialized her great-aunt in a sparkling essay; she also dashed off a little skit called "Freshwater" to amuse her fellow Bloomsberries. One of the things that Pattledom and Bloomsbury shared, after all, was a love of theater and a passion for dressing up and putting on amateur theatricals.

Collapsing several time periods, Woolf's skit conjures up the antic excitement of life chez Cameron at Dimbola Lodge. Act I opens with Charles Cameron having his long white hair and beard washed while his wife is busy trying to persuade anyone who comes her way to sit — and sit! — in front of her camera. The Camerons await only the arrival of two sturdy coffins before setting sail for Sri Lanka, but in the meantime, their neighbor Alfred Tennyson drops by for a visit. The poet laureate is fleeing Farringford, his nearby property, for it has been invaded by American poetry enthusiasts. Tennyson begins to recite his famous poem "Maud" but is interrupted by the painter Watts, who is agonizing over how to draw the big toe of Mammon in his latest allegorical painting.

All this gets on the nerves of Nelly (Ellen Terry), Watts's wife, model, and muse, and she skips off to the beach for a swim. There she encounters Lieutenant Craig, a handsome naval officer, and they fall into each other's arms. Craig, let it be noted, was the name that in real life Ellen Terry chose as a surname for her children. Returning to Dimbola, Nelly informs her "signior" husband, Watts, that she is leaving him. The skit ends with the unexpected arrival, dea ex machina, of another of the Camerons' neighbors on the Isle of Wight — Queen Victoria. Her Majesty declines to sit, literally or figuratively, but she confers a peerage on Tennyson and the Order of Merit upon Watts, all of course in memoriam of dearly departed Albert.

"Freshwater" is a romp that Virginia Woolf, with her hands full of more important literary projects, put to one side. But it was clever and said something she wanted said about the Victorian era, so in 1935 she revised the text and organized a new performance. The revised "Freshwater" was put on before a small audience of friends in the London studio of Vanessa Bell and Duncan Grant, and the cast list, in Woolf's own handwriting, has come down to us.

That list is fascinating, for it shows the comic yet insightful way Virginia Woolf was mapping Pattledom onto Bloomsbury. Virginia Woolf was in love with her artist sister, so it is no surprise that she cast Vanessa Bell as their great-aunt Julia Cameron. Virginia's husband, Leonard Woolf, a radical thinker with a love of Ceylon, was a natural to play Charles Cameron, a man aching to get back to his plantations on that distant island. As for having the unconventional and highly sexed modernist painter Duncan Grant play the part of the staid and impotent old Victorian fuddy-duddy George Frederick Watts, that was a marvelous joke of Virginia's that all Bloomsbury could appreciate. And what more could Virginia's beautiful seventeen-year-old niece, Angelica Bell, an aspiring actress, want than to play the part of that legend of the English stage, Ellen Terry, when Ellen too was a frisky teenager?

3

High Society

SARAH PRINSEP and Julia Cameron had once been queens of Calcutta society, and after their move to England, they quickly found ways to attract England's best and brightest to their homes. All the same, the legend of their grandfather the Chevalier de l'Etang, in Queen Marie Antoinette's circle at Versailles, seems to have been etched into their souls, and they longed to be more than rich and bourgeois. England had its own caste system, and for a Pattle to be invited to a ball by a duchess around 1850 was about as difficult as it would be thirty years later for a Mrs. Smith from Duluth to be invited to one of Mrs. Astor's Manhattan soirees.

Marriage was the traditional way up the slippery pole of English society for young women, and the two youngest Pattle sisters were eager to climb. Their older sisters, Adeline, Sarah, and Maria, had all been seen as beauties when they came out, but Virginia and Sophia were simply stunning. William Makepeace Thackeray—of whom much more in Part II of this book—once recalled, in an essay for the humorous magazine *Punch,* that poets had composed odes in celebration of the beauty of Virginia Pattle and that people rioted when she appeared in the streets of London. Not by chance, the Prinsep and Cameron homes provided the two youngest Pattle heiresses with the perfect frame for their beauty and French-accented charm.

Sophia Pattle (1829–1911) rose into the lower ranks of the peerage by marrying Lord John Dalrymple, the younger son of a noble Scottish family. "Dal" was a charmer, as Lady Strachey would later tell Virginia Woolf, but the Scottish nobility was known for being poor but too proud to earn money, so "Dal" was probably an expensive acquisition. Sophia might have done better with the successful artist William Holman Hunt. The John Dalrymples had only two children, but one of them was a boy who grew up and had children himself, so Lord Dalrymple managed at least to fulfill the most important duty of a nobleman — the provision of a viable male heir. Consequently, as we saw in Chapter 1, the Dalrymples, ably represented by the Indian scholar William Dalrymple, are still going strong in the twenty-first century.

After her husband's death, Lady Dalrymple retired to France, which indicates that she might have had financial problems. France in the late nineteenth century was cheap, and the French, who had once cut off the heads of their own aristocrats, loved an English milady. Sophia Dalrymple, Hermione Lee mentions in her biography of Virginia Woolf, was known to the Stephens as "the disreputable Monte Carlo aunt," but she seems to have kept in contact with her family in England. In 1906, hearing that her Stephen great-nephews were planning to travel through Montenegro on horseback, Lady Dalrymple sent a letter and a newspaper clipping warning them about the danger of brigands.

Sophia had managed to raise her family into the peerage, but in the British studbook, Scottish peers ranked above Irish peers but below English peers, and her older sister, Virginia Pattle (1827–1910), easily eclipsed her. With her marriage to Charles Somers-Cocks, direct heir to his father, the 2nd Earl Somers, Virginia Pattle soared close to the very top of the English peerage.

Given the huge estates and great wealth of Earl Somers, it was clearly Virginia's beauty and sparkle, not her money, that captured the heart of Charles Somers-Cocks. According to one account, Virginia Pattle was acclaimed as the top debutante of her year, which, if true, means that her family now had the social influence to get a daughter presented at court. On the death of her husband's father, Virginia duly became Countess Somers, and in her twenties and thirties she lived the life of an acknowledged beauty and hostess in the highest ranks of society. Her husband adored and deferred to her, but Virginia's brilliant success was marred by her inability to give the earl her husband the male heir he counted upon. Thwarted in this most atavistic of female desires, Virginia Somers determined to push her heiress daughters, Adeline (this would be Adeline the third) and Isabella Somers, up onto the top rungs of the English peerage. As Virginia Woolf remarks in her "Sketch of the Past," "Aunt Virginia, it is plain, put her own daughters, my mother's first cousins, through tortures compared to which the boot or the Chinese shoe is negligible, in order to marry one to the Duke of Bedford, the other to Lord Henry Somerset. (That is how we came to be, as the nurse said, well connected.)"

Countess Somers succeeded in achieving her ambitious goals, at least in the beginning, at least in part. Her older daughter, Adeline Marie Somers, married George Russell, the 10th Duke of Bedford, and the younger girl, Isabella Somers, did almost as well, becoming the wife of Lord Henry Somerset, a younger son of the Duke of Beaufort. The Russells and the Somersets, like the Somerses, were the English equivalent of the *noblesse d'épée* and rather looked down at the upstart Saxe-Coburgs and their tacky new places at Balmoral and Osborne.

George Russell's primary residence was Woburn Abbey, one of the greatest estates of England, and he also owned a large chunk of central London around the eponymous Bedford Square. English history is peppered with Russells — including the great twentieth-century philosopher, mathematician, activist, and Nobel Prize winner Bertrand Russell. Alas, things did not go well for George and Adeline Russell. They had no children, and George died of diabetes at forty, leaving the title, the estate, and, interestingly, the guardianship of his illegitimate Indian daughter (India keeps popping up in this story!) to his brother. Adeline Somers Russell's glory days as mistress of Woburn Abbey were short. Virginia Woolf recalled how the duchess had come to Kensington to see her mother, and behind the folding doors that Julia Stephen pulled across when talking privately with women friends, went on her knees weeping as she told how her husband had just died at the abbey. Thereafter the life of Adeline, Duchess of Bedford, it was said in her own family, was magnificent and very unhappy. The fate of Adeline's sister, Isabella, however, was even worse, and her disastrous marriage became a cause célèbre of the Victorian era.

Isabella Somers (1851–1921) was a deeply Christian young woman whose secret ambition, according to her biographer Ros Black, was to become a nun. Instead, she found herself married to dashing Lord Henry Somerset, second son to the Duke of Beaufort. The Somersets' main country seat was (and is) Badminton House, and through the Plantagenet John of Gaunt, the family claims (distant) kinship with the present English royal family. Elizabeth II, her husband and (distant) cousin Prince Phillip, and all the Windsors trace their lineage back to the early-fifteenth-century Joan Beaufort, Queen of Scots. Further along in English history, the name Somerset crops up regularly. Lord Raglan, for example, the gentleman who pioneered a fashion in sleeves after losing an arm at the Battle of Waterloo and went on, alas, to command the calamitous British invasion of Crimea in 1854, began life as Lord Fitzroy Somerset.

Lord Henry Somerset secured Isabella's hand and large fortune by flattering and flirting with the girl's beautiful mother, Countess Somers. This was hardly a recipe for conjugal happiness, and Lord Henry proved to be not only duplicitous but violently abusive. From his teenage years he had shown an undisguised preference for persons of his own sex, and he married solely because Isabella Somers's money would enable him to live in style and provide him with opportunities for social advancement. For some time after the wedding, Henry refused to consummate the match, claiming, with aristocratic panache, that he wished to forsake society and pursue a life of chastity on Christian principles — in the company of a few chosen male friends. He still was in urgent need of money, however, and when his father-in-law, Earl Somers, refused to advance him any more, Henry saw no choice but to go to bed with his wife and try for a child. When Isabella gave birth to a healthy male, to be known as "Somey" in the family, there was great rejoicing with the Somersets at Badminton House and the Somerses at Reigate Priory.

His dynastic responsibilities met, however, Henry saw no reason not to follow his own tastes and explore the gay underworld that linked Blackfriars to Mayfair. He installed his lover, Walter Dalrymple (a relative of Sophia's husband, Sir John Dalrymple, and thus one of his wife's cousins), at his London townhouse, and there they entertained young noblemen of similar tastes, along with a series of male prostitutes. To Isabella herself he was not merely indifferent but cruel, telling her outright that he would never return to her bed or give her the children she wanted. He snubbed her in public, and on one occasion threatened her with a small knife. Henry told Isabella that, if she ever told anyone the truth about their marriage, he would make her life a misery.

Isabella was desperate for an unofficial separation, but since her husband derived almost all his income from her father, he would not let her go. Isabella appealed to her parents, but Earl and Countess Somers were above all anxious to avoid a scandal that would cast shame on the whole family. Then, on February 3, 1878, things came to a head.

Returning home from lunch with her parents, who were staying at a hotel, Isabella was told by a servant that her husband had taken his disreputable friends into his son's room to admire the boy as he lay sleeping. Faced with what she perceived as a direct physical and moral threat to her child, Isabella went to her husband's desk, found letters that proved the nature of his relationships with his male friends and hangers-on, and copied sections of them. The Pattle women, as I have said, had smarts and guts.

Isabella got the child up, carried him over to her parents, and courageously returned home. Discovering the loss of his son and seeing that his papers had been disturbed, Lord Henry stormed over to the hotel, crazy with rage, and accused his in-laws of child abduction. Alarmed by Henry's anger, caring at last more for their daughter's safety than their own social status, the Somerses dispatched a servant to get Isabella out of her husband's house before his return. She arrived at the hotel in her dressing gown, with her hair down her back, one slipper on and one off.

In 1878, the Married Women's Property Act was still four years in the future, and children were by law the property of the father. A mother had no legal guardianship rights. Lord Henry was not unhappy to get rid of his wife, but he was furious to have his child, the passport to his future, taken from him. With the full support of his parents, whose affection for Isabella died as soon as the ducal succession was in question, Lord Henry went to court, confident of victory, to regain physical possession of his son and heir.

At this time, homosexuality was officially anathema in Victorian England, its propensities and practices fiercely denounced by clergymen, educators, and doctors, and, at least on the books, subject to severe punishment under the law. All the same, Lord Henry was right to be confident that he would prevail in the court of law and in public opinion. His well-connected friends launched a vicious attack on Isabella in the press, casting her as a frigid harridan who had driven her husband away, and the court refused to accept as evidence the letters she had copied as proof of her husband's homosexual liaisons.

At the end of the trial, when making his ruling, the judge acquitted Lord Henry of the "horrible and foul crime" of which he stood accused by his wife. He simply could not believe, the judge said, that "Lord Henry Somerset could be so bad as to seek to pollute the rising mind of a child." All the same, little Somey was, "if things remain as they are [that is, if Lord Henry's elder brother had no male children], the heir of the premier Duke of England" and the grandson, moreover, of Earl Somers, a former Lord Chancellor of England. On the basis of the child's lineage and glorious prospects, not on the evidence of spousal abuse and immorality, the judge granted Lady Henry Somerset custody of her son until he was sixteen.

It was a moral victory for Isabella Somers, but it came at a very heavy cost — to her, not to her husband. There was in England an unwritten law that the dirty linen of the aristocracy must not be washed in public, and the homosexual activities of many highborn gentlemen were either ignored or regarded with benevolent cynicism. Queen Victoria knew full well that many of her grandsons were gay, and if royal wives didn't make a big fuss when coming upon hubby in flagrante delicto with the stable boy, why should Isabella Somers make a fuss? Morality in matters sexual was considered ineffably bourgeois. Of course, Lady Henry's mother had been born a Pattle!

So, according to the inflexible law of the beau monde, it was Isabella who had to be punished. Eager not to offend the Somersets, the officers of the law moved with elephantine deliberation, giving Lord Henry plenty of time to escape across the Channel, lest opinion turn against him. Thereafter he led a carefree new life in Italy, "the land of Michelangelesque young men," as Quentin Bell elegantly puts it, and affordable even for a younger son on a small allowance.

Isabella, meanwhile, found herself banished for life from London society. Shades of Downton Abbey — when visiting her sister, Adeline, the Duchess of Bedford, Isabella was obliged to escape down a servants' staircase whenever the duchess's mother-in-law arrived. Encouraged by middle-class relatives like her first cousin Julia Jackson Stephen, Lady Isabella Somerset, as she preferred to be known after the scandal, turned to good works, notably the support of poor women with alcoholic husbands, and she had a notable career as a philanthropist.

Relations between the Somersets and the Somerses were never cordial, but Somey remained loyal to his mother. When he married, he did not invite his father to the wedding, with the result that all the Somersets boycotted the event. Worse, Lord Henry Somerset's older brother, on succeeding to the title of 10th Duke of Beaufort at age forty-eight, married his longtime mistress, who produced a son and heir. Sadly — or not, depending on your point of view — the task of producing two male heirs in succession proved too much of a strain for the Beaufort men, and in due course Somey's grandson David Somerset, Isabella's great-grandson, became the 11th Duke of Beaufort. The Pattle bloodline, one might say, came out on top.

❧

Virginia Woolf was never close to her Somers great-aunt or her first cousins once removed, but their lives intersected with hers in several interesting ways. As the documentation brought forward in the Somerset child custody trial shows, the "gay life" was at least as common in the Mayfair culture of Isabella Somers circa 1878 as in Virginia Woolf's Bloomsbury circa 1918. The big difference was that the women of Bloomsbury knew, accepted, and indeed joked about the fact that so many of their male friends were homosexuals.

More directly, Virginia Woolf's aristocratic relatives shaped her youth because they powerfully shaped the relationship between her parents. As we shall see in Part III, from her teenage years as a notable beauty to her death as a gaunt, gray-haired, though still middle-aged matron, Julia Prinsep Jackson Duckworth Stephen managed to project an air of glamour. In the middle- and upper-middle-professional milieu she inhabited in her last years, part of that glamour was due to the fact that Julia could, if she chose, claim French nobility among her ancestors and English aristocrats as her close relatives. Julia Stephen was far too refined to brag about "my poor cousin the Dowager Duchess of Bedford" or "that dreadful person Lord Henry Somerset who ruined the life of my cousin Isabella," but friends were happy to do it for her.

No one was more susceptible to Julia's glamour than her second husband. A stubbornly independent man who worked for a living, Leslie Stephen was proud of his own ascetic, intellectual, ethical heritage as a Venn-Stephen. The Pattle clan loyalty emerged whenever there was a family marriage or a death, so, when Julia and Leslie married, Julia's aunt Virginia, Countess Somers, loaned them her smaller estate for their honeymoon. When Maria Pattle Jackson died in 1892, Julia Stephen was prostrate with grief over the death of her mother, and she and Leslie went to live for six or eight weeks in a little house at Chenies in Buckinghamshire loaned to them by Julia's cousin, the Dowager Duchess of Bedford.

The Bedford-Beaufort connection was one of the things that made Julia Jackson the epitome of beauty, grace, and distinction in Leslie's eyes, and it would be one of the forces that shaped their relationship when they married. No one better than Leslie understood that, by marrying him, Julia had moved down several notches in the complex hierarchy of the English bourgeoisie and become a woman who needed, for the first time in her life, to worry about money. As we shall see, while superbly playing the part of the self-sacrificing Victorian "Angel in the House," Julia Stephen was empowered by her husband's highly eroticized adoration and sense of indebtedness.

For Leslie and Julia's children, their mother's aristocratic relatives formed a vague but agreeable backdrop to humdrum Kensington life, and Virginia's husband, Leonard Woolf, picked up on it as soon as they became engaged. In his autobiography, Woolf accurately identified his wife's class background: "The children of Sir Leslie Stephen had, at the turn of the century when their father died, broken away from the society into which they were born. That society consisted of the upper levels of the professional middle class and country families interpenetrated to a certain extent by the aristocracy." Leonard saw, resented, and envied that class's "assurance of manner," which could easily change into "insolent urbanity," and he felt himself excluded from it despite his education at a public school (meaning, in British terms, a private school) and at Cambridge University. "I was an outsider to this class because, although

I and my father before me belonged to the professional middle class, we had only recently struggled up to it from the stratum of Jewish shopkeepers. We had no roots in it."

George Duckworth, Julia's oldest son and Virginia Woolf's older half-brother, was particularly aware that his mother had come down in society by marrying Leslie Stephen. As an adult, George's goal was to use the fortune he had inherited from his father, Herbert Duckworth, to move the family back up into the higher reaches of English society. Following the deaths of his mother and of his sister Stella, George decided that his own rise in society might still be achieved by following the old Pattle strategy: finding upper-class husbands for his beautiful stepsisters. Perhaps, George thought, Vanessa and Virginia Stephen, like Virginia Pattle Somers, Adeline Somers Russell, and Isabella Somers Somerset before them, might snag an earl or a duke. This plan was a dismal failure, as each of George's Stephen sisters in turn hated to play the part of a society miss. Perhaps the family gossip about the disastrous marriages of their mother's cousins Adeline and Isabella did their part in convincing Vanessa and Virginia that marrying up the social ladder was a recipe for disaster.

In the annals of Bloomsbury, however, George Duckworth's social climbing played an important role. In 1904, following the death of Leslie Stephen, George was all set to move into 46 Gordon Square in Bloomsbury with his four Stephen half-siblings and continue in his in loco parentis role with Vanessa and Virginia. Then providentially, as it seemed to his half-sisters, Lady Margaret Herbert, the stepdaughter of the Dowager Countess of Caernarvon, agreed to marry George, and the two set up their own household. Had George Duckworth continued to live with his sisters, taking precedence over their brother Thoby, there would have been no Bloomsbury group.

❧

Virginia Woolf was contemptuous of her brother George's social snobbery, but when she started to envisage a career in journalism, she turned for support to her intimate friend Violet Dickinson, who moved on the edges of high society, and to Violet's close friend Lady Robert Cecil. As their correspondence proves, Nellie Cecil, herself a semiprofessional writer, did her best to get Virginia Woolf launched in the world of journalism in 1907. Relations between the two women cooled after Virginia's marriage, but when Virginia's second novel, *Night and Day,* was published to admiring reviews in 1919, Lady Robert invited Virginia (but, I note, not Leonard) to lunch to meet her highly aristocratic French relatives the Bibescos — "my first appearance as a small Lioness," Woolf remarks.

Once she became a literary celebrity, Woolf was no more immune than her friend Lytton Strachey to the pleasures of being invited to exclusive parties or having intimate teas with titled ladies. She engaged in a warm, if guarded, friendship with Lady Ottoline Morrell, whose Cavendish-Bentinck ancestry could be traced back to a (male) lover of William III. More important, when the immensely aristocratic and extremely handsome Mrs. Harold Nicolson, alias Vita Sackville-West, invaded her world, Mrs. Woolf was, as we shall see in Chapter 17, ready to be seduced.

In December 1936, then at the height of her career, Virginia Woolf was asked to give a talk to the Bloomsbury Memoir Club on the topic "Am I a Snob?" The text we have of this talk shows Woolf at her charming and graceful best. Yes, she says up front, I am a snob and have been ever since girlhood, since the Stephen family of Kensington "had floating fringes in the world of fashion." If she received a letter bearing a coronet, that letter was always displayed on her desk, which, Woolf admits, was a little pathetic of her, given that several of the male members of the Memoir Club had so much greater reason to advertise their friends in high places. Her dear friend Desmond MacCarthy, Eton and Cambridge, never boasted that his appointment book was packed with meetings scheduled with the noble and mighty. As for her other great friend Maynard Keynes, also Eton and Cambridge, he would happily discuss "pigs, plays, pictures," but you would have to learn from someone else that Mr. Keynes had just been summoned to No. 10 Downing Street by Prime Minister Baldwin and begged, almost on bended knee, to join the cabinet and save the nation.

Having showered her friends Desmond and Maynard — both present in the room when she gave her speech — with delicate compliments and established the social eminence of Bloomsbury, Woolf gives a humorous account of a casual dinner she had had with her friends the Thynnes — the Marchioness of Bath and her daughters, the Ladies Katherine and Beatrice Thynne — and its contrast with a sumptuous lunch for forty close acquaintances given by Margot Asquith, Lady Oxford. For Woolf, Lady Oxford, gleaming in emeralds, brilliant of wit and spiteful of tongue, fell far below Lady Beatrice, who could not spell and dressed like a bag lady. "I want coronets," writes Woolf, "but they must be old coronets that carry land with them and country houses; coronets that breed simplicity, eccentricity, ease; and such confidence in your own state that you . . . feed the dogs bloody bones from table with your own hands."

After such opportunities to break bread with the top people, Woolf tells us, she would emerge onto the street and view "the butchers' shops and the trays of penny toys through an air that seemed made of gold dust and champagne . . . If you ask me if I would rather meet Einstein or the Prince of Wales, I plump for the Prince without hesitation." But having owned up to her own snobbery and absolved her friends of the same sin, Virginia Woolf steers her charming and apparently nonchalant talk into two directions designed to please those of her listeners who did not get regular invitations to No. 10 or Buck House. Snobbery comes in different shades, Woolf argues, and there is an aristocracy of writers that aristocrats recognize but fail pathetically to understand. And to end her talk and give her Bloomsbury friends the kind of red meat they expected from their Virginia, Woolf illustrates the absurd snobbery of so many in the aristocratic set by narrating the course of her own "friendship" with Lady Sybil Colefax.

Learning that Sir Arthur Colefax, Lady Sybil's husband, had suddenly died, Virginia was full of sympathy and hurried off to pay a condolence call. She found the Colefax townhouse empty and its mistress stripped of pretense. It was all too clear that it was the loss of her house and the auctioning of her furniture and silverware that Sibyl mourned, not the husband who had paid for them all. She was taking the opportunity of her move to dismiss her maid Fielding, who, after thirty years of service, was going blind and dared to shed tears for her dead master.

In Virginia Woolf's last glimpse of her former friend, Lady Colefax ventures out in her Rolls-Royce, her facial color restored, her shell intact, ready to do battle if not with the wealthy hostess Lady Curzon, a former vicereine of India, then at least with the ambitious Mrs. Ralph Wigram. As she steps into her car, Sibyl seeks to impress her literary friend Virginia one last time, by remarking how she had once met Henry James — whom she refers to as "dear old "H.J."

Virginia Woolf had, of course, known Henry James as a beloved family friend when she was a girl. She knew that nobody who knew "the Master" ever referred to him by his initials. Henry James, and before him her adoptive grandfather William Thackeray, and implicitly Woolf herself, were all aristocrats in the illustrious world of letters, a world to which literary snobs like Lady Sibyl could only aspire.

PART II

Virginia Woolf and the Thackerays — A Legacy of Literature, Money, and Madness

Virginia Woolf and Her Seven Siblings

Three Duckworths, One Thackeray-Stephen, and Three Stephens

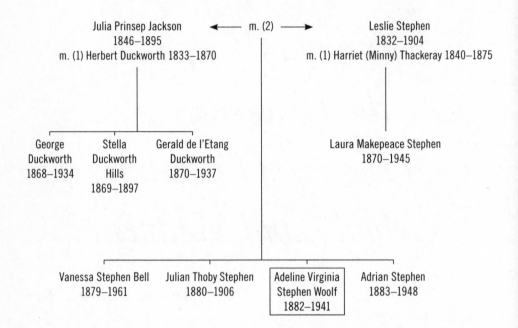

Julia Prinsep Jackson
1846–1895
m. (1) Herbert Duckworth 1833–1870
    ◄─── m. (2) ───►
Leslie Stephen
1832–1904
m. (1) Harriet (Minny) Thackeray 1840–1875

George
Duckworth
1868–1934

Stella
Duckworth
Hills
1869–1897

Gerald de l'Etang
Duckworth
1870–1937

Laura Makepeace Stephen
1870–1945

Vanessa Stephen Bell
1879–1961

Julian Thoby Stephen
1880–1906

Adeline Virginia
Stephen Woolf
1882–1941

Adrian Stephen
1883–1948

4

Finders Keepers

OH DEAR, surely not Thackeray, my Woolf-loving readers will be exclaiming! If we must go all stuffy and venture into literary influence, why not Jane Austen or George Eliot or Charlotte Brontë, whom we have actually read? Woolf wrote brilliantly about so many Victorian writers, especially the women, but she barely makes even a passing reference to Thackeray. And surely, to speak of a legacy from Thackeray is far-fetched. There was, after all, no blood relationship between Woolf and Thackeray, and he died almost twenty years before she was born.

But a legacy did come down to Woolf from Thackeray, part legal-financial, part literary-cultural, and part psychological-medical, and it inflected the course of her life in subtle structural ways. To illustrate how the legacy worked, and how easy it is to miss, I want to take a careful look at something apparently random and inconsequential — some old pieces of paper at the back of a closet.

෨

In the New Year of 1906, the tall, narrow house at 22 Hyde Park Gate, Kensington, where Virginia Woolf had been born and had lived her whole life, lay deserted. She and her brothers Thoby and Adrian and her sister Vanessa had fled the parental ghosts and, in defiance of their smarter friends, rented 46 Gordon Square in Bloomsbury, near the British Museum. The new place was roomy, with high ceilings and windows that let in some light, and it was blessedly affordable for four young people who lived the upper-middle-class life on inherited money but felt in no way rich. If a Bloomsbury address signaled downward mobility, so be it, said Vanessa Stephen, who had engineered the move.

Thoby Stephen had for several years been enjoying a bachelor's life in London under the guise of studying the law, and he was now charged by his older sister with finding a tenant for the old parental home. It was one more piece of drudgery Thoby had to shoulder in his post-Cambridge existence, and he was gloomy but unsurprised when no eager lady appeared waving her husband's check in response to his advertisement. No one, it seemed, was keen to occupy a house with so many stairs, so little garden, and sub-basement servant quarters calculated to scare off even the lowliest of scullery maids.

And then it happened, the find of a lifetime, or so it seemed to the excited Thoby. At the back of a closet at Hyde Park Gate, he came upon ten dusty old sheets of paper covered with writing and drawings — and suddenly Apollo drove his chariot through the Kensington drizzle, scattering golden guineas down on his obedient English devotee. The paper, Thoby was quick enough to recognize, was part of "Lord Bateman," a poem by William Makepeace Thackeray, a writer and illustrator whose fame had only grown brighter in the years since his untimely death forty years earlier.

In great excitement, Virginia Woolf wrote to her friend Violet Dickinson: "Thoby made £1000, *one thousand pounds,* by selling 10 pages of Thackeray's Lord Bateman. George [Smith, of publisher Smith & Elder] sold it to Pierpont Morgan. So all bar [that is, Thoby's expenses to train as a barrister] and Greek expenses [see below] are more than paid for."

At last, after two long years watching his father yield to a malady too terrible even to be spoken aloud, all was sunshine in Thoby Stephen's life. After the lotus-eating of his Cambridge years and a spell of wild oats in London, he felt ready at last to follow in the footsteps of his uncle Sir James Fitzjames Stephen, Baronet, Queen's Counsel. Now at last, thanks to the Thackeray find, without laying out any part of the meager three thousand pounds left him by his father, he felt all set financially to start on the risky but prestigious life of a barrister. He could also finance a summer expedition to Greece and Turkey for himself and his siblings, a scheme he had long nurtured.

If we are to believe the portrait of her brother that Virginia Woolf offers in *Jacob's Room,* a dozen years of ancient Greek at school and university had barely equipped Thoby Stephen to stumble through *Agamemnon* or *Oedipus Rex* in the original, and he knew little of ancient civilizations. All the same, he and his friend Lytton Strachey were convinced that they understood the old Greeks better than anyone and that if he, tall, broad, magnificent Thoby Stephen, were to stroll the agora in Athens, the ghost of Socrates would appear and hail him as a "fine fellow."

Now these gratifying assumptions were to be tested on Greek soil — and in between serious tours of the ancient sites on the Peloponnese, Thoby thought he would make a marital scouting trip to the Euboean peninsula. There, at Achmetaga, her family's Greek estate, pretty, vivacious Irene Noel was spending the summer. Irene was her rich father's heiress and was being pursued by several young men, including Thoby's good friend Desmond MacCarthy, but Thoby thought he stood a good chance with her. He was by now quite aware that his strong, silent brand of masculinity had just as devastating an effect on young women as on young men — women just felt unable to say so straight out.

In the same letter in which she told the great news to Violet Dickinson, Virginia wrote, "By the way, don't say anything about Thoby's sale of the Ms. Or his price. It is rather a secret I think." The secrecy was not surprising. Thoby Stephen was not related to the dead Thackeray and had no inheritance rights to any of the writer's private papers. At the time of his death, William Makepeace Thackeray's estate had been split in half between his two daughters, Anne and Harriet (Minny) Thackeray, and they both married and produced legitimate children. In 1906, Anne Thackeray Ritchie and her two children, Hester and William Ritchie, along with Laura Makepeace Stephen, Minny's daughter with Leslie Stephen, all had a better right than Thoby Stephen to claim their grandfather's writing and reap the profit.

But the legal status of William Makepeace Thackeray's private papers had never been clearly resolved, and none of the Thackeray heirs came forward to exercise their hereditary right. The copyright of the writer's published work belonged to his publishing house, Smith & Elder — that much at least had been determined. After William Thackeray died unexpectedly, in December 1863, his friend and publisher George Smith paid the Thackeray daughters the very considerable sum of ten thousand pounds for the copyrights to all of their father's work. This earned the gratitude of the two women, but purchasing the rights to Thackeray's literary estate was also a smart business investment on the part of Smith & Elder. Thackeray continued to sell well and, perhaps conscious of this, George Smith allowed Anne and Harriet Thackeray to keep in their possession all of Thackeray's manuscripts and private papers. After the death of his wife, Minny Thackeray Stephen, Leslie Stephen was given the pride of the collection, the manuscript of *Vanity Fair*, Thackeray's most famous novel, plus another illustrated manuscript. He also became the trustee of what his biographer Noel Annan describes as "a dowry for Laura [the child of his marriage to Minny Thackeray] which later reverted to his family [that is, the children of his second wife]." Of this "dowry," more later.

Given how much money a few sheets in Thackeray's hand could obtain in 1906, one can only speculate on what Leslie Stephen got for the *Vanity Fair* manuscript, and after receiving these generous gifts, Stephen did not contest the right of his sister-in-law, Anne Thackeray Ritchie, to the rest of the Thackeray papers. Over the years, these rose markedly in value and, with the tacit approval of the copyright holders, came to constitute a kind of piggy bank for the Ritchie family. By putting some of her father's less important documents up for sale, Anne Thackeray Ritchie was able to afford some important luxuries for herself, such as travel abroad, and also pay the boarding-school fees for her son.

Lady Ritchie was known in the Stephen family to be generous to a fault, and when and if she heard of Thoby's windfall, she was probably happy that the Stephen children should share a little in the inherited Thackeray loot. As for Laura Stephen, locked away in an asylum, where her "dowry" conveniently paid for all her expenses, she had neither the literacy nor, by reason of her attested insanity, the legal authority to make any claims to any part of her grandfather's literary estate.

Thus, on the surface, the discovery and sale of the valuable Thackeray autograph was simply a case of finders, keepers. The sheets had at some point drifted into the possession of Thoby's father, Minny Thackeray's widower, Leslie Stephen. They had been found and kept by Leslie's oldest son in Leslie's house, or, more precisely — since in this book I am being a stickler about who inherited what from whom — the house Leslie had inherited from Julia, his wife and Thoby's mother. As a widow, Julia Duckworth had purchased the house (under a different street number), and after Leslie married her, he moved into his new wife's house with his daughter, Laura. The renumbered 22 Hyde Park Gate then became the family home for all eight Duckworth and Stephen children. After Julia's death, Leslie, as her widower, took complete possession and ownership of the Hyde Park Gate property, and on his death, the house formed part of his estate, its rental and eventual sale value presumably, like the rest of his assets, to be divided equally among Vanessa, Thoby, Virginia, and Adrian.

The year 1906 was indisputably a landmark year in the life of Virginia Woolf. As we shall see in Chapter 12, somewhere on his dream tour of Greece and Turkey, Thoby Stephen contracted typhoid, and he died of the disease upon his return home. Free of their older brother's control, and with his sorrowing friends from Cambridge clustering around them, Vanessa and Virginia both achieved a new autonomy and, eventually, chose husbands, Clive Bell and Leonard Woolf, who had been Thoby's close friends at Cambridge. Those two men, while interpreting marriage in very different ways, would last Thoby's sisters a lifetime. So you can say without exaggeration that, if that Thackeray manuscript had been thrown unread into the dustbin by some efficient housemaid, Bloomsbury might never have bloomed, and Virginia Stephen might never have become Virginia Woolf.

And once you start putting the names Thackeray and Stephen together, a pattern in the family carpet begins to emerge. Far from being a random, one-off, serendipitous event, Thoby Stephen's discovery in the closet was a final, dramatic instance of the way that the fortunes of Leslie Stephen and his second family were shaped by their connection to the Thackerays. Over two generations, money flowed from the Thackerays to the Leslie Stephens, making possible their primary residence at Hyde Park Gate and at Talland House, their summer retreat in St. Ives, Cornwall. These two properties constituted the two contrasting worlds of her childhood that Virginia Woolf would etch into English literature.

The money originated with William Makepeace Thackeray, who earned it with his writing and drawing. As a young man, Thackeray had inherited a large fortune from his Anglo-Indian father and then gambled it away. His subsequent drive to succeed as a writer was fueled by his determination to win back the affluent lifestyle that had been his as a boy and ensure that his daughters, Anny and Minny, should never experience the financial problems that had weighed him down in his twenties and early thirties. Thackeray succeeded, but at great cost to himself. He died intestate and unprepared at fifty-two but leaving an estate that, divided equally between his daughters, guaranteed them a financially secure future. He also left them an immense legacy of affection and goodwill, not only in England's literary community but in the world of European culture at large. That cultural legacy would, in his lifetime and after his death, promote the success of his writer daughter Anne, who proudly carried her father's name with her even after she married. It would also advance the career of the man whom, after Thackeray's death, his daughter Minny chose to marry — Leslie Stephen.

As Leslie's daughter Virginia would note decades later in *A Room of One's Own,* for someone struggling to make it in English publishing, an unearned income of, say, five hundred pounds a year could make all the difference between success and failure. When he began his career as a writer, her father, Leslie Stephen, did not have anything near that sum. As he admitted in a letter to his second wife, Julia, during their courtship, in his first years in London after resigning from his Cambridge fellowship, he had gotten something of a reputation around London of being a "notorious penny-a-liner" — that is, a writer who received as little as one penny for each line he put in print. To any young man eager to be a journalist, Leslie wryly remarked to Julia, he would recommend taking over the management of a pub instead.

But then, almost despite himself, Leslie Stephen found himself married to a woman who could offer him a lot more than "five hundred pounds a year." During the eight years of his marriage to Minny Thackeray, Leslie enjoyed a level of domestic comfort and social prominence that he had never before known. He allowed his capable and provident wife the daily management of what was now their joint fortune and then, when she died, he assumed control as well as ownership of Minny's estate. This included real estate, securities, best-seller manuscripts, and many *objets de vertu,* as William Thackeray had been a discerning and keen collector. Leslie Stephen sincerely grieved for his wife, but he had always aspired to live as a "gentleman," by which he meant a man not obliged to work for money, and now a gentleman was what he found himself to be. With the fortune he had inherited from Minny Thackeray, Leslie Stephen was at last able to pursue his scholarly interests in peace and write his book on moral philosophy.

After a few years as a widower, Leslie Stephen found himself more and more attracted to his friend and neighbor Julia Jackson Duckworth. Some ten years earlier, as an impecunious bachelor, Leslie had seen in Julia Jackson his ideal woman and had stood back in the shadows when Herbert Duckworth swept her off her feet. As the daughter of an independently wealthy woman and the wife and widow of a wealthy man, Julia had been accustomed to an affluent lifestyle, and she would lose her widow's income and the financial support of the Duckworths if she remarried. All the same, Leslie Stephen thought he might have a chance with Julia. Having inherited property from his first wife, he was now a "gentleman" like Herbert Duckworth. And as an aspiring man of letters he could benefit from the valuable literary network that Minny's famous father, William Makepeace Thackeray, had built up.

George Smith, an influential figure in English literary circles, had been not only William Makepeace Thackeray's publisher but probably his best friend. Smith & Elder published most of Thackeray's novels, and as publisher and editor the two men had launched the highly regarded and financially successful literary magazine *Cornhill.* Smith was deeply attached to the Thackeray daughters, Anny and Minny, and after their father's tragically sudden and early death he determined to do everything he could for them. When Minny married Leslie Stephen, Smith knew that Stephen would prefer not to live on this wife's fortune. He recognized that Stephen was a proud and stubborn man, still fighting to make his way in the literary world. And so, in a characteristic act of thoughtfulness and generosity, George Smith offered Leslie Stephen the editorship of *Cornhill* at five hundred pounds a year. That was a salary to make Stephen's competitors salivate, and it proved a poor investment for Smith &

Elder. Stephen worked hard as an editor, but *Cornhill* steadily lost subscribers during his tenure. When Stephen suffered a nervous breakdown from stress, he was eased out.

Undeterred by the *Cornhill* debacle, some years later, when the widowed Leslie Stephen was married to Julia Duckworth, George Smith offered him the editorship of Smith & Elder's latest venture, the *Dictionary of National Biography,* again at a generous salary. The *DNB* was a high-prestige publication that in the end cost George Smith seventy thousand pounds, some twenty thousand pounds more than he had estimated, but it was the making of Leslie Stephen. As his biographer Noel Annan puts it, the *DNB* was "Stephen's most important bequest to posterity." Lord Rosebery, one of England's prime ministers, declared it "the monumental literary work of Her Majesty's reign." If Leslie Stephen today is remembered in literary history as anything more than Virginia Woolf's father, it is as the first editor of the *DNB.*

Thanks to the generosity of George Smith, Leslie Stephen gained professional status, the veneration of young male historians, the adoration of his wife, Julia, a knighthood, and, for the first ten years or so of his second marriage before he collapsed again, a regular, guaranteed salary. Editing the *DNB* put the meat and potatoes and bread and butter on the table of the Stephen family during Virginia Woolf's childhood. The inheritance from Minny Thackeray provided the gravy and the jam.

Could Leslie and Julia Stephen have managed a private school education for their Stephen sons without his salary as editor of the *DNB*? Probably not. If he had not had the financial cushion of Minny's money, would frugal Leslie, while on a walking tour in Cornwall, have felt able, on impulse, to please Julia and the girls by arranging to buy the lease on Talland House? I wonder. And without the Thackeray connection, would there even have been a Stephen family? Would Julia Duckworth have agreed to marry Leslie Stephen if he had been not only the poor, awkward, ill-clad intellectual she had known as a teenager, but also a widower saddled with a child? If his first wife had not been Julia's Kensington neighbor, the affluent and stylish Minny Thackeray, would Leslie Stephen have gotten within hailing distance of her?

Along with money and connections, Minny Thackeray bequeathed one more important thing to her husband, Leslie, and to the woman who would be his second wife, her dear friend Julia Duckworth. That bequest was her sister Anne Thackeray. Anne lived with Leslie and Minny for much of their married life and moved back in with Leslie after Minny's death. She met Julia Jackson when Julia was a young teenager, and the two remained lifelong friends. In the first days after Julia's death, Anne was the only visitor Leslie would see, and during Leslie's final illness she visited him often. Virginia Woolf wrote, after Anne Thackeray Ritchie's own death, "I feel as if we owed more than we can ever say to Aunt Anny for what she was to mother and father as well as what she was to us. I think they loved her better than anyone."

And, for the aspiring writer Virginia Woolf, Anne Thackeray Ritchie was not just a marvelous auntie. She was also a muse or what we might now label a role model. There, sitting across the tea table at Hyde Park Gate, was a woman like the White Queen in *Alice* — blinking and squinting and dripping butter on her skirt, yet a witness to Victorian greatness and possessed of a clear memory of everything she had experienced from the age of two. Anne remembered sitting on the knee of Dickens, walking the sands near Farringford with Tennyson, and spending weeks at Casa Guidi with the Brownings. Franz Liszt (on piano) and Joseph Joachim (on violin) had played for her. Charlotte Brontë had sat silently opposite her at dinner. She had risked social opprobrium by exchanging cards and visits with George Eliot in England.

But Anne Thackeray Ritchie was not just a woman who had known famous people. She was a professional writer, someone who produced a steady stream of books, had a small but faithful readership, and who looked anxiously every quarter for her editor's check to come in the mail. Anne Thackeray Ritchie was living proof that, with enough talent, enough grit, and the right connections, a woman could make it in the misogynistic world of English publishing — and also be a good wife, a wise mother, and a loyal friend.

And deep in the Thackeray past was a story of the tragic madness of Anne's mother, Isabella Shawe Thackeray, a story that never made it into the carefully scoured pages of Leslie Stephen's *DNB* but that Virginia Woolf as a girl may have picked up from snatches of conversation between her mother and Anne. Though not a drop of Thackeray blood ran in Woolf's veins, that history of insanity would have its baleful influence on Virginia Woolf. It lived on, at a sanitized distance, in the person of Laura Makepeace Stephen, Virginia's half-sister, the "real" niece whom Anne Thackeray Ritchie loved so much, as we shall see in Chapter 7, and could do so very little to protect.

Virginia Woolf read all of her Aunt Anny's large literary output. More important, the essays, reviews, and novels of Anne's father, William Make-peace Thackeray, were foundational texts in Woolf's literary education. Along with the novels of Walter Scott, Thackeray's works were read aloud to her by her father when she was a girl, and she in turn would read them aloud as her sister Vanessa painted or sewed. "When I read Dickens and Thackeray," Vanessa Bell would later recall, "it is Virginia's voice that I hear." A quote from Thackeray, inscribed on a piece of chocolate-colored card, hung in the hallway at 22 Hyde Park Gate. As Woolf recalled, it began: "What is it to be a gentle-man? It is to be tender to women, chivalrous to servants . . ."

As a writer specializing in a mixture of fiction, commentary on contempo-rary mores, and English social history, Thackeray spoke to Woolf, so directly perhaps that, in a kind female Oedipal rebellion, she wrote almost nothing about him. He was in certain ways a throwback to the England of Sterne and Addison, Defoe and Fielding, that Woolf adored and did write about, but he was also an eminent literary Victorian. Quotations like the one in the Stephen family's hall made it hard for Woolf and her generation of Edwardian writers to get past the life of bland conventionality and professional plaudits created for Thackeray postmortem by his *DNB* editor son-in-law Leslie Stephen. As the accredited and lauded chief literary biographer of his day, Leslie Stephen followed a policy of systematic whitewashing and bowdlerization. In all litera-ture, he shied away from any kind of "indecency" and considered any revela-tion of personal weakness in his subject to be a betrayal of a biographer's trust.

In recent years, biographers like John Aplin and Henrietta Garnett (Vir-ginia Woolf's great-niece) have begun the task of stripping off the whitewash and revealing William Makepeace Thackeray as he really was — a witty, sen-sual, epicurean artist unhappily marooned in Albertian England. Today we can glimpse how much — like his contemporaries Dickens and George Eliot — Thackeray suffered the tyrannies, hypocrisies, and repressions of the Victo-rian era. Like all Oedipal and Electral struggles against the writers and culture of the parental generation, Virginia Woolf's Bloomsbury was the continuation as well as the denial of the high Victorian era. To understand the Bloomsbury society that Virginia Woolf did so much to create, we need to delve back into literary history and tell the stories of her surrogate grandfather, William Makepeace Thackeray; his wife, Isabella; his older daughter, Anne, the sibyl of Kensington; his younger daughter, Minny; and his granddaughter, Laura Makepeace Stephen.

5

William and Isabella

LESLIE STEPHEN, in his black moods, called himself a second-class mind, and he was right. His first wife's father, William Makepeace Thackeray, on the other hand, was first rate in every way that mattered in a man except looks — a talented artist, a good man of business, a London hostess's favorite guest, a literary man's best friend, a redoubtable clubman and bon vivant, a writer of genius, and, on top of it all, a devoted son, loyal husband, and attentive father. Though he never sold as many copies as his friend Dickens, Thackeray in his lifetime was widely adjudged to be the greatest living writer of English prose.

For the English novel, the middle decades of the nineteenth century are a golden age when — to name only some of the most famous — men like Charles Dickens, William Makepeace Thackeray, Anthony Trollope, and William Wilkie Collins and women like George Eliot, Elizabeth Gaskell, and Emily, Charlotte, and Anne Brontë churned out masterpieces that won glowing reviews, sold like hotcakes, and are still popular today as books, movies, and television series. But while enjoying the praise of their fellow citizens and earning serious money, the Victorian novelists lived at a time when their creative canvas was severely limited by popular taste, and their private lives were subject to invasive scrutiny and public censure. The urbane realism of Henry Fielding in

Tom Jones and the philosophical meandering of Laurence Sterne in *Tristram Shandy* were long gone, and an English writer or artist or composer eager to find *la vie de Bohème* of Balzac, Flaubert, and George Sand had to cross the Channel and speak French.

When *Vanity Fair*, Thackeray's first and greatest success, was coming out in serial form in 1848–49, England was schizophrenic about sexual morality. Prince Albert was at the height of his power and influence, busily purging the Court of St. James of lustful aristocrats and with his wife, Victoria, setting a standard to all England of solid, monogamous, patriarchal, big-family, low-church Christian values — all the things Bloomsbury circa 1910 would mock and desecrate. The Methodists in Thackeray's day were evangelizing the working class and advocating a new puritanism. There was a brisk market in anti-masturbatory devices for young men, and middle-class girls caught touching their genitalia were whipped, put to bed with their hands bound, and even subjected to cruel restraints of leather and iron. Scientists preached the gospel of female frigidity and female fragility. Doctors prospered from an epidemic of hysteria — "womb sickness" — as affluent women opted for the invalid couch over the double bed and flocked to expensive spa hotels that catered to their social and even sexual needs. Prostitution was heavily regulated by the British government, regularly condemned in the press, and minutely analyzed and documented in governmental white papers, yet London had more brothels per square mile than any other capital city, and sadomasochism was known in reportedly libertine France as *le vice anglais*. Homosexuality was threatened by severe punishment under the law and anathematized from the pulpit but, like the elephant in the room that no one cares to notice, was accepted as an inescapable but unavowable fact of life by polite society, the English press, and the Metropolitan Police.

To any serious observer, these sexual facts on the ground were key features of Victorian psychological and social life, yet they were largely taboo topics for English fiction writers, who were expected to be spotless exemplars of Victorian morality. For Thackeray, even more than for his great rivals Charles Dickens and George Eliot (Mary Ann Evans), the increasing puritanism of contemporary English society was not just a professional straitjacket but a source of intense personal stress. Thackeray died at fifty-three, Dickens at fifty-eight, and George Eliot at sixty-one.

ॐ

William Makepeace Thackeray came from money, and, as for so many of the characters in our story, that money came out of India. Born in Calcutta (the colonial name for Kolkata) in 1811, William was the only child of an ill-suited couple, Anne Becher Thackeray, a beauty and a devout Calvinist, and Richmond Thackeray, an urbane, pleasure-loving man. Richmond Thackeray and his father before him had made a large fortune by assuring the East India Company a regular supply of elephants.

On his magnificent estate, Richmond Thackeray maintained an Indian mistress to whom he was much attached and who bore him at least one child, a daughter, Sarah (Sarah Thackeray Blechynden), whom he remembered lovingly in his will. Richmond's marriage to Anne Becher seems on his side to have been part caprice, part convention: English men in India were expected to acquire English wives and needed legitimate heirs. On her part, marriage was the only way Anne could escape her mother.

At only fifteen Anne Becher had fallen madly in love with a young officer, Henry Carmichael-Smyth. When Anne Becher was told, by her very respectable grandmother, that her soldier love, Henry, had died in the wars against Napoleon, Anne wept and believed she had been told the truth. When Anne's very disreputable mother (the wife of two, possibly three, men in India) dragged Anne off to Calcutta to find a husband, the girl agreed to marry Richmond Thackeray, a wealthy man old enough to be her father. Soon after her marriage, things came close to tragedy for Anne, still a teenager, when she went into labor with her first child.

It was the monsoon season, a storm broke out, and her husband, Richmond, was away from home. As the storm became a hurricane, all the servants ran out of the house in fear, and Anne took refuge in a tiny inner room and, after many hours, gave birth to her son, William Makepeace Thackeray, alone and without assistance. William had an unusually large head, and as a result of that tortured birth, Anne was never able to have another child. Adultery, dark-skinned mistresses, difficult childbirths — subjects like these were pushed to the extreme edges of the novels of Dickens and Thackeray, though not, let it be noted, from the novels of George Eliot and Elizabeth Gaskell or the poetry of Elizabeth Barrett Browning.

Sometime after the birth of Anne's son, who should appear out of the blue at a party in Calcutta but Henry Carmichael-Smyth, the young officer Anne had loved and who had reportedly been killed on some distant battlefield in Europe. Henry was still passionately in love with Anne, despite what seemed to him her betrayal of their love, and the pair were joyfully reunited. It is a story worthy of Kipling, and one that Anne Becher Thackeray's writer grand-daughter, also called Anne, would delight in hearing and telling. Richmond Thackeray died of an infectious disease when his son, William, was four, and Anne sent the boy back to England. After observing the accepted period of mourning, Anne married Henry Carmichael-Smyth, and the two returned to England, where mother and son were rapturously reunited. Anne Thackeray Carmichael-Smyth gave her only child the unwavering love and attention that, as Freud would later contend, propel boys toward achievement. As for Henry Carmichael-Smyth, like the noble Dobbin in *Vanity Fair,* he loved his wife's son as his own.

A large, plain, indolent, awkward boy of great charm and subtle mind, who loved to draw and was very happy at home in the country doing not very much, William at age ten was, like most boys of his class, sent away to board-ing school. Thackeray would later recall his years at Charterhouse as an edu-cation in intellectual sterility and physical pain. The two separate disfiguring breaks in Thackeray's nose, so obvious in photographs, were lasting marks of the fights he was forced into at his exclusive school.

Though an indifferent student of the Greek and Latin that constituted vir-tually the whole curriculum at school and university in England, William still gained admittance to Trinity College, Cambridge. His father, after all, and many Thackeray relatives were old Cantabrigians. From the father he never really knew, William inherited an appetite for lovely, capricious women and a discriminating palate for beautiful things, which his doting mother and step-father gave him pretty much free rein to indulge as an undergraduate. None-theless, when Thackeray came into the large fortune left him by his father, he promptly left the university. His close Trinity friends Alfred Tennyson and Richard Monckton Milnes had already been obliged to leave Trinity without a degree when their fathers could no longer pay the bill, and they were now embarking, in very different ways, on a literary career. Thackeray was eager to follow their example, confident that in London or in Paris, where he was almost equally at home, he could find success.

Within a couple of years, Thackeray had run through almost all of his inheritance in the cafés, alehouses, theaters, gambling dens, and brothels that proliferated in both great capital cities. He then proceeded to waste most of his parents' savings too on some bad Indian bank investments and an ill-conceived radical newspaper. By the age of twenty-five he was essentially bankrupt and decided what he needed was a wife and children to steady him. There was a deeply romantic and familial side to Thackeray's character, rooted perhaps in the strange love story of his mother and Henry Carmichael-Smyth, and while eyeing the stunningly beautiful Sophia and Virginia Pattle and deciding regretfully they would never eye him, William went in hot pursuit of a young Irish woman, Isabella Gethin Shawe.

No one could understand why William Thackeray was so determined to marry eighteen-year-old Isabella Shawe. She had no money and, indeed, nothing to recommend her aside from a sweet face and a light touch on the clavichord. Very shy, very innocent, and very ignorant, Miss Shawe simply could not hold a candle to William's mother — tall, imposing, brilliant, still exceptionally beautiful in her forties and now the uncrowned queen of the tiny self-absorbed Francophobic Anglo-Indian community in Paris. Like the Carmichael-Smyths, the Shawes had moved to Paris because it was cheap and out of the reach of English debtor law. The impoverished widow of an officer in the Indian army, Isabella's mother, Mrs. Shawe, had been forced to rent out Doneraile Court, her family estate in County Cork, and she was depending upon her older daughter, Isabella, to marry money. Young Thackeray, with all his debts and his hazy-crazy plans to be a writer and illustrator, was exactly the kind of son-in-law she did not want.

Given Mrs. Shawe's strong opposition and the tyrannical hold she had over her daughters, Isabella and Jane, the courtship went nowhere for a while. A slip of a girl who barely reached the shoulder of her tall, bulky suitor, Isabella was initially intimidated by the idea of becoming Mrs. William Thackeray. She once asked William whether she would still be able to sleep with her sister if she married him. But William wooed with passion and poetry and funny drawings, and as the two were of age, they were married at the British embassy in Paris.

Sex proved after all not a problem between Isabella and William — earlier sowing of wild oats can have its pluses for a bridegroom — and in the first weeks both were happy to spend the day in bed. When money problems became too pressing to ignore, William and Isabella moved to rented accommodation in London, where he could be close to the publishing industry. Isabella proved to have no taste or talent for housekeeping, so the couple lived in bohemian squalor as well as constant fear of the bailiffs. Nonetheless, William was beginning to make a name for himself as a writer and cartoonist, and Isabella played her piano in the middle of the domestic chaos and joyfully felt her baby kick inside. William Makepeace Thackeray would remember those first years of marriage as the happiest in his life, which tells us something about the unhappiness he felt in the years of his fame.

When Isabella went into labor with her first child, she was at first attended by her husband's mother, who, alongside her Calvinism, had become a devout believer in homeopathy. Mrs. Carmichael-Smyth had managed to birth her son, William, in India without any assistance, and she saw no reason why, with her help, her daughter-in-law should not produce a healthy child. But Isabella was little and her husband was a big man with a very big head, and the baby got stuck in the birth canal. Mother and daughter might both have died if William had not arrived on the scene, sized up the problem, and gone out to find a doctor with forceps. The Thackerays called their daughter Anne Isabella, and they adored and spoiled her. As a toddler, little Anny was chubby and plain of face but precocious and affectionate and voluble, the image of her brilliant, exuberant father.

But even as Thackeray was finding a public and seeing his way out of debt, things began to go very wrong at home. Isabella became pregnant almost immediately after her difficult first delivery, and when Jane, the Thackerays' second child, died before her first birthday, Isabella plunged into grief and depression. She was almost immediately pregnant again, however, and in 1840, a third daughter, Harriet, to be known thereafter as Minny, was born many weeks premature. Swaddled in cotton wool according to the medical practice of the time, Minny seemed all too likely to follow baby sister Jane to the cemetery. She survived, thanks to Jessie Brodie, the young Scots woman who devotedly served the Thackerays as both nurse to the infants and maid of all work. For the rest of her life, Minny Thackeray would be seen as a fragile being, forever wrapped in metaphorical cotton wool by her adoring father and older sister.

By this time, William had set indolence aside as a single man's luxury and put his broad shoulder to the journalistic wheel. He was publishing a steady stream of articles, satirical essays, and travelogues, many of them illustrated with his own drawings, but still he had more debt than income. Since even a palatable Irish stew was beyond Isabella, William felt justified in fleeing domestic chaos, but his increasingly frequent absences made his wife only more depressed and more angry. Things became explosive between the two in 1839, when, claiming that he had to meet an urgent magazine deadline, William went off to Belgium. According to Henrietta Garnett, who has combed the Thackeray family archive, his former French mistress was waiting for him there. William at this point was about twenty-eight, Isabella about twenty-one.

The result of this Belgian escapade was disastrous. On his return to London, William found Isabella alternately raving and catatonic. A visit to the seashore being seen at this time as a sovereign remedy, Thackeray duly removed his wife, almost-three-year-old Anny, and baby Minny to Margate, a pleasant holiday resort on the south coast of Kent made famous by the painter J.M.W. Turner. Walking along Margate beach one day, Isabella suddenly rushed into the waves with little Anny and pushed her down under. Suddenly recalled to her senses, the mother pulled her terrified, sputtering child out of the sea, and walked back to the sand. Astonishingly precocious, Anne Thackeray had a clear memory of that day but never blamed her mother for what had happened.

Unable to manage a wife who was raving and threatening to harm her children, Thackeray borrowed more money to take his family to Ireland. The

Shawe women were back at Doneraile Court, and Thackeray assumed that his mother-in-law would wish to take charge of her daughter and infant grand-daughters. At sea, the nightmare only got worse. Somehow, somewhere in the strait between Southampton and the Isle of Wight, soon after the Irish ferry had left port, Isabella Thackeray managed to throw herself out the window of the privy into the sea. As William wrote in anguish to his parents in Paris the next day, for some twenty minutes no one on board missed Isabella. But then she was spotted, floating on her back and calmly paddling with her hands, and the crew was able to fish her out. After this, William never left Isabella's side during the day, and before he fell asleep at night, he attached to his wrist a cord that was also wrapped around her waist.

Once in Ireland, the sad little family trekked to the mother's childhood home and were obliged to take lodgings nearby, since Mrs. Shawe would not receive them at Doneraile Court. In a fury that poor Thackeray was begin-ning to recognize, his mother-in-law hurled imprecations, blaming him for her daughter's condition and barely deigning to look at her granddaughters. Mad-ness, Thackeray was discovering to his cost, ran in the Gethin Shawe family.

Driven away by his mother-in-law, William took his family back over the Irish Sea, managed to borrow more money in London, and then set off across the English Channel to Paris, where the help of his parents could be counted on. Anne Thackeray Ritchie retained a clear memory of the long coach journey at night from the French coast to Paris. An energetic and voluble three-year-old, she kept talking and fidgeting. Fearing Anny would wake her troubled mother and fractious baby sister, William lost patience. He told little Anny that, if she did not stop being naughty, he would snuff out the lantern and leave her in the dark. It was a terrible lesson in obedience, if understandable, given the situation. From this point on, Anne Thackeray determined that, if she could only be by her father's side and be sure of his love, she would strive to please him and be the perfect daughter.

Over the next months, William took his wife to a series of notable sana-toriums in Europe, often taking Anny to visit her mother in the institution, hoping that the madness was temporary and that love for him and her child could bring Isabella back. Nothing worked. The mental disease specialists of the day proved unable to do anything for Mrs. Thackeray and declared her incurably insane. William was now faced with a terrible choice. As long as Isabella lived — and her leap into the sea had proved that her body was strong if her mind was deranged — William under English law could not get a divorce. The easy thing to do would have been to consign Isabella to the asylum at Chaillot just outside Paris, return to London, and ask his parents to keep an eye on his wife. No one would have blamed Thackeray for doing this. He needed to earn money for his family, and Chaillot had an excellent reputation in the medical world.

But William saw with his own eyes how dirty and ragged Isabella became within weeks of being institutionalized. It seemed all too likely that her life would be made wretched and even cut short if she was left in an asylum. Though he had renounced the Protestant orthodoxy of his mother, William Thackeray had a strong faith in God and followed a code of ethics. He retained a clear and present memory of Isabella as a lovely young woman, singing and dancing about the house with her baby, so he brought her back to England, where he could watch over her. William established Isabella in a home of her own, under the care of an English couple who proved loving and capable.

For a time, William confided his daughters to the care of his mother and stepfather in France, returned to London, and buckled down to writing. The lives of his wife and his young daughters, as well as the financial well-being of his parents, depended on his finding success as a novelist and journalist. He wrote in spurts, putting himself under immense deadline pressure, and over the next twenty-five years he produced a flood of novels, essays, and articles, and made a great deal of money. He coped with the stresses of his life by eating too much and drinking even more.

But even as he found success with the reading public, Thackeray was faced with difficult decisions as a father and as a man. He was a pleasure-loving, cosmopolitan man who liked to have sex with women and loved the company of handsome, intelligent people of both sexes. He was, in fact, very like his father, Richmond Thackeray, but he found himself in an increasingly puritanical England, not in easygoing India circa 1800. After sampling the great smorgasbord of sexual delicacies laid out for men in London and Paris, William had in his mid-twenties decided in favor of loving conjugal sex — with tragic results. Now, barely thirty, he found himself tied to a wife who was incapable of satisfying his needs while he competed in a literary market that expected its authors, male and female, to lead blameless lives.

Internationally, the best money in literature came from fiction, but the large and lucrative English market for novels included a higher percentage of women than in any other country except the United States. To succeed in fiction writing circa 1845, you had to cater to the tastes and understand the values of a wide range of female readers. There were the aristocratic women who aspired to be fashionable in literature as well as hats. There were the wives and daughters of the affluent bourgeoisie who had too much time on their hands. There was the small but growing cadre of educated women who were hammering at the doors of the great universities and the learned professions. There was the large group of newly literate, curious, and ambitious factory girls and lady's maids who had access to books and magazines through their employers and their local libraries. All these female readers embraced, or claimed to embrace, the new doctrine on heterosexual morality promulgated by Prince Albert and his queen wife.

If he had left his two daughters permanently in the care of his mother, William could probably have followed his pleasures and been publicly commended to boot. The streets of central London at night, one gathers from historians of the era, were patrolled by literary gents, hats pulled down over the eyes, wrapped up to the nose in mufflers, taking notes on lowlife in the slums for the edification — or so they claimed — of their middle-class readers. Thackeray could also have sent his daughters to boarding school at a very young age: Anny and Minny were bright little girls, and unlike many men of his time, he was not opposed in principle to educating women. Boarding school, my readers will remember, was the solution to domestic problems arrived at by the widowed Reverend Patrick Brontë in 1824. Unable, in his remote Yorkshire parish, to find a wife willing to take on the care of his six young children, Brontë thought it best to send his four oldest daughters to Cowan Bridge School. There, freezing, psychologically abused, and chronically malnourished, the two eldest, Maria and Elizabeth, quickly succumbed to tuberculosis at the ages of eleven and ten.

For William Makepeace Thackeray, in the end there was no choice. Both fastidious and traditionalist in his views, Thackeray felt a strong if critical allegiance to his caste; the raffish life of his good friend Wilkie Collins, who had two mistresses and a serious opium habit, held no appeal for him. He could not imagine being happy without his daughters, so, as soon as he had the means, he rented a house in leafy Kensington, hired a servant or two, bought a little furniture and some bits of crockery, and wrote to his mother to bring the girls to their new home. Minny missed her grandparents, for she was their pet, but Anny, reunited at last with her father, felt from the first day that finally all was right again in her world.

Today William Makepeace Thackeray would win praise as a model single father, a man who worked hard for his family, adored his kids, and showed a rare understanding of their needs. Instead, Thackeray's refusal to be separated from his children brought the full glare of public scrutiny upon him. England expected its writers to respect the contemporary sexual shibboleths not only in the words they printed but in their private lives. The idea that a man in the prime of life, with, rumor had it, a checkered past, and known to be permanently separated from his wife, should dare to live with his minor female children, superintend their education, and form their characters was unacceptable to the English public.

The English press, which found it highly lucrative to combine moralism with sensationalism, claimed a duty to protect those young motherless Thackeray girls, so journalists were on the lookout for anything that might suggest William Makepeace Thackeray was not leading a spotlessly celibate life. Thus, when Thackeray rushed into print to praise *Jane Eyre,* the controversial new novel by the unknown Currer Bell, people jumped to the conclusion that Thackeray, under a pseudonym, had written the book himself, basing it upon his own conjugal life. When Charlotte Brontë came forward as the author of *Jane Eyre* and dedicated the second edition of her successful novel to Thackeray, this was seen by some as further proof that, while keeping his mad wife under restraint in Camberwell, William Makepeace Thackeray had engaged in an adulterous relationship with his children's governess.

Events like the *Jane Eyre* fracas confirmed for Thackeray that any hint of misconduct would affect sales of his books and place him and his family in financial jeopardy. His irony, his hatred of cant, his religious skepticism, his cynical take on contemporary life all jarred with the increasingly sectarian, sentimental, jingoistic temperament of even the male readers of his time. Furthermore, as his many aunts and cousins and female friends impressed upon him, any hint of immorality on their father's part would cast a shadow over the reputation of Anny and Minny. Thackeray's solution was twofold. As a professional writer, he would give the English reading public what it expected. As a private citizen, with the active support of his male friends who were committed to secrecy — theirs as well as his — he would satisfy his legitimate sexual needs behind the anonymous doors of London houses where discretion was factored into the price and on the Continent, where an Englishman of means could fade into anonymity.

Thackeray, his friends, his family, his daughter Anne who became his literary executor, and his (eventual) son-in-law Leslie Stephen, first editor of the *Dictionary of National Biography,* guarded the secrets of his personal life successfully, even more successfully than the comparable set of people did for Thackeray's friend and rival Charles Dickens. It is only thanks to the adventitious discovery of a coded diary and some advanced literary sleuthing that we can state, as a fact, that Charles Dickens had a secret life, maintaining his mistress Ellen Ternan in secret locations in England and traveling on the Continent with her incognito. It seems eminently possible that William Thackeray, whose sexual and familial situation was much more dire than that of Dickens and whose livelihood also depended on conforming to the sexual prudery of the English reading public, also had a secret life.

In the nineteenth century, evidence of that secret life became public only once, at Thackeray's funeral. Some two thousand soberly clad men arrived at the cemetery to pay tribute to the great man and were shocked to see a group of gaily dressed women, hair flying in the wind, gathered around the open grave. The painter John Millais confided to his diary that the women were from Thackeray's favorite brothel, women who had loved him and also wanted to pay their last respects.

ॐ

In our twenty-first century, our interest in a book seems to be inseparable from our curiosity about its author. That confusion is something the resolutely anonymous novelist "Elena Ferrante" anathematizes, but I am not convinced she is right in every case. If someone picks up a novel by Charles Dickens because she has heard about the invisible woman in his life — to use Claire Tomalin's phrase denoting Ellen Ternan — well, why not? Dickens is a terrific read.

One reason why we are fascinated by Queen Victoria and repelled by Prince Albert is that their youngest daughter, Princess Beatrice, failed to scrub from the historical record the documentary proof that Queen Victoria had been a passionate woman who could not wait to get into bed with her husband at night. Comparable evidence for Albert's sexual appetite has not been forthcoming, though several renegade royal historians, including Lytton Strachey, suggest that Prince Albert, the rigidly faithful husband and father of nine, loved men, not women. In our LGBTQA age, if tomorrow some documents turned up in an obscure German archive showing that Albert of Saxe-Coburg and Gotha had been seduced by his tutor as a boy and had several aristocratic men lovers at Bonn University, the prince consort would be dug out of the historical graveyard and given a whole new life.

Virginia Woolf was painfully aware of the dilemma a biographer faced when dealing with aspects of a subject's life that went against contemporary moral standards. In her second novel, *Night and Day,* she creates a character, Margaret Hilbery, based very closely on Anne Thackeray Ritchie. Mrs. Hilbery is writing the biography of her famous poet father Richard Alardyce, and she is unable to progress past his twenties, as she cannot decide whether to reveal or conceal Alardyce's sexual adventures as a young man. She sees that there was an indissoluble link between Alardyce's creative genius and his extramarital affairs: "She had been her father's companion at the season when he wrote the finest of his poems. She had sat on his knee in a tavern and the haunts of drunken poets and it was for her sake, people said, that he had cured himself of his dissipation, and become the irreproachable literary character that the world knows, *whose inspiration deserted him*" [my emphasis].

If we substitute "novels" for "poems" we have here Woolf's condensed summary of the tragedy of William Makepeace Thackeray's life. It would be interesting to know if this perception was something that Anne Thackeray Ritchie confided to her or whether she had deduced it for herself on the basis of her wide reading in Victorian social and literary history.

The more one looks at the sex lives of the great Victorian writers and artists, the more obvious it is that they were no less perverse and polyamorous than the members of the Bloomsbury group. Historians, novelists, and playwrights like Steven Marcus, Peter Gay, Phyllis Rose, Tom Stoppard, and Colm Tóibín have shown that the Victorians were, if anything, queerer, because secrecy and shibboleth spiced up the sexual stew.

The difference between the Kensington of Thackeray and the Bloomsbury of Woolf, as we shall see later in this book, was not what happened in the bed or the brothel or the hayloft, but what was said and written about what happened, where, and with whom. In regard to sexual activity, a code of silence for men and of ignorance — or feigned ignorance — for women prevailed in mid-Victorian England, and the funeral of William Makepeace Thackeray illustrates this very well.

In defiance of the unwritten Victorian rule barring women from going to the cemetery, Anne and Harriet Thackeray insisted on accompanying their beloved father to his grave. Arriving at the burial site, they saw the unknown, incongruously dressed women being urgently shooed away by black-clad male mourners. They had seen women like that before many times — in the streets just off Pall Mall and Drury Lane and driving brazenly out in the Bois de Boulogne. Behind black veils, the faces of the Thackeray sisters betrayed nothing, and in all her many autobiographical works, Anne Thackeray Ritchie never made any mention of what had happened.

6

Anny and Minny

GROWING UP, Virginia Woolf and her sister Vanessa suffered from a superfluity of family. Though their parents had each been one of only three, and Aunt Caroline Stephen had considerately remained single, in Virginia's generation there had been an explosion of cousins. Uncle Fitzy Stephen and his wife, Mary, contributed seven, Aunt Adeline and Uncle Henry Vaughan another seven, while Aunt Mary and Uncle Herbert Fisher came in with an outrageous eleven. Any or all of the aunts and uncles, with clutches of cousins, might at any time descend on the Stephens in Kensington, and whereas Leslie could escape to his study, his daughters were trapped next to the teapot, murderously close to wishing that their family had been more vulnerable to the measles, whooping cough, tuberculosis, and diphtheria that still cut swaths through the infant population of England.

But there was one aunt whose arrival at 22 Hyde Park Gate was greeted with pleasure by all six Stephens, and that was Aunt Anny — Anne Thackeray Ritchie as she was known to her loyal readers, Lady Ritchie as she became after her husband's knighthood — and she was, of course, not really a relative at all. Aunt Anny did not come very often and rarely quite when expected, but when she came, deaf Leslie smiled and cupped his hand to his ear, Julia looked twenty years younger, and Virginia and Vanessa waited in joyous suspense to hear what the dear, dotty old lady would come out with next. Perhaps the tale of how, as a little girl, she had been taken by her father's friend to an apartment in Paris and told to be absolutely quiet and listen while a pale, thin gentleman played his latest composition — and the man was Chopin. Or the tale of her arriving a week earlier than arranged to stay at Down with the Charles Darwins, and how lucky she had been to get her dates wrong, since a week later poor Charles was dead.

Anne Thackeray Ritchie came to the Stephen home because she was one of Julia's oldest and closest friends, because Leslie Stephen had once been her sister's husband, and because Anne was determined to let nothing come between her and the Stephen family, which included not only Vanessa, Thoby, Virginia, and Adrian, but also Anne's only niece by blood, Laura Makepeace Stephen.

ॐ

When, finally, William Thackeray and his daughters were reunited in Kensington, Anny and Minny Thackeray entered some fifteen years of settled happiness and growing affluence clouded only by their father's regular bouts of ill health.

Life in Kensington was a little staid, as a host of redoubtable women helped Thackeray maintain his façade of irreproachable respectability. These ladies included a battery of Thackeray-Ritchie aunts, and notable friends such as Adelaide Kemble Sartoris, the retired opera diva, and her sister Fanny Kemble Butler, once a famous actress. In the early Kensington years, aware that he must not seem to be neglecting his daughters' education, Thackeray employed a series of governesses, carefully choosing, due to the fracas over *Jane Eyre,* the ugliest women he could find. Unfortunately, the governesses proved as ignorant as they were plain, and by the age of fifteen, Anny declared she would have no more of them.

Thackeray's next solution to the problem of providing a live-in female chaperone for his daughters was to welcome Amy Crowe into his household.

She was the penniless orphan daughter of Thackeray's painter friend Eyre Crowe, and she became a second sister to Anny and Minny and a third daughter to William. When Amy married Edward Thackeray, a dashing army officer who was one of William's second cousins, the large Thackeray clan rejoiced, and when in 1865 Amy died in India after giving birth to her second daughter, they grieved. Edward brought his tiny daughters, Anne and Margaret Thackeray (called Annie and Margie in the family), back to England, and Anny and Minny took the infants into their home and served as their adoptive mothers until cousin Edward remarried and took his children back.

Anny and Minny Thackeray grew up to be the epitome of respectability, their reputations untarnished by even a breath of scandal. They were Victorians in a way Leslie Stephen would later celebrate as rectitude in his *Dictionary of National Biography* and Lytton Strachey later still would mock as hypocrisy. But the social conformity of the Thackeray sisters was a far more complex thing than either Stephen or Strachey understood. If we look behind the façade that William Makepeace Thackeray so carefully created to hide his private life, we can see that Anny and Minny as young women had a better introduction to "Vanity Fair" than did either Leslie or Lytton, whose travels in Europe and cultural links to Europeans were neither deep nor extensive. That the two women were in no way infected by Becky-Sharp-itis is, I think, to their credit and their father's. Thackeray was arguably the most acute social critic of the England of his day. He gave his daughters the key to his life and his library and then, for the most part, he respected their minds enough to allow them to use those keys as seemed to them best.

As Virginia Woolf knew from her wide reading in the lives and work of women writers, the free use of a father's library was essential to any number of famous and achieving women. Anny and Minny Thackeray had that freedom. Though they did not learn Latin and Greek like their contemporaries Elizabeth Barrett, Florence Nightingale, and George Eliot, they had superb French, along with good Italian and German, so *The Divine Comedy* and *The Decameron* were theirs, along with Goethe and Schiller, *La Princesse de Clèves,* and the letters of Madame de Sévigné. On the shelves of Thackeray's library, the unexpurgated works of Shakespeare, Ben Jonson, and Milton jostled books by his beloved eighteenth-century writers — Steele, Addison, Fielding, Sterne,

Swift, Pope, Diderot, Rousseau, Voltaire — all authors whose works appeared on neither the shelves nor the syllabi of the governesses and female academies charged with the education of "young persons" (that is, unmarried girls). Novels could take girls like Anny and Minny into a thousand different worlds and minds, turn their heads with romance, and lay bare the traps of passion. Thackeray was also interested in the genre of folktales, newly popular due to the research done by German scholars such as the Grimm brothers. In fairy tales, the Thackeray women found the immemorial plots of human life, and when she was older, Anne would write several successful books in which she imagined modern versions of classic tales like "Beauty and the Beast" and "Little Red Riding Hood."

And unlike the invalid Elizabeth Barrett — a scholar of Greek but a prisoner in her own home, as Virginia Woolf, in *Flush,* would so sympathetically show from the point of view of the poet's equally captive dog — the Thackeray sisters were able to flesh out their literary adventures with music, opera, art, architecture, and the experience of everyday life in foreign countries. That they began their traveling life poor and ended it rather rich only extended their range of experience.

Paris had been William Makepeace Thackeray's second home ever since his first year of freedom as a Cambridge undergraduate. Once Thackeray came under the spotlight of the English press, he, like his friend Dickens, escaped scrutiny by traveling in Europe, and it was not by chance that the subjects Thackeray chose for his novels after *Vanity Fair* required extensive field work abroad. Anny and Minny and their father were culture vultures when that was hard, indefatigably trekking through churches, galleries, and museums all over France, Germany, and Italy. A man of superb taste and a collector, Thackeray trawled antique shops and curio stalls, and his daughters went with him. Ardent music lovers all three, the Thackerays went to symphony concerts, attended exclusive salons to hear the latest string quartets, as Proust would do a generation on, and they had many a night at the opera. Virginia Woolf and Vanessa Bell as adults would also spend as much time as they could afford in Europe, and they would explore the worlds of music, theater, and ballet, but they did so only after the death of their father. Leslie Stephen never went near an art gallery, hated music long before he went deaf, and, according to his biographer Noel Annan, attended the theater only a couple of times, in order to see in the flesh the famous beauty Lillie Langtry, one of the Prince of Wales's mistresses.

Anne and Minny were intelligent and observant young women, and if indeed their father had a secret life, their travels together abroad must have offered them some clues to it. Just by walking and driving at night through the streets of great European cities and seeing the world through their father's sharp, cynical eyes, Anny and Minny were exposed to things that an English miss was not supposed to see. The opium-eaters in the salons. The scantily dressed girls on the street corners. The drunks littering the pavement. The emaciated beggar infants drugged into sleep. In Paris or Berlin or Venice, let us picture two intelligent young women lying awake in the heat of their shuttered room while next door, over much wine, their famous father and his European friends converse late into the night. These would be fast-paced conversations in several languages, in which things were discussed that English artists and writers were not free to explore in their published work — free love, for example, which many believed in and some practiced. Exposed to the very best of European culture from their teenage years, the Thackeray sisters were as cosmopolitan as they were Victorian, and their experience of life with their father was much richer and broader than that of Vanessa and Virginia Stephen with their parents a generation later.

Did Anny and Minny notice that their father's old and famous friend Elizabeth Barrett Browning was often under the influence of opium? Of course, but they were not shocked. Opium products were an integral part of their world, and laudanum, a liquid form of opium, was available by the pennyworth in England on every town street. When the Thackeray women once paid a visit to their father's old Cambridge friend Richard Monckton Milnes at Fryston, his family place (known in the gay underworld as the Yorkshire Sodom), were they surprised when the red-haired teenage waif Algernon Swinburne, Monckton Milnes's latest literary protégé, got up to read his shockingly sensual poem "Les Noyades"? Of course, but their father and his Cambridge friend the archbishop of York were in the audience listening to Swinburne too, and they clapped, so where could be the harm?

Did Anny and Minny know that the reason the illustrious father of their friend Katy Dickens Collins had left his wife, Catherine, was that he was in a relationship with a young actress? Well, yes. Their father had caused a furor at his club by remarking he had seen Dickens and Ellen Ternan together in the street. Did Anny and Minny understand that they could be friends with George Eliot when abroad, but could never entertain her in their home because she was an adulteress? Quite certainly. Did they hear that their father's writer friend Wilkie Collins kept not one mistress and her children, but two? Possibly.

And even in the beautiful new house that Thackeray had custom-built and meticulously furnished on Palace Green, Kensington, facing the royal palace, occasional stories surfaced from the days before Victoria and Albert cleansed the Augean stables of English society, stories for the writer Anny to set down in her diary. Thus, Thackeray Ritchie tells how her paternal grandmother, the deeply religious and extremely proper Anne Becher Thackeray Carmichael-Smyth, in the days immediately before her death in 1864, became a little addled and amazed her granddaughters by telling them the story of how, as a young teenager, she was coerced into her first marriage and had had to give birth to their father all alone.

❧

William Makepeace Thackeray loved both his daughters, but he was still very much the patriarch, the son of an exceptionally beautiful woman to whom he was exceptionally close, and a man who chose Isabella Shawe as his wife because she was small, pretty, compliant, ignorant, and his inferior in every way. How a woman looked still mattered to Thackeray much more than how she thought, and from Anne's infancy he convinced himself that this daughter was too clever and too plain to ever attract a husband. His daughter Anne, Thackeray once wrote ruefully, was "a man of genius."

Anne from earliest childhood worshiped her father, and she accepted his judgment. At fifteen she became Thackeray's amanuensis and undertook some of his professional correspondence. At eighteen she published her first essay in

Anne Thackeray as a young woman

Cornhill, the magazine her father edited, and began a modestly successful career as a writer of fiction and memoir. Inchoate feelings of dissatisfaction and yearning, often expressed as illness, as it was among so many affluent Victorian women, possessed Anne as she grew into adulthood. To be a writer, to be perhaps "a man of genius," was not enough for her, as it was not enough for that other plain woman of proven genius, Mary Ann (or Marian) Evans (George Eliot).

Minny, early on, was assigned a different destiny. A tiny, calm, obedient child, very unlike her turbulent sister, she was the family pet and pretty like her mother. William Thackeray expected Minny to marry and bear the sons he and his mother longed for. That, as adults, plain Anny could cast her spell over a whole room of people and sweet Minny could complete a literary assignment on deadline for her sister if Anny was too ill to do it, did not seriously affect the female roles assigned to the two sisters in their father's lifetime. As the years passed, Minny remained tied to her father's coattails just like Anny, and both women started to feel that life was passing them by.

But when Thackeray was discovered dead in his room, everything changed for Anny and Minny. Their father had been their idol and the center of their lives. When their widowed grandmother Anne Carmichael-Smyth also died, one year to the day after her son, the Thackeray sisters were doubly bereft but also free to set up house together without a chaperone. According to British law, in the absence of a will and a male heir, Thackeray's two daughters each inherited a half of their father's estate. That included a gracious home with modern conveniences in a superb location, furnished with choice art and antiques. It also included several other real estate properties, Thackeray's copyrights, and the huge mass of his private papers. The house on Palace Green was sold for ten thousand pounds, a profit of six thousand pounds, and all but its most precious contents were sold at auction. Then, as we saw in Chapter 4, William Thackeray's great friend and publisher George Smith, of Smith & Elder, "rode round to offer 10,000 pounds for all of Thackeray's copyrights," as Henrietta Garnett puts it, "thereby earning the girls' undying gratitude and making the best bargain of his life."

By 1865, the Thackeray sisters between them were able, for eighteen hundred pounds, to buy 16 Onslow Gardens, a pleasant home in Kensington, hire a staff of five and a private carriage service, start a series of intimate little dinner parties, pay visits to their many friends in England such as Adelaide Sartoris and Julia Cameron, and travel abroad in style. Living prudently (and Minny was good at keeping her sister's spendthrift tendencies in check), they could envisage living the rest of their lives in modest affluence bordering on luxury, lives very different from — for example — that of their friend Caroline Stephen. She lived in shabby gentility with her widowed mother and, in recent years, her bachelor younger brother, Leslie.

Leslie Stephen was destined to become Virginia Woolf's father when he was fifty years old. He was largely responsible for her education. And, as we shall see in Chapter 10, the final seven years of his life were an experience of torture for both Virginia and her sister Vanessa. To understand the familial world in which Virginia Woolf came to maturity, it is illuminating to take a brief look at the world of all-boy schools and all-male colleges in which Leslie Stephen was formed as a father to girls.

❧

Around the turn of the nineteenth century, the families of both of Leslie Stephen's parents had been active members of the influential evangelical movement to abolish slavery in the British Empire known as the Clapham Saints. The Stephen family was famously frugal and high-minded, committed to a patriarchal family life founded on biblical precedent. When Leslie and his older brother, Fitzjames, were children, the undisputed head of the family was their father, a dedicated, overworked, frustrated, disregarded, and deeply neurotic top official at the Colonial Office; his uncertain temper and deep gloom kept his family in thrall. As a child, Leslie Stephen was sickly and anxious, his mother's pet, a boy with a taste for mathematics that promised well, and a talent for drawing that no one encouraged but that would come down to his daughter Vanessa and to her descendants. Leslie was sensitive and loved poetry, but poetry and drawing were not what a Victorian father wanted to see in his son, and, fearing that Leslie was in danger of becoming effeminate, James Stephen sent both Leslie and Fitzjames to Eton as day boys.

Although the headmaster of Eton had assured their father they would be well treated, the Stephen brothers were relentlessly tormented by both the poor scholarship boys and the wealthy boarders. In the biography he wrote of his brother, Leslie says that he survived Eton mainly because "Fitzy" was a large, strong youth who learned to fight back and hit hard. Finally, James Stephen realized that Eton was proving more boxing ring than study hall, and he allowed his two sons to withdraw from school and study with private tutors for the entrance examinations, called "Little Go," for Cambridge University.

As undergraduates at Trinity College, Cambridge, Fitzy was content to "go out for the poll," that is, take the common examination and then head off to London to train as a barrister, but Leslie opted to compete in the mathematical Tripos. This set of examinations was designed as a marathon plus a high-hurdle course to identify and list the top students, called "Wranglers." It was divided into "bookwork" — during which, as fast as quill would go, the candidates regurgitated random sections of the huge mass of material they had learned by heart — and "problems," which were designed to take more time to solve than any student less brilliant than the young John Maynard Keynes would need. Part I of the Tripos lasted for three days, at which point there was a break for the examiners to fail, or "plow," the poorest students. Those men left standing did another five days of testing, forty-four and one-half hours in all. The Stephen family feared that Leslie was too weak and nervy to withstand the extreme stress of the mathematical Tripos, but he proved them wrong. In a very strong field, he placed 20th out of 143 and secured an ecclesiastical fellowship at Trinity Hall, a Cambridge college not to be confused with Trinity. Stephen was required to take holy orders in the Church of England, put his signature to a statement subscribing to the church's Thirty-nine Articles, officiate at services at the college chapel, and serve as a spiritual guide to the young men.

As a fellow at Trinity Hall, Leslie Stephen was happier than ever before in his life as he had plenty of time to devote to his favorite new activity — coaching the college rowing crews. Leslie had pulled an oar as an undergraduate without ever being part of a winning eight, but he proved a very good coach. A tall man with long legs and excellent wind, he loved to run along the towpath with a bullhorn, urging his crew on, and in the company of enthusiastic, hearty, unintellectual men some three or more years his junior, he bloomed. Throughout his life, Stephen would find companionship and respect mostly with men younger than himself, disciples not colleagues, men willing to learn from him and submit to his dictates in the way a crew obeys a coach.

But Cambridge undergraduates were "up" for only three eight-week terms a year, so Leslie Stephen had lots of time on his hands during the vacations, especially the "long vac," the four months from June to October. Having no interest in mathematics per se, he began to read voraciously in English philosophy — Hobbes, Locke, Bentham, Mill — though not the German philosophers, like Kant and Hegel, whom he considered effete and decadent. The more he read, the more the strict Puritan faith of his Clapham Saint family fell away from him. He was forced to realize that he did not believe in God and to see that his hours conducting evensong, giving funeral elegies for students who died in manly competition, and counseling young men were hypocrisy, a mockery of basic moral values as propounded by John Stuart Mill. Like George Eliot, Leslie Stephen came to proudly embrace a severe secular code of ethics that did not rely on divine sanction and expected no heavenly reward for good deeds.

In good conscience, he felt impelled to inform his college and, worse still, his father that he had ceased to be an observing Christian. Faced with the death of God and the end of the collegial life in which, for the first time, he had been seen as a strong man and a leader, Leslie Stephen fell into the first of the mental breakdowns to which men in his family were subject. After clinging to Cambridge college life for two more years, Leslie moved in with his mother and his sister, Milly, in Bayswater, an unfashionable part of London.

Seeing his younger brother depressed and at a loss, the energetic Fitzy, now a successful barrister and journalist, encouraged Leslie to "write for the periodicals" and introduced him to editors. On philosophy, politics, literature — whatever subject the ex-mathematician Leslie Stephen could mug up, it didn't really matter — he could write an essay and, with Fitzy's network, could find a journal willing and eager to publish it — as long as he did not expect to earn a living wage. Eager to discover whether the fiercely pro-Southern English press was telling the truth about the American Civil War, in 1863 Stephen paid a long visit to the United States. There he found three prominent Yankee intellectuals — Charles Eliot Norton, Oliver Wendell Holmes, and James Russell Lowell — who were kindred spirits and would become his friends for life.

But it was his discovery of mountaineering that really saved Leslie Stephen from the dark depression occasioned by his crisis of faith and the loss of his Cambridge nest. He spent as much time as he could in Switzerland, first as a member of a group, later as a leader and publicist for the English gentleman's latest craze — scrambling up high icy peaks in the wake of the local guides. In the opinion of many of his climbing companions, Leslie Stephen did not climb for the views or indeed for the fellowship, since he walked in resolute silence. Climbing was a contest between him and the mountain and one that he could, with great effort, win, each time he went up. Knowing himself to be strong, tough, and agile, Leslie gained the confidence to believe that he could conquer difficulties of all kinds, perhaps even find the courage to court and propose to a woman.

For despite what he himself had, quite literally, preached to the young men of Trinity Hall, Leslie Stephen discovered that his personal needs could not be satisfied by virile friendships, arduous study, forty-mile tramps, and summer *randonnées*. Other Englishmen of Stephen's class, as his biographer Noel Annan briefly acknowledges, found sexual partners among the climbers and guides in the mountain huts, but Leslie Stephen seized upon marriage as the solution to his sexual and social problems. Though without religious faith, he retained the uneasy conscience of his abolitionist Clapham Saint forebears, and reportedly — for we are speaking here of the apostle of biographical bowdlerization — he resisted the sexual opportunities that the London of his day offered even to poor men like himself. When, in 1867, he began, awkwardly, hesitantly, looking around for a suitable woman to marry and bear his children, his family and friends quickly mobilized to help him find a wife.

In his rather painful excursions into Pattledom, where he felt himself an insignificant outsider, Leslie Stephen's eye had lighted upon Mrs. Prinsep's dazzling teenage niece Julia Jackson. Many years later, as a mournful old man, Leslie Stephen could still devote three packed, ecstatic pages to evoking the "absolutely faultless" beauty of the young woman who would, in the end, become his wife. Once, he tells us, sitting in a skiff on the river Thames, he happened to look up at a bridge and catch sight of Julia Jackson silhouetted against the sky, and experienced a never-to-be-forgotten rapture. But, ever the rational, fact-oriented, depressive materialist, Leslie Stephen realized that, though he looked up at Miss Jackson from afar as if at a holy vision, she barely saw him even when he was standing right next to her. And in fact, on the night when he happened to see Julia on the bridge, Stephen was expertly feathering his oars to impress two other young ladies — the Misses Thackeray.

৵

Stephen had long known the Thackeray sisters by sight, but then, all of a sudden, a mere acquaintance was becoming a friendship, and perhaps something more. Leslie would return from the city to find Miss Anne Thackeray and her sister, Minny, taking tea at his mother's house and chatting with his sister, Milly. He found them both excellent company and models of their sex, but his eyes passed quickly over Anne — ebullient, brilliant, lovable, but plain of face and inclined to dominate the conversation, especially when it came to the book business. Miss Minny Thackeray was different. She was perhaps, Stephen thought, as a recent connoisseur of female beauty, a trifle yellowed round the edges, but pretty, feminine, and charming. She listened well, was adept at sending buttered teacakes in the direction of hungry men, and talked modestly of managing the household while dearest Anne went forth and conquered the world of letters. Anny, declared Minny proudly, was a genius just like their father.

Leslie saw in Minny a woman who could be counted upon to grace his hearth, manage his household, welcome his friends, and defer to his superiority as man and mind. Leslie also wanted children, and from the expert way Minny managed the two little daughters of Edward Thackeray, he could see that she had the makings of an admirable mother. For her part, Minny Thackeray quickly seized upon Leslie Stephen as the husband her happiness required, a man who could be shaped and molded, a man who would do.

Harriet "Minny" Thackeray's modesty, her domesticity, her love of family and loyalty to friends were much praised in her lifetime and celebrated by her husband many years after her death in the so-called *Mausoleum Book.* Those qualities were all quite real. They were also part of a role that she played, which was calculated to appeal to a naive prospective suitor like Leslie Stephen. As recent historians have documented, Minny was perhaps not as brilliant and talented as her older sister, but neither was she a second Isabella Gethin Shawe. The name Minny can mislead us today. Though small of stature and weak in body, Harriet Thackeray was no mouse.

Like many intelligent Victorian women born into the affluent middle class, Minny Thackeray knew how to exploit illness and to play, for her own purposes, the role of innocent passivity. Far from being a sweet little lamb, she was spoiled, not a little selfish, capable, pragmatic, and, within the life prescribed for her by her father and society at large, accustomed to having things her way — a cleverer, nicer version of George Eliot's character Rosamond Vincy in *Middlemarch.* One can imagine opera lover Minny singing with Rosina in *The*

Barber of Seville, "I am a sweet little woman, glad to do as I am told — BUT I do have my little weaknesses, and if someone takes me the wrong way, I can be a viper." Her father knew this and chuckled about a woman's wiles. Her sister knew this and loved Minny the more for being strong of mind if not body. Her husband, by his own written account, seems never to have known it. In eight years of marriage, Leslie Stephen never understood what a clear-sighted, decisive, sophisticated, self-willed woman he had in Minny Thackeray.

But to return to the courtship days of Leslie and Minny, while clearly seeing the advantages offered by marriage in general and by marriage to the wealthy, well-connected Miss Minny Thackeray in particular, Stephen did not fall head over heels in love. In fact, he found it hard to make up his mind to propose. So, when his mother and sister suggested he meet up with the Thackeray sisters in his beloved Switzerland, Leslie Stephen agreed, but no sooner had he arrived than he lost his nerve. To the assembled women's shock and dismay, Leslie took off for the high Alpine huts and climbed some more mountains. Once back at home in London, however, persuaded that it was not the work of a gentleman to refuse a proposal that a young lady had been led to expect, he proposed, assured that he would be accepted. And he was — on one condition. "I cannot conceive of life without my sister," we can imagine Minny saying. "In our home together, dearest Leslie, there must always be room for Anny."

And Leslie agreed. What choice did he actually have? Leslie liked facts, and given the fact that he was barely able to meet his own meager expenses, the new Stephen household would have to be established at 8 Onslow Gardens, Kensington, which Anny and Minny owned jointly. It would run for the foreseeable future on Thackeray money, with Anny and Leslie-Minny (who as husband and wife, according to English law, became one single legal entity, that is, the husband) sharing expenses. And apart from the financial advantages, there were social ones too. Leslie was often out of the house on journalism business in London, and he still intended to take long mountaineering holidays in the Alps. On weekends in England he was beginning to organize a group of younger men for what he called tramps — day hikes for as long as forty miles. Anne would be company for Minny when her husband was away. If children came along, as Leslie devoutly hoped, Anny would be the perfect aunt. And Anny and Minny, though so different in temperament, got on so well. Late in life, Leslie Stephen likened the relationship between his first wife and her sister to that between a "popular author and his wife," a remark both snotty and insightful from a man whose own erudite tomes never sold many copies. Leslie Stephen, his friends at the club agreed, was a lucky dog to have gotten the wealthy Miss Minny Thackeray for free, and as a bonus, her sister as a paying guest in her own home.

If there was one issue that separated the two Thackeray sisters, it was their mother, but even Isabella Shawe Thackeray seems never to have become a source of open conflict between the two. Anny could not forget the day when Isabella had almost drowned her in the sea at Margate, but she never stopped loving her mother. After their father's death, the Thackeray sisters maintained Isabella in her own home on the south coast, at not inconsiderable expense, and Anny went to see her mother when she could. Over the decades, Isabella became calmer, more aware, more responsive to old songs, old poems, and old memories, and mother and daughter developed a loving relationship. At the age of seventy-five, Isabella died in Anne's arms, the two of them watched over in turn by Anne's friend, Julia Jackson Duckworth Stephen. The relationship of Isabella and Anne Thackeray was a triumph of love over adversity.

Why Minny was never expected by either her father or her sister to take her share of Isabella's burden is an important part of the Thackeray bequest to the Stephens. The surface reason was that Minny Thackeray was an infant when Isabella fell into madness, and had no memories of her mother. The deep reason was that William Thackeray feared that exposing Minny to her mad mother might push Minny into madness too. William Thackeray saw his older daughter, Anny, as strong and resilient like himself. He saw Minny as weak and vulnerable like Isabella. Jane Shawe, Isabella's sister, also went mad late in life, and William feared that Minny might have inherited the insanity that ran in her mother's family.

This idea that Minny might go mad if placed under extreme stress, as her mother had done, was more fear than fact. Minny Thackeray was an eminently rational and practical person, a good deal more sane, in many ways, than her mildly manic-depressive sister Anne or Minny's extremely neurotic husband, Leslie. But the fear of inherited madness was passed on by William Thackeray to Anny, who took on the role of Minny's protector when their father was gone. When Minny married, her father's fear of Minny's mental vulnerability was passed down once again to Minny's husband, Leslie Stephen.

The fear of what might be called the Shawe-Thackeray inheritance had, as we shall see in the next chapter, tragic consequences for Leslie and Minny's child, Laura Makepeace Stephen, but it would also cast a shadow over the adult life of Virginia Woolf. She, of course, bore no genetic relationship to the Shawe women, but her parents were convinced that madness was a trait that women, as the weaker sex, inherited, suffered from, and could pass on to their children. The severe mental illness from which Woolf suffered from her mid-teens regularly created havoc with her life, but she had also to bear the fear that, in modern terms, madness was part of her genetic makeup and could affect her children.

ॐ

As it turned out, Minny Thackeray Stephen needed none of operatic Rosina's traps to ensnare a husband and keep him happy in her thrall. From the time of their honeymoon, spent inevitably in Switzerland, but in a luxury hotel, not a mountain hut, Leslie loved being married to a delightful, accommodating, intelligent woman who could pay for the luxuries she had grown up with. He and Minny got on perfectly in society and in bed, and she afforded him pleasures and comforts he had barely dreamed of in youth. Theirs was a very happy marriage.

Leslie had a fine mind and worked hard, and, propelled by the Thackeray connections and Minny's delightful dinner parties, his professional career blossomed and bore fruit. As we saw in Chapter 4, a few years into the marriage, the editorship of Thackeray's beloved *Cornhill* was offered to Leslie by George Smith, William Thackeray's publisher and devoted friend, at the splendid salary of five hundred pounds a year. Thereafter Stephen's reputation and earnings grew steadily, and after some seven years of marriage, during which he had lived in houses owned or rented, in fact if not law, by his wife and her sister, he was able to purchase a home for his growing family. Minny, who had her father William Makepeace Thackeray's gift for drawing and his refined taste in art and furnishings, joyfully undertook to design and decorate her new home.

Anny was more and more away with friends and relatives, writing her books, living her own life, and the Thackeray sisters seemed, at last, to accept that life must carry them apart.

If there was a shadow over the married life of Leslie and Minny, it was Minny's ill health. Both Stephens were anxious to have children, but Minny found it hard to conceive and harder to bring a child to term. Her first child, a son, was a late miscarriage. Her second child, a daughter named Laura Makepeace, was born, as she herself had been, months premature. When, four years later, Minny became pregnant again and, despite complications, seemed likely to bring the child to term, both Stephens were overjoyed.

In November of 1875, the Stephens were sitting down to dinner in their new home when their dear friend Julia Jackson Duckworth dropped in, as she often did, to discuss some philanthropic mission with Minny. The Stephens begged Julia to sit down and share the delicious soup puree Minny had ordered up from the kitchen, but Julia insisted on rushing away. As she later recorded, her two friends' shining love and happiness formed an unbearable contrast with the darkness of the widowed life that had been hers for five years.

Just hours later, Minny Stephen awoke, complaining of terrible pain, and then went into convulsions. She was suffering, it seems clear, from eclampsia, a condition attendant on pregnancy that still kills women today. The doctor was called but there was nothing to be done, and Minny Stephen died in horrible pain. It was Leslie's birthday, and he never celebrated that day again.

Minny's death was the first great tragedy of Leslie Stephen's life, and he feared he would never recover from his loss. For Anne Thackeray it was the third great tragedy, following on her mother's fall into insanity as a young woman and her father's untimely death. Minny was the person Anny loved most in the world now that her father was dead, and sisters, unlike wives, cannot be replaced. All the same, Anny knew from grim experience that the clouds would part someday and that she had best enjoy the sunshine when at last it came.

For some two years, Leslie and Anny clung together for support. They gave up the house that was stamped in Minny's image and moved for comfort into a property Minny and Anny had inherited from their grandmother, at Hyde Park Gate in Kensington. The house was virtually next door to Julia Duckworth and her children. Brother- and sister-in-law mourned, each in his and her way, but imperceptibly each was also reaching out to the future. Thanks to the old and close friendship between Anne and Julia, and the physical proximity between the two families, Leslie was able to get close to his neighbor Mrs. Duckworth in ways that did not endanger her reputation — talking in the evening, walking in Richmond Park, baring their souls in long, regular letters. Anne Thackeray, meanwhile, was discovering to her incredulous delight that the pleasure she had always felt in the company of her cousin Richmond Ritchie was fully reciprocated.

Anne had known Richmond literally from birth: she was eighteen years his senior, and his mother and her sisters were her father's first cousins. Members of the large and sociable Thackeray-Ritchie clan were forever visiting one another in Kensington or Windsor and traveling on the Continent in large, luggage-laden packs. Richmond was a handsome and charming boy who grew into a brilliant young man, winning a Kings Scholarship to Eton, a champion at fives — a ball game played at Eton — elected to the exclusive club called Pop, and duly proceeding on to Trinity College, Cambridge. An outstanding student, Richmond was reading for the classics Tripos and expected to go on to a remarkable career. His success was important, as his mother was a widow with a small income and many children.

But Richmond was also strong-willed, and when he decided that Anne Thackeray, though so very much older, was the most wonderful woman he had ever met and he wanted to marry her, he could not be dissuaded. As for Anne herself, as she later wrote, she loved Richmond very much, but not enough to be unselfish and send him away. Their relationship became passionate, and when Richmond proposed, Anne accepted. He left Cambridge in a hurry and took a junior but paying position at the Colonial Office, and the wedding date was set for a day in late August when the bridegroom could get twenty-four hours' leave.

No one in the Ritchie-Thackeray family was happy about the marriage, but everyone loved Anny, so they quickly accepted her as Richmond's wife. Julia Duckworth rejoiced that her old friend Anne had at last found someone to love her and offer the chance of happiness after so much pain. But Leslie Stephen was outraged. Leslie rated women on their looks, not their brains, and he had never seen Anne Thackeray as attractive. Like her father, he assumed that she would never marry. Leslie Stephen had married, in a sense, two Thackeray women, not one, and after death had snatched one away from him, the second remained to be counted on. Now the second was entering into an almost incestuous relationship with a man young enough to be her son. How could Leslie Stephen be expected to bear it?

The conflict over Anne's engagement to Richmond deepened the rift in the relationship between Anne and Leslie that had already arisen over the treatment of his daughter, Laura. Minny and Anny saw quite clearly and early on that, in comparison to the little daughters of Edward Thackeray whom they had temporarily adopted, Laura was slow to develop both physically and mentally. Minny's response had been to love her child, meet her special needs with sympathy and intelligence, and help her overcome her problems. Anny endorsed her sister's approach.

Leslie faced up to his child's problems only after his wife died and he became wholly responsible for her. Laura became, as he saw it, naughty and willful, and her conduct aggravated her father's grief and loneliness and made him angry. Anne was willing to take on the care of her niece, as she had once done for her small cousins, but Leslie would have none of that. He thought Anne was being weak and told her that he would deal with his daughter as he saw fit. If Anne persisted in interfering, she would no longer be welcome in his home.

Leslie's view of Laura and his plan for her were very much the result of the counsel and support he was receiving from Julia Duckworth. By the time Anne and Richmond were engaged, Leslie Stephen had finally persuaded Julia Duckworth to become his wife, and Julia was convinced that her husband must take a very firm line with his child. Thus, even as relations between the Thackeray-Ritchies and the Stephen-Duckworths were smoothed over enough to bring Leslie and Julia to Anne and Richmond's wedding, beneath the surface Leslie Stephen's feelings toward his former sister-in-law were still raw, and he lashed out to wound her as, he felt, she had wounded him.

Thus, in preparation for his remarriage, Leslie made a will that included guardianship provisions for his daughter, Laura. Anne Thackeray, Laura's devoted aunt, was the obvious choice as guardian, but Leslie Stephen passed over her. Instead he appointed Anne's new husband, Richmond Ritchie, a young man he loathed, and his own wife-to-be, Julia Duckworth. Leslie further stipulated that Julia should henceforth exercise over Laura the full rights and authority of a mother.

Anne Thackeray Ritchie had deeply loved and sought to protect her sister, Minny. When Minny died, the love and protection were extended to Minny's daughter, a child in obvious need of both. Having been thrust out of Laura's life, Anne Thackeray Ritchie could hardly have been blamed had she refused to have anything more to do with Leslie Stephen. But she did not. Taking courage from her new married happiness, she kept the lines of communication open between her own family and the family of her friends Leslie and Julia. They had made it plain that they would resent and fear any attempt to interfere in Laura's care. That was nonnegotiable. But at least Anne could come to the Stephens' house every now and then, ask to see her niece, take her in her arms, and watch, if only from afar. It was not much, but it was something. And in Julia and Leslie's two daughters, Vanessa and Virginia, so different yet so alike in their aspirations, close allies yet rivals for familial love and affection, Anne could see something of herself and Minny.

ॐ

There are strong parallels between Anne Thackeray Ritchie and Virginia Woolf. Both were exceptionally sensitive and intelligent, and both were subjected to tragic bereavements early in life that left them mentally scarred. If Virginia was, from time to time, mad, Anne was subject to periods of mental and physical collapse throughout her life. In an age when eccentricity was almost the norm, she was seen as more than a little crazy. Both Anne and Virginia, when not ill, were exceptionally loving, creative, hardworking, and achieving. From the age of four, Anne had known the inside of a mental asylum, though as a visitor, not a patient, and her life was inflected by the problem and the inheritance of madness.

Like Virginia Woolf, Anne Thackeray waited for years before finding a man she felt able to marry. Both Richmond Ritchie and Leonard Woolf were, in different ways, controversial partners, and in choosing them against the advice of friends and family, Anne Thackeray and Virginia Stephen each took a leap of faith that paid off.

And of course, and above all, both Anne Thackeray Ritchie and Virginia Woolf were not just writers but authors who published articles and books, found a dedicated readership, earned fees and advances, and knew their trade. Both wrote memoirs and autobiographical essays.

Anne Thackeray Ritchie was aware of a number of good women writers of the late eighteenth and early nineteenth centuries whose books were out of favor. She wrote a series of short biographies in an attempt to make sure these women were not erased from the annals of literature. Her efforts were often in vain, but a generation later, Virginia Woolf would take up the same challenge, with much greater authority and lasting effect.

੨੭

Leonard Woolf was introduced to "Aunt Anny" in the months after his marriage to Virginia and, while noting that her genius was "a shade out of control," took to her immediately. "I was taken to be exhibited to many of Virginia's relations whom hitherto I had not met. The most interesting was Lady Ritchie ... Aunt Anny, as she was always called ... was a rare instance of the child of a man of genius inheriting some of that genius." During World War I, when Anne Thackeray Ritchie lived almost exclusively in her house at Freshwater on the Isle of Wight, she and the Woolfs saw little of one another. Both in her published essays and reviews and in person, Lady Ritchie was prone to lament how far the new generation of novelists fell below the standards of the Victorian greats such as her father, and Virginia Woolf, who had published her first novel in 1915, took those remarks personally. In 1915 Woolf suffered an extremely serious mental breakdown, from which it took her more than a year to recover, and, with travel in wartime difficult, she was unable to get to the Isle of Wight to see her dear old friend and clear the air.

Thus, when Lady Ritchie died in 1919, Virginia and Leonard were truly sad and eager to mend bridges with the Ritchie family. Both Woolfs at once published obituaries that offered thoughtful and loving tribute to the dead woman. For the *Times Literary Supplement* of March 6, 1919, Virginia Woolf wrote:

> She will be the unacknowledged source of much that remains in men's minds about the Victorian age. She will be the transparent medium through which we behold the dead. We shall see them lit up by her tender and radiant glow. Above all and forever she will be the companion and interpreter of her father whose spirit she has made walk among us not only because she wrote of him but because, even more wonderfully, lived in him . . . many are today turning to the thought of her, thanking her not only for her work, but thanking her more profoundly for the bountiful and magnanimous nature in which all tender and enchanting things seemed to grow — a garden one might call it where the air blew sweetly and freely and the bird of the soul raised an unpremeditated song of thanksgiving for the life that it had found so good.

Virginia Woolf's style in this obituary, written I think under the influence of emotion, seems forced, almost like a parody of Thackeray Ritchie's famously loose, flowing, euphuistic style. The Ritchie-Thackeray-Cornish clan disliked Virginia's obituary and were further enraged by the portrayal of Lady Ritchie as Mrs. Hilbery in Woolf's new novel, *Night and Day,* also published in 1919.

No one who knew Anne Thackeray Ritchie could fail to recognize whom Virginia Woolf had in mind when, in the opening pages of the novel, she describes the mother of her protagonist, Katharine Hilbery: "[Mrs. Hilbery's] large blue eyes, at once sagacious and innocent, seemed to regard the world with an enormous desire that it should behave itself nobly and an entire confidence that it would do so, if it would only take the pains . . . [s]he was clearly still prepared to give everyone any number of fresh chances and the whole system the benefit of the doubt."

Mrs. Hilbery is the daughter of Richard Alardyce, a great Victorian poet — a composite of Thackeray Ritchie's father, William Makepeace Thackeray, and her great friend Alfred Tennyson. The novel opens at the Hilberys' London home, which contains a small private museum devoted to the great poet's memory. A similar shrine, devoted to her father, could be found in all the homes of Anne Thackeray Ritchie.

Night and Day is Virginia Woolf's most conventional and least known work, essentially a highly autobiographical romance novel in which the two protagonists, Katharine Hilbery and Ralph Denham, must both choose between two suitors. A struggling barrister, Denham lives with his large, financially strapped family in Hampstead, a then benighted region of London so distant from the Hilbery world of Chelsea, Belgravia, and Kensington that, at one point, Katharine literally cannot think how to make her way home from Denham's house. Katharine finally chooses Ralph Denham, a character based on Leonard Woolf, after he is able to convince her that he respects and values her as much as he loves her and will never force her to obey his wishes or conform to his ideas.

Katharine needs a husband because, in her late twenties, she is frittering away her life, pouring tea for her mother's aging cronies — who include a wickedly accurate version of Henry James — showing new visitors around the shrine to the Great Alardyce, keeping track of the mounds of the poet's personal papers heaped up in the study, and trying to make her mother commit two consecutive sentences of the biography to paper. In her letters, Virginia Woolf says that she is basing Katharine on her sister Vanessa, and clearly Woolf, in her portrayal of the Hilbery ménage, is drawing on memories not only of the Ritchie family but of the frustration and stress she and Vanessa had suffered in the last years of their father's life at Hyde Park Gate.

A superficial reading of the opening of the novel might lead one to conclude that Katharine Hilbery is a slave to her selfish mother and to the memory of her dead grandfather. However, as the novel progresses, we see that in Mrs. Hilbery, Woolf sets out not to critique and mock Anne Thackeray Ritchie but to celebrate and immortalize a most beloved old friend and the kind of mother she herself longed for. Maggie Hilbery, herself happily married to a devoted and congenial man, is keenly aware of her daughter's situation and, while knowing how much she will miss her daughter when she marries, is eager for Katharine to find a life of her own. Ralph Denham meets Katharine because her mother has invited him to tea, and at the end of the novel, Mrs.

Hilbery, in a move worthy of Oscar Wilde or P. G. Wodehouse, breaks the impasse between Katharine and Ralph and disposes of Katharine's fiancé, William Rodney — a carefully heterosexualized but still recognizable version of Lytton Strachey. Even as Katharine and Ralph walk the rainy streets of London and debate the possibility of a meeting of two minds, male and female, Mrs. Hilbery, their dea ex machina, sizes up the situation, makes a decision, and acts.

Comedy is something we look for in Virginia Woolf's letters and diary but not her novels. In *Night and Day,* however, where she sorts her four young characters neatly into two pairs as in a drawing room comedy, she indulges her gift for funny dialogue, as the following set of Hilberyisms illustrates:

> "Mr. Fortescue [the Henry James avatar] has almost tired me out. He is so eloquent and so witty, so searching and so profound that, after a half hour or so, I feel inclined to turn off all the lights." (page 12)
>
> "Dear things, dear chairs and tables. How like old friends they are — faithful, silent friends. Which reminds me, Katharine, little Mr. Anning is coming tonight." (page 12)
>
> "I don't know what's come over me. I actually had to ask Augustus the name of the lady Hamlet was in love with as you were out Katharine, and Heaven knows what he mayn't put down about me in his diary." (page 56)

As Woolf herself recognized, her Mrs. Hilbery is the best thing in the book, and if Anne Thackeray Ritchie had lived another six months, I think she would have loved it, laughed with it, learned from it, and written to her beloved adoptive niece Virginia that perhaps the twentieth-century novel had some things going for it after all.

7

Virginia Woolf's Mad, Bad Sister

WHEN FREDERIC Maitland, one of her father's most loyal disciples, gratifyingly determined to undertake an official biography of Leslie Stephen, he
wrote asking Leslie's daughter Virginia to read, on his behalf, the many letters her parents had exchanged during their courtship. Maitland had married
into the Stephen family — he was the husband of Florence Fisher, one of Julia's
nieces — but all the same he felt a delicacy about reading personal correspondence. Such were the conventions of British biography circa 1905, and Frederic
Maitland was a rising Cambridge historian with lots of other fish to fry.

Woolf was gratified to be contacted by Maitland. In 1905 she was recovering from a serious mental breakdown, still under suicide watch by friends
and family members, and ordered by her doctor, Sir Charles Savage, to eat a
lot more and read as little as possible. Bored, frustrated, ready to throw all her
medications down the toilet along with the medical men who had prescribed
them, Woolf eagerly agreed to do all she could to advance Maitland's work.

This raised alarm bells with several family members, notably Jack Hills,
who had once been married to Virginia's dead half-sister, Stella Duckworth.
Indignant to hear that Hills considered her the last person qualified to read
her parents' letters, Woolf dived right into them. In the early years of their
relationship, Woolf discovered, both her parents had been obsessed with the

problems posed by Leslie's "idiot" daughter, Laura Makepeace Stephen. Hills had been appointed Laura Stephen's legal guardian after his wife's death. Laura was some twelve years older than Virginia, and by the time Virginia emerged from the nursery, Laura was already spending time away from the family or was sequestered with an attendant somewhere in the family home. We do not know how much the two sisters interacted.

Jack Hills need not have worried about crazy Virginia letting any cats out of the Stephen family bag. No one better than Woolf, who had just emerged from a private clinic for the affluent insane herself, appreciated the sensitivity of the Laura revelations. She told Maitland that the early letters between her parents added no facts of importance to the understanding of Leslie Stephen's career, and she extracted a few, carefully chosen passages that the disciple-biographer could cite to humanize his august subject. A Trinity don of delicate health — he would die as a young man in the year the Stephen biography was published — Maitland was happy to take her advice. As far as I can judge from Woolf's letters, Frederic Maitland would have been happy to allow Leslie Stephen's talented daughter to not only ghostwrite but type up the whole volume to be published under his name — a fact not lost on the ambitious Miss Stephen.

What the Stephen courtship letters — now in the Berg Collection in the New York Public Library — show is that, in the long and tortured months when Leslie Stephen was striving to persuade Julia Duckworth to marry him, he found in his daughter, Laura, a way to involve Julia actively in his life. The child posed a challenge closely tailored to Julia's interests and skills, and in letters and doubtless in conversation too, Leslie and Julia agonized over what to do about Laura. The agreement they finally reached was a key factor in turning their friendship into marriage.

Unfortunately, as Virginia Stephen knew all too well and Maitland probably knew or at least guessed, Julia and Leslie Stephen had not solved the Laura problem. Far from it. If indeed there was a skeleton in Leslie Stephen's closet, Laura was it, and as the Leslie Stephen school of biography saw it, the closet must be left firmly closed.

The image of closet and closure is all too apt. Laura Stephen had been largely separated from the rest of the family all through her teens and was put in a mental asylum in her early twenties. The skeleton image is not apt. The oldest Stephen daughter was very much alive when Maitland was writing the laudatory biography of his mentor.

ॐ

When Laura was born, not even three pounds in weight, Minny Stephen at once bonded with her tiny daughter and, unlike many women of her class, was intimately involved in her care. Of course, the Stephens had a reliable nurse and a staff of maids to provide twenty-four-hour assistance, but Laura Stephen owed her survival to her mother.

Laura, or Memee as she was called, was an unusually small infant and had a great deal of pain from teething, often waking the household with her screams

Minny and baby Laura with their dog, Troy

at night. As a result, she developed a strong dislike of meat, so her mother allowed her the nutritious, easily chewed foods she liked, such as goat's milk and fresh fruit. Slow to walk, Laura was also slow to talk, and even slower to make sense. She loved to sing and dance around and hum and babble away in a weird mixture of English and German (Louise Beinecke, her nurse, was German), which her mother declared enchanting. In a letter to her sister, Anne, Minny gave a sample of Laura speak — or rather, Laura song: "I was so surprised at Memee suddenly beginning to strum on the piano and shouting a long ballad all de children are mumbled down stairs Polly put the kettle on Cooky take it off again where's me little children gone."

Victorian fathers were not expected to show much interest in their infant children, especially if they were girls, but in this Leslie Stephen was the exception. When he came home at night, he would, according to Anne Thackeray Ritchie, head straight for the nursery to find his wife and daughter, and happily join in the prevailing baby worship. To his great friend in America, Oliver Wendell Holmes, Leslie Stephen wrote:

> It is true that my baby is the best of all possible babies. That child's head contains an amount of brains wh. would astonish any humble phrenologist. She can't talk much but her expression indicates an amount of humour & of feeling wh. few persons possess. She is not appreciated by the general public because she does not weigh as much as some babies & the public goes by weight in regards to babies but she is a baby to be proud of to anyone who has an eye to the best qualities in human babies.

The Thackeray documentation shows that for her first four years, Laura Stephen led the privileged life of children of her class, big-sistered by Annie and Margie Thackeray, her mother's informally adopted daughters, taking seaside holidays with the children of relatives and friends like the Duckworths, carried off to the Continent for long stays in comfortable hotels with her doting parents. Her slowness to speak did not go unnoticed, but she was a natural mimic and very funny. She was no doubt very spoiled, but she was a beautiful, good-natured, affectionate little person, and beauty and sweetness of nature were the key requirements for little Victorian girls.

But then, literally from one day to the next, disaster struck. Laura's mother died of eclampsia in the last months of pregnancy as we have seen, and during the mourning period no one seemed to remember Laura was there, much less care about what she was feeling. The five-year-old now found herself in the care of her father, a man whom she adored but who was sunk in his own grief and frequently went off, leaving his child with relatives and friends. Annie and Margie Thackeray, who had loved and protected Laura, went back to India to live with their father, Edward Thackeray, and his new wife. All the same, Laura still had her aunt Anny and her dog.

Soon after Minny's death, Anne Thackeray moved back in with her brother-in-law and niece, first at Leslie's house at 8 Southwell Gardens and then, after Leslie sold that house for a splendid forty-one hundred pounds, at the house in Hyde Park Gate near Julia Duckworth. Brother- and sister-in-law clung together in their sorrow at first, but after a time they began to clash fiercely, over money matters and the management of Laura. Leslie Stephen was increasingly aware of his daughter's cognitive problems and angry with what he regarded as her refusal to learn and conform to an educational schedule.

Anne Thackeray wanted to continue her dead sister Minny's system for handling the child. She would have willingly taken on the care of Laura, as she had done for Annie and Margie, but Leslie considered Laura spoiled and selfish. That the little girl's mopes and fits of passion and refusals to cooperate could be an expression of trauma following the loss of her mother apparently never occurred to him. He found Laura to be a burden, and saw the laxity of Anne and nurse Beinecke as the cause of the child's inexcusable refusal to be a loving support to her father in his misery. So, after terrible quarrels, Leslie told Anne that he would tolerate no further interference from her in his daughter's upbringing. Wounded, frustrated, fearful for Laura but on the brink of a new life as Richmond Ritchie's wife, Anne Thackeray moved out of the Hyde Park Gate house she owned jointly with Leslie, and within months was married.

Thus, within a couple of years Laura Stephen had lost her mother, her adoptive sisters Annie and Margie, the love of her father, and the affectionate and supportive presence of her aunt. And even as Anne Thackeray was taking a swift, unexpected swerve into marriage, Leslie was doing the same, as he grew ever closer to his neighbor and friend Julia Duckworth.

To the black-clad Julia Duckworth, the black-clad Leslie Stephen reported in the years 1876 and 1877 that he was in torment. He had finally been forced to recognize serious cognitive and emotional problems in his daughter, now seven. Not only was Laura verbally incomprehensible and slow to learn, but she was also increasingly unruly, disobedient, even perverse. Julia was sympathetic and full of advice. On the subject of educating small children, she felt herself an expert. Her own daughter, Stella Duckworth, one year older than Laura, was a model of obedience and decorum, a tiny, exquisite, mute version of her beautiful mama. Julia's sons, George and Gerald Duckworth, were doing well at prep school, both on track to enter Eton as boarders on the strength of the trust funds left them by their affluent papa.

The problem with Laura, as Leslie and Julia chose to see it, was that she had inherited the madness that ran in her mother Minny Thackeray's maternal family. Leslie had perhaps heard his sister-in-law, Anne Thackeray, tell the story of how her mother, Isabella Shawe Thackeray, had tried to drown her as a tiny girl and how her father, William Makepeace Thackeray, had always feared that his fragile younger daughter, Minny, might have inherited her mother's madness.

Leslie could report from certain knowledge that his mother-in-law, Isabella Thackeray — still very much alive — had been incurably insane from her mid-twenties and that her sister, Jane Shawe, had headed down the same path later in life. Isabella's daughter Anny Thackeray was, Leslie and Julia agreed during their courtship, while immensely lovable and quite a literary talent, not the most rational of women. Did Anny not persist in seeing silver linings where Julia and Leslie saw only thunderclouds? Was Anny capable of sticking to a budget or making a simple statement based on statistics? Was she not married to a boy half her age? Leslie Stephen, encouraged by Julia, came to see Laura's unnerving mood swings from apathy to violence as reminiscent of the child's maternal grandmother as a young woman.

The idea that Laura Stephen had inherited insanity from her mother's family held sway in the Stephen family for the next two generations or more, even as evidence steadily built up that, if indeed Laura Stephen was congenitally disposed to insanity, she could just as easily have inherited it from her father as from her mother. Let us review the evidence.

Leslie Stephen's biographer Noel Annan clearly lays out that both Leslie and his father, James Stephen, were subject to frequent deep depressions and occasional mental breakdowns. They were afflicted with "neurasthenia," to use the Victorian medical parlance, or something like bipolar disease in ours, and if there is a "gene" for "neurasthenia," it was expressed in severe and mild forms over at least three generations of Stephens. Following a blow on the head from a sail, J. K. Stephen (known in the family as Jem), one of Sir Fitzjames Stephen's sons and Laura's first cousin, became violently insane in his mid-twenties and starved himself to death at thirty-three in a mental institution. As a result of Jem's tragic end, his father, Fitzjames, became unhinged with grief, was removed from the bench, and died two years after his son.

Leslie's older son, Thoby Stephen, Laura's half-brother, was notably uncommunicative, had an odd accident involving another boy and a knife at prep school, and was later sent home from his boarding school after trying to throw himself out a window. The school said he had been sleepwalking but, again according to Noel Annan, Thoby repeated this apparent attempt at suicide when he was brought home. Further down the years, Leslie's third daughter, Virginia, Laura's half-sister, made her first attempt at suicide at fifteen, had to be forcibly restrained from throwing herself out the window at the institution where she was confined, and lived her life thereafter in fear of the next psychotic episode.

As we shall see later in this book, the legendarily tough, redoubtable Vanessa Stephen Bell was mysteriously incapacitated on her journeys to Greece in 1906 and Turkey in 1911, and she suffered two major mental breakdowns in later life. Adrian, the youngest of Leslie Stephen's children, was considered too fragile to be sent away to school and was educated from home in a private day school until he began to prepare for entrance to Cambridge. After years of aimlessly seeking a profession, Adrian Stephen settled, to the dismay and scorn of his older sisters, on a career as a Freudian analyst. Psychoanalysis, as Vanessa cattily pointed out to Virginia, did not require any exams or paper qualifications, and the two sisters giggled over the fact that their little brother (a hulking six foot five) was now encouraged by his own analyst to see them as the cause of all his problems. Adrian Stephen is the forgotten sibling in the Virginia Woolf story, but I wonder if analysis led him to figure out that Virginia was not the only "crazy" person in his family.

ಎ➥

Several attempts have been made to diagnose what was "wrong" with Laura Stephen. When Laura was about eighteen, Leslie Stephen brought in a friend, the eminent Victorian psychologist Sir Charles Savage, and he reinforced Leslie and Julia's idea about inherited lunacy by giving it as his expert opinion that the girl was not only an "idiot" but incurably insane. The same doctor had been consulted in the case of Jem Stephen and, eerily, for decades he would be Virginia Woolf's doctor too. A hundred years or so after Savage, the biographers Hermione Lee and Henrietta Garnett suggested that some form of autism may have been at the root of Laura's problems. Theirs is an informed guess at best, since autism had yet to be diagnosed or studied in the late nineteenth century. So, once again, let us review the evidence.

Certain things can be established when the Thackeray sources are set next to the Stephen ones. Laura Stephen was born many weeks premature, weighing less than three pounds. That she survived at all is a tribute to the power of cotton wool and a mother's love. All the same, it seems certain that, without the breathing support available now in our specialized preemie units, Laura's immature lungs inhibited the normal development of her brain.

The Thackeray papers also provide excellent evidence that, even by our exacting twenty-first-century standards, Laura as an infant and small girl received exemplary care. Minny Thackeray Stephen was the ideal mother for her child — intelligent, devoted, responsive, and able to afford the best. Minny had a strong social network, headed up by her live-in sister, Anny.

For almost five years Laura Stephen knew nothing but love and affection and care. Even in the second summer after Minny's death, Laura spent a happy holiday in the Lake District with her father and his sister, Milly Stephen. Her aunt even managed to persuade Laura to eat some meat, and the little girl was behaving well enough to be rowed across the lake by her father for a visit to the reclusive and highly particular art critic John Ruskin. Now a sturdy seven-year-old, Laura took hill walks with her mountaineer father and his dog, Troy, whom she adored.

But by the age of eight, back in Kensington, separated from her aunt Anne, the girl had become a problem that Leslie Stephen could not cope with alone, or so he confessed to Julia Duckworth. And in a conscious spirit of self-abnegation and social commitment that astonished her family and friends (how could the charming Mrs. Duckworth, wrote Henry James, consent to become "the receptacle of Leslie Stephen's impossible taciturnity and dreariness?"), Julia agreed to take on not only her neurotic friend, but his ungovernable child.

And once he remarried, like so many fathers in real life as well as fairy tales (remember Cinderella?), Leslie did what he had said he would do in his will and gave Julia the same jurisdiction over his daughter, Laura, that the child's mother would have had. To bring up and educate daughters was, in Victorian society, properly the province of women, and Leslie Stephen now had a proposed dictionary of twenty-six volumes to edit.

Julia preferred sons to daughters and made no secret of it. She adored both her Duckworth sons, who so closely resembled her darling Herbert, and Gerald ceased to be her pet only when Adrian was born. Julia saw Laura as not just intellectually backward but emotionally entitled, and that was something she could not tolerate in a small girl. Laura had been spoiled and needed to be brought under firm control. Louise Beinecke, the German nurse who had been with Laura since birth, had to be dismissed and replaced with a person who understood discipline. The child's peculiar tastes for things like goat milk must not be indulged. Meat was good for Laura, and she must be forced to eat it. She must learn to read and write. Her strange little dances and odd little songs must stop. A good steel surgical corset would do wonders for her deportment.

It is plain, from the details about Laura given in the biographies of Anne Thackeray Ritchie, that the drooling, violent, ungovernable, moronic Laura Stephen inscribed into the literature surrounding Virginia Woolf and Vanessa Bell emerged after her father remarried and after Laura came under the control of her new stepmother.

Laura Makepeace Stephen as a young girl

Julia might well have tolerated, pitied, or even felt affection for her step-daughter, had Laura been a nice, obedient, quiet, fragile, affectionate idiot. But she was not. Laura had the Stephen strength and the Stephen will, and she had once known love, so she resisted the new regimen forced upon her. She spat out gobs of the meat she was forced to eat, stammered, stuttered, howled, and occasionally threw things like scissors. Her stepmother responded with enforced isolation.

Julia Stephen was not guilty of conscious malice and, as we shall see, she had her hands full with a demanding husband, three older children and four younger ones, a large household, and a tight budget. She also took on a massive load of private and public philanthropy. For the next twelve or so years, Julia did her duty, as she saw it, by the child of her husband and her dead friend Minny Thackeray, but she found it impossible to love Laura. Julia had abjured all faith in God, but she still saw the world in terms of good and evil, and Laura, to her mind, was wicked and deserving of punishment. In her frustration and fury and pain, the teenage Laura, once such a pretty little girl, began to look ugly, uncouth, and unfeminine, and that alienated her even more from her family. Ugliness and lack of feminine charm were sins against the aesthetic creed of Pattledom, and that was a creed Julia Stephen still lived by.

At times Leslie Stephen, who worked in the house and could not entirely ignore what was going on between Laura and Julia, intervened, and he was the one who managed to teach Laura to read. One odd, discrepant little anecdote from the Woolf-Bell literature that testifies to Laura's ability to speak and understand has Laura reading *Alice's Adventures in Wonderland* aloud to her new little brother, Thoby. When Anne Thackeray Ritchie came to the house, Laura would run in, full of joyous excitement, to embrace her aunt and make an effort to communicate. But by the time Laura was in her mid-teens Anne had serious health problems, marital difficulties, and extensive professional commitments, and she came only rarely to Hyde Park Gate.

And then, as we try to trace exactly how Laura Stephen as a teenager moved into screaming, violent insanity, we have to take into account the fact that she was living in the same house as the Duckworth boys. Could Laura's symptoms be interpreted as a frightened, powerless, handicapped girl's reaction to sexual abuse? Here again we need to carefully review the evidence.

According to the testimony of Virginia Woolf, Gerald Duckworth in his teens and George Duckworth in his early thirties committed abusive acts upon her and Vanessa. One of the things that have made Woolf an iconic figure for third-wave feminists is that she felt safe enough to confide to friends the sexual abuse she had suffered at the hands of her older half-brothers. In the discussion of Laura, it is important, I think, to distinguish between what Virginia Woolf in 1939–40 said Gerald did to her as "a very small child" — so perhaps in 1888 — and what she told the Bloomsbury group Memoir Club in 1921–22 that George did to both her and Vanessa circa 1900. I will be discussing the issue concerning George in Chapter 10.

As the war with Hitler's Germany became a terrifying daily reality to people in the United Kingdom, Virginia Woolf found herself probing her earliest memories in an unfinished, tentative, and brilliant piece now known as "A Sketch of the Past." As she looks back, Woolf notices that, as a girl, she had felt a kind of rapture when looking at the pattern on a dress or a view of the sea and was yet so repulsed by her own body that she avoided even glancing at herself in the mirror. Trying to reconcile those contradictory facts in her life — sensual delight, corporeal disgust — Woolf suddenly recalls something that had happened to her when she was very young. This was something she had never before confided in anyone, never talked about. At Talland House one summer, her half-brother Gerald, who was some twelve years older, lifted her onto a slab in the hall, put his hand up her knickers, and began to "explore [her] body." She had wriggled and stiffened in resistance, yet the hand did not stop but "explored [her] private parts." Her reaction, Woolf tells us, "must have been strong since I still recall it. This seems to show that a feeling about certain parts of the body; how they must not be touched; how it is wrong to allow them to be touched; must be instinctive."

This is a radical statement, and as late as 1995, Quentin Bell was still dismissing it. What Gerald Duckworth did as a teenager to Quentin's aunt when she was a small child, Bell wrote, was the kind of thing children commonly do to children. Bell is discounting the importance of his aunt's experience. His darling, crazy aunt Virginia was simply too prone to go off the wall over nothing, he is saying as her nephew and biographer. But, as we are now coming to understand in the twenty-first century, it is precisely because acts like Gerald Duckworth's are common that they are egregious. What Gerald did to her was within the family, at the hands, quite literally, of a family member, and with almost casual ease, so she had no recourse at the time. Thereafter there was no person whom she could tell what had happened and how she had felt, so the memory festered. Gerald, she testified, had made the most intimate parts of her body into something sordid and repulsive.

As we now know, for Virginia Woolf, a single incidence of sexual abuse triggered an intense reaction with lifelong consequences, and she was able, decades later, as a celebrated writer and mature thinker, to advance a code of morality on the basis of her experience. On the most primal level, Woolf wants us to understand, a boy who uses a small girl's body for sexual exploration without her consent and despite her resistance is abusive. That families and society permit such abuse to occur and allow it to go unnoticed, as if it is just the way of things, is part and parcel of the abuse.

Today these insights are central to our understanding of child sexual abuse. When Woolf was developing her ideas in 1940, they were revolutionary. And, given the psychological damage done to Virginia Woolf as a girl by the Duckworths, it seems legitimate to wonder how Woolf's sister Laura, twelve years older, a girl with severe developmental handicaps growing into adulthood as an outlaw within the family, might have fared at the hands of the same young men.

We know that George and Gerald knew Laura Stephen well, much better than their four younger half-siblings knew her. Gerald was exactly the same age as Laura, George two years older, and as small children they had all three, under the watchful eyes of their mothers, Julia and Minny, played together on the sand at the seaside. George and Gerald probably decided early on, as spoiled little boys will, that Laura was "not all there." When their mother married Leslie Stephen, the young Duckworth boys were not pleased to share her with a crusty, depressed old man and stand by as he and his imbecile girl moved into their own home.

George Duckworth, as Virginia Woolf would later describe him in a talk to the Memoir Club, was intellectually backward and not made for self-reflection. She might have been equally caustic on the subject of Gerald, had his private publishing company not published her first two novels. When their mother produced four siblings in six years — Vanessa, Thoby, Virginia, and Adrian — the response of the Duckworth brothers, away at school for much of the year, was pragmatic. They never doubted that they would always come first with their mother, and they could take comfort in the fact that they were socially superior to Thoby and Adrian (who did not have a rich papa or get into Eton), and that Vanessa and Virginia, like Stella, had inherited the Pattle beauty and were likely to be a credit to them. But there was one person in the family on whom the brothers could take out some of their repressed resentments and frustrations about their mother's second marriage — Laura Makepeace Stephen.

George and Gerald saw Laura draining time and energy from Julia that they felt were rightfully theirs, and they complained bitterly that Laura was backward and out of control and mortified them in front of their friends. Picturesque examples of Laura's behavior were passed on by the Duckworths to the Stephen children, who were receptive, since they got even less of their mother's love and attention than their half-brothers did.

Did the Duckworths' antipathy toward Laura Stephen take the form of sexual abuse? Could the violent behavior attributed to Laura Stephen in her teenage years have been a healthy but unavailing cry for help? It seems all too possible. Let us remember that the Duckworths were healthy young males whose education from the age of eight segregated them from women and accustomed them to receiving and administering physical abuse. Eton, the Duckworth boys' secondary school, was a hormonal powder keg, a hierarchy set up to allow the older boys to exploit younger boys as domestic servants (fags) or, if they were beautiful, as sex toys behind the closed door of the study. This victimization occurred with the tacit connivance of the headmaster and the teachers, who had their own favorites among the older boys and who intervened in their pupils' relationships mainly to administer public floggings on the bare buttocks. Imagine what such an education in sadomasochism might predispose a teenage boy to do if left alone with an unloved, handicapped teenage girl.

From the time of Leslie and Julia's marriage, when the two households were merged in Julia's house, George and Gerald lived for many weeks of the year in the same house as Laura. She had her own room somewhere upstairs and her own version of Grace Poole — the servant entrusted with supervising Rochester's mad wife in *Jane Eyre* — but what care and protection that person afforded is not known. Laura was clearly more alone and more vulnerable than her younger sister would be ten years later, when George began to abuse his position as head of the family. The Duckworth youths as teenagers crossed Laura on the stairs and saw her at meals; if she used one of the three water closets that served the whole household, they could catch her coming in and out. The opportunities for abuse were there, and, as Vanessa half-jokingly told friends in later life, their half-brothers were good at seizing opportunities.

But what about Julia Stephen? Was she not a stern disciplinarian who would never tolerate any improper behavior in her home? Well, yes and no, and modern studies have eloquently shown that, all too often, the wives and mothers of sexual abusers do not come to the defense of the abused, preferring for complex reasons to look the other way. Julia Stephen was often away from home or at least out of the house on her many errands of mercy, and we know for a fact that her preference for the boys and young men in her household led her to protect her large, priapic, and violently deranged nephew Jem Stephen when he began stalking her daughter Stella. When Leslie Stephen ventured to express fears for Stella's safety, Julia told him, "I cannot bar my door to Jem," so Stella was obliged to slip out of the room or down the backstairs to avoid him, and her sisters were instructed to tell Jem that Stella was out.

James "Jem" Stephen

One can feel sympathy for poor doomed Jem, the pride of his family throughout his school and university career, and still feel that Stella was a victim too, and that Julia might have been a little more protective of her daughter. Louise DeSalvo, who bothered to read the poetry that Jem wrote at Oxford, has convincingly shown that the family's golden boy was obsessed with images of violent sexual abuse toward women long before he went mad. That the poetry and the images won prizes and the admiration of his peers only shows that many Victorian men found sadism normal, even amusing.

And if Julia Stephen was so cavalier in defense of her own daughter, what would she have done had she spotted her darling boys interacting — inappropriately, shall we say — with Laura? Raised a finger in reproof, sent her sons to their rooms, complained to Laura's companion of letting her roam the house alone, but not much more, I think. Boys will be boys, after all, and Julia Stephen felt that Laura was enough to try the patience of a saint. The Duckworths were young lords of the universe, convinced of their own irreproachability, and their doting mother would have believed whatever they told her.

All of this is supposition, of course. There is no hard evidence that Gerald and George Duckworth abused Laura Stephen. How could there be? Of all the people who recorded memories about life at 22 Hyde Park Gate, Laura's is a testimony we do not have. As a child she did not learn to write, and even when Aunt Anny came to see her, the two were not permitted to be alone together. All the same I think it is important to raise this question: if the mentally fragile Virginia Stephen was permanently wounded by what George and Gerald did to her, what effect might the brothers have had on Virginia's developmentally challenged, possibly autistic half-sister Laura Makepeace Stephen?

❧

Isabella Shawe Thackeray, my readers will remember, was for some fifty years looked after by reliable people in a series of private homes, her care supervised by her husband and then by her older daughter, who loved her and visited her regularly. Under this system of loving care, Isabella, who seems to have been schizophrenic, became happier and more responsive with the years, able to communicate a little through the music she had always loved.

Laura Stephen, in contrast, whose development was retarded by so many tragic circumstances but was not psychotic, was placed in an institution for the insane as a young woman and remained in institutional care until her death. How old Laura was when she was institutionalized is hard to determine, but that very lack of a hard date or a remembered transition tells us that she had long since been set outside the Stephen family circle.

Leslie Stephen was reluctant to send Laura to an asylum. When he could move off his treadmill of anxieties, he was a loving, reasoning, ethical man, and his nephew Jem's suicide in the asylum must have weighed upon him. According to one account, it was George Duckworth, speaking man to man as the eldest son, who insisted to his stepfather that Laura must be institutionalized as she was putting Julia's life at risk. Asked to choose between his eldest daughter and his wife, Leslie chose Julia. It is not chance that Laura left the family around the time that the invalid Maria Pattle Jackson, Julia's mother, moved into a bedroom next to her daughter's at 22 Hyde Park Gate.

As far as I can tell from the various accounts, Laura lived with her family until her late teens. She was then sent to live in the country for most of the year but continued to spend the summers at Talland House in St. Ives with the Duckworths and the other Stephens for a year or two after that. It was at Talland House that Gerald Duckworth felt able to set the child Virginia on the hall table and finger her genitals.

In her early twenties, Laura was committed to Earlswood, "an idiot asylum" in Redhill, a London suburb, and then to an equivalent one in Southgate, where she could also be readily visited from Kensington. In the early years Julia Stephen went to see Laura at the institution, often with her daughter Stella. After Julia's death in 1895, one of the many family burdens assumed by Stella was to visit Laura, but in 1897 Stella died too.

Ever since his marriage Leslie had found it difficult to be in the same room as Laura, but flickers of the love he had felt for his first child as a little girl still burned, and all his life he was haunted with guilt and a sense of responsibility. For as long as he could, Leslie visited Laura in the institution, and when he became seriously ill with cancer, he sought to ensure that Laura would be protected. In 1897, after Stella's death, Leslie wrote to his teenage son Thoby,

"I want you to remember her [that is, Laura] and see that she is properly cared for." When Thoby died in 1906, less than three years after his father, first Jack Hills, Stella's widower, then Katharine Stephen, one of Leslie's nieces, became Laura's guardian, but Laura outlived her too. When Laura died, she was apparently in some kind of medically supervised living situation near York, a city in the Midlands far from the homes in London and Sussex of her surviving brother and sisters.

Laura's best support during her sad life came from her mother's side of the family. While Laura lived with the Stephens, Anne Thackeray Ritchie stayed as much a part of her niece's life as she could. After Laura was institutionalized, even though it must have been inexpressibly painful, Anne visited Laura just as she had once visited her own mother, taking her out for jaunts or having her visit. After Lady Ritchie died, her daughter Hester Ritchie Norman continued to keep in touch with Laura, and to invite her to stay occasionally. Belinda Norman Butler, Hester's daughter, remembered Laura Stephen clearly, and her testimony is startling: "She was perfectly all right, really. Of course, she had some companion to look after her. She was craggy-looking, with the Stephen nose, like Leslie's. She was tall and thin and dressed in black lace. She was utterly sweet to us. She was *nice* to us. When we broke something once, I remember she helped us to pick up the pieces of some china we had smashed. She laughed and was kind and didn't scold us."

But even more important to Laura's comfort and safety was the money she had in essence inherited from her Thackeray mother. After Minny's death, Leslie made an agreement with his sister-in-law, Anne Thackeray Ritchie, that a generous sum of money accruing to Leslie as Minny's husband and widower would be put into a trust fund for Laura. Intended initially, perhaps, as a dowry, the fund was later used to place Laura in a private institution. Any money left over from covering Laura's expenses was to be reinvested in the 4 percent funds and inherited at Laura's death by her next of kin — her father and his other children. Laura's expenses never amounted to more than a few hundred pounds a year, but there seems never to have been any question of using all of Laura's "dowry" to set her up in a private home with caretakers, as her grandmother Isabella Thackeray had been.

There is no account of any of the other four Stephen children ever visiting Laura. After Leslie's and Thoby's deaths, and presumably after Katharine Stephen could no longer act as guardian, Vanessa and Virginia were occasionally asked to make some decision about Laura's care, but they kept a determined distance. Laura Stephen remained one family matter on which her sisters saw eye to eye with George and Gerald. When George Duckworth died in 1934, Virginia Woolf wrote to Vanessa Bell, "Leonard says Laura is the one we could have spared."

When Laura, age seventy-four, died of stomach cancer in 1945, a few years after Virginia Woolf's suicide, the lawyer for Laura's estate had difficulties locating her next of kin, Adrian Stephen and Vanessa Bell. He needed to tell them that they had inherited 7,800 pounds (some 400,000 in today's pounds), minus death duties, from Laura Makepeace Stephen.

There is a definite irony in this considerable legacy. There is nothing in the record to suggest that Laura's sisters and brothers had ever shown any love, sympathy, or even pity for her. Vanessa, who was nine or ten when Laura left the family, certainly remembered her but firmly put those memories away. Virginia, some three years younger than Vanessa, did volunteer some memories to the Memoir Club in the 1920s. Describing the house at 22 Hyde Park Gate where she had been born and spent her first twenty-three years, Woolf recalls that it accommodated not one household but three, for besides the three Duckworths and the six Stephens, "there was Thackeray's grand-daughter, a vacant-eyed girl whose idiocy was becoming daily more obvious, who could hardly read, who would throw scissors into the fire, who was tongue-tied and stammered and yet had to appear at the table with the rest of us."

Virginia Woolf was famous for her frankness, her willingness to put the unspeakable into words, but she cannot bring herself to say "my half-sister Laura Stephen." Did she herself see the throwing of scissors, or is she merely using for narrative effect details picked up from her parents' letters or passed on by her older siblings and half-siblings? The phrase "Thackeray's grand-daughter" makes of Laura Stephen not a tragically handicapped human being but a kind of cruel joke played by fate on an illustrious writer, and one that another illustrious writer can best appreciate.

Woolf's remark about there being three households at Hyde Park Gate indicates that, by the time she was getting to know her Kensington world, Laura was hidden away. During the holidays in St. Ives, however, in a smaller, more horizontal house with open doors and windows, things were different. Laura was taken along to Cornwall, or sent by train on what was a complicated journey requiring several changes of train and platform. One summer, Laura got off the train at the wrong place but managed to negotiate her way to St. Ives. This incident again suggests that Laura's mental incapacity and inability to communicate were exaggerated.

For years, Laura was certainly there at Talland House, hovering at the edge of the family cricket game, sitting on the family's little private beach, playing in the sand as she had done once long ago with her mother at Freshwater, singing perhaps in a little moment of pleasure, casting a shadow even when people did their best to ignore her. In all the evocations of the summers at St. Ives that Virginia Woolf wrote in her fiction and in her autobiographical essays, she never mentions Laura. Her presence would destroy the remembered magic of Talland House, so it is edited out.

But it is easier to excise a person from a memoir than from memory. Virginia Woolf was an exceptionally observant, sensitive, and articulate child and she certainly saw, heard, and took note of the fate of her half-sister. When Laura disappeared from the family, Virginia was perhaps ten. Who knows exactly what she was told, but as she grew up some news of her sister would surely have come her way after different family members returned from their visits to the mental institution. At fifteen, blindsided by the deaths of her mother and her sister Stella, Virginia had a bout of suicidal madness, and thereafter she lived with the nightmare that she herself might be condemned to live with mad people or die in a madhouse like cousin Jem. The mere sight of "idiots" caused her to feel repugnance and panic. Had she ever gone to the asylum at Edgehill or Southgate with her mother or her father or her sister Stella, Virginia might have looked into Laura's face and seen a likeness — the long, thin figure, the Stephen nose, their father's nose, her nose. She did not go.

ॐ

One of Leslie Stephen's last memories of his first wife, Minny, was of her sitting in a sunny Alpine meadow and playing happily with "Memee." This name touchingly combines "me," "Mummy," and *m'aimer,* and Laura probably coined it for herself.

Love is often not enough in life, and Minny might not have been able to save her daughter from what society termed "insanity," but there can be no doubt that, had Minny lived, Laura would have continued to know love. Minny's father, William Makepeace Thackeray, had been unable to save his wife from her madness, but Isabella Thackeray lived out her long life in her own home with responsible caregivers, and when she was dying, her daughter Anny was by her side, holding her hand. Julia Stephen was there too, united in female love and friendship. Minny Thackeray Stephen, counseled by her sister, would have tried to find a similarly humane solution for her daughter, and we know that Minny was a woman with a strong will, a good mind, and ample means.

When we compare the life of mad Isabella Thackeray to that of her supposedly mad granddaughter, and even to that of Virginia Woolf, it becomes all too apparent that, in the history of mental health, progress does not follow a simple upward curve, and care too often depends on the individual decisions and actions of family members.

PART III

The Angels of Hyde Park Gate

8

Julia Prinsep Jackson Duckworth Stephen

VIRGINIA WOOLF became a novelist in part because, through imaginative projection and writerly craft, fiction enabled her to feel close to her dead mother. Sustained versions of Julia Stephen occur in *The Voyage Out* (1915), *Jacob's Room* (1922), and *To the Lighthouse* (1927). Fragments of her pop up in other novels.

Woolf had a kind of adoration for her mother, but as the sixth of Julia's seven children, in a family where Father came first, Grandma a close second, and sons counted for more than daughters, Woolf did not know her mother in even the quotidian yet intense way that the lucky ones among us know our mothers.

To be close to Mother, to hold her undivided attention, to feel an intimate bond with her, was something that Virginia and Vanessa Stephen did not have as children. It was something they yearned for, especially since they could see that each of their four brothers, in different ways and at different times, had it. The lack of that primal bond punched a hole in the emotional fabric of both sisters, and they suffered from it all their lives.

From toddlerhood, Virginia was an exceptionally quick, articulate, vivid, affectionate child. By roaring and wailing and climbing out onto window

*Julia Stephen with Virginia. Of all the pictures in Leslie Stephen's family
album of Julia with her children as babies, this is by far the most beautiful.
It is attributed to H. H. Cameron, possibly one of Julia Cameron's sons.*

ledges, she did everything she could to attract attention, but in the big household at 22 Hyde Park Gate, she could never hold it for long. "Can I remember
ever being alone with [my mother] for more than a few minutes?" Woolf later
asked herself, and she was almost glad when she fell ill as a child, since then
Julia would come to her bedside and take care of her. At other times there was
always someone barging in to demand Julia's immediate attention, and getting
it — a sibling, a visitor, a supplicant, a servant, a dog, Father! Julia Stephen,
Woolf tells us, "was living on such an extended surface that she had no time
nor strength" for her daughters. The Stephen family snap of Julia and Leslie
sitting side by side on the couch and reading intently, with little Virginia's face

Virginia peeps up from behind the sofa where her parents are reading.

peeping up behind them, is emblematic of the way Virginia interacted with her parents — with easy familiarity but largely unnoticed.

In her memoir essay "22 Hyde Park Gate," Woolf refuses to blame her mother. She had worshiped her as a child, and, as an adult, she still adores her — so quick, so funny, so definite, so active, and so very beautiful. As Virginia remembered it, life with Mother, the first thirteen years of her life, had been happiness for everyone. It was a humdrum happiness, an organized and choreographed succession of events, which could be boring, like the daily winter walks in Kensington Gardens, painful, like the visits to the dentist, or joyful, like the annual transfer of the whole big clan to St. Ives in Cornwall for the summer, but always reliable. "What a jumble of things I can remember [of Mother]," writes Woolf, "but they are all of her in company; of her surrounded; of her generalized; dispersed; omnipresent, of her as the creator of that crowded, merry world which spun so gaily at the center of my childhood."

But then, quite suddenly in 1895, Julia Stephen died at the age of forty-nine, and of that merry world "nothing was left. In its place a dark cloud settled over us; we seemed to sit all together cooped up, solemn, unreal, under a haze of heavy emotion . . . a finger was laid on our lips." For Virginia her mother's death seemed the greatest tragedy imaginable. She was traumatized into silence and amnesia, her precious memories of her mother overlaid by the pious, black-edged version of Julia enshrined in the memorial volume her father put together for the edification of her and her siblings, which they would name the *Mausoleum Book*.

It was not until 1909 that Woolf felt able to make her first attempt to free Julia Stephen from the textual mausoleum Leslie Stephen had constructed, and only with the publication of *To the Lighthouse* could Woolf finally lay her mother's ghost. By this point, a fierce rejection of the Victorian past had swept over England, and in all too many ways Julia Stephen was the personification of Victorian values. By the late 1920s it was all too clear that, for a Virginia Woolf as we know her to come into existence, her mother had had to die young. Could anyone imagine Julia Stephen allowing a fortuneless Jew like Leonard Woolf to come within hailing distance of one of her daughters?

As the mother of a daughter and an admirer of Virginia Woolf, I confess I find it hard to forgive Julia Stephen for failing to see anything special in this daughter. Why could the woman not give up a couple of her paupers and neglect a few of her invalids and offer this marvelous child the attention and focused affection she craved and needed and deserved? But there are two sides to every mother-daughter dyad, and before we choose sides, it behooves us to dive deeper into the short and complicated life of Julia Prinsep Jackson Duckworth Stephen. We owe it to the woman who shaped the young Virginia so powerfully to gather the known facts and piece together a story that is neither the Golden Legend of her biographer husband nor the modernist refractions of her novelist daughter. If we start at the beginning—in Pattledom, where

Woolf's parents played out the first act of the complex drama of their lives — perhaps we can understand if not forgive.

ॐ

For the teenage girl Julia Jackson, Pattledom, the vibrant social group that gathered around her Pattle aunts Sarah Prinsep and Julia Cameron, had been home as long as she could remember. The first glimpses that the thirty-year-old struggling journalist Leslie Stephen had of Julia were around 1864 when he came as an occasional, unimportant visitor to the Prinseps in Kensington and the Camerons on the Isle of Wight.

Among the seven Pattle sisters, Julia's mother, Maria, was considered by many to be second in beauty only to her younger sister Virginia, Countess Somers, but Maria did not soar into the peerage. Instead she married John Jackson, a doctor in the medical branch of the East India Company in Bengal. According to Lady Strachey, Lytton's mother, who had known all the Pattles back in their India days, John Jackson was a handsome and engaging man, so perhaps Maria married for love. But this was a period when doctors were more like barbers than lawyers in status; they entered private homes by the trades-man's entrance, and Jackson was poorly remunerated. In their early years of marriage the Jacksons lived in Calcutta (Kolkata), where Maria had been born and where her sisters were already queens of society. It was there that she and John Jackson had three daughters, Adeline, Mary, and Julia.

When the two older Jackson girls were old enough, they went to England to live with their Pattle aunts. Sending small children back "home" from India for their safety was not uncommon at that time, but when, claiming ill health, Mrs. Jackson left India with her toddler daughter Julia, never to return, she was doing something a little bold and unusual. She was striking out on her own to a new continent and a new culture, as her grandmother Thérèse de l'Etang and her mother, Adeline Pattle, had done before her, and thereby making the key decision that her three daughters should all be English, not Anglo-Indian. Her inherited share of the Pattle estate made Maria financially independent of her husband, and with the help of her more affluent older sisters, she was able to set up her own household in the south of England.

Life on two continents may have flouted the conventions a little, but it seems to have suited the Jacksons. According to the sparse information we have on him, Dr. Jackson found his medical practice and research in infectious disease absorbing, and he proved remarkably resistant to the infections that killed off so many Europeans every year in India. When Jackson was offered the paid leave due him, he declined to leave Bengal and rejoin his wife and daughters in England for even a few months. Virginia Woolf and Quentin Bell would have liked their ancestor much more if he had had a local concubine or some servant boys to fill in for an absent wife, but Jackson was reportedly a very religious man, and family documents give no hint of scandal. Certainly, when at last Dr. Jackson retired from the Indian army medical corps and returned to England, he lived in amity with his wife in rented homes, most latterly in salubrious Brighton. Maria, though ailing and immobile, was a charming hostess and managed to compete a little with her sisters Sarah and Julia by welcoming guests like Anne Thackeray and attracting her own small circle of devotees. As we shall see, the rising poet Coventry Patmore was foremost among the young men who gathered around Maria Jackson.

By the time of Dr. Jackson's return to family life, his older daughters were on the edge of matrimony, and the youngest Jackson girl, Julia, had no memory at all of her father. Julia had come to regard her uncle Henry Thoby Prinsep as father in all but name and would remain deeply attached to him all her life. When she and Leslie Stephen had their first son, he was named Julian Thoby Stephen, and always known as Thoby. After Julia's death, her uncle Thoby Prinsep's cane was found in its usual place, next to her bedside.

Leslie Stephen stood on the edge of the illustrious crowd of people gathered at Dimbola Lodge and at Little Holland House, and he was intimidated by the beauty of the Pattle women and the high social and intellectual caliber of the men they and their husbands attracted to their homes. When he first set eyes on Maria Pattle Jackson's youngest daughter, Julia, Leslie Stephen thought she was the most beautiful girl he had ever seen, and he watched Julia from a cautious distance, observing the relationships she had with her parents and sisters. Some thirty years later, Leslie Stephen's reactions to the Jackson family were still fresh in his mind, and he recorded them in the *Mausoleum*

Book; his observations shed important light on the balance of parental power during the childhood of Virginia Woolf.

Stephen observed that it pleased the titular and revered overlords of Pattledom, Henry Thoby Prinsep in Kensington and Charles Hay Cameron in Freshwater, to give their wives free rein. Prinsep was reserved and often ill. Cameron, a tall, strange old man, wrapped in shawls against the sea winds, hid as much as possible from his wife's friends and her camera, and observed her wild extravagance and restless energy with wry amusement. Adoring their husbands, happy to pay obeisance to patriarchal power, and reveling in the affluence that India had afforded their families, Sarah Prinsep and Julia Cameron were free to do much as they liked, to entertain and be extremely decorative, to "drape and arrange, pull down and build up, and carry on life in a high-handed and adventurous way," as Virginia Woolf would later put it. But what most struck contemporaries about the Pattle women was the intensity of their attachment to one another. The sisters indulged in a regular round of visits to one another's homes, and when apart they were in daily communication by letter, or later, telegram. Even in an age when large Victorian families like those of Queen Victoria and Florence Nightingale hung together like small clans, the Pattles took sister-sister, mother-daughter, aunt-niece relationships to a new level.

Looking back on Pattledom in 1895, Leslie Stephen remembered that one family member stood outside this charmed circle of husband worship and sisterly affection — Dr. John Jackson. The man was perfectly respectable, even jolly, and yet he sat in the wings, leaving the stage to his beautiful wife and daughters and largely ignored by his wife's relatives and their friends. Leslie Stephen noticed this because he stood outside as well. In Leslie Stephen's words, written thirty years on, "Somehow Jackson did not seem to count — as fathers generally count in their families. Mrs Jackson was passionately devoted to her children and was, beyond all doubt, a thoroughly good wife. But I could not perceive that she was romantic as a wife. The old doctor was respected or esteemed rather than ardently loved — or so I fancied. And this was the more obvious because of the strength of the other family affections."

Stephen himself came from a family structured on almost biblical patriarchal lines, and he lived at a time when a man like his older brother, Sir

Fitzjames Stephen, could create a panic over the boiled beef and carrots at lunchtime by simply raising an eyebrow. It is thus unsurprising that it struck Leslie Stephen as anomalous, even heretical, how little John Jackson "counted" with his wife and daughters, how little affection he inspired in the breasts of his extravagantly affectionate womenfolk. And it is not happenstance that this old memory came back strongly to Leslie in the agonizing months following Julia's death.

While explicitly eulogizing his dead wife's manifold perfections for the benefit of her children, Leslie Stephen was implicitly probing the truth of their marriage. While asserting his scholarly expertise by collecting documents, putting dates and facts together, and refraining from conclusions, Leslie yet shows a dim and painful awareness that in fact he was to his own family what Jackson had been to his — indulged yet peripheral, almost superfluous. Julia had allowed Leslie the familial primacy he needed and demanded, but had it perhaps been merely an appearance of primacy? Was it possible that Julia's "ardent love" had not been for him but for the women in her family and her woman friends? Was it even possible that his first wife, dear little Minny, who kept her sister by her side for seven years of their eight-year marriage and had a large circle of female friends, had done the same? Was there a pattern of female love and friendship here that a different biographer, a different memoirist, might uncover?

Cast suddenly into emotional disarray by Julia's death, Leslie Stephen was abruptly questioning his patriarchal assumptions. He was seeing that exercising the power vested in men by matrimony could come at a terrible cost, not only to wives like Julia, who wore out young and welcomed death, but also to husbands like himself, who were left to mourn in solitude. Such thoughts were too terrifying to contemplate for long, so deaf old Leslie Stephen returned to the comfort of his library and his book of household accounts and took out his conflict and his doubt on his daughters.

As we shall see in Chapter 10, Virginia as a young woman observed her father, loved her father, pitied her father. The two of them shared a passion for literature and literary history. For long silent hours they would sit side by side, reading. Virginia knew her father as she had not known her mother. He remained an ineradicable presence in her mind, heart, and memory, but for that very reason she refused to forgive him. Just before her suicide, in the midst of a war to the death against fascism, Woolf returned to her father and questioned if the Hitlers and Stalins of the world might be the terrible product of the male human being's insatiable need for women to love him.

୭৶

In the year 1866, when Leslie Stephen turned away from Pattledom to pursue Minny Thackeray — though, as we have seen, not too fast! — Julia Jackson was in her late teens and at the height of her beauty. She was an intelligent girl, thoughtful, articulate, even a trifle acerbic, but there was nothing of the bluestocking in her. Unlike her contemporaries Florence Nightingale or Elizabeth Barrett, Julia Jackson never set her mother all atwitter by demanding lessons in ancient Greek or statistics. All the same, it was Julia's personality as much as her beauty that made an impression, especially on men. Her youngest daughter, Virginia, remembered her mother as mesmerizing, and to judge from memoirs of the period, Woolf had it right. Maria Jackson once boasted that any man who happened to encounter her daughter Julia in a railway carriage wanted to marry her.

Even as a little girl Julia was so lovely that artists like Dante Gabriel Rossetti and William Holman Hunt begged to paint her portrait, and after some years Mrs. Jackson relented and allowed her daughter to pose — suitably chaperoned, of course. Following the George Watts–Ellen Terry debacle we saw in Chapter 2, even an English artist could not wholly be trusted. Aunt Julia Cameron was also on hand with her camera to take the haunting photographs of her Jackson niece that would be handed down in the Stephen family. Yet even as admiration was part of the air Julia Jackson breathed, she gave the impression of being unaware of the effect she had on people. She did not need to flirt — just pose — and her apparent lack of coquetry made Julia all the more attractive in a high Victorian culture obsessed with the purity of its "young persons."

Julia Jackson was eyed longingly by poor young men like Leslie Stephen and received marriage proposals from at least two successful older ones, but until she turned twenty she remained serenely single and devoted to the care of her gracefully ailing mama. Then, on a holiday in Venice with members of her family in the summer of 1866, passion entered her life in the shape of the handsome, blond, old-Etonian barrister Herbert Duckworth. The two fell quickly, deeply, madly in love, became engaged to be married within a couple of months, and, to the beaming approval of both families, were wed in the spring of 1867.

The announcement that Julia Jackson was to marry Herbert Duckworth caused no little consternation in her circle of acquaintance. Valentine Cameron Prinsep, Julia's artist cousin, arrived with the news of the engagement at a dinner party given for Leslie Stephen and a few of his friends by the Thackeray sisters. As Henrietta Garnett elegantly puts it in her biography of Anne Thackeray Ritchie, the news "dropped like a stone into their soup plates. Julia had appeared as a vision, beyond the reach of ordinary mortals . . . Collectively they had placed her on a pedestal and now Herbert Duckworth had plucked her down."

Who was this man whom young Julia Cameron seized upon as perfection in spats? This turns out to be a tricky biographical question because Leslie Stephen, Julia's second husband, is the source of almost everything we know about her first. Stephen prided himself on his rationality, his mastery of the facts, and his meticulous research. However, if there was one man in the world who could not write a fair and objective portrait of Herbert Duckworth, it was Leslie Stephen.

Leslie had inherited Julia's private papers, and there he found a trove of Jackson-Prinsep-Cameron letters, which allowed him to recapture the period in Julia's shining youth when he had first met her. There was also a small number of letters exchanged by her and Herbert Duckworth during their courtship and marriage. Reading those carefully preserved letters put Leslie on the rack, but he persisted. They confirmed what Leslie had known ever since he had been drawn back into Julia's orbit after his first wife's death. Julia had fallen in love with Herbert Duckworth almost at first sight and adored him after he made her his wife. She remembered their few years together as the happiest period in her life, the culmination of a cloudless youth. Though she was far too high-minded to rhapsodize about her first marriage in the presence of her second husband and her Stephen children, and never talked about Herbert even to her closest friends, Julia had never forgotten him. In her heart, she always mourned and missed him.

His dead wife's first marriage was an open wound in Leslie Stephen's psyche because for him Herbert Duckworth did not exist merely in a few letters. The two men had known each other. They had both been at Eton, though Stephen was one year older and a day boy, and both, like their fathers, had gone on to Trinity College, Cambridge. Leslie recounts in the *Mausoleum Book* how, as a second-year student he had arranged to meet his cousin, G. B. Atkinson, in Trinity Street. Atkinson failed to appear and, when questioned later, cheerfully admitted that he had stood up his cousin Leslie in favor of paying a call on Herbert Duckworth, who had, in Cambridge parlance, just "come up." Duckworth, Atkinson raved, was "the perfect type of the public school man."

Leslie Stephen professes to be joking when he tells this story, but many a truth is spoken in jest, and on such youthful slights a lifetime of resentment can be built. Atkinson was probably not the only Cambridge man ready to pass over a shabby, unkempt intellectual like Stephen Minor (Stephen Major, that is, Leslie's brisk, assertive older brother, Fitzjames, being quite another affair) in favor of debonair Duckworth Minor.

With the unconscious condescension and self-revelation that today makes reading the *Mausoleum Book* so fascinating, Stephen concedes that Julia's first husband had some good points. Let me annotate in italics the way he continues after his "joke" about the Atkinson incident. Herbert Duckworth was

in all seriousness [*really?*], not only a thorough gentleman in the best sense of the word, but had the outward indications of the character which may be valued a little too warmly by men like Atkinson [*!*] . . . He was good at fives . . . and at other games, without being excessively devoted to athletic pursuits [*such as climbing in the Alps and writing groundbreaking books about alpinism, like Leslie Stephen*]: he was capable of passing examinations creditably, though he did not aim for distinction at the Senate House [*unlike Stephen, the Wrangler and former Cambridge mathematics don*], and altogether was the kind of man who might be expected to settle down as a thorough country gentleman with all the very real merits that belong to that character. A man of honour, of fair accomplishments and interest in books, he was fitted to take his place in any society, without being the least of a dandy or a fop.

Ah, yes, damning with faint praise, and then the killer double negative — "without being the least of a dandy or a fop." Translation: *Herbert Duckworth was a perfect representative of that subset of English upper-middle-class males that morons like Atkinson aped but that real men of real brain and sinew like Leslie Stephen despised.*

However hard he tries to be fair and to paint the Duckworth marriage in Julia's bright colors, Leslie Stephen could not, in his heart of hearts, forgive his wife for having once upon a time fallen for a man with a handsome face and a superb tailor. Only another man, Leslie Stephen might have said, can really know a man, can get below the surface and judge the substance. Duckworth had been the kind of boy who had made his life torture at Eton.

Stephen also knew that the Duckworth family fortune was made in cotton, and this, I think, is a crucial point in the Leslie-Herbert rivalry. Cotton, in early-to-mid-nineteenth-century England, meant trade with the slave-owning American South. It was the cotton magnates, fearful for their industry, who almost managed to drag England into the American Civil War on the side of the South. The Stephen-Venn family, on the other hand, were founding members of the abolitionist group known as the Clapham Saints, in the van of the campaign to abolish the slave trade and make slavery illegal throughout the British Empire. Leslie's father, James Stephen, spent his life as an official at the Colonial Office trying to enforce the law and stamp out slavery in all British colonies. In the big fives match of life, the Duckworths and the Stephens had been playing on opposite sides.

But marvelous, saintly Julia had adored Herbert Duckworth. The letters proved it.

ॐ

Unlike Minny Thackeray Stephen, the newlywed Julia Jackson Duckworth had no trouble getting pregnant and bringing a child to term.

Julia Duckworth circa 1867, pregnant with her first child, George

Barely a year after her wedding, she gave birth to her first child, George Herbert Duckworth, a big healthy baby and the image of his handsome blond papa. In 1869 Julia neatly balanced the family with a baby girl, Stella, in her own beautiful likeness, and within a couple of months of Stella's birth Julia had to give up breastfeeding her daughter as she was pregnant again. It was looking as if the Herbert Duckworths might have one of the enormous families — eight children, ten, eleven, who knew? — in which the well-fed Victorian bourgeoisie specialized.

But if large families were common at this time, so were women's deaths in childbirth among the rich as well as the poor. Middle-class parturients in England were now advised by their doctors to entrust themselves to male obstetricians instead of midwives, even as most members of the medical profession refused to see any connection between childbirth mortality and a doctor's un-washed hands. Florence Nightingale was forced to close her new obstetrics unit at St. Thomas's Hospital because of an iatrogenic epidemic of puerperal fever. Women approaching their third or fourth delivery date were encouraged to write letters of farewell to be read, in the event of their death in childbirth, by their surviving children.

It is possible that when Julia Jackson became pregnant for the third time in three years, some alarm bells went off in Pattledom, but if her mother mewed and her aunties clucked, Julia Duckworth remained serene. She was seen, and remembered herself, as rapturously happy during the three or so years between twenty-one and twenty-four. She spent those years pregnant or lactating, but clearly she welcomed Herbert back into her big bed as soon as she could. To Julia Duckworth — as the story goes — the discomforts of pregnancy, the te-dious reclusion that Victorian middle-class society imposed upon women in their final months, and the pains of delivery without anesthesia were to be taken in stride. She was beautiful, she was married to a man she adored, she was effortlessly fertile, she bore healthy children, and all was right in her world. Just as she had once been the picture-perfect Victorian virgin, Julia was now the pattern Victorian wife.

Herbert Duckworth was not quite the handsome drone in the Bertie Wooster mold that Leslie Stephen deemed him. Instead of living as a coun-try gentleman on his allowance from the pater, Herbert went in for the law. He became a barrister, a profession for which he had excellent qualifications — a solid intelligence, the Eton-and-Cambridge old boy network, good looks, the manners of a gentleman, and an interest in money. He may not have worked long hours, but to judge by the important inheritances he left to his children, Duckworth did well in the law, a lot better than Leslie Ste-phen did in writing and editing, even with the support of the Thackeray network. By 1870, however, Herbert, thirty-seven, was finding his legal prac-tice a strain. To satisfy his doctors and please his wife, who, trained by her mother, fretted over his health, he decided to stop riding the legal circuit for a while and devote himself to his family. Julia was delighted. The only blot upon her married life arose when Herbert went away on business or failed to meet her at the time stipulated in his latest telegram. Now Julia had Herbert by her side and under her eye and could count on his being nearby when the new baby came.

And so it came about that, as Julia was approaching the time of her confinement, the Duckworths were visiting the family of Julia's sister Adeline Jackson Vaughan at Upton Castle, the Vaughans' romantic but comfortless ruin in Pembrokeshire, West Wales. On a beautiful September day, Julia and Herbert went walking in an orchard. That day was etched into Julia's memory, but since she seems never to have described it to her daughter Virginia, we are free to set the scene.

We see the handsome, elegant young husband and the radiant, heavily pregnant wife on his arm, the chubby little blond two-year-old waddling along with his nurse, the sweet baby girl asleep under a tree in her perambulator. The husband reaches up to pick a fig from the tree above him, doubles over in agony, and goes quickly back to the house. In a few hours, a doctor is hastily called, but nothing can be done. An abscess has burst, and within a few hours Herbert Duckworth is dead. Six weeks later, Julia Duckworth gave birth to a second son, a delicate baby she named Gerald de l'Etang Duckworth, after Antoine de l'Etang, her distant aristocratic ancestor.

"Devastated" is a cliché word for young grieving widows, but it graphically describes Julia Duckworth in the first months after her husband's death. It was as if the country about her had been laid waste. Perhaps the most poignant pictures Julia Cameron ever took were of the sorrowing Mrs. Herbert Duckworth, thin yet classically beautiful in her high-necked black dress, fair hair pulled back in the severe knot she would wear for the rest of her life.

At first, Julia Duckworth's grieving for Herbert was in the high histrionic mode patented by Queen Victoria after the death of Prince Albert in 1861. Stella Duckworth remembered her mother recumbent upon Herbert's tomb, begging audibly for death. Even eight years after Herbert's death and only months before her own remarriage, Julia Duckworth caused a small sensation at the sweaty August wedding of Anne Thackeray and Richmond Ritchie, by appearing among the other brightly clad guests in black velvet, heavily veiled in black, and flanked by her small daughter, whose somber mask mirrored her own. There is a self-dramatization here that was part of Julia Duckworth's complex personality, but her grief was nonetheless sincere, and like Victoria, she laid the burden of her loss upon her daughter, Stella, not her sons.

Julia explained her state of mind during the time after Gerald's birth in an astonishingly acute and self-aware letter she wrote to Leslie Stephen in the year before they were married. Here we can see that, if Virginia Woolf as a literary critic was indebted to her father, as a psychological novelist she owed much to her mother. Julia wrote to Leslie:

> I was only 24 when it all seemed a shipwreck, and I knew that I had to live on and on, and the only thing to be done was to be as cheerful as I could and do as much as I could and think as little. And so I got deadened. I had all along felt that if it had been possible for me to be myself, it would have been better individually, and that I could have got more real life out of the wreck if I had broken down more. But there was Baby [Gerald] to be thought of and everyone around me urging me to keep up, and I could never be alone which sometimes was such torture. So that by degrees I felt that though I was more cheerful and content than most people, I was more changed.

Perhaps one of the reasons Julia Duckworth found comfort with Leslie Stephen was that he too came to weddings dressed in black and never urged her to "keep up."

Money is often a problem for widows, but it was one problem Julia Duckworth did not face. Herbert Duckworth had been a man of means, he left his family well off, and his father was good to his widow, taking her and the children into his home. Learning a lesson, perhaps, from the wild extravagances that had sent her aunt Julia Cameron into exile in Ceylon, the widowed Mrs. Duckworth led a life that was affluent but not extravagant, sociable but not social. She was a devoted and idolized mother, a loving and attentive daughter and sister, and, while careful to be a good steward to the patrimony of her three young children, she was generous with money as well as time in her support of local charities.

After the death of her father-in-law, she moved away from the Duckworth house in central London and bought a house for herself and her children in a newly developed and, at the time, fairly inexpensive street in Kensington called Hyde Park Gate. It was probably no accident that Hyde Park Gate was only a short walk from the site of Little Holland House, where Julia Duckworth had once been so happy; its owners tore down the house and redeveloped the property after the Prinsep lease ran out. Thoby Prinsep's house had been low and rambling, surrounded by meadows and full of light; by contrast, Julia's chosen home for the rest of her life was a tall, dark row house, with only a tiny dank garden at the back. The woman liked to torture herself.

And while she seemed all serenity and reason, admirably managing her household, her children, her family, and her philanthropy, and impressing her friends, the mind of Julia Duckworth was in turmoil. It was as if hitherto her life had been a sunlit garden and suddenly, without warning, without reason, the sun went out, and she was left alone in darkness. No one had thought Julia Jackson needed any formal education as a girl. Education was for Unitarians like Elizabeth Gaskell or the daughters of poor clergymen like the Brontë sisters. No one, certainly, had thought Julia Jackson had it in her to be the next George Eliot or even the next Anne Thackeray. But after Herbert Duckworth died, Julia dove deep into her mind and began to read and think seriously. One of the people whose work she read, and found convincing, was her atheist philosopher friend and neighbor Leslie Stephen.

Her husband's death had destroyed a happiness that Julia Duckworth had assumed to be her inheritance. It changed her understanding of life and her place in the world, and in this change, a perverse, masochistic form of egotism played its part along with grief and loss. This egotism would have a profound effect upon her daughters, on Stella in particular. God had played a cruel trick upon Julia, and she was sure that she had not deserved it. Ergo, as she firmly and irrevocably decided, there was no God, there was no heaven, there was no salvation, there was no joy. There was only affection, only duty, only self-sacrifice, only pain. Julia Duckworth told her suitor Leslie that for her the world after Herbert's death was forever "clothed in drab . . . shrouded in a crape veil." She lived her words.

Proximity, as we have seen, was perhaps the first thing that permitted the relationship between Leslie and Julia to grow into friendship, then marriage. Anne and Minny Thackeray had known Julia Jackson as a teenage girl. When Herbert died, Anny came to Julia with sympathy and support. After Minny died, Julia reached out to Anny in turn and supported her in her grief. The Thackeray sisters, who had been so happy with their father in Kensington, had inherited from their grandmother an income property in the new development at Hyde Park Gate. Thus it seemed only natural for Anne, her brother-in-law, Leslie, and little Laura to move to Hyde Park Gate and be close to Julia.

The development of the relationship between Leslie and Julia hinged on the assumption that they were both grieving inconsolably for a spouse who had been suddenly and unmercifully taken from them at a moment of supreme happiness. For Leslie, this was a half-truth. Julia had always been his ideal woman. Minny Thackeray — as her husband saw her — was a dear little thing in her way, but a mere child and certainly not a great beauty. Minny had in a sense been a stopgap until Leslie could explore real, passionate conjugal love with Julia Jackson. And though he certainly did not say this to Julia, Leslie Stephen, as we have seen, had never had much use for Herbert Duckworth and was eager to show her what marriage to a real man could bring.

When Julia finally agreed to marry him, Leslie knew that he was not Julia's ideal man. He knew it was pity rather than love that conquered her resistance to his repeated proposals. He also knew that Julia was making, in the eyes of her family and friends and no doubt in her own, a big sacrifice in marrying him. Julia Cameron wrote to her "cherished" niece Julia: "I have so long felt that Leslie was your fate . . . I felt of him 'the shadow sits and waits for her' . . . I felt that sitting ever close to you — tall, wrapt in gloom, companionless and silent, he would make an appeal to you which would be powerful because of the vastness of his intellect." Anne Thackeray Ritchie also saw the marriage as a sacrifice on Julia's part. "My hope is for Leslie and Julia's happiness and sweet Memekins' [that is, Laura's]. I think it is very noble and generous of Julia to give up her liberty and her *prestige* [Thackeray Ritchie's emphasis] and her money and everything to comfort and cheer up Leslie."

෨෯

To say that the family Virginia Woolf was born into was complicated is an understatement. If we strip away the Victoriana — the black-and-gold wood paneling, the crimson velvet curtains blocking the light, the servants bustling up out of the gas-lit sub-basement with silver tea sets and down again with full chamber pots — we find a very twenty-first-century family.

First, we have Leslie and Julia, two busy, well-to-do people who own a house in town and rent a holiday home by the sea and can afford seven live-in servants, plus additional help with the laundry and the garden, but still feel poor in comparison to relatives and friends. Each partner has been married before, and they carry heavy emotional baggage as well as four children, George, Stella, and Gerald Duckworth and Laura Stephen, into the marriage. When four more children arrive in rapid succession, things get really stressful. The Stephen and Duckworth children have little in common, but they all live in the same house, and the nuclear family of ten is framed in a huge extended family of bosomy aunties, booming uncles, and creepy cousins, to say nothing of a mother-in-law who is always demanding attention, whether in person or via the mail, which is delivered several times a day.

To say that Julia Stephen had her hands full is an understatement. No sooner has she married Leslie Stephen than she is pregnant, and when Vanessa, her fourth child, is born, she is past denying how painful and debilitating childbearing is. Over the next four years, three more children arrive, each, as everyone could see, a drain on Julia's physical reserves. All the same, Julia's biggest worry is not her seven children, plus Laura, but her husband, the big baby who will never grow up and go away.

The saintliness of Julia was in ratio to Leslie's orneriness, for even in an era when wives were expected to sacrifice themselves to the comfort of their husbands, Julia Stephen's friends and relatives considered her husband to be exceptionally difficult. In *The Voyage Out,* with her characters Ridley and Helen Ambrose, Virginia Woolf makes the first of her fictional attempts to evoke what her parents' marriage was like. Helen starts the novel in grief. For a period of months if not years, she is leaving behind her two small children, whom she adores — especially the little boy — and giving them into the care of an evangelical nanny she does not trust. Given her domestic cares and responsibilities, why, we might ask, is Helen Ambrose setting out for South America?

Well, we gather as the novel progresses, Helen's scholar husband, Ridley, is overworked, needs a holiday, fancies a season in a relative's hacienda in South America, and could not possibly survive such a trip without his wife.

In the early pages of the book, we find Ridley, on the first day away at sea, entering the cabin study dedicated to his personal use and suddenly reduced to a trembling heap of anxiety and resentment. The table is wobbly, the chair the wrong height, and the door leaky. Helen shoos Ridley out, organizes a new chair and table from the crew, and gets down on her hands and knees with a hammer and a piece of thick cloth to make a doorstopper, so her husband's feet don't feel the cold sea air. Smiling, all right in his world, Ridley Ambrose once again becomes absorbed in the preparation of a new edition of the Greek poet Pindar, which, the reader cannot help feeling, the world could probably manage without. At the end of the novel, when his niece Rachel is dying upstairs, all Ridley can do for his frantic and exhausted wife is to drive her and everyone else in the house mad by muttering poetry and singing ballads. Leslie Stephen memorized yards of poetry as a boy and was famous among family and friends, especially as he aged and grew deaf, for reciting aloud and humming old tunes under his breath.

In *The Voyage Out,* the exertions of Helen Ambrose to serve her husband when on vacation give us an inkling of the complex household machinery Julia Stephen set up at 22 Hyde Park Gate. Each morning, water must be carried upstairs to fill the hip bath in the master's dressing room, as he cannot be expected to compete with other members of the family for the single bathroom. (The Stephens were not, I suspect, a particularly fragrant bunch, Leslie apart.) After breakfast, Leslie Stephen retired to his fifth-floor aerie to labor on his dictionary and scholarly books. Heavy volumes crashing to the floor are a sign the master is at work, so quiet must reign throughout the rest of the busy household. One of the maids must go up regularly and, without making a sound, empty his study chamber pot, since descending to one of the three lavatories on the lower floors would break his chain of thought. Meals carefully planned by the mistress to please the master's palate and promote his digestion must be served precisely on time.

Such material demands were taxing, but Julia was a highly efficient household manager, so she coped. Far more wearing to Mrs. Stephen, if not to the second parlor maid (remember that gas-lit sub-basement where the staff of seven live-in servants moldered?), was Mr. Stephen's incurable angst. Was he not just a third-class mind? Did any of the coming young men like Maitland really admire him? Would all of his work be forgotten within a year of his death? Only Julia could combat these night terrors, but when at last Leslie fell asleep, she often lay awake, racked with fatigue and anxiety.

And then there was sex, a word not uttered, a subject not raised in the Stephen home or addressed at all in the *Dictionary of National Biography*. Sex is also an issue that Virginia Woolf — so quick with off-color gossip in her letters and so slow to feel desire in her life — skates circles around in her many accounts of her parents' marriage. Trampling down shopworn Victorian shibboleths was one thing. Imagining her father and mother in bed, copulating, quite another.

Yet, for Julia Stephen, a woman who managed to produce seven children by two husbands in less than ten years, and died worn out at forty-nine, sex was like the elephant in the room, heard, felt, smelled, but never alluded to. Leslie Stephen was a tall, strong, healthy man who came from a lineage of passionate males, a man who blossomed in the company of young, beautiful women and could be outrageously rude to old, ugly ones, a man who ventured for the first and only time into a theater to ogle Lillie Langtry. Leslie had desired Julia ever since she was a teenager, and finding her at last in his bed must have been an immense pleasure. Julia, for her part, no doubt found that sexual intercourse was a sure way to calm her husband and get him off to sleep. And then, what better way can a woman find to bolster a man's self-esteem and allay his morbid anxieties about status and legacy than to present him with four healthy, beautiful, bright children (so different from poor Laura!), two strapping boys and two beautiful girls?

Julia was thirty-two when she married Leslie Stephen. Many women in their thirties and forties are at the height of their sexual responsiveness, and Julia had lived without sexual intimacy for nine years. Perhaps she was just as eager as her husband for the pleasure and release of tension that sex can afford. Woolf's portrait of her parents as the Ambroses in *The Voyage Out* and the Ramsays in *To the Lighthouse* hint at a happy sexual relationship as well as an intellectual companionship between Leslie and Julia. Maybe they had a lovely time in bed. We shall never know. What we do know, in the absence of Bloomsbury-style conjugal confessions, is that Julia's pattern of behavior in her second marriage was very different from that of her first.

According to the letters she kept and that Leslie Stephen found after her death, Julia's three-year marriage to Herbert Duckworth was one long honeymoon. Friends and family remarked that, even when pregnant or nursing, Julia Duckworth clung tight to her barrister husband, going on the legal circuit with him when she could, pining for him when he was away. Her mother and sisters, who had been hitherto the focus of her love and attention, had to defer to a husband's superior claims. In her second marriage, however, especially during the first ten or so years, Julia ran her life in a very different way. It was now Julia who was often away from home on extended visits, and her husband's wants and needs, along with those of her children, were not infrequently subordinated to those of her extended family or even her friends.

Now, let it be noted up front that Julia Stephen was not leaving her family for pleasure — not, for example, to go to a spa for health reasons in what amounted to a vacation, as her mother had often done without raising any eyebrows. No, Julia Stephen left home on errands of mercy to attend people she loved who were in pain and threatened with death, and in a period when hospitals were for the indigent and private institutions were for the mad, no one questioned her doing so. Sick people with means in the last decades of the nineteenth century remained in their homes, received house calls from their physicians, and were nursed by their female relatives, with the variously useful help of paid attendants. (Remember Sarah Gamp, the drunken, thieving bed nurse in Dickens's *Martin Chuzzlewit*?)

In a household afflicted with sickness, no one could turn chaos into order quicker than Julia Stephen. If needed, she was ready to do the ugly, disgusting jobs — holding the chamber pot, mopping up the vomit, stripping the soiled sheets, changing the dressing — that today, if we are lucky and affluent, we mostly delegate to professionals. And when practical help was of no avail, Julia Stephen would sit next to a dying man, hold his hand, and keep back her tears until the body was washed and decent enough for inspection and the time for lamentation had come. She did this many times, and in my book that makes her a heroine. Perhaps it makes her a saint in yours, though "saint" was a word rarely uttered without irony in the Stephen house.

In 1883, Julia Stephen's friends and relatives persuaded her to publish a little pamphlet called *Notes from Sickrooms,* in which she advised other women on how to properly care for their ailing loved ones. Julia's advice is practical and uncomplicated, yet following it was labor-intensive. Sick people require perfect quiet and neatness, she wrote, an unlimited supply of clean laundry, tempting and nutritious food, and a perfectly smooth bottom sheet. Crumbs are always finding their way into the bed, observes Mrs. Leslie Stephen, and even the tiniest crumb will cause discomfort and distress. Above all, the nurse must carefully observe her patient to ensure that his needs are met, with consideration for his particular wishes, tastes, and habits.

From what Julia Stephen does not say in her *Notes from Sickrooms,* she neither believed in miracles nor placed much faith in doctors and medical science. Doctors, after all, had been powerless to help Herbert Duckworth and Minny Thackeray Stephen. Like Florence Nightingale, whose best-selling *Notes on Nursing* she had read, Julia knew that even the most devoted and attentive care was not always enough and that a home nurse must be prepared for the job of providing strong and loving support to her patient in the last days and hours of life.

Since Julia Stephen did not believe that when you died, you went on to a new and better world, unlike Nightingale in the nineteenth century or Mother Theresa in the twentieth, she was unwilling to offer the dying the consoling prospect of heaven and a reunion with the beloved dead. But to those who said that only the religious woman can be entrusted with the care of the dying, Julia Stephen's response was that, on the contrary, since this is the only life we have, helping to ease pain and make life's end as smooth as possible was a woman's supreme duty. This was Julia's credo and she lived by it.

The list of the many people she nursed and who, quite literally in some cases, died in her arms, is long. There was her father-in-law, Mr. Duckworth, and her beloved uncle Thoby Prinsep. He had been almost blind and an invalid for many years when he entered his final illness, and he died soon after the Stephens were married. Julia looked after him on his deathbed, keeping his cane as a memento. Soon after, pregnant with Vanessa, she was back on the Isle of Wight, taking care of her aunt Sarah Pattle Prinsep, who did not survive Uncle Thoby very long.

Next on Julia's list was her sister Adeline, who suffered not only from an incurable disease but from the indifference of her self-involved phony of a husband, Henry Halford Vaughan. In 1881, Adeline died in hideous pain, and it was Julia, not her husband, who was by her side at the end. Julia reported the death in an agonized letter to Leslie. Julia and Adeline had been deeply attached, and Adeline, as she saw death coming, must have begged Julia to do what she could for her children, living in an isolated spot under the care of the oldest girl. Certainly, over the next years Julia found it necessary to return to Pembrokeshire in West Wales (not an easy journey from Kensington) to the house of a man who had treated her sister abominably so as to do what she could for Adeline's children.

Then in 1883 Julia left four-year-old Vanessa, three-year-old Thoby, two-year-old Virginia, and baby Adrian, only three months old and hitherto breastfed, at home so that she could be at the deathbed of her friend Susan Lushington. When Anny Thackeray Ritchie sat beside the bed of her dying mother in 1894, Julia Stephen managed to arrive in time to give help and observe the death, sitting in the background, silent, calm, observant, ready.

But the person to whom Julia gave the most care and attention and time by far was her mother. Like not a few women of means in her day, Maria Jackson enjoyed ill health for much of her life. Her pain was real, and increasingly so, but it also allowed her to be where she liked, avoid many things she found disagreeable, and continue to be the most elegant and well-rested of the famous Pattle sisters. Care for their ailing mother first devolved upon the two oldest Jackson daughters, for whom Maria showed a marked preference, and after Adeline married at eighteen and Mary wed soon after, the health of Mrs. Jackson took a turn for the worse. She suffered from "rheumatism," was in constant pain, found movement difficult, and traveled about to spas in England and on the Continent in search of health. With Adeline and Mary fully occupied with demanding husbands and a growing pack of small children, Maria now relied on her remaining daughter, and Julia, then in her late teens, rose to the challenge, becoming the favorite daughter in return. One of the miracles that Herbert Duckworth managed to perform was to replace his mother-in-law as the chief focus of Julia's affection and keep Maria at arm's length. But after Herbert's death, Maria Jackson and Julia Duckworth returned to what we might now diagnose as their old codependency.

At some point in her forties or early fifties, Maria Jackson had a bad bout of rheumatic fever, and from that point became a complete invalid, unable to get out of bed without support or do anything for herself. She and her husband took a house in Brighton, but they spent a good deal of time with their daughters, especially Julia. In 1887, John Jackson finally met an illness he could not lick, and despite the best nursing care his daughter Julia could give, he died, at age eighty-three. This was when Maria Jackson took up permanent residence with the Stephen family at 22 Hyde Park Gate. There she lived for four or five years, immaculately groomed, an immobile scented idol regarded with wonder but little affection by her four youngest grandchildren, who resented almost as much as their father the love and attention their mother showered upon this tedious old woman.

In the *Mausoleum Book,* Leslie Stephen claims he was happy that his mother-in-law spent more and more time in his house as she grew older and more infirm, and that he loved and esteemed her. That he was happier with Maria in the house may be believed. With her mother just upstairs, Julia now had almost no reason to go away, so Leslie saw more of his wife. That he appreciated Maria Jackson I doubt. Leslie Stephen had little use for women in general, often upsetting his wife and daughters by his rude remarks about female visitors, and Maria Jackson was the kind of idle, decorative woman he despised. When once for Christmas Maria gave him a volume of poems by Coventry Patmore, her dear friend and favorite poet, Leslie sent the book back to her. He preferred stronger literary meat, he told his mother-in-law.

Such flashes of open conflict in the household may have been rare. Maria was bedridden, and on those occasions when she spent time with the family in the reception rooms, she was no doubt charming and eager to keep the peace. By the testimony of Anne Thackeray Ritchie, who took refuge with the Jacksons in Brighton after Leslie Stephen turned her out of the house at the time of her marriage, Maria was a gracious, restful presence, and excellent company in the great Pattle tradition. All the same, the fact that Mrs. Jackson was installed in the bedroom right next to Julia and Leslie's bedroom and his dressing room cannot have been entirely comfortable for the married pair, and of course her care put a strain on the whole household. With three flights of stairs for her maid to negotiate, carrying brass cans of hot water, full commode pans, and trays of tempting little delicacies, Mrs. Jackson made a lot more work for the staff, and thus for the mistress of the house. Julia Stephen had now to divide herself between two people, each of them accustomed to being the principal focus of her love and care. The strain can be read in the photographs taken of her at the time. It is not, I think, incidental that Laura Makepeace Stephen was sent away from Hyde Park Gate for good at about the time that Maria Jackson moved in.

Virginia Woolf has nothing very nice to say about her maternal grandmother. Biographers like Hermione Lee, who have taken a look at the trove of Maria Jackson's letters that Julia Stephen left at her death, have painted a rather damning portrait of Maria, and one that it has pleased me so far to echo. It would be easy to argue that Julia Stephen was the victim not only of a tyrant husband but of a parasite mother, but it would also be wrong, at least in part. According to Leslie Stephen in the *Mausoleum Book,* Julia and Maria enjoyed each other, and were happier together than apart: "I do not think that either of them [Maria and Julia] ever said a word which could give pain to the other. They relied continually upon one another — I have never seen nor can I imagine the relation between mother and daughter more beautiful and perfect. Our 'darling of darlings' loved her mother so well that it might seem as if they had been alone together in the world."

It is honorable in Leslie Stephen to write this, and I think we should take his testimony at face value. He had seen these women together ever since Julia was a teenager and knew them as well as anyone. No man wished more than he to be first in his wife's affections, yearned to become himself the person who never gave her pain, to be with her as if they were alone on earth.

Maria Jackson, age seventy-four, died in 1892. Following her mother's death, as we saw in Chapter 3, Julia Stephen was so prostrated with grief that she and Leslie went to live for six or eight weeks in a little house at Chenies in Buckinghamshire, loaned to them by Julia's cousin the Duchess of Bedford. As usual, the Pattle women rallied round one another in times of trouble, and

Leslie and Julia could both be away since by this time Stella Duckworth, age thirteen, was considered old enough to manage the house and take care of her younger half-siblings.

Given his wife's frequent long absences, the grumpiness for which Leslie Stephen is legendary becomes more understandable and even forgivable. Leslie came, as I have noted, from a family in which the father's needs and desires came first, and he lived in a society that believed this to be right and proper. Leslie adored Julia, he wanted her in his bed, and with each year he came to rely on her more and more. When she was not at home he missed her atrociously, and this made him angry, resentful, and truculent.

Leslie's ability to rule in his own home was made more difficult, a little paradoxically, because he was so often there. He did go into central London on dictionary business, and he managed to get away from time to time, especially when depression and overwork brought him close to a breakdown. In the early years of their marriage, with Julia's smiling approval, he went on strenuous walking holidays with friends, like the one in Cornwall during which he saw Talland House and impetuously decided to buy the lease on it. Once he took a longish trip to the United States and reconnected with old friends like Oliver Wendell Holmes. However, unlike his lawyer-professor brother-in-law Henry Vaughan, or his other brother-in-law Herbert Fisher, aide and adviser to the Prince of Wales, Leslie Stephen did most of his work in his fifth-floor attic study at 22 Hyde Park Gate, and when he was there Julia felt able to leave. Leslie could protest, he could groan, he could lament, he could write long letters telling Julia all the home news and begging her to come back soon because the children were sick again and he missed her so dreadfully, but he somehow could not produce the inner bull elephant seal and fire off a telegram: "Come Home At Once, Your Husband."

Passionately in love, dazzled by his wife's beauty, and not a little in awe of her lofty social connections, Leslie Stephen could not find it in his heart or in his code of ethics to exercise the power over his wife granted him by English law. Thus, part of the complex dynamic in the Stephen marriage was Leslie's seesawing between unreasonable demands and abject apologies. "I'm not as bad a husband as Carlyle, am I? Tell me I'm not!" can be paraphrased as the refrain in many of his letters to his absent wife. But then she came home and he often ran cantankerous, penny-pinching Carlyle a close second in the parlor while exerting his conjugal rights in the bedroom, as Carlyle did not.

Leslie could not change. He could not help himself. He had to punish Julia — because she had been so very happy with Herbert Duckworth, because she was so very attached to those rather tiresome women, her mother and her sisters, because she found it so easy to live in harmony with her women relatives and friends, because she placed their needs ahead of his own. And Julia knew this, accepted it as a woman's lot in life, got away from the stresses of home when she could, and grew thin and tense.

Given the emotional and practical complications her absences caused, it was surely not just a sense of duty that sent Julia Stephen away from home for lengthy visits, on top of the afternoons she dedicated to charitable activities when at home in both Kensington and St. Ives. If Julia had been asked, she would probably have said that it was not a question of making a hierarchy of love (I love my mother more than my husband and my little children) but of identifying need. Adeline and Maria needed her more; she was the best person to serve those needs. It was also a question of secular morality. To go to a house of pain and death was hard, it was exhausting and agonizing, but the burden was hers to bear as she chose. She had built a household machine that could function in her absence. Leslie and the babies would miss her, but they would manage.

Julia Stephen's nobility of soul stands the test of time since the evidence for it is so strong and was offered in many cases by people whose lives barely touched upon hers, people she had no obligation to notice, no need to help. She was a Samaritan, not a Pharisee, her goodness practical and hands-on, not ideological and abstract. If a poor person needed a coat, she would make sure to find one and put it in a parcel. If a letter of support and friendship was needed, she wrote one by return mail. If a local family lost a breadwinner, she would be sure to hear of it and launch a relief fund. Her life philosophy of doing good in the world because good work is urgently needed, not because good work wins an eternal reward, is one to honor. Virginia Woolf — who for some years taught working-class women at night school, organized a Cooperative Society seminar series in her Richmond home, wrote endless letters about household help for her sister, and was very handy with brown paper and string — honored her mother's code more, I think, than she is usually given credit for.

As we have seen, when she was a recently bereaved widow, Julia Duckworth longed for moments of solitude, of being left to herself. "I could never be alone," she wrote to Leslie Stephen, "which sometimes was such torture." Once she remarried, moments alone were even rarer and more precious. Thus, even if the tram she caught on Kensington High Road was cold, even if the platform at Paddington Station was rain-swept, and the railway compartment dirty, still she was alone, free to chat if she felt like it or read her book or think without interruption or comment. She was independent, she was anonymous, she was free. In her mother's overstuffed house, in her sister's ruined castle, she had a room to herself. When not busy with the invalid, she could retire at night to her bedroom, where there was no husband hungry for sex, no baby hungry for milk. Going off on an errand of mercy was not a rest, but it was a change, a kind of tonic, and one the Stephens' strict code of ethics allowed Julia to take without guilt.

For twenty-five years after she was numbed by Herbert Duckworth's death, Julia soldiered on. After eight years of widowhood, she agreed to embrace the solemn pleasures offered by a second marriage to a ravaged and worthy man she knew depended like a child on her love and support and whom she loved and esteemed but did not desire. She felt simple joys — the beautiful baby on her knee, a boat ride out into St. Ives Harbour with the older children, a perfectly conceived dinner party like the one with the *boeuf en daube* that Virginia Woolf stages for Mrs. Ramsay in *To the Lighthouse.*

That Julia Stephen was a woman of beauty and charm is something we take largely on trust. In the snapshots taken of her during her second marriage, we see a painfully thin woman with haunted eyes and a big nose, severely dressed and coiffed, more hag than goddess. Posed, as she often is, next to her daughters, the contrast is painful to see.

She looks sixty, not forty, to our modern eyes. People who knew Mrs. Stephen remembered how, when she believed herself unobserved, Julia looked sad. The camera goes further than mere sadness, capturing images of a woman etiolating from stress and overwork. The things for which Julia was famous with family and friends — the speed, grace, and economy of her movements,

Julia Stephen with her oldest daughter, Stella Duckworth

the bite and ebullience of her conversation, her intoxicating laugh — could not be captured by black-and-white still photography.

"Mesmerizing" is a word that was often applied to Julia, and one of her achievements was to take a leaf out of her aunt Julia's Pattle playbook and project an image of elegance and distinction that did not rely on fashion. Julia Stephen, according to her daughter Virginia, would clap an old deerstalker hat on her head before haring down the lawn to scoop up a perplexed young male visitor and immediately cast him under her spell. Wrapping her old gray cloak about her as she hurried to the Kensington High bus stop, she somehow, according to the grieving testimony given after her death, managed to strike mail carriers, porters, and painters alike as a perfect lady. When dining out, Julia would put on her evening dress, choose a set of jewelry with the help of her admiring daughters, and sally forth to charm the company, raising her arms and shaking her bracelets in a gesture all her friends loved.

Let us praise Julia Stephen for managing somehow to be beautiful even (to use her own words) when clothed in perpetual drab and shrouded in a crape veil. And if she put on a show of her own devising, why should that be held against her? When Mahatma Gandhi returned a celebrity to chilly England dressed in his homespun loincloth and shawl, was he aware of the effect he was making? Of course. Those who do good in the world need to develop their own stagecraft, their own iconography, and they are entitled to the satisfactions of virtue.

Did Julia Stephen see herself as a saint? No — she was far too busy to even contemplate the idea, and she tells us so in the very first paragraph of *Notes from Sick Rooms:*

> I have often wondered why it is considered a proof of virtue in anyone to become a nurse. *The ordinary relations between the sick and the well are far easier and pleasanter than between the well and the well . . .* Illness has, or ought to have, much of the leveling power of death. We forget, or at all events cease to dwell on, the unfavourable sides to a character when death has claimed its owner, and *in illness we can afford to ignore the details which in health make familiar intercourse difficult.* [my emphasis]

It is there. The acerbity, the psychological acuity, the refusal of conventional pieties, the easy style — some of the very things for which Virginia Woolf will become famous.

∂∾

The way that Julia Stephen managed to make self-sacrifice alluring and charity work glamorous was remarkable, but it posed an existential problem for all three of her daughters. Stella, as we shall see in the next chapter, sank deep into the domestic altruism and public philanthropy her mother advocated, and she was exploited, not prized, for doing so. Vanessa, taking the opposite tack, took strength from her talents and ambitions as a painter, practicing overt obedience and inner resistance. As for Virginia, she came in midlife to see her mother, or the pious, saintly mother Leslie Stephen had pressed upon her in the *Mausoleum Book,* as perhaps the greatest threat to her existence as a writer.

She said this most clearly and poignantly in a short essay called "Professions for Women," which was published after her death. She opens by saying that her profession was writing, and that was a lucky thing since a writer can achieve a lot with a ream of paper and some pens, whereas an artist needs to hire models, and musicians need good instruments and a place to perform. But then Woolf recalls how, when she settled down to write reviews of male writers for publication, she would be "bothered" and "tormented" by a phantom figure she identified as "the Angel in the House": "[The Angel] was intensely sympathetic. She was immensely charming. She was utterly unselfish. She excelled in the difficult arts of family life. She sacrificed herself daily. If there was chicken, she took the leg, if there was a draught she sat in it. Above all — need I say it — she was pure."

The phantom Angel whispers to Woolf that she should strive in her reviews to "flatter" and be "sympathetic and tender." "'Use all the arts and wiles of our sex. Never let anybody guess that you have a mind of your own. Above all be Pure,' said the Angel. And she made as if to guide my pen. I now record the one act for which I take some credit to myself . . . I turned upon her and caught her by the throat. I did my best to kill her . . . Had I not killed her she would have killed me. She would have plucked the heart out of my writing."

The Angel is quite clearly Woolf's mother, Julia Stephen, and to second-wave feminists like me, that passage in "Professions for Women" was a revelation, a call to arms. To find fulfillment and achievement, to realize one's destiny, one might need symbolically to wrestle with one's mother, even kill her in a new version of the death of Laius at the hands of his son, Oedipus.

As Woolf indicates in her essay, the Angel in the House is a specific cultural reference to the codification of female perfection set forth in a long narrative poem by Coventry Patmore, which was first published in 1854. Patmore's *The Angel in the House* is a paean to his ideal woman — an adoring wife and self-sacrificing mother, devoid of vanity and self-interest, striving tirelessly to serve the needs of her family, happy within the walls of her little domestic kingdom, bowing her head before blame and praise alike. Patmore's Angel was Chaucer's Patient Griselda Redux — but with a nice, grateful, admittedly exigent but certainly not sadistic Victorian spouse like . . . well . . . like Leslie Stephen. Patmore dedicated the poem to his first wife — who, unsurprisingly one cannot help but think, was deceased.

By the time Virginia Woolf and her sisters Stella and Vanessa were growing up in the last decades of the nineteenth century, Patmore's poem had become a touchstone of the age. It was cited in rebuke of female subversives such as Florence Nightingale's marvelous aunt Julia Smith and Nightingale's equally marvelous first cousin Barbara Leigh Smith Bodichon. These women and their friends and colleagues financed, founded, and staffed the first women's colleges, clamored for access to all the learned professions, agitated for a working wage for women in the labor force, demanded equal rights for women under the law, and pressed for the vote. These were the kind of women whom Julia Stephen disliked, denigrated, and opposed. These are the kind of women Woolf would honor and celebrate in great feminist essays such as *A Room of One's Own* and *Three Guineas*.

But in the Stephen household at Hyde Park Gate in Kensington, the Patmore poem was much more than a cultural icon for the age. Julia Stephen knew Coventry Patmore well. As we have seen, he was the favorite author of her mother, Maria Pattle Jackson. He was a frequent guest in the Jackson home. When Julia Jackson was a girl, Patmore was an author she was encouraged to read, a man she was encouraged to listen to, a man at hand to mold her at an impressionable age. Julia Stephen possessed a signed copy of *The Angel in the House* and she, even more than most women of her class and era, was indoctrinated with Patmore's message. She quite consciously labored to be the Angel of 22 Hyde Park Gate, and perhaps Leslie Stephen is not wholly to be blamed for the fact that that is exactly the way he memorialized her for her children, and for posterity, in the *Mausoleum Book.*

Dissatisfied with her 1915 attempt to capture the lived reality of her parents' marriage in her first novel, *The Voyage Out,* Woolf in 1926 began writing *To the Lighthouse,* and was astonished to find how easily and quickly the book came to her. In the later novel, Julia Stephen comes alive as Mrs. Ramsay, the epitome of loving and lovable female loveliness in an old deerstalker hat. After reading the novel in manuscript, Vanessa Bell wrote to Virginia: "It was like meeting her [their mother] again with oneself grown up and on equal terms." Woolf herself said that, when *To the Lighthouse* was done, "I ceased to be obsessed with my mother. I no longer hear her voice. I do not see her."

For me and many other readers, *To the Lighthouse* is Woolf's greatest work, a landmark in English literature, but for all Woolf's genius, she could not quite release Angel Julia from a house that became a mausoleum. I for one still find it hard to like and relate to Virginia Woolf's mother the way I do, for example, to her great-aunt Julia Cameron or her adoptive aunt Anne Thackeray Ritchie. They were two stalwart and unrepentant Victorians, yet somehow it is Julia Stephen, a younger woman possessed of such beauty and charm, who personifies the stereotypic Victorian values. She is the Angel/Demon against which Virginia Woolf, Bloomsbury, and much of modern culture found it necessary to rebel.

9

Stella Duckworth Hills

LAURA MAKEPEACE Stephen managed to survive asylum living for fifty years, but Virginia Woolf's other half-sister, Stella Duckworth, was dead at twenty-eight. Most of what we know of Stella comes from the autobiographical pieces that Virginia Woolf wrote long after Stella's death — "Reminiscences" of 1904–5, written for the Memoir Club, and the incomplete "A Sketch of the Past" of 1939–41. As Woolf remembered it, the key to Stella's life and character was the relationship she had with her mother. Stella and Julia, Woolf tells us, were inextricably bound together in a web of love and dependence and sacrifice. Woolf wrote her memoir essays under a powerful compulsion to record and to honor the lives of the mother and sister she had loved so much and lost so early. But the examples of Julia Stephen and Stella Duckworth also led Woolf to consider the question of what is lost and what gained when women reflexively put the wishes and needs of others before their own.

☙

Stella Duckworth was weaned earlier than her two brothers, and she was only one year old when her father died, too young to have any memories of him. Then, for about seven years, she lived by the side of a mother who, as we saw in the previous chapter, had been plunged into a pit of grief and despair. As Woolf reconstructs her older sister's life as a child, Stella lived "in the shade of [her mother's] widowhood; saw that beautiful crape-veiled figure daily; and perhaps took then the ply that was so marked — that attitude of devotion, almost canine in its touching adoration, to her mother; that passive, suffering affection; and also that complete unquestioning dependence."

Julia decided early that her daughter Stella was slow, and as an adult, Stella would laughingly tell friends that she was very stupid because she had had rheumatic fever as a child. However, the belief that Stella was of low intelligence — not totally unrelated to the belief that Laura Stephen was an insane moron — was reinforced when her mother married the fiercely competitive scholar Leslie Stephen. Julia herself, who had an excellent mind though she had never gone to school, found an education in her second marriage and rose triumphantly to the challenge of becoming not only the wife but the intellectual companion of a very erudite man. But things did not go so well for Stella. As Woolf testifies in "Reminiscences," the cult of books and learning that Leslie and Julia created in their Kensington home and that she herself fitted into so well had crippled Stella. Unlike her brothers, who were no brighter yet moved smoothly through Eton and Trinity College, Cambridge, for Stella there was no escape. Stella, Woolf says, "was not clever, she seldom read a book; and this fact had I think an immense influence upon her life. She exaggerated her deficiency, and, living in close companionship with her mother, was always contrasting their differences, and imposing on herself an inferiority which led her from the first to live in her mother's shade. [Julia] was . . . ruthless in her ways, and quite indifferent, if she saw good, to any amount of personal suffering."

Here, Virginia Woolf as an adult clearly sees what she had not seen as a child — that their mother had made Stella suffer and had been self-righteously indifferent to the pain she was causing. Virginia had inherited their mother's quick wit and acerbic tongue and feels obligated in conscience to make an act of contrition to the long-dead sister who had not.

If we parse the available information on the household at 22 Hyde Park Gate, it becomes clear that it was Stephen family dynamics, not some nineteenth-century version of the IQ test, that kept the label of stupidity pinned on Stella's back for so long. None of the Duckworths were exactly known for intellect and scholarship—not Herbert, if what Leslie portrays is to be believed, and certainly not Herbert's sister, the rich, splendidly preserved, and confidently mindless Aunt Minna Duckworth. Gerald Duckworth founded a successful publishing house, so presumably had a head for business to go with his inherited money. But Gerald's older brother, George, according to Virginia Woolf's cutting account in "A Sketch of the Past," was exceptionally dim, a Wodehousian figure, flunking every exam he took and getting jobs in the political establishment solely on the basis of connections.

For Leslie Stephen, almost no one was clever enough, and he and Julia passed their low assessment of Stella's intellectual capacities on to their Stephen children. As long as their mother lived, Vanessa, Thoby, Virginia, and Adrian all learned from their parents to look down their long Stephen noses at Stella, and the fact that Stella was routinely charged with unpleasant tasks, such as taking them to the dentist, did not advance her in their estimation. The young Stephens were addicted to toffees, bull's-eyes, and jam roly-polies, and their teeth rotted out fast. When, after an excruciating session of drilling without anesthesia at their exclusive London dentist's office, they were treated by their older sister to ice cream out of her own pocket, they were mollified but not exactly grateful. As children will, they had figured out that Stella, like all the Duckworths, was rather rich, so it seemed to them only fair that she should share a bit of her ample pocket money.

Vanessa, Thoby, Virginia, and Adrian loved to give one another weird nicknames—Virginia was "the Goat," Vanessa "the Saint," Adrian "the Wombat." Stella was "the Old Cow," a nickname assumed to be affectionate but surely hurtful.

৵

When her mother remarried and began to produce a crop of smart, funny, entertaining babies, the pall of gloom under which Stella Duckworth had grown up lifted, but a heavy burden of domestic responsibilities quickly fell on her shoulders. Stella was only ten years older than her oldest Stephen sibling, Vanessa, but Stella was the oldest child at home, and by her mid-teens she was being left in charge of the big household for weeks on end. The evidence points to the fact that it was Stella who allowed Julia Stephen to build her reputation as the perfect nurse, Stella who burnished Julia's halo as the Angel of Mercy.

Julia Stephen, as we have seen, was accustomed at a moment's notice to fly forth to tend the sick and dying—in West Wales this month or the Isle of Wight the next. Julia had put a superb domestic machine in place and, as she saw it, all her teenage daughter had to do was keep it oiled and running. In Julia's absence, Stella would do her best, and if that was not very good, since she was supposedly not very bright, everyone in the family, from the little scrubber in the scullery to the baby in the nursery, could look forward to Julia coming back and picking up the pieces. And indeed, once the star returned, Stella the understudy retired backstage and took up the tedious things that always needed doing in a large family—darning, piecing the sheets, sorting the linen closet, settling the tradesmen's bills, replying to the letters that flew in each week from the horde of relatives. Reading may not have been Stella Duckworth's favorite pastime, but given her domestic duties, can we wonder that she rarely opened a book?

For all this hard work and heavy responsibility, Stella received little gratitude and less praise. Leslie was fond of his stepdaughter and could see how hard she tried, but it was his wife who fulfilled all of Leslie's most urgent and intimate needs, and if Julia was away and things at home did not quite run with the beautiful precision he could expect from his wife, Leslie felt entitled to complain. As for Julia, she was never quick to praise, and when she came back home, no doubt physically weary and emotionally drained from her sickbed ministrations, she would fall upon Stella, counting up all the things the girl had done wrong and wondering why someone whom she had taken such pains to train could be so inept. It was easy for Julia Stephen to convince herself that she was not only offering her eldest daughter a model of female philanthropy but also preparing her for her future as a wife and mother. Once, when Leslie saw Stella weeping and ventured to suggest to his wife that she had been unduly harsh on the girl, Julia was taken aback. "I ask of my daughter no more than I ask of myself," said Julia, a stereotypically Victorian reply that is not endearing.

Since Julia had so little time, she had Stella teach the smaller children their first lessons, and it did not take long for the Stephen children to notice that Stella was hardly more advanced in her studies than they were. Thoby was easily bored and dismissive of authority, but by the age of six he was in school, so it was Virginia, who loved to read and soaked up information fast, who most resented the times when her parents were too busy to attend to her and deputed Stella to supervise her work. In "A Sketch of the Past" Virginia Woolf remembers how she used her precocious reading ability to engage the attention of her parents, especially her father; she quickly observed that she had something in common with him. "How proud, priggishly, I was, if he gave his little amused snort when he found me reading some book that no child could understand. I was a snob, no doubt, and read partly to make him think me a very clever little brat."

Vanessa was much less judgmental than Thoby and Virginia. From the age of three, as the oldest Stephen, Vanessa had found herself holding the baby and spooning mush into the toddler, so it was no stretch to put herself in Stella's shoes as the Stephens' version of Cinderella. Vanessa, like Thoby, was not that interested in schoolwork, but unlike Stella, she had her own claim to excellence, and one that both her parents encouraged in a girl. If Virginia was soon cast as the clever sister in the family, Vanessa was the artistic one, and she slowly developed a close bond with her older sister in part because Stella was the first to encourage her to develop her talent as an artist.

Like most affluent young girls, Stella had been taught a little music and art, and Julia had her teach her younger siblings to play the piano and draw. All four Stephens would become dedicated music lovers in adulthood, but as children, only Adrian showed either taste or talent for the piano. With her elementary drawing lessons, however, informed by the marvelous how-to-draw books written by the Stephen family friend John Ruskin, Stella struck gold. Thoby, like his father as a boy, loved to draw. As an adult, Thoby Stephen would illustrate his letters with remarkable little line drawings of people he met and creatures from the natural world, especially his beloved birds. As for Vanessa, when she was perhaps six Stella gave her a set of colored chalks. This was not an expensive gift, but once offered the means to experiment with color, Vanessa became totally absorbed and mysteriously happy. Vanessa Bell's fame as a painter is rooted in her use of color, and, as she would later recall, the chalks offered a life-changing experience. Stella had seen something in her and thought about how she could help.

Quiet, placid, useful, sitting in the background or to the side, Stella was always on hand, a constant feature on the landscape of Stephen family life, but more, indeed, like a cow than a traveler or even a shepherd. That Stella might be an independent being, with ideas and wishes of her own, apparently did not occur to her mother or anyone else at Hyde Park Gate. From girlhood Julia had dedicated herself unstintingly to her mother, Maria Jackson. She expected comparable devotion from Stella, and more indeed, since the demands on her, as a mother of eight, all living in the same house, were so much greater. As for Stella's having a will of her own, Julia did not tolerate willfulness in any of her girls. And Stella accepted Julia's harshness as the price to be paid for Julia's love and society. Knowing herself to be indispensable, even if no one ever said so, she was content to be her mother's assistant at home and backup when Julia was away.

Having an adult sister had very real advantages for Vanessa and Virginia. Stella spared them many of the burdens of home life, so they had time to read and write, draw and paint. At the same time, as they grew older, they could see that Julia and Stella had a symbiotic relationship that excluded them, and this they grew to resent. Vanessa and Virginia found themselves set outside the dominant household pairings of Julia/Leslie, Julia/Maria, and Julia/Stella, and, separated from their brothers by schooling, they were thrown back upon each other for company, understanding, and support. As young girls, they created a dyad of their own, a fierce, intimate, protective alliance that, given the paucity of parental attention, could turn at any moment into competition and rivalry.

As Virginia Woolf looked back on her childhood in "A Sketch of the Past," she remembered feeling a subtle detachment in Stella that was a barrier to intimacy. Every morning until lunch, every evening from teatime on, Stella was reliably there at Hyde Park Gate, busy, kind, and generous with time and money, and yet maintaining a psychological distance. This combination of surface obedience and inner reserve set Stella apart from her highly articulate and often rambunctious younger siblings. It allowed them to dismiss her as all Duckworth and no Pattle.

In several of her novels, Virginia Woolf sought to cross that remembered barrier to intimacy with Stella by creating older-sister characters and showing how a complex inner life can exist under a woman's mask of sweetness, compliance, and service to family. With Eleanor Pargiter in *The Years,* for example, Woolf uses the freedom of fiction to throw aside the stereotype of the mean, frustrated old spinster and bestow on Eleanor the long, happy life that her sister Stella was denied. Well into her thirties, Miss Pargiter exists, it seems, merely to serve her father and numerous younger siblings. Her only outlet is her charity work in the slums every afternoon, and her endless committees. But Eleanor's father finally dies, and she then has money of her own to swap the fusty, neglected family home for a modern flat and travel the world. Eleanor is a valiant volunteer to the end, but in the last scene of the novel we see her a sprightly seventy-year-old, attending a terrific party where she is surrounded by a lively band of affectionate young relatives. Eleanor Pargiter in *The Years* is a little eccentric, but she is not pathetic and she is not tragic. Unlike real-life Stella, fictional Eleanor does not marry, which may be sad, for she might have liked to, but she also does not run the risk of pregnancy. Fictional Eleanor is a happy, fulfilled single woman, and she does not die. I love the character of Eleanor Pargiter. She is one of the reasons why I think we need to take notice when, very quietly, Virginia Woolf does something revolutionary in fictional characterization.

It is tempting to follow Woolf's lead and imagine a rich inner life for Stella Duckworth, but the sad truth is that we have too few documents to get us past the pictorial record of a beautiful, attentive, unsmiling girl seated to the side in the family album pictures. A few of Stella's letters survive, along with a pocket diary in which, following her mother's death, she frantically listed the tasks she needed to complete each day. Vanessa Bell read that diary in 1910 and remarked, in a letter to her sister Virginia, that she was surprised, given the extraordinary domestic burden that her older sister had strapped to her back, that Stella had lived to see her twenty-eighth birthday.

We can only guess what Stella Duckworth was thinking and feeling as she smilingly served tea while Leslie Stephen shouted and his lady visitors twittered into his ear trumpet. The impulse to write and record was not in Stella as it was in her younger sisters, and if Stella confided in her friends Susan Lushington and Lisa Stillman, they never came forward with memories and letters. This is an irreparable loss. Just think how flat and impoverished our understanding of Vanessa Bell and Virginia Woolf as young women would be if friends like Margery Snowden, Violet Dickinson, and the Vaughan cousins had not lovingly kept their letters.

2♥

When Stella Duckworth turned eighteen, she "came out," in the parlance of the day, and her life was expected to change quite soon. As teenagers, young persons of independent means like Stella were carefully protected from impecunious clergymen and lascivious dancing masters, but once they put their hair up and let their skirts down and had been painstakingly introduced to a selection of eligible young men, they were expected to marry. Late Victorians considered matrimony to be the sacred duty and personal mission of all young women, and a wealthy young woman came under special pressure to marry, since she was believed to need a husband who could manage her fortune and sire sons to inherit her money.

All went well at first. Stella was one of the most successful "young persons" of her year — charming, modest, and, unlike her little sister Virginia ten years later, far too nice and socially adept to make any young man on the dance floor feel stupid or ill-informed. Stella was also very beautiful — perhaps, the family album suggests, the most beautiful of Julia's three much-admired daughters.

Decades after Stella's death, Virginia Woolf remembered how exquisitely pale and prone to blush her sister had been — "a phantom loveliness." Stella was also the daughter who most resembled her mother as a young woman — Leslie Stephen certainly thought so — and I find it interesting to conjecture how exactly that resemblance played out between the two women.

By the time Stella was twenty, Julia Stephen was looking much older than her years. In the family group photos taken in 1894 or 1895, Julia, forty-eight, looks older than her husband, Leslie, even though he was fourteen years her senior.

The Duckworth-Stephen family at Wimbledon circa 1894

For a woman who had been an acclaimed beauty since puberty, it cannot have been easy to see those pictures enshrined in the family album. When she looked across the table at Stella, so much like the lovely young self who had been captured by Aunt Julia Cameron's lens and who still haunted a dark corridor downstairs, did Julia Stephen feel maternal pride or female jealousy? Versions of the "Mirror, mirror on the wall, who is the fairest one of all?" struggle between Snow White and her wicked stepmother are, after all, played out every day.

Virginia Woolf insists that Julia had no reason to be jealous of Stella. The Julia Stephen in her forties that Woolf as memoirist calls up from the dead is not the gaunt woman we find frozen and silenced in the family snapshots. She is not even the subtly shaded Julia that Woolf the novelist gives us as Mrs. Ramsay in *To the Lighthouse*. Instead, the Julia of "Reminiscences" and "A Sketch of the Past" is a dazzling, quicksilver beauty, forever in motion, witty, surprising, bending the whole world to her charm. The Julia of Woolf the memoirist is in fact less the Julia whom Virginia herself came to know as she emerged from childhood than the Julia of Leslie Stephen's *Mausoleum Book,* which is odd, given how much Virginia and her siblings claimed to hate and resent that book.

Young men quickly clustered about Stella Duckworth, many of them introduced by her older brothers, George and Gerald. "Stella's coming out," writes Woolf, "and her success and her loves, excited many instincts long dormant in her mother; she [that is, Julia] liked young men, she enjoyed their confidences; she was intensely amused by the play and intrigue of the thing; only, as she complained, Stella would insist upon going home long before the night was over, for fear lest she [Julia] should be tired."

Stella received several proposals of marriage and declined them all, with her mother's support. No longer the autocratic mother enforcing her will, Julia had become an almost mischievous confidante. As Woolf describes it, Julia and Stella would have great fun, sitting together in close conference, rating each suitor in turn, and laughingly deciding in the end that none of them would do.

Marriage is, of course, not for everyone, and not every woman likes men. A Victorian woman like Stella Duckworth, with the means to support herself, might have weighed the risks and benefits of marriage and motherhood and decided rationally she had best stay single. But as her later actions proved, Stella did want to have a husband and children, and there was at least one suitor to whom she was far from averse, so her insistence on remaining unmarried for eight years after she came out is hard to explain. Julia's ready complaisance in her decision is, on the surface, even more inexplicable, since Mrs. Leslie Stephen was famous in her circle for being a hopeless romantic and an indefatigable matchmaker of the Rodgers and Hammerstein "Hello, young lovers . . . I've had a love of my own" variety. She was instrumental in arranging the marriages of young friends and relatives like Kitty Lushington and Leo Maxse, Florence Fisher and Frederic Maitland, and her friends surely assumed that, as she savored her debutante daughter's success, Julia's thoughts were dwelling on trousseaus and wedding cake.

Her mother's love of matchmaking is, indeed, something Virginia Woolf features and delicately satirizes in *To the Lighthouse.* Her character Mrs. Ramsay is quite aware that in the eyes of the unprepossessing bachelor William Banks, she herself is the perfect woman, but she does her charitable best to push the contentedly single artist Lily Briscoe into his arms. With Paul Rayley and Minta Doyle Mrs. Ramsay is more successful, as their engagement comes about in the general euphoria caused by her legendary *boeuf en daube,* but even this triumph is short-lived. Within pages, the novelist tells us offhandedly that Paul and Minta were ill suited and did not live happy ever after.

As she returns to the events of her mid-adolescence, Virginia Woolf circles around the transformation in the relationship between Julia and Stella that occurred when Stella came of age. Given Julia Stephen's fierce espousal of woman's traditional roles as wife and mother, given the power a Victorian mother wielded over her daughters (remember Oscar Wilde's Lady Bracknell!), and given Julia's exceptional personal ascendency over Stella, how did it come about that she merrily gave way when Stella rejected one eligible young man after another? How did it come about that Stella, once the most compliant of children, now developed a backbone, and her mother meekly accepted this sudden new assertion of autonomy? Refusing to pass judgment on this turn of events in the lives of the two dead women, both of whom she loved so much, Woolf instead deploys her narrative skills and gives us a detailed account of the first time that Jack Hills proposed to Stella Duckworth, an event to which she was at least in part an eyewitness.

Of the several young men who proposed marriage to Stella Duckworth in her late teens and early twenties, John Waller Hills was the frontrunner. Eton- and Oxford-educated, Hills was a close friend of the Duckworth brothers and had become a regular guest at the Stephen dinner table by the time Stella came of age. "It was very natural," Woolf writes in "A Sketch of the Past," "that when [Hills] was living alone in Ebury Street, very hard-up, very hard-worked, stammering, and lonely, that he came to my mother for sympathy." Leslie Stephen despised Hills as a man of facts, not ideas, but even he never thought for a moment that it was Stella's money that Jack wanted. Anyone with eyes could see that he was not only passionately in love with Stella but unreservedly devoted to her. For Jack, Stella was never a stupid Old Cow. She was always a shining star.

And so, Jack Hills arrived one day, ready to go down on his knees and propose to Stella Duckworth in form, with the approval of all in the family and in the expectation of being accepted. As readers who love Jane Austen will know, a marriage proposal in an upper-class nineteenth-century household was always a choreographed event, and Stella cannot have been taken unprepared by what Jack wished to say to her. Within minutes of beginning their private interview, however, she rejected his proposal out of hand. She then ran up to her room, where she was heard sobbing bitterly. Jack promptly went in to see Julia, who had been waiting to know how things had gone. Jack fell weeping into Julia's outstretched arms, expecting, and finding, the balm of maternal sympathy that he had never experienced with his own mother.

Julia liked Jack Hills very much. She looked on him almost as a son, and she felt very sorry for him when she saw Stella making him so unhappy. According to what Jack told other family members, when he turned to Julia after Stella rejected his proposal, Julia showed herself at her most charming and sympathetic. On the other hand, what passed between mother and daughter when Jack had gone and Julia went upstairs to Stella's room, we do not know. No record exists of their conversation. The subsequent chain of events makes it clear, however, that Julia issued no diatribe and no ultimatum. She did not thunder: "How can you be so cruel to that delightful, deserving young man? You are a shameless hussy, leading him on and then dismissing him." Or: "I shall be very seriously displeased with you, Stella, if you do not reconsider your silly, unkind decision to reject Jack. I would like you to keep to your room for the next days and give more serious, considered thought to your future."

Something odd is happening here between daughter and mother, and Virginia Woolf gives us the clue to it. There was something "beautiful" about the bond between her mother and her oldest sister, Woolf tells us, but also something "excessive" and "morbid." The blame for that, Woolf asserts, lay with Stella, who was reading her mother's mind in a way that made Julia uncomfortable: "What her mother felt passed almost instantly through Stella's mind; there was no need for the brain to ponder and criticize what the soul knew. [Julia] would no doubt have liked some brisker resistance, some intellectual opposition, calling out a different kind of care. [Julia] may have felt that the tie [of Stella to herself] was too close to be wholesome and might hinder Stella from entertaining those feelings upon which she [Julia] set so high a value."

Reading that passage, one can sense Virginia Woolf imagining her own ideal for a mother-daughter relationship, one as close as that between Julia and Maria and between Julia and Stella, but free of the excessive and the morbid. Perhaps, she hints, had her mother only been able to live a few more years, she herself and Vanessa could have given Julia "brisker resistance," "intellectual opposition," "a different kind of care."

Whether, in fact, when Vanessa and Virginia turned eighteen in their turn and took their place in adult society, Julia Stephen would have tolerated, much less appreciated "resistance" and "opposition" from them, one may take leave to doubt. If you follow Woolf's line of analysis, however, it becomes clear that, however Julia Stephen might rhapsodize about the joys of married life and preach marriage and motherhood as a woman's solemn duty to society, Stella Duckworth knew that in fact these were not things her mother wanted for *her*. By remaining single, Stella might appear to disappoint Julia while intuiting, without Julia ever needing to say a word, what it was that Julia really wanted. To keep Stella for herself, and, if she were to die, for Leslie.

Jack Hills was a lovely young man, but since he already treated Julia as a mother, she had no need to be his mother-in-law. To see her beautiful eldest daughter walk blushing down the aisle would have been gratifying, but what Julia really wanted and needed, as her strength waned and familial pressures mounted, was not to be the mother of the bride on a single day but to have Stella by her side every day, forever, perfectly trained, passionately willing, forever subordinate, eternal moon to Julia's sun.

Julia had produced three daughters, so she could afford to have one remain a spinster dedicated to the care of herself and the aging, exigent Leslie. Vanessa and Virginia were both very pretty little girls who promised to be beauties in Julia's image. When the time came, Julia would feel able to exercise her maternal authority and make sure that her younger daughters married and supplied Julia with jolly sons-in-law and enchanting grandchildren. Stella, whose "almost canine" adoration often irritated Julia, would be perfectly happy as the chief bridesmaid, the maiden aunty, standing with a smile behind Grandma's big chair.

In the third volume of his autobiography, Leonard Woolf in his eighties would write of his vicarage neighbors at Rodmell, the Hawkesfords, "Next to the war memorial in Whitehall, there should be another to the millions of daughters who gave their lives to looking after selfish parents and the millions of Marys who gave their lives to looking after the Mrs Hawkesfords."

છ

As a small girl, Stella Duckworth had trotted behind her mother when Julia went out on her charitable visits. In her teens she graduated to the committee meetings of various reform societies, and toward the end of her mother's life, she dealt with many of the written demands for assistance — a winter coat, a job for the widow's eldest son, a recommendation for a servant — that flooded into Hyde Park Gate every day. It was through Julia that Stella came to know the social reformer Octavia Hill, and when Stella was over twenty-one and permitted to do social work independently from her mother, she began volunteering to assist in Hill's campaign to resettle London's slum dwellers in decent accommodation. Private philanthropy, which was central to the lives of so many Victorian women, offered the perfect cover for Julia's increasing frailty and Stella's self-sacrifice. If Stella had chosen not to be a wife and mother like Julia, the two could claim that she had perhaps taken the finer way, treading the noble path of charitable good works where Julia had gone before.

For the next six or so years, having apparently given up all thought of marrying, Stella Duckworth spent her discretionary hours working on Octavia Hill's housing projects. By 1900, having taken over the management of extensive properties belonging to the Commissioners of the Church of England, Hill was at the head of an organization that ran seventeen thousand housing units. The success of Hill's system depended on establishing close relationships with renting families and being extremely firm about rent collection. Every week, a group of women — at first volunteers, later paid employees, but all women — would spread out and visit each of the Hill-financed homes to collect the rent and assess the domestic situation.

I suspect that Miss Hill played a more important and satisfying part in

Stella Duckworth's life than we shall ever know, though exactly how she contributed to Hill's organization is unclear. She may have been one of the women volunteers who went around each week to collect the rent money. We do know that Stella even in her twenties could get leave to go into slum areas of London only if she took one of her young sisters or brothers along with her as a kind of chaperone. None of the children, unsurprisingly, enjoyed these exhausting and sometimes painful sorties out of prim and proper Kensington. Only Virginia, of the four young Stephens, seems to have understood what her older sister was trying to accomplish and tried to emulate her.

In her life, Woolf, with some distaste and much irony, engaged in several kinds of educational projects for poor women, and in her fiction Woolf almost obsessively sets a frame around the middle-class privilege her characters enjoy. She juxtaposes her protagonists against a flower seller straight out of *My Fair Lady,* ragged urchins throwing stones into the river off the Embankment, men on the dole flogging postcards, a charwoman on hands and knees, scrubbing. Her female characters are often political and social activists. In *The Years,* Rose Pargiter goes to jail for her work on the campaign for Irish independence, and the Pargiter cousins Magdalena and Elvira D'Elroy, partly out of straitened means and partly as an ideological statement, live in a noisy, ugly flat in a working-class neighborhood of London, far from the quiet elegance of their childhood home. Mary Datchet in *Night and Day* is part of the new cadre of women professionals who, unlike Stella Duckworth, got paid for their work for charitable organizations and could — barely! — afford to rent a room of their own and live independent lives.

⁊

In 1895, twenty-six-year-old Stella Duckworth's brothers, seeing her droop and wither, decided they must do something about getting her married. George and Gerald Duckworth were not pleased with the way their mother had allowed Stella to be so silly about men. To have a sister fade into spinsterhood might, inexplicably, be acceptable to Mother and Father, but the brothers felt it cast a shadow upon their own social eligibility. The possibility that their very own sister might age into a version of fierce, unfashionable, man-hating Octavia Hill was, to say the least, alarming to George and Gerald. Thus, in the spring, her brothers devised a plan whereby Stella would accompany them on a tour of the Continent, and they made sure that Julia would give her full approval and cooperation. Theirs would be a cheerful party of friends, the brothers said, and after all, Mother had met Father in Venice and fallen in love. Perhaps the magic of Italy could work again.

Stella did not want to leave Hyde Park Gate. She, unlike her stepfather and siblings, looked at Julia Stephen with clear eyes. She had known her mother as a young, beautiful woman, and she saw the thin face and gaunt body. Bearing so much of the domestic and philanthropic burden her mother had taken on, Stella appreciated that Julia was having to work harder and harder to maintain her image as the Angel in the House and was being destroyed in the effort.

In the New Year of 1895 Julia Stephen came down with a bad case of influenza, and as the time neared for her oldest children to leave on their Italian tour, she had only just gotten out of bed. Seeing her mother so obviously pale and weak, Stella begged to be allowed to stay in Kensington, but George and Gerald used all their male charm and brotherly authority to overrule her. Julia herself, always eager to please her older sons, told Stella she was a goose to worry and insisted that her daughter take this lovely holiday. Thus, at the beginning of April the three Duckworths sailed for Europe, and Vanessa, sixteen, suddenly and uncomfortably found herself promoted to the position of Chief Daughter.

Stella's fears for her mother were well grounded. Soon after her Duckworth children left, Julia Stephen fell ill again and was forced back to bed. The doctors began to suspect rheumatic fever, a common and survivable disease at the time but dangerous for someone like Julia, whose physical reserves were depleted and whose morale was low. Reading between the lines of the cheery letters she was receiving from home, Stella guessed that things were going very badly wrong in Kensington. There was something frantic about Vanessa's communications, and when had Leslie Stephen ever had any idea of what to do in a medical emergency, so for once Stella put her foot down. She and her brothers must pack up and return home as quickly as possible. As a result of Stella's premonition of disaster, the Duckworths got home in time to take over the direction of the sickroom — George did very well with Harley Street men — but ten days after their return, in the early morning of May 5, Julia Stephen died.

For thirteen-year-old Virginia, her mother's death appeared at the time to be "the greatest disaster that could happen," and it was not until May 1939, only two years before her own death, that Woolf was able to give a full account of what she herself saw, felt, and thought when her mother lay dying and dead in the big bed on the second floor.

Lachrymose deathbed scenes were a staple of Victorian fiction — Dickens, with Little Nell, Sydney Carton, and Jo the crossing sweeper, made them a specialty. Virginia Woolf hated these scenes, and in her own fiction she went to extremes to avoid them. In the last part of *To the Lighthouse,* Mrs. Ramsay, whom we have grown to love and whom we have seen triumphant at her dinner party, dies in an aside, her creator refusing to engage our morbid pity. Thus, one of the things that the mature Virginia Woolf analyzes in her account of her mother's death was that she had felt herself, out of the blue, involved in a melodrama. Everyone except her had an assigned part and took satisfaction in playing it for the public. The doctor, stoic in defeat, hands behind his back, walks off into the lightening day. Father stretches out his hands and howls like a tortured animal. The older brothers swathe their younger siblings in towels and give them warm milk and brandy before solemnly ushering them into the room to kiss the warm cheek of their mother, who has died only minutes earlier. Bewildered, rebelling against any prewritten script for the emotions, Virginia in those first hours observes it all dry-eyed, restraining a laugh behind her hand at the newly hired nurse's practiced weeping.

Two people in the earlier deathbed scene Woolf recalls are resolutely themselves. Julia herself, and Stella. When Virginia is ushered in to say her last goodbye, Julia says, bracingly, unsentimentally, "Hold yourself straight, my little Goat." As for Stella, she had foreseen that her mother might soon die and prepared as best she could. Julia had been Stella's lodestone, the center of her life, the person she loved best, but in the extremity of grief and loss, as in the routine of daily life, Stella's thought was for others. Virginia, scrupulously focusing on her own feelings and reactions, tells us in her final account of her mother's death what Stella did for her.

Once again, according to Victorian custom, thirteen-year-old Virginia is led into the parental bedroom and confronted for a second time with her mother's corpse, now neatly laid out. The urge to giggle at other people's dramatic grieving has gone. The trauma that will send her into her first nervous breakdown is near, and Stella, the person who this time accompanies Virginia to the viewing and holds her hand, registers Virginia's acute distress.

"Her face looked immeasurably distant, hollow, and stern," writes Woolf of her mother. "When I kissed her, it was like kissing cold iron. Whenever I touch cold iron the feeling comes back to me—the feeling of my mother's face, iron-cold and granulated." Instinctively, Stella acts to make the dead woman real again, alive in memory if not in fact, to be loved and cared for, not feared. "Then Stella kissed her [Julia's] cheek and undid a button on her night gown. 'She always liked to have it like that,' she said."

Back in the nursery, Virginia tells Stella that "when I see mother, I see a man sitting with her." Stella is shocked and frightened, and this vision of the man was probably a first symptom of Woolf's approaching retreat into delusion. Stella again shows acute psychological perceptiveness. She does not say something sensible and insensitive like "Don't be so silly, child. This is no time for your fancies." Instead Stella contemplates the picture her little sister has conjured up and says, "It is nice she [Julia] should not be alone."

Perhaps Stella, the daughter who never knew her father, welcomed the notion that a man who was not Leslie Stephen sat by her mother's side in the hour of death. Perhaps Stella in her non-intellectuality and Virginia in her imagination both took comfort in an idea that Julia herself had once entertained in the first days of her widowhood—that Herbert was on hand, waiting for her to die, so that they could be reunited.

❧

The burden of the big household at 22 Hyde Park Gate had proved beyond the strength of Julia Stephen, and she had barely taken her last breath when her daughter Stella took up that burden. Stella managed the household with efficiency and diligence, but far more important than her housekeeping skills were her empathy and emotional wisdom. At first, their mother's death sent the Stephen children into shock, and for many months they were terribly sad and shaken. But then, finding that Stella offered them a semblance of normal life and a space to recover, they accepted these gifts as their due, eager to move on with life. They were young — Adrian, the youngest, was only ten; Vanessa, the oldest, only fifteen — full of ambition and joie de vivre; and, as Thoby was the first to admit openly, it was silly to keep on weeping. No tears, however bitter, could bring their mother back.

Their father, Leslie Stephen, however, could not move on. The very idea of moving on was anathema to him. He was, he declared, utterly and forever inconsolable, and it was his children's first duty to mourn as he did and give him their unconditional love and unquestioning support. Withdrawing to his study, Leslie read old letters and began to write his commemoration of Julia's life, purportedly so that the children would never forget or fail to reverence their mother. In the evenings, Leslie descended for a silent dinner and then sat in the darkened parlor, weeping and raging at his fate.

Leslie's titanic misery cast a pall over the whole household, but it fell with especial weight on Stella's shoulders. That his wife's oldest daughter might bear a sorrow as heavy as his own, that his duty as a father might be first and foremost to comfort her, was something Leslie Stephen could never stretch his mind to.

In losing Julia almost as suddenly and early as he had lost his first wife, Minny Thackeray Stephen, Leslie felt he was reliving his worst nightmare. At the same time, wives, for a man like Leslie Stephen, were in the end replaceable, and even as he railed at the incomprehensible atrocity of his double tragedy, Leslie had the consolation that his dead wife had bequeathed to him a stand-in for herself, inadequate of course, but good enough to serve. After the death of his first wife, Leslie Stephen had turned for comfort and support to Minny's sister, Anne Thackeray. When Anne — cruelly, incomprehensibly to Leslie's mind — deserted him to marry her young cousin, Leslie found Minny and Anny's dear friend Julia Duckworth at hand to bind up his widower's wounds. Now Julia too was gone, and in his torment of mourning and self-pity, Leslie again turned to a woman for the sympathy and support he saw as his patriarchal right. That woman was Stella, and her hardest hours in those early hard days were spent sitting in the red plush living room, crushed to her stepfather's bosom as he wept over the loss of her mother.

What are we to make of this tableau? One of the fascinating things about Victorian fiction, letters, and memoirs is the way atavistic impulses bubble up as an unconscious subtext. Stella Duckworth had lived in Leslie Stephen's home as his daughter since she was a small girl, but she was not his daughter, and the fact that she looked so very much like her mother as a young woman makes her stepfather's growing dependency on her both weird and unwholesome.

Let me be clear. We are not speaking of literal incest here. There is no evidence that Leslie Stephen ever made what was once called an improper advance to either his sister-in-law, Anne Thackeray, or his stepdaughter, Stella Duckworth. He never asked either of them to take his dead wife's side of the bed. What he did was ask, indeed expect, them to dedicate their lives to his care and welfare, as his dead wives had done. And he actively, as by right, sought to close off the possibility of their becoming wives to other men.

George Duckworth, who still lived at Hyde Park Gate and had taken on the role of head of the house, should have seen what was happening and protected his sister from their stepfather's emotional exploitation. He did not, out of stupidity and emotional obtuseness but also out of an unacknowledged cupidity that paralleled his stepfather's. With Leslie holed up in his study and monopolizing Stella in the evenings, George was in loco parentis to his Stephen sisters, with consequences we will be discussing in the next chapter.

Released from her adoring bondage to her mother and without the blinders of male privilege like her brothers', Stella could see that things at 22 Hyde Park Gate were very wrong. For her dead mother's sake as well as for their own, Stella was willing to do everything she could for her brothers and sisters, but she could not and would not be a surrogate Julia for her stepfather. She saw that her sisters were in urgent need of a mother's protection as they came into womanhood, and that, as an unmarried woman, she herself lacked authority in the family.

Finding Jack Hills by her side again, solid, down-to-earth, dependable, a man of facts, not ideas, a man who loved her and was willing to wait in the hope she might love him, a little flame of hope was lit in Stella Duckworth's heart. Perhaps self-sacrifice was not always the best course of action. If, perhaps, rather than give up and give way, she chose to decide and act, chose self-ful-fillment over self-sacrifice, everything for everybody would, in fact, be better. Perhaps she, like other women, like her mother, could have a husband and babies as well as parents and siblings. Perhaps this is what Jack Hills told Stella when he took her out into the garden of the Stephens' rented vacation house at Hindhead for a talk that lasted hours. What we know is that Jack proposed marriage for the third time and that this time Stella accepted. To the astonishment of the Stephen family, waiting nervously in the house as dusk turned to night, the two walked in, pink with delight, and announced their engagement.

Of the love between Stella and Jack, Virginia Woolf writes in a kind of rapture that tells us a lot about her own decision to marry Leonard: "The marriage would have been, I think, a very happy marriage. It would have borne many children. And she might have been alive . . . And it was through that engagement that I had my first vision — so intense, so exciting, so rapturous was it that the word vision applies — my first vision then of love, love between man and woman. It was to me like a ruby, clear, intense . . . This color, this incandescence, was in Stella's whole body. Her pallor became lit up, her eyes bluer. She had something of moonlight about her that winter."

Once he had recovered from the shock of Jack's proposal and Stella's acceptance, Leslie Stephen nurtured a steadily growing rage at what he saw as Stella's betrayal. The scorn he had long expressed for Jack was now thickly marbled with jealousy, and he refused to give his blessing to the match. Delighting in Stella and Jack's happiness and fearing that Leslie's volcanic temper would wear down Stella's resistance, family and friends rallied in defense of the young couple, and little by little the deaf old man came to see that his position was indefensible. Since Stella herself remained strong and resolute before his attacks, Leslie negotiated. If the ungrateful young pair would get married, they must at least move in with him, Leslie insisted, and here practical Stella saw a way to compromise. The house at 24 Hyde Park Gate was up for sale and Stella bought it. The Stephen and Hills households would be separate but close.

For eight long months, Leslie did his best to cloud his stepdaughter's joy, and the Duckworth brothers further complicated things by decreeing, apparently on the grounds of propriety, that Stella and Jack must be given as little time alone together as possible. Unsurprisingly, all this opposition from his fiancée's family did not sit well with Jack, who had already been waiting for Stella for almost ten years, so Stella had her hands full placating the four most important men in her life. Nonetheless, as the wedding approached, Stella seemed to the world a new woman, a model of efficiency, sure of her choices and eager to be married, every inch Julia's daughter.

Brides are traditionally busy people, but Stella Duckworth was busier than most. She had no mother to plan her wedding, Jack's mother proved disengaged, even hostile, and Jack himself was too busy preparing for his next set of law exams to be of practical help. There was the new home at 24 Hyde Park Gate not just to buy but to remodel and redecorate with new furniture, new curtains, new almost everything. And then there were the arrangements for the actual wedding, which Stella found time to take on only six weeks before the event.

In 1897, when few businesses and even fewer private individuals in London had telephones, household errands and social calls ate up the afternoons of middle-class women, and preparations for a shopping trip were more like the ascent of Everest than an email to Amazon. Every visit had to be planned and confirmed by mail, and all too often, after a long trip across London by bus and tube, a woman would arrive to find the shop closed. Just getting the dresses for the bride and for bridesmaids Vanessa and Virginia took many tiring treks over to the dressmakers and much tedious standing on stools to be pinned and fitted. Meanwhile, the regular schedule of housekeeping at 22 Hyde Park Gate had to be rigorously followed, and Stella or Vanessa had to always be at home to pour Father his tea and offer him the choice of seedcake or spiced buns.

A letter that Stella Duckworth wrote to her brother Thoby on March 11, only weeks before the wedding, gives an idea of the long list of jobs that the bride-to-be needed to check off every day. Thoby was an undergraduate at Cambridge and living on a slim allowance, and Stella knew that neither he nor his father had seen any reason for Thoby to acquire morning dress. Knowing how perfectly outfitted her Duckworth brothers would be and not wishing the Stephen men to come off like poor relations, Stella hurriedly penned the following:

My Darling Thoby, I want you to do something for me so attend very carefully will you go to a good tailor. I dare say the one you went to for those trousers wd [*sic*] do and get yourself a black tail coat and a nice pair of grey trousers. I expect it will have to be made for you so I am telling you in good time. The suit will cost between £3 and £4. I expect you had better ask what it will cost then I will send you the money to pay the bill with. You must also have a new topper [top hat] but we have time to choose that in London. Adrian has been staying in with a feverish cold. He is almost well now but he has his exeat [permission to be away from school] & so stays till Tuesday.

Your loving S.D.

All the while, finally in charge of her fortune as well as her life, Stella continued to make her visits to workhouses. She was actively planning with Octavia Hill the construction, at Stella's own expense, of some cottages for poor Londoners in Lisson Grove, Marylebone. And Stella did not neglect one charity case who especially depended on her — Laura Stephen.

The only person at 22 Hyde Park Gate in Julia Stephen's lifetime who both loved and respected Stella was Laura Stephen. Laura was just one year younger than Stella, and the two had known each other from the days when Laura's mother, Minny Thackeray, was alive. Given Laura's difficulties with speech and inability to write, the nature and extent of the relationship between these two women can only be conjectured. But we know that Stella was never mean to or impatient with anyone and that, when Laura was finally committed to an institution in her early twenties, Stella visited her. After Julia's death in 1895, Stella seems to have taken on the primary responsibility for Laura along with the rest of her burdens.

This, at least, is what I deduce from two terse remarks in Virginia Woolf's journal for 1897: "[January 12] Stella went to Laura and was away for lunch and tea." Then, two days later, "Stella was away all morning and afternoon at Laura." These two comments are interesting both because they are the only two places I have found in the early journal where Virginia refers to "Laura," and because of the date — some three months before Stella's wedding, and as we have seen, an exceptionally busy and fraught time for the bride-to-be. Why exactly Laura needed such focused attention we can only guess, but it seems all too likely that Laura was extremely upset to hear of Stella's marriage, and needed Stella's personal reassurance that she would not be deserted. In general, news of Laura was kept from Virginia, but it was so unusual for Stella to take two long afternoons off from her family and her fiancé that Virginia picked up on it and marked it in her diary.

With the exception of Leslie, Virginia was the one in the family who seemed most deeply disturbed by Stella's upcoming marriage. With all the emotional turbulence swirling about her, Virginia, who had barely recovered from the trauma of her mother's death, was again haunted by hallucinatory visions, irrational fears, and thoughts of taking her own life. Dr. Savage and other specialists were summoned, and once again the patient was ordered to walk and eat more, do no lessons, and read and write as little as possible. Leslie took long walks in Kensington Gardens and talked books with Virginia, but Stella was the person with whom Virginia was calmest and most comfortable, so Stella took Virginia about with her and kept her close when they were at home.

Cast all too often in the role of unwanted chaperone to Stella and Jack, Virginia had a chance to look over her sister's fiancé at close quarters and did not much like what she saw. As Leslie had often observed, Jack was no intellectual. He was also not blond, handsome, and immaculately turned out like the Duckworths, nor tall, broad, and sinewy like the Stephen men. Schoolboy Adrian already towered over Jack. At fifteen, as she herself would later remember, Virginia Stephen was "extraordinarily unprotected, unformed, unshielded, apprehensive, receptive, anticipatory," a moth newly emerging from its chrysalis, wings still wet and fluttering.

The passion between Jack and Stella, which she remembered with such passion as a woman, had disturbed Virginia as a young adolescent. She had been given the "basic facts of life" and, oddly, it had been Jack Hills who gave them. Not content with offering the younger Stephen girls a concise summary of human reproduction, however, Jack Hills had gone further. He told Vanessa and Virginia that men not only thought about sex and talked about sex among themselves all the time, but they actually "had women." To Virginia this was incomprehensible. At sixteen, a keen student of ancient Greek, she knew about "sodomy" from Plato, but when it came to the social mores in her own world she was a complete innocent. The idea that men and women in the present were living by different moral codes, and that the purity men preached so constantly was for women only, baffled and upset her.

But even Virginia became cheerful as the wedding came near, and the delights of being a bridesmaid were made manifest in a most becoming custom-made dress and "a pendant gold watch from Dent's of Pall Mall" — a gift from the groom but no doubt shopped for by the bride. When Stella Duckworth walked down the aisle, the whole congregation was bathed in the radiance of her happiness, and when in April 1897 the married couple set off for their honeymoon in Italy, Virginia and her siblings all looked to the future with fresh hope. With Jack and Stella just doors away at Hyde Park Gate, perhaps home would cease to be a mausoleum to Saint Julia.

But then, a mere two weeks later, the young couple sent word that they were returning at once to Kensington. Stella was feverish, often in great pain, and unfit for travel. She urgently needed to consult her English doctors. Obviously the Italian honeymoon to which Jack Hills had looked forward so passionately had been a disaster, not an idyll.

Louise DeSalvo has a very dark reading of Jack Hills and his pursuit of Stella Duckworth. DeSalvo sees Hills as another version of the Victorian sadistic misogynist and reports that Violet Dickinson told Vanessa Bell that Stella's death was caused by her bridegroom's persistent and feral lovemaking on their honeymoon. I feel that DeSalvo is overstating her case here. Violet Dickinson was a close friend of the family at this time, but how she could have known what happened between Stella and Jack in Italy is unclear.

After the Hillses returned home, Virginia became increasingly nervous, irritable, scared. After happening to see several road accidents on nearby Kensington High Street, she refused to go out of the house: Woolf would re-create this feeling of irrational fear in her character Rhoda in *The Waves*. At the same time, Virginia resented the attention Stella was getting from family and friends and referred to Stella once in her diary as a fat cow who could bounce out of bed if and when she chose. If this seems unjust and harsh, let us keep in mind that the news of Stella's pregnancy would have been kept from the younger girls, increasing Virginia's confusion and distress.

Any resentment Virginia may have felt toward Stella was quick to pass. Stella was her surrogate mother, and, when Virginia came down with a bad cold, she was allowed to sleep in Stella's dressing room. Late at night, when Stella was seized by the agonizing pain that signaled the end of her illness and her life, George Duckworth had to carry the sleeping Virginia out of number 24 and along the street.

In the years to come, Virginia Woolf and her sister Vanessa would both agonize over the events of Stella's illness. How could such a happy, healthy young woman have been allowed to die? Based on the confused medical reports, a modern diagnosis might be that Stella Duckworth Hills was having recurring attacks of appendicitis. It is possible that Stella was pregnant when she returned from Italy or became pregnant soon after. With pus leaking into her abdomen, Stella was fighting off one round of infection after another, so her health would decline and then improve for no reason clear to medical science at the time. Her pregnancy complicated everything, and the best her eminent physicians could do was offer enemas and opiates and express cautious optimism.

When the appendix burst, there was nothing to be done. Confronted with a dying woman in agony, implored by her family to do something, anything, the doctors agreed to operate, but it was pointless. On July 19, 1897, Stella Duckworth Hills died of septicemia, much as her father had done twenty-six years earlier. Can one wonder that Virginia Woolf thought doctors usually did more harm than good?

After Stella died, Virginia had a major mental breakdown, making several suicide attempts. The shock and sorrow of losing both her mother and her sister in two years had upset her fragile mental equilibrium, but terror of an uncertain future also played its part in her collapse. A hypersensitive girl with a brilliant mind, teetering on the edge of adulthood, Virginia was appalled by the lessons on womanhood she had received from the two dead women.

In the eyes of their family and of society at large, both Julia and Stella were exemplary women who died young—forty-nine and twenty-eight—each after shedding her life blood on the altar of family. Did this mean that, to be a woman, one must give up the self and sacrifice to others one's own ideas, dreams, ambitions, and desires?

Virginia Stephen and her sister Vanessa adored their mother and loved their sister Stella very much. But they did not wish to be like them. In the future, each sister, in interactive but competitive ways, would set out to become a new kind of woman. For the time being, however, they had to put their longing for independence and their creative dreams on hold as their father made his long, agonizing journey into death.

10

A Close Conspiracy

FOR VIRGINIA and Vanessa Stephen, the death of their mother had been a tragedy, but Stella was there to take up the care of the household and Father and Laura, and they moved on. They were young. Vanessa turned eighteen, glided through ballrooms in satin and long, white gloves, much admired and with at least one young man — George Booth, the highly eligible son of old family friends — reportedly ready to go down on his knees, ring in hand. In the age of Victoria, death — women dying in childbirth, infants succumbing to diphtheria, young adults struck down by tuberculosis — paid regular visits to every family, so the Stephen sisters, though immensely sad because their mother had died, did not feel themselves singled out by fate. But when Stella Duckworth Hills died, unremarkable misfortune turned to silent disaster for her younger sisters.

The teenage Virginia Stephen, who was finding a refuge in ancient Greek literature, came to see her life as a mixture of Sophoclean tragedy and Gothic horror. "I do not want to go into my room at Hyde Park Gate," Virginia Woolf wrote in 1940, "I shrink from the years 1897–1904, the seven unhappy years. Not many lives were tortured and fretted and made numb with non-being as ours [hers and Vanessa's] were then."

That she was writing this in Sussex, as German bombers passed overhead on their way to London and she and Leonard made plans to commit suicide in the event of a Nazi invasion, was not incidental. That the fragmentary and incomplete and astoundingly beautiful and sad piece that would be called "A Sketch of the Past" was one of the last things she wrote is not incidental. The horror of war and the imminence of death by her own hand brought Virginia Woolf back in thought and memory to when she and her sister suddenly found themselves "fully exposed" at one and the same time to "the full blast of that strange character," their father, and to the smothering, sentimental, eroticized control of their older half-brother, George Duckworth.

When they were girls, Vanessa had dared to aspire to be a painter, Virginia to be a writer, but as they came into adulthood, both felt their ambitions smothered in the cradle like bastard children. The Victorian rituals and paraphernalia of mourning — the letters of condolence on notepaper edged in black, the wardrobe changes from black grosgrain to gray linen to white dimity — came to seem a mockery to them. To survive, Vanessa and Virginia formed a "close conspiracy," "a little sensitive center of acute life, of instantaneous sympathy, in the great echoing shell of Hyde Park Gate" ("A Sketch of the Past," page 143; further pages from this work are cited in the following sections).

Virginia cried out for mothering, and though older family friends like Anne Thackeray Ritchie, Violet Dickinson, and Beatrice Thynne did their best to give it, most of Virginia's mothering came from Vanessa. It was Vanessa, a strong, loving, reliable presence to whom nothing need be explained, who formed the center of Virginia's emotional matrix. Before sexologists like Havelock Ellis identified lesbianism as a feature on the social landscape, Englishwomen circa 1900 still quite unselfconsciously kissed and clung to one another, but the Stephen sisters were unusually demonstrative in their affection. Well into her twenties, Virginia had a way of sitting on Vanessa's knee and demanding to be petted as if she was five years old. "Sometimes," remarks Nigel Nicolson, a family friend and the coeditor of Woolf's letters, "Virginia loved her [Vanessa] almost to the point of thought incest."

ॐ

In the initial months after Stella's death, the grief of her sisters, along with their rage and bewilderment at the way she had been allowed to die, had to be suppressed, diverted, deferred. In the eyes of the world the feelings of Vanessa and Virginia seemed inconsequential in comparison to those of the bereaved males — the two widowers, Leslie and Jack, and Stella's brothers, George and Gerald — and each young woman reacted to the trauma of loss in ways that would set a pattern for their lives.

Virginia, "a porous vessel afloat in sensation, a sensitive plate exposed to invisible rays" as she later remembered herself, became delusory, refused to eat, and tried to kill herself. Virginia Woolf, we can now confidently assert, was afflicted by a severe and incurable mood disorder, and grief could, as her later life would show, be a trigger for it. Dr. Savage and the other medical experts consulted at that time were not using the word "mad" for Virginia, but, following the definitive consignment of her older sister Laura Stephen to an asylum, it hung in the air.

Virginia's breakdown was a dramatic expression of her grief and brought her the care and attention she craved. As a child Virginia had been a nervy, nerdy, will-o'-the-wisp of a child, yet sturdy and energetic, good at stump cricket, handy with a fishing rod. She read constantly and had lightning bolts of brilliance. One summer, when the pilchards finally crowded into the harbor at St. Ives, she wrote an account of the event and submitted it to the local paper. She did not score her first publication, but her brother Thoby, always so silent and hard to impress, told Nessa, who told Virginia, that he thought Virginia "might be a bit of a genius" (page 130). When she felt ignored or wronged, the girl Virginia would erupt into wild, vitriolic speech, her face turning bright red.

If Vanessa began in the family as "the Saint" or "Maria," Virginia was "the Goat" or "Billy," ready to kick you when you least expected it, or the monkey or "the apes," a mischievous simian collective, full of tricks, ready to bite. But after her breakdown of 1897–98, Virginia came to seem fragile, unreliable, and dependent. For the rest of her life Woolf would fight to establish herself as a caring subject, not just an object of care.

Vanessa meanwhile seemed calm and stalwart. She shouldered the triple burden of Father, household, and Virginia without fuss, and sealed tight the coffer of her own grief. Refusing to delve into emotion when she felt most injured or to dwell on the past, she moved through the unhappy present with a silent, steely determination to have her way as soon as she could. In comparison to her younger sister, Vanessa Stephen appeared to come through the double tragedies of her family unscathed, but the suppression of emotion came at a great psychic cost, twisting her nature in ways that, as we shall see, would shape the course of her life and the nature of her relationships with those she loved most.

ॐ

On the surface, life in the household of Leslie Stephen between 1897 and 1904 was humdrum, ritualized, conventional, often pleasant. As the sizable pack of letters to friends from this period attest, Vanessa and Virginia led a life of devoted usefulness and steady activity. They had been given "the rule of the house," and with all three older brothers in residence (Adrian was now at Cambridge University), they were responsible for supplying their men with good food, clean laundry, starched collars, and lavender-scented sheets.

One of the innovations that occurred after Stella's death was that Vanessa and Virginia, who had hitherto shared a bedroom, were given two separate bedsitting rooms on the fourth floor by George, who decorated the rooms at his own expense. During their free hours, between ten and one, Vanessa went off to the Royal Academy of Art to lose herself blissfully in problems of line and perspective, while Virginia went up to read and write in her diary and notebook and work on her Greek. After lunch, the Stephen women were permitted to receive visitors or put on their hats and gloves and go out to do errands — as long as one of them at least was home sharp at 4:30, to superintend the preparations of Father's tea. Then, presiding over the tea urn, they would take on the society manners they had learned from their mother and keep the conversational ball rolling smoothly, despite Leslie's pathetic requests to know what people were saying and his belligerent comments when the responses were shouted down his ear trumpet.

In the summer months, daily life was more varied and healthy, with opportunities for long walks and rides on horseback or bicycle and the simple pleasures, like butterfly hunting and wildflower collecting, that Virginia associated with the happy past at Talland House, in Mother's day. But beneath the surface, beneath what Virginia Woolf calls the "cotton wool" of unthinking, unreal "normal" life, a cauldron of bitterness, frustration, and fury seethed in silence in the hearts of two young women of exceptional talent and energy coming into adulthood.

The Leslie Stephen family had always been a microcosm of the general patriarchy in which men came first, as of right. With both Julia and Stella gone, Vanessa and Virginia now had to cater to and cope with their father's blind egotism, insatiable neediness, and cataclysmic rages. As Woolf reconstructs it, Leslie Stephen had been given to sudden eruptions of uncontrollable fury even as a boy. His mother tolerated them because his health was delicate. Subsequently, Leslie's two wives smoothed his feathers, deferred to him, bolstered him, allowed him to "say exactly what he thought, however inconvenient, and do exactly what he liked" (page 110). As Virginia Woolf writes, "it never struck my father, I believe, that there was any harm in being ill to live with" (page 109).

Between them, Minny and Julia had managed to turn a solitary, awkward bachelor, happiest when pitted against the elements on an Alpine crag, into an acceptably social being, taciturn and abrupt but willing to go out to parties in full evening dress, his beautiful wife on his arm, happy to be at the head of a big silver-laden dinner table at home, carving the roast for the assembly of friends, chatting amiably to the charming young lady strategically placed on his right. In the adoring warmth of the domestic setting his wives afforded him, Leslie Stephen had no need to rage. He felt like what he longed above all to be — a genius like Milton or Lord Byron or his father-in-law Thackeray, since to a genius all is permitted. This is the Leslie Stephen that Virginia Woolf so brilliantly portrays as Mr. Ramsay in *To the Lighthouse*.

But after Julia died, Leslie stopped going out, stopped traveling, stopped taking his great "tramps," became immured in his deafness, and found in neither of his remaining daughters the mirror of adoration to which he was habituated and addicted. Her father was, Woolf analyzes, "a man in prison, isolated. He had so ignored, so disguised his own feelings that he had no idea of what he was; and no idea of what other people were" (page 146).

Leslie Stephen still had a small group of young acolytes who came at times to pay their respects and listen to his perorations, and to them he never showed any sign of temper — he was always mild-mannered if terse, self-deprecating, modest about his life's achievements even when they were finally acknowledged with a knighthood. With his sons, especially Thoby, for whom he felt immense love and pride, Leslie tried out his old Trinity Hall boathouse manner, seeking manly fellowship and merry collegiality and finding forced smiles and grudging attention. To his sons Leslie Stephen seemed stuck in a remote past, more grandfather than father. Only with his daughters did Leslie feel able to express his sense of cosmic grievance, his bitter awareness of how far below genius he had fallen in his own estimation. Being with Father "was like being shut up with a wild beast," Virginia Woolf writes, with herself "a nervous gibbering little monkey . . . mopping and mowing and leaping into dark corners and swinging in rapture across the cage," and he "the pacing, dangerous, morose lion; a lion who was sulky and angry and injured; and then suddenly ferocious, and then very humble, and then majestic; and then lying dusty and fly-pestered in a corner of the cage" (page 116).

Virginia Stephen thought her father was a brute, but she also loved him, admiring the clarity of his thought, honoring his steady passion for the life of the mind, and seeing the pathos of his life. Silently, unapologetically, unreservedly, Vanessa hated the old man and wished for his death. In the two main partnerships of her post-Kensington life — with Clive Bell and Duncan Grant — Vanessa showed that she could tolerate almost anything in a man as long as he was not, in Woolf's phrase, "ill to live with."

ॐ

The problem of life with Father was, as the extant correspondence shows, one that could be shared with sympathetic women. To friends like Violet Dickinson and the Vaughan cousins, particularly after Leslie Stephen had his first operation for cancer, Virginia could write humorously that their household was constantly invaded by lachrymose old women. Aunts and cousins and elderly women friends came to sit and twitter unsought consolations as the sisters, grim-faced, poured tea and passed the mounds of cake and cucumber sandwiches ferried up on silver trays from the penumbral basement. But with Leslie deaf, absorbed in his books and his woes, and indifferent to the family around him as long as his material needs were met, George Duckworth became the man of the house. "And so," Woolf writes, "while father preserved the framework of 1860, George filled in the framework with all kinds of minutely teethed saws; and the machine into which our rebellious bodies were inserted in 1900 not only held us tight in its framework but bit into us with innumerable sharp teeth" (pages 131–32).

George's social aspirations for himself and his family were the obvious part of the problem he posed to his sisters. George's aim, Woolf sarcastically remarks, was to marry a woman with diamonds, employ a groom with shining buttons, and have entrée to court, and he appeared to have what it took to make a splendid marriage. He was, by his early thirties, private secretary to the rising politician Austen Chamberlain, was said to lead a blameless life (Jack Hills once assured Virginia Woolf that her brother George had been a virgin when he married), had more than a thousand a year in unearned income, and was unfailingly of service to women. George Duckworth was always ready to offer a hand out of the carriage, an umbrella in a surprise shower, or a carefully rehearsed compliment. He was handsome, six feet tall, with tightly curling black hair and the ears of a faun, and when he left for the office around 9:45 each day, he was immaculately turned out, from the top hat he shined up with the velvet cloth on the hall table to his "ribbed socks and perfectly polished little shoes." "When Miss Willett of Brighton saw George Duckworth 'throwing off his ulster' in the middle of her drawing room," records Virginia Woolf in her Memoir Club paper, "she was moved to write an Ode comparing him to the Hermes of Praxiteles — which my mother kept in her writing table drawer" (page 166).

But George had little piggy eyes and was, Virginia Woolf says, abnormally stupid, so perhaps he bored even the matrons and misses of Mayfair. Certainly, after several aristocratic young women had eluded his grasp, he seized with desperation on the need to take first Vanessa and then Virginia into society. Given the sad demise of his mother and his sister Stella, it was his, George Duckworth's, duty in life to introduce the Stephen girls to some "nice" people, people far above the ugly old bluestockings like Mrs. Humphry Ward, the weedy academics like Fred Maitland, the fuddy-duddy writers like Henry James, and the has-been painters like William Holman Hunt who still collected around his stepfather in Kensington.

During the London season, one of his sisters must accompany George to the dinners, and parties, and balls, and country house weekends for which the gilt-edged invitations piled up so gratifyingly on his mantelpiece. With a gloriously beautiful, marvelously intelligent sister on his arm, George Duckworth would no longer appear a dim bachelor whose Somerset ancestors had been in cotton, but a saintly young man, a golden halo encircling his black curls.

But George Duckworth did not see his Stephen sisters as just potential social assets in his quest to find a titled bride. He was, his sister Virginia opined, a man of powerful passion, and on one occasion he came close to acknowledging that he used her and Vanessa to take the edge off his sexual needs. When Virginia was just eighteen, George came to her bedsitting room — the room he had set up for her in the old nursery — and presented her with a small, inexpensive enamel pin. He and Vanessa, George said, had quarreled the night before. He had insisted that she accompany him to a party and she insisted that she would not go. This obdurate noncompliance, George obscurely intimated to Virginia, was a serious matter. Vanessa was forcing both himself and his brother Gerald into leaving the parental home and taking refuge in the arms of whores. Ergo, tonight Virginia must take up the part Vanessa was refusing.

And, as she relates it, Virginia did, not totally impervious to the romance of donning long gloves and satin slippers. She was whisked off to a dinner party given by Lady Carnarvon, the former vicereine of Canada, a lady whom George was once observed kissing and whose daughter Lady Margaret Herbert he would finally marry in 1906. Finding that Lady Carnarvon, though wearing a modest selection of the diamonds she had inherited from Marie Antoinette, was a pleasant enough woman, Virginia relaxed enough to suggest to the assembled party that men and women should get together to read and discuss the dialogues of Plato. At this, an icy silence fell over the dinner table, and things went no better at the theater, where the Carnarvon party, to its shock and horror, was treated to a finale in which a young man hotly pursued a young woman and finally managed to jump her. Virginia had actually understood very little about the risqué French comedy, but Lady Carnarvon was mortified, so the evening had not been a success. After being dragged off to yet a third party by George, Virginia got home to the silent house in the small hours of the morning, undressed, got gratefully into bed, and put out the light "when the door opened" and "someone entered."

> "Who?" I cried. "Don't be frightened," George whispered, "And don't turn on the light, oh beloved. Beloved —" and he flung himself on my bed and took me in his arms.
>
> Yes, the old ladies of Kensington and Belgravia never knew that George Duckworth was not only father and brother, brother and sister to those poor Stephen girls, he was their lover also. (page 177)

In a continuation of this set of memories, Woolf says that such an incursion happened more than once, that George himself switched off the light, that he would lie next to her in bed "cuddling and kissing and otherwise embracing me in order, as he told Dr Savage later, to comfort me for the illness of my father — who was dying three or four stories down of cancer" (page 182).

The reference to Dr. Savage is important. It seems that, when Virginia Stephen was institutionalized with a major mental breakdown in 1904, George Duckworth may have played a part in her paranoid hallucinations, and her doctor questioned him about his relationship with his sister. Certainly, biographers of Virginia Woolf have fallen upon these two passages and pointed the finger at George Duckworth as the cause of Woolf's inability to experience sexual pleasure and even the trigger for her madness. In her controversial 1989 book, Louise DeSalvo argued that Virginia Woolf's madness was the result of sexual abuse. Quentin Bell and Hermione Lee, while much more cautious in their parsing of the evidence, also come to the conclusion that the sexualized conduct of George and Gerald had a devastating effect on Virginia Woolf's whole life.

In the opinion of Quentin Bell, the nephew of both George Duckworth and Virginia Woolf, to his aunt Virginia as a late teenager "Eros came with a commotion of leathern wings, a figure of mawkish, incestuous sensuality. Virginia felt George had spoiled her life before it had fairly begun. Naturally shy in sexual matters, she was from this time terrified back into a posture of frozen and defensive panic." The biographer Hermione Lee is even more incisive: "There is no way of knowing whether the teenage Virginia Stephen was fucked or forced to have oral sex or buggered. Nor is it possible to say with certainty that these events, any more than Gerald Duckworth's interference with the child Virginia, drove her mad. But Virginia herself thought that what had been done to her was very damaging."

ॐ

When Virginia Woolf produced these revelations about (by this time) Sir George Duckworth to the Memoir Club in 1920 or 1921, others backed up her account. Older women, like her Greek teacher Janet Case, recalled feeling uncomfortable at the way George would kiss and embrace his sisters in public. Above all, with her usual dry humor, Vanessa Bell laughingly admitted that whatever George had done to Virginia, he had done to her too. She too had been provided by George with a bedsitting room of her own one story up from his, into which he could enter late at night with silent impunity. In fact, the available evidence makes it clear that Vanessa, not Virginia, was the principal target of George's predations. It is also clear that her reactions at the time were more complicated than the visceral repulsion felt by her younger sister.

Vanessa Bell at the beginning seemed admirably fitted for the role of society belle that her brother George planned for her. When she first appeared in 1898, with her black lace over a white underdress sparkling with brilliants, a perfect amethyst gleaming at her throat and a blue enamel butterfly pinned in her chignon — both the gifts of George — she took people's breath away. It was Virginia who sat in the ballroom reading *In Memoriam* while Vanessa danced every dance. It was Virginia who froze out young men at dinner parties with her erudite conversation, while Vanessa, who almost prided herself on not being an intellectual, was adept at keeping the conversational ball rolling in mixed company. Vanessa was reduced to tears when an evening dress she had made from a green upholstery fabric was greeted with cold contempt by George — "Tear that thing up"! — but it was Virginia whose bloomers fell down. Vanessa had possibilities, and George fussed over Vanessa's wardrobe, paid for her to have dresses from a fashionable *couturière,* gave her expensive jewelry and, to the envy of her brothers who were mad about hunting, a thoroughbred horse.

But then, as we have seen, things came to some kind of head between Vanessa and George. They had a violent quarrel over an invitation to Mrs. Maud Russell's select soiree, and George felt obliged to call in help from Virginia. Could it be that Vanessa simply could no longer bear the prospect of George coming to her room after the party? Certainly, it is at this point, according to Vanessa Bell's biographer Frances Spalding, that Vanessa became romantically involved with Jack Hills, her sister Stella's widower.

After Stella's death, Jack Hills had continued to be welcomed as a member of the Stephen-Duckworth family. He went on holiday with them, and Vanessa and Virginia were each allowed to take long walks with Jack as he clutched their hands and poured out not just his grief but his sexual frustration. That Jack Hills should fall in love with Vanessa is not hard to understand. He emerges from the memories recorded of him by Virginia Woolf and Vanessa Bell as a heterosexual man educated in the homosexualized culture of the boy's boarding school and the men's college, struggling throughout his twenties to find some honorable way to satisfy his sexual needs.

Attracted by beautiful, sympathetic Julia Stephen, Hills, as we have seen, fell passionately in love with her oldest daughter, and for almost ten years he loved and desired Stella Duckworth. But when, finally, they were married and permitted to be alone together on their honeymoon, things did not go smoothly between them. In a matter of weeks, Hills was back in Kensington, with Stella hedged in again by her stepfather and four brothers and with her needy younger sister often installed in her dressing room. For the first months of his marriage, his wife was intermittently ill, then, overnight, she was dead, and once again Jack Hills was consumed by frustrated sexual desire. But then, on holiday with the Stephens, there, holding his hand, listening raptly, full of sympathy, was Vanessa. And she looked so astonishingly like his dead wife — not the care-worn twenty-eight-year-old Stella whom he had married, but the incandescently pale eighteen-year-old Stella who had first lit the flame of his passion.

The Duckworth brothers may have been obtuse, but they knew that their old friend Jack was eaten up with sexual frustration, and they had tried to keep him and Stella apart during his eight-month engagement. Either they let down their guard after Stella's death or they were not present at the rented house at Painswick in 1900 when Jack and Vanessa went off on their long walks. So it was an immense shock to uncover, on the family's return to Kensington, the burgeoning love affair of Jack and Vanessa.

One evening, George came to Virginia's room and, in his usual round-about way, begged her to explain to her sister that, in England, it was impossible for Vanessa to marry Jack. Such a marriage was incestuous and therefore forbidden under English law. Virginia agreed to talk to Vanessa. She had never much appreciated Jack, and the idea that Vanessa might marry and leave her with father and brothers alarmed her. But when she tried to put George's case against the marriage to her sister, Vanessa was taken aback and very angry. Virginia, she felt, out of need, out of fragility, had betrayed her. "So, you too take their side," Vanessa coldly said, and though Virginia rallied to Vanessa's cause, a tiny crack now ran through the golden bowl of the sisters' relationship.

Stella's brothers may have been officious and ill-informed (Jack and Vanessa could easily have gone to France to be married, where it would have been both legal and far from rare), and they did not need Virginia's help in bringing Jack Hills to heel. But the Duckworths were not wrong in scenting something incestuous about the love that flared so quickly between Vanessa and Jack Hills. If a young woman was desperate to get away from home, marriage was indeed the obvious way to do it, and eligible young men like George Booth had once clustered around Vanessa. With the mourning period for Stella now over, the same young men could have come back, to the applause of society. A creepy repetition compulsion was at play in the family group at Hyde Park Gate, a preference for endogamy over exogamy that would have fascinated Freud. Mad Jem Stephen, too injured to conceal his passions, had pursued his cousin Stella round the house with rape in his heart. Leslie Stephen, after his wife's death, had clasped Stella to his bosom in part at least because she looked so astonishingly like his wife, Julia, as a young woman. Now Jack was wanting to marry Vanessa, a young version of his dead wife.

George Duckworth played a key role in ending Vanessa's relationship with Jack Hills, and perhaps to make amends, in 1900 he invited Vanessa to take a trip to Paris with him, at his expense. In 1902, George and Vanessa set off together again, for a more extensive trip to Rome. Both vacations were no doubt taken with groups of friends, but this is supposition, and the simple fact that Vanessa went away for weeks with George and his friends is surely a little odd. If Vanessa loathed and feared George, as we know from her own testimony that Virginia did, why did she agree to travel with him and give him more opportunities to express his feelings for the sister he addressed as "Beloved"? Did George behave with propriety, or did he take advantage of the times when they were alone together? If so, what was Vanessa's response?

Well, we can't even hazard an answer to those questions because we do not have the letters Vanessa is known to have written to Virginia when she was away. All we have is a letter from Virginia to George, telling him she had heard from Vanessa that she was having a splendid time in Paris with him: "My dear old Bar . . . Nessa's letters are frantic with excitement. My only fear is lest she find it all too fascinating ever to leave it. Don't let her get engaged to a charming French marquis — I am sure they have not the constitution of good husbands. And don't let her see too many improper studios — The artist's temperament is such a difficult thing to manage and she has volcanoes underneath her sedate manner."

Here Virginia, our future novelist, shows remarkable insight into her sister's character, and she is almost alarmingly prescient of Vanessa's future life. But the most interesting thing about this letter is that George Duckworth kept it all his life and thus allowed us to read it. If Vanessa was determined to get away from the Kensington past, George wanted to remember it.

The issue of the sisters' letters to each other is an important one to consider as we examine this period in their lives. The letter from Virginia to George is one of many written by the Stephen sisters from the final Kensington period that have come down to us. Letters from his sisters were among the papers left by Thoby Stephen when he died in 1906, and both Virginia and Vanessa wrote regularly to their female Vaughan cousins and their cousin-in-law

Madge Symonds Vaughan. The real trove of correspondence from this period was, however, addressed to two close friends, Violet Dickinson and Margery Snowden. Violet Dickinson was an old friend of the Stephen family, and a support to both sisters, but for Virginia she conceived a passion. Violet was perhaps the second person in Virginia Woolf's life to use the word "genius" of her, and Violet hoarded Virginia's letters. These would eventually number an astonishing 450, "recording a love that had grown old," as Woolf's editor Nigel Nicolson puts it. And if Violet was smitten by Virginia, Margery, an art school friend, was smitten by Vanessa and kept all her letters.

Demonstrably, preserving important letters was a practice built into the culture of the Stephen family and their friends and, given that Vanessa and Virginia Stephen circa 1900 had yet to prove themselves remarkable, their biographers have reason to be thankful for it. Yet the very wealth of information that has come down to us serves to hide a massive hole in the documentary evidence. Not a single letter from Vanessa to Virginia or Virginia to Vanessa has survived from their Kensington years. Yes, we know from Virginia's 1900 letter to George in Paris that, while Vanessa was away with their brother, she and Virginia corresponded regularly. What we do not have is any of those letters from Vanessa, or Virginia's replies.

The lack of any extant letters from before 1897 between the sisters is unsurprising. Since they lived under the same roof and took all their vacations together, they had no occasion to write to each other. However, once Vanessa began to leave home to visit friends or travel with George, the sisters are known to have corresponded almost every day. As Vanessa Bell told her daughter, Angelica, many years later, keeping in touch by mail was a small but key part of the maternal care that Vanessa gave and Virginia craved.

If you write and receive a great many letters, as these women both did, most of them will get thrown in the waste bin or lost in the move. But if only chance or neglect was at work here, one would expect at least some stray little postcard to have turned up. Letters from Vanessa were important to Virginia. They were a lifeline that kept her going as she worked in Vanessa's absence to keep their ailing father happy and the household ticking along. The letters would be something she kept and reread. I would lay odds that, as late as March 1904, when she was rushed into a private clinic, somewhere in her upstairs room at Hyde Park Gate, Virginia Stephen had a bundle of letters tied up in ribbon and marked "Vanessa."

The dates of the letters that have come down to us offer a hint as to how and when the Kensington letters might have gone missing. The first two extant letters in the sisters' correspondence were written by Vanessa to Virginia on October 25 and December 7, 1904. The first letter we have from Virginia to Vanessa, a brief note ("We missed you today. Here is a check . . ."), is tentatively dated by editors to October 1907. The first substantive letter from Virginia to Vanessa was written on August 4, 1908.

From this point until Virginia's death in 1941, the sisters kept at least some of their letters to each other, thus opening a door into their lives and their relationship for posterity. We know when they stopped by the fishmongers and asked the maid to bring in the dessert, what they liked for tea and avoided for dinner, where they bought their books and their paints, the way they handled menstruation. We know that they were both capable of whipping up a sponge cake, making quarts of strawberry jam, planting and weeding large gardens, and keeping chickens and ducks. We know that they could name every butterfly in their flowerbeds and mend their own bicycle tire punctures. Once you enter the great mound of firsthand evidence left to us by the Stephen sisters, you begin to feel that you know more about them than about women in your own family.

Bu this plethora of later information makes all the more significant the fact that the first two items in the sisters' correspondence date to late 1904. This was the year their father died. It was the year Vanessa, Thoby, and Adrian moved from Kensington to 46 Gordon Square, Bloomsbury. It was the year that Virginia fell into her most dangerous nervous breakdown to date, and thereby lost control over her possessions for some seven months. The first letters Woolf would keep hold of for the rest of her life were, precisely, two letters from Vanessa from that difficult period in her life in 1904–5, when Vanessa acted as Virginia's de facto legal guardian. They were letters that provoked in Virginia a growing resentment at being separate from her surviving family and treated as a helpless object of care. They were letters to which Vanessa never had access.

For, while Virginia was away being cared for by friends, her siblings were moving to their new home, and the efficient Vanessa was entrusted by her brothers with the job of emptying out the parental home in preparation for tenants. It was Vanessa who made the main decisions about what to take, what to store, what to give away, and what to throw out, and her charge would have extended to packing up the things her sister had left at Hyde Park Gate when she fell ill. Thus, it is interesting to find Vanessa Bell declaring in that very first extant letter, of October 25, 1904, that she was not at all sure it was a good idea to keep one's letters.

Vanessa was moved to write this because Frederic Maitland had undertaken the biography of their father, Leslie Stephen, and Virginia had been entrusted with the delicate task of reading her parents' private papers and deciding what the biographer might see and what he might publish. As we have seen, Jack Hills, Stella's widower, had been especially concerned that Maitland might delve into the issue of Laura, for whom he served as legal guardian, and, to Virginia's indignation, he expressed doubt that Virginia was the proper person to represent the family's interests. Vanessa, it seems, was somewhat of Jack Hills's mind. She told Virginia, "I am glad that I shall never be celebrated enough to have my life written. There's something horrible to me, which I expect the true literary mind does not feel any sympathy with, in any third person's reading what was meant to be only between two. I shall burn all my letters someday."

Virginia, as Vanessa implies in her letter, saw the keeping of old correspondence differently. Already at age twenty-two, Woolf saw letters as vital historical documents and an important literary genre. At twenty-seven, as we shall see, Woolf would be busy writing a "biography" of her sister Vanessa based on the letters her father had put together when writing the *Mausoleum Book*. All her life, Virginia Woolf searched the familial past, reading old documents, stirring up memories, reminiscing with her younger brother, Adrian, who also found comfort in the old days. She wrote sketches of the past, memories of Hyde Park Gate, and in her novels she offers versions of family members — her parents in *To the Lighthouse,* Stella in *The Years,* and Thoby in *Jacob's Room.* In 1941, in what proved to be the last months of her life, she was still drafting

"A Sketch of the Past," and the letters she and Vanessa had exchanged between 1897 and 1904 would have been of immense value to her. It is hard to imagine that, at the time of her father's death, in February 1904, Virginia Woolf threw away or destroyed all of the letters Vanessa had written her.

But, as she confessed in that first precious letter we have, Vanessa Stephen was not a literary scholar, and old letters seemed to her more dangerous than precious. As she set about the enormous task of clearing out the contents of 22 Hyde Park Gate, it is not hard to imagine Vanessa coming upon her letters to her sister, and her sister's to her, and deciding that certain family matters were best kept from prying eyes. When, her job well done, Vanessa Stephen locked the front door of Hyde Park Gate and walked away, she intended to put the past behind her. In the years ahead, as we shall see, she will systematically edit old Kensington friends and relatives out of her world. By the 1930s, as her son Quentin Bell once observed with amusement, if she picked up the phone and heard the voice of her oldest brother, now Sir George Duckworth, she pretended to be the maid.

She and her older sisters, Stella and Laura, and to a lesser degree, her younger sister, Virginia, had all been subjected to forms of abuse that Vanessa Stephen was determined to put out of mind and off the record. In this determination to shut away, close off, and deny events of a sexually subversive nature, Vanessa Bell, often heralded as an avatar of female sexual liberation, was in fact much closer to her Victorian father, who saw it as his duty to wipe all stain from the public image of his biographical subjects, than to her uninhibited modernist sister Virginia.

PART IV

Old Bloomsbury

11

From Cambridge to Bloomsbury

BLOOMSBURY IS a small district close to everything in central London, home to upmarket offices, institutions of higher learning, and medical facilities, and characterized by its squares, with their delightful little fenced-in, tree-shaded gardens. Today the area is peppered by blue National Trust plaques informing the alert tourist that Roger Fry had his Omega Workshops here, and Lytton Strachey a pied-à-terre just around the corner from his beloved British Museum. In the center of Tavistock Square is a portrait bust of Virginia Woolf. Today Bloomsbury is very select — though not, as I discovered in 2017, rock-on ritzy like Hyde Park Gate — but in the summer of 1904, when Vanessa Bell moved herself and her siblings there, Bloomsbury was shabby and a tad bohemian, though not actually scabrous, like Paddington. The Stephen children's new address at 46 Gordon Square made their Belgravia and Kensington acquaintances shudder, but for Vanessa, that was no small part of its attraction. She was closing the door on her old Kensington life, and if the Maxses and the Ritchies and the Booths now hesitated to visit the Stephens, *tant mieux!* After her celebratory visit to Paris following her father's death, in February 1904, Vanessa Stephen was becoming decidedly Francophile.

The plan to move to Bloomsbury and rent out 22 Hyde Park Gate had been set in motion in the period 1903–4, as Leslie Stephen's life was obviously coming to an end. Gerald Duckworth, long eager to have a bachelor flat of his own, was fully behind the move, and George had to give up his plan to move in with his younger siblings when he became engaged to Lady Margaret Herbert. The loss of George was not mourned by any of the Stephens, but it tightened the finances of the move. Luckily some Pattle descendant in the family diaspora proved willing to pay several hundred pounds for the Stephens' portrait of their great-aunt Virginia Somers, which helped with the refurbishing, and Vanessa was already envisaging a lighter, sparer look for her living space. Vanessa, Thoby, and Adrian adored their new home and at once found themselves caught up in a happy whirl of social events. Their marvelous cook from Hyde Park Gate, Mrs. Sophie Farrell, and Maud (no surname available), her friend the parlor maid, had moved with the Stephens from Hyde Park Gate, so they were well looked after at home, and in the evenings they joyously got all gussied up and went to parties. Thoby was observed, to the surprise of Vanessa, enthusiastically waltzing one young lady after another around a ballroom.

Virginia had been involved in the house hunting, but the death of their father, though long anticipated, was harder for her than for the other three Stephens. For some months, she was carried along, spending some chilly, somber weeks in Pembrokeshire and then whisked off to France by Vanessa. Leslie Stephen had been too parsimonious to finance trips to the Continent for his children, even his sons, so Vanessa, who had gone abroad twice with George, was determined to give her siblings a taste of Parisian living. Virginia had seemed to enjoy herself while she was away, but, as she was to discover in the years ahead, hectic activity, especially paired with emotional distress, was a reliable trigger for her mental disorder. When she got back to Kensington, it hit her hard that she was losing her childhood home, with all its memories, that Father was at last irrevocably dead, that she missed him and yet was horribly glad he was gone. Virginia was once again, as after the deaths of her mother and her sister Stella, beset by hallucinatory voices, refused to eat, could not sleep, tried to kill herself, and came once again under the care of Dr. Savage.

On Savage's advice, Vanessa kept her sister out of London for some four months, and Virginia was shuttled about the countryside to live in the homes of protective and watchful friends — Violet Dickinson in Welwyn, Aunt Caroline

Stephen in Cambridge, Madge Symonds Vaughan in Giggleswick, Yorkshire. Virginia was grateful for the kindness of friends, but as her mania receded, she felt bored and unsettled, and food and sleep remained a problem. "Oh how thankful I shall be to be my own mistress and throw their silly medications down the slop pail!" Woolf wrote to Violet Dickinson. "I never shall believe, or have believed, anything any doctor says — I learnt their utter helplessness when Father was ill. They can guess at what's the matter but they can't put it right." She resented being excluded from the new post-Kensington world, and found attempts to negotiate with Vanessa frustrating. "Nessa contrived to say that it didn't much matter to anyone, her included, I suppose," wrote Virginia to Violet from her aunt's home in Cambridge, "whether I was here or in London, which made me angry, but then she has a genius for stating unpleasant truths in her matter-of-fact voice."

Given permission at last to go home, Virginia Woolf at first reveled in the simple pleasures of being alone in her own room for hours at a time and allowed to explore London with no one but her dog. She kept very busy at her standup desk, as she was now determined to make her way in the world of publishing, and her friends Violet Dickinson and Nelly (Lady Robert) Cecil were eager to use their influence on her behalf. Beginning with reviews and little sketches and essays for a women's religious periodical called the *Guardian,* Woolf graduated with remarkable speed to writing regular if anonymous pieces for that august periodical the *Times Literary Supplement*. Within a year, modest checks for three guineas and five pounds began landing on her doormat, harbingers of better commissions to come and a welcome addition to the income of a woman with some hefty medical bills who needed to come up with her share of the rent and expenses at Gordon Square. Little by little, Virginia felt better able to go out in the evenings for small parties, enjoyed meeting up with old friends, and began to feel at ease in the new social circle her siblings had developed. Very soon the high point in her week became her brother Thoby's "at homes" on Thursday evenings.

Those "Thursdays" are what Virginia Woolf, in a paper she delivered to the Memoir Club in late 1921 or early 1922, calls "Old Bloomsbury." It was, as she records, in the months between early 1905 and summer 1906 that the

Bloomsbury group first emerged — so let us now figuratively hop on the tube as far as St. Pancras Station and catch the train for the short ride to Cambridge. The Bloomsbury group, everyone agrees, came out of Cambridge.

With three exceptions, all the foundational members of the Bloomsbury group — Thoby and Adrian Stephen, Lytton and James Strachey, Maynard Keynes, Clive Bell, Desmond MacCarthy, Leonard Woolf, and Saxon Sydney-Turner, plus the ancillary members Roger Fry, E. M. Forster (known as Morgan), Harry Norton, Gerald Shove, and Goldsworthy Lowes Dickinson — were undergraduates at Cambridge University. The three main members of the Bloomsbury group who could not put B.A. M.A. (Cantab) after their names were Duncan Grant and Vanessa Bell, two painters dedicated to their art who did not give a toss for Cambridge, and Virginia Woolf, who certainly did.

A number of the Cambridge men (Fry, Lowes Dickinson, MacCarthy, Forster, Lytton Strachey, Sydney-Turner, Woolf, Keynes, James Strachey, Norton, Shove, in order of election) were Angels, that is to say members of the Cambridge Conversazione Society, and this turned out to be highly relevant to the evolution of the Bloomsbury group. Small, self-selecting, highly secretive, and disproportionately influential, the Society, as it was known to its members, had its own customs and its own jargon. Its undergraduate members were known as Apostles because only twelve could be members at any one time. Those being considered for membership in the Society were referred to as embryos. Apostles, once they graduated, became Angels. Deeply immersed in philosophy and lovers of Plato, the members of the Society dubbed themselves "real" and dismissed everyone else as merely "phenomenal."

The moral philosophy and code of conduct that would distinguish the Bloomsbury group has often been traced back to a single paragraph in *Principia Ethica,* the early masterwork of the Apostle G. E. Moore:

> By far the most valuable things which we can know or can imagine are certain states of consciousness, which may be roughly described as the pleasures of human intercourse and the enjoyment of beautiful objects ... That it is only for the sake of these things — in order that as much as possible of them may at some time exist — that any one can be

justified in performing any public or private duty; that they are the *raison d'être* of virtue; that ... they form the rational ultimate end of human action and the sole criterion of social progress; these appear to be truths which have been generally overlooked.

Convinced that Moore had provided them with a philosophical basis for their personal conduct, Lytton Strachey and John Maynard Keynes, as both Apostles and Angels, were influential in transforming the Society from a place where homosexuality flourished unobserved to a place where homosexuality was zealously canvassed and actively practiced. These two men subsequently became leaders of the Bloomsbury group, and Virginia Woolf, in her 1921–22 account of the group between 1904 and 1914, states unselfconsciously and with complete accuracy that "Old Bloomsbury" was obsessed with "buggery" — this being the group's preferred term for homosexual acts.

ॐ

The Cambridge of the Bloomsbury group was the construct of a specific period and a specific caste. Let us think of it for the time being as "Cambridge" in quotation marks, a group of elite young men that came into full flower in the early nineteenth century. This "Cambridge" had only a name in common with the small, nondescript town in the fens, and it was only one small but defining part of Cambridge University. In the years when the seeds of Bloomsbury were germinating, the colleges that composed Cambridge University had an unofficial hierarchy. Trinity and King's were at the top and Downing and Selwyn somewhere at the bottom, with all the others (St. John's, Clare, Queens', Christ's, St. Catharine's, Jesus, Pembroke, Emmanuel, Peterhouse, Magdalene, Fitzwilliam, Corpus Christi, and Trinity Hall) jostling for their places in the middle. "Cambridge" was, almost to a man, Trinity and King's.

I say "to a man" since, at least until the 1910s when the Newnhamites Katherine "Ka" Cox, Alix Sargant-Florence, Fredegond Fisher, Karin Costelloe, Frances Marshall, and the Olivier sisters, Bryn, Noël, Marjorie, and Daphne, clamored for membership, "Cambridge" was to all intents and purposes an exclusive men's club. The (then two) women's colleges, Newnham and Girton, stood outside the college hierarchy, a position symbolized by the long, hilly bicycle ride that separated the village of Girton from Cambridge. By 1882, Newnham and Girton students had been given leave to attend university classes and lectures and to sit the university Tripos examinations. They were not precisely Cambridge undergraduates, however, since it was not until 1947 that Cambridge University bestowed degrees upon women.

The men of "Cambridge" distinguished themselves by looking for approval, status, and ideas not from their dons or their parents or society at large, but from one another. As Clive Bell would later write in his 1933 paper to the Memoir Club, "We were anarchical in our disrespect and in our skepticism; we had broken more successfully with the public school tradition; we were desperately serious about art and frivolous about almost everything else. We were not ashamed of being childish, of playing stump cricket, ping pong & racing pennies along the coping of Trinity Bridge; we were never boyish."

Most "Cambridge" men went in for classics and moral sciences, Triposes that did not require a man to get up in the morning, and it was a mark of intellectual superiority in them to leave university lectures and classes to the women. Girtonians and Newnhamites, it was darkly whispered at Trinity and King's, had been known to lose sleep over exams and even typewrite their supervision essays.

Enrolled in the shortest, least-demanding course of higher education known to the civilized world, the men of "Cambridge" were joyfully free to create a lifestyle and forge a philosophy. For as little as nine terms of only eight weeks each, plus a few weeks at the end of each year for exams and the big June festivities known as "May Balls," a "Cambridge" man was free to do pretty much as he liked at any time of the day or night, in the company of men very like himself, who lived conveniently fifty paces across the courtyard or two flights down the staircase.

To take examples from the members of the Bloomsbury group, Saxon Sydney-Turner might read Plato and Lucretius in the original as easily as you or I read our email. Harry Norton might devote himself to higher mathematics while Roger Fry spent his days fossicking around between the chem lab and the Fitzwilliam Museum. Lytton Strachey and Leonard Woolf might gather around the charismatic young philosopher George Moore and argue the night away over what exactly was meant by the true or the good, and whether one could know if that chair there was, epistemologically speaking, really there. Thoby Stephen or Clive Bell might punt and picnic, row crew and ride to hounds, take long walks, eat a great many hot buttered muffins at teatime, get roaring drunk at night, leave his living room in a sordid mess of empty bottles and cigar butts, and retire to bed happy, knowing that, by the time he arose, his gyp would have cleaned it all up. In most cases, "Cambridge" men did some combination of all the above, but if Sydney-Turner, Fry, Norton, and Moore got scholarships and starred Firsts, they did not boast about them. If anything, the "intellectuals," to use Clive Bell's word, looked with envy at men like Bell and Stephen, who barely scraped a Third in Tripos exams but projected an image of easygoing, socially accomplished, outdoorsy virility.

"Cambridge" around the turn of the twentieth century had a mythic status in the minds of upper-class Englishmen. It was alma mater (benevolent mother) to a young man who, at eight or seven or even six years of age, had been delivered by his treacherous biological mother into the hands of the prep-school matron, whose job it was to make sure the right starched collars got back to the right boy and to dollop out cod liver oil. "Cambridge" was a cozy womb where such a man felt nourished, comforted, protected, cherished. It was, memoirs of the period breathlessly concur, an intoxicating, life-changing, never-to-be-forgotten experience. It was as if, like the prisoners in Plato's *Republic,* young men emerged in Cambridge, dazzled, from the dark cave of mere representation into the sunshine of reality — and if that comparison seems far-fetched, remember that "Cambridge" men were force-fed classical Greek and Latin from the age of six. In a social caste that tended to dismiss religious faith as old hat, "Cambridge" filled a deep spiritual need. As E. M. Forster put it, at Cambridge "body and spirit, reason and emotion, work and play, architecture and scenery, laughter and seriousness, life and art — these pairs which are elsewhere contrasted were there fused into one. People and books reinforced one another, intelligence joined hands with affection, speculation became a passion, and discussion was made profound by love."

Virginia Woolf knew "Cambridge" could not have been hers, even if she had gone to Newnham, like some of her girl cousins. She both longed for the experience her brothers and friends had known at the university and dismissed it as a pillar supporting male privilege. In an incomplete and unpublished review of *Euphrosyne,* a small collection of poems brought out in 1905 by four of her "Cambridge" friends, she remarked caustically: "One would think that life was a very poor business save for those three or four years at College & that if he failed to enjoy those, you had not much to promise him in this world or the next — unless indeed there is some kind of university in the fields of Paradise."

Virginia Woolf was right to be caustic. *Euphrosyne* sank like a stone.

In a section of his 1933 *Essays in Biography,* John Maynard Keynes, who, as the government's top economist, had lent the Bloomsbury group much of its luster, made a strong, even emotional case that Bloomsbury had grown out of the Cambridge Conversazione Society, and specifically from the philosophical ideas of his fellow Apostle and revered friend G. E. Moore. Following the publication of Keynes's book, this claim was genially contested by Clive Bell in a talk he gave to the Bloomsbury Memoir Club. Bell asserted that Keynes, who was some two years younger than Thoby Stephen, Woolf, Sydney-Turner, and himself, had become part of the Bloomsbury group only some years after he went down from Cambridge.

Asserting the primacy of "phenomenal" Cambridge over "real" Cambridge, Bell insisted that the first stone in the "foundation for Bloomsbury" had been laid by the Midnight Society. This was a play-reading group that Clive himself, along with Thoby Stephen, Leonard Woolf, Lytton Strachey, and Saxon Sydney-Turner, started at Trinity. In the typed draft of his speech to the Memoir Club now in the Wren Library at Trinity College, Cambridge, Bell fondly recalled how, when they had finished reading the week's chosen play, in the early hours of the morning the Midnight Society members would partake of cold pie and punch. In the ensuing inebriation (we are not talking Hawaiian punch here), they would pour out into Great Court and Nevile's Court around 5 a.m., "chanting the better-known verses of Fitzgerald's Omar Kayam to the tune of Abide with Me, or the choruses from Atalanta in [Calydon]. The Goth [Thoby Stephen] sang loudest and most heartily and most completely out of tune."

"Atalanta in Calydon" is a not unimportant detail here. The poem was the first success of Algernon Charles Swinburne, and as far as I have been able to make out through its fog of verbiage and pseudo-Greek allusions, it celebrates the joys of hunting, but it was its homosexual subtext, apparent to male readers at the time, that made it a success.

For it was not mere happenstance that both Keynes and Bell were writing these accounts of the origins of Bloomsbury in the early 1930s. This was a time when many prominent men in England were denouncing Bloomsbury as a noxious collection of effete homosexuals and their sycophantic female acolytes. The artist and critic Wyndham Lewis led the attack from the British art world. The novelist D. H. Lawrence paid a visit to Cambridge, and after an evening at high table with Lytton and Maynard at their most wittily scatological, denounced them and all their kind as corrupt and unclean. Bertrand Russell, himself an Angel, opined that the Cambridge Conversazione Society lost its claim to intellectual superiority when it became militantly homosexual under Keynes and Strachey. Russell had a point. The letters of Strachey and Keynes prove that they elected "embryos" like Arthur Hobhouse on the grounds that they were handsome and thus potential "catamites." "Catamite" is a very old English word for a young male lover.

In the 1930s, homophobic criticism of Bloomsbury was still voiced only in private, but it was dangerous. Ever since the last decade of the nineteenth century, public opinion in Britain, inflamed by the popular press, had become increasingly homophobic, and for the first time, upper-class gay men who cruised the streets and bathhouses of London for working-class sex partners, as many of them did, ran a small but real risk of discovery, prosecution, and imprisonment.

Since the death of Lytton Strachey in 1932, the Bloomsbury man at particular risk in this climate of opinion was John Maynard Keynes. From his schoolboy days at Eton and right into his thirties, Keynes had a series of passionate relationships and numerous casual couplings, which for some years he systematically recorded in his diary. In his conversation and in his correspondence with his like-minded Apostle Lytton Strachey, the young Keynes was forthright about his sexual tastes and activities, and he subscribed with great enthusiasm to Lytton's gospel of the higher sodomy as laid out by Plato in the *Phaedrus*.

While living as a fellow of King's, a college famous for homosexual dons like Oscar Browning, Keynes enjoyed a measure of protection. He once jokingly remarked that he had been shocked to find himself the only man in Cambridge who was not openly an "invert." But once Keynes became influential in government and diplomatic circles and moved to London, he needed to exercise extreme caution in his private life. It would take only one disgruntled lover to make a call to a London newspaper (the "blackmailer of Bordeaux" is one notation in Keynes's diary) to put the great economist's career in jeopardy.

In 1925, to the horror of his last known "catamite," Sebastian Sprott, and to the exasperated incredulity of his old chum Vanessa Bell, John Maynard Keynes, soon to become the 1st Baron Keynes of Tilton, got married to the tiny, effervescent, quintessentially feminine Russian ballerina Lydia Lopokova. Needless to say, in his 1933 autobiographical essays, Keynes gives not the slightest hint that he was (or had been until recently) an active homosexual, and that several of the men he refers to admiringly in the book (Lytton Strachey and Duncan Grant, for example) had been not just his friends, but his lovers.

As Keynes took steps to rub the homosexual text off the blackboard of his life, he confidently expected his "Cambridge" friends to rally to his side, and no one was in a better position to do this than Clive Bell. As the acknowledged Don Juan of Bloomsbury, Clive was just the right man to put a new spin on the tricky issue of homosexuality from Cambridge to Bloomsbury.

In the draft of his talk to the Memoir Club, Clive Bell took a subtly different approach from the one Virginia Woolf had taken in her talk some ten years earlier. He did not contradict what she had said about Old Bloomsbury's "obsession with buggery," but he insisted that both he and his best friend, "the Goth," who might rightly be considered the father of Bloomsbury, thought it was a huge joke.

> The Goth [Thoby Stephen] and I were not in love though later when we had both gone down Lytton occasionally amused himself by pretending that we were ... the Goth and I used occasionally to discuss what he called (referring I imagine to a correspondence with Leonard [Woolf]) the Singhalese vice. He was then inclined not to censure, but to [illegible] and I to laugh ... My relations with the Goth, intimate

and affectionate at the same time [were] wonderfully impersonal as our correspondence shows . . . There is little or nothing about the feelings, no gossip, not a word about what is called unnatural vice — and next to nothing about natural.

This is a clever piece of rhetoric. Bell was able to refer openly to Lytton Strachey's homosexuality since Lytton had died in 1932. He could reliably cite Leonard Woolf, the husband of Virginia and another man with impeccable heterosexual credentials, to suggest that homosexuality is a foreign vice, endemic in Asian cultures like that of Sri Lanka, and perhaps an unfortunate byproduct of Britain's colonial past. As Clive Bell would have it, in the Cambridge he knew, homosexuality was not a vice. It was an interesting matter for intellectual discussion and casual conversation but not a subject for reproof or censure. He and the Goth happened to desire women while Lytton desired men, but they all three lived together like the three men in the tub. Among true friends, it did not matter who was "gay" and who "straight," to use the terms of today.

This seems, at face value, a very modern position to be taking in the early 1930s. Many of us in twenty-first-century American society would agree that the barrier separating the gay and the straight should be a permeable membrane, not a wall, a matter of interactions between individual men and women in specific contexts, not of fixed categories. Part of the importance and the mystique of Bloomsbury is that copious documentation exists to prove that the group endorsed, lived, and promulgated this view from the very early years of the past century.

However, once you look at the hard evidence on British homosexual life provided by historians like Graham Robb and Matt Houlbrook, it becomes plain that this tolerant attitude, this delicate and affectionate balance between men of different sexual tendencies and activities, was not new to Bloomsbury. It was, in fact, eminently Victorian. In the twentieth century it would be forced to move underground, but as recent television chronicles of the private lives of prominent men such as Princess Margaret's sometime husband Antony Armstrong-Jones and the political leader Jeremy Thorpe reveal, it was still going strong in Oxford in the 1940s and 1950s.

What distinguished Bloomsbury from "Cambridge" was the grafting of two women, Vanessa Stephen Bell and Virginia Stephen Woolf, onto the all-male, gay-straight-who-cares? stock and, for a brief but key moment in his Memoir Club talk, Clive Bell recognizes this. "The second stone" in the foundation of Bloomsbury, he tells us, "was laid, it is my belief, when I went to stay with the Goth at Fritham [one of Leslie Stephen's summer rentals], and met the two Miss Stephens, but that event is far too exciting & significant to be touched on . . . It deserves an evening to itself."

On the surface, this statement is a graceful acknowledgment by Clive Bell of the presence in his audience of Mrs. Bell and Mrs. Woolf. But what Clive, with his studied yet perfunctory bow to Vanessa and Virginia as the two mothers of Bloomsbury, fails to point out is that, whereas "Cambridge" had indeed for generations pieced homosexuality seamlessly onto homosociality, it was ignorant and suspicious of women to the point of enmity. This was an issue that both the founding mothers had been obliged to meet head-on.

For if the Apostles were all men, as were all the members of the Midnight Society, this was not just because the women of Girton and Newnham were all locked away behind high walls by eight o'clock every evening — though they were. By their own free testimony, Thoby Stephen, Clive Bell, and Leonard Woolf, the three Bloomsbury men who identified as straight and are known to have had sex with women before marriage, did not see their love affairs and the women they slept with as subjects for conversation and comment. Women were not interesting per se, and discussion of ladies who might become wives was off limits among gentlemen. In contrast, the love affairs between male friends were a subject of absorbing interest, and as Bell volunteered in his Memoir Club talk, he and Stephen and Woolf, all straight men, discussed "buggery" all the time, both in private and in semiprivate groups like the Apostles.

Between the men of "Cambridge" or the men of "Oxford" and young women of their own class, there was, the novels and memoirs of the period indicate, an abyss that could be bridged only by a proposal of marriage. Whether gay or straight, whether enthusiastic copulators like Bell and Keynes or aching virgins like Sydney-Turner and (until his late twenties) Lytton Strachey, they all were united in a profound alienation from women, which could at any moment turn into overt misogyny. This was true even of the most outstandingly heterosexual man in "Old Bloomsbury," Thoby Stephen, Virginia Woolf's adored older brother.

Thoby Stephen was a complicated man. In his childhood, according to Noel Annan, inertia seems to have alternated with neurotic attacks verging on the suicidal, not unreminiscent of those that would afflict his sister Virginia. Notably reticent, Thoby had in him a resistance to meeting the expectations of others that aroused the respect of his peers if not his superiors. In adulthood, that resistance manifested itself in a kind of animal impassivity—Henry James, who had known the Stephen children from infancy, once called Thoby Stephen "a big mild mastiff." After scraping into Cambridge University on the strength of his family connections, Thoby came down after four years with a third-class degree and began to read for the bar. He had no obvious enthusiasm for the law at the outset, and a barrister's life was a risky one. Energy and verbal fluency were the main engines of success, but good social connections and an independent income certainly helped. Thoby Stephen was not brilliant, not articulate, and not wealthy.

Seen from the outside, Thoby Stephen was a failure, but in the eyes of his father, who, to use Virginia Woolf's word, "demonstratively" worshiped him, of his friends from his prep schools, Evelyn's and Clifton College, and finally of his fellow undergraduates at Cambridge, Thoby Stephen more than made up for all debits with muscular masculinity. Once installed in his rooms at Trinity College, Thoby Stephen, some six foot four and broad of shoulder, found himself swimming in a sea of admiration, an object of explicit desire for gay Lytton, of silent envy for straight Bell, Woolf, and Sydney-Turner.

In the section of "A Sketch of the Past" where she discusses how she and her brother interacted during their father's final years, Woolf says that she and he would argue vigorously over books and ideas, but never speak of anything personal or exchange confidences. Thus, as she puts it, Thoby Stephen passed from boyhood to adulthood before her eyes "without saying a single word that could have been taken for a sign of what he was feeling." Thus, as I would put it, Thoby Stephen, an adult living in the same house as his father, and with great influence over the older man, led a secret life of his own far from his family and closed his eyes to what his father and elder stepbrother were doing to his two sisters.

Julian Thoby Stephen, age twenty-six

In her 1922 novel *Jacob's Room,* Virginia Woolf stretched her imagination and staged a little scene that explores the homoerotic current that ran silently beneath her brother's friendships with other men. In the novel, Jacob Flanders, the protagonist Woolf based on her brother Thoby, is sailing around the Scilly Islands off Cornwall in the small boat of his university friend Timothy Durrant, a character based in part on Thoby's close friend Clive Bell. Tiring of the Shakespeare play he has brought along for light reading, Jacob plunges into the sea for a swim — and if the modern reader assumes that he must be wearing a bathing suit, that reader would be wrong. When Jacob gets back in the boat after his swim, one might equally assume that he would towel off and put his clothes back on, but again one would be wrong. Jacob puts on his shirt and then sprawls in the bottom of the boat to dry off, naked from the waist down, calmly, confidently offering to his smaller, plumper friend at the tiller a full view of his magnificent male assets.

The importance of this scene lies in its sexual ambiguity, and here Woolf had a radical insight into the male society of her period that is easy to miss. This is not a gay seduction scene. Flanders and Durrant are not homosexual, and they do not want to have sex together. But they come from a class of boys who grew up in an all-male culture where homosociality blends imperceptibly into homosexuality, where boys and men, quite literally, are often thrown into a bed with each other. Flanders is the son of a poor widow, while Durrant is affluent. He owns the boat and stands at the tiller. To establish dominance in the male hierarchy, Flanders, sure of his straightness, unselfconsciously borrows from the gay playbook. Flanders is big, and both men know that is what counts.

Woolf then contrasts Jacob's cool display of raw masculinity with his best friend on the boat with his silent, awkward behavior in mixed company. The sailboat moors near the home of Timothy's widowed mother, and it turns out that in these social circles, packing a dinner jacket, however crumpled and salt-soaked, is de rigueur, whereas a bathing suit and a towel are not. Jacob is given a very warm welcome by Mrs. Durrant and, as for Timothy's sister, Clara Durrant, she is struck dumb with admiration for tall, broad, handsome Jacob. Jacob finds Clara attractive as well, and the two are allowed a few minutes alone, picking fruit for lunch, but it is not enough. Clara is inhibited and inexperienced, and Jacob rarely says much of anything to anyone, so nothing of any significance happens between them.

Back in London, Jacob and Clara occasionally meet, but he is busy reading Sophocles and Marvell with his Cambridge friend (a version of Lytton) and cavorting at bohemian parties. Nothing is said between Jacob and Clara, and while he goes off to fight in World War I and die, Clara stays at home to pour the tea and watch the rain fall. Here, in a few brief paragraphs, Woolf illustrates the sad, silly result of the social chasm separating English-public-school-educated men from women of their own social caste.

In real life, as opposed to his sister's imaginative reconstruction of him, a strong strain of active misogyny seems to have emerged in Thoby Stephen after he left Cambridge, moved back home to Hyde Park Gate, and began to move in mixed company. He was happiest in his evening sessions with Lytton Strachey, under whose guidance he found his way through the Elizabethan poets and the eighteenth-century wits, the more obscure the better. The two friends also reveled in ancient Greek plays like *Lysistrata,* even though they were obliged to read them in the bowdlerized English versions created by Victorian scholars like Benjamin Jowett. Unlike their friend Saxon Sydney-Turner or indeed Thoby's sister Virginia, neither the Goth nor "Strache" could ever really wrap his head around Greek grammar.

In a letter to Clive Bell, probably from the spring of 1903, soon after they came down from Trinity, Stephen enthusiastically urges Bell (at this point "Cambridge" men always used surnames among themselves) to read Aristophanes' play *Lysistrata.* This, my reader will remember, is the comedy in which the female protagonist, Lysistrata, seeks to convince the women of Athens that they could end the Peloponnesian War if they would only refuse to sleep with their men until a peace is negotiated. In his letter to Bell, however, Stephen chooses to cite a passage from the play that has nothing, or nothing apparently, to do with the central theme of women attempting to exercise power:

> Have you read the Lysistrata of Aristophanes? It is beyond glorious throughout and there is one passage that pleased me more than a little. 'Once upon a time there was a certain youth called Melancthon who fled from marriage and departed to the desert and dwelt upon the mountains; there did he hunt the hare — aye he had a certain dog — and never did he come back to his home for the loathing he felt. So did he hate all the female [illegible] and so do we like Melancthon — all we who are wise.' Rather a locus classicus that I think for hunting with Artemis rather than yielding the heart to Aphrodite.

So, even as young Thoby Stephen was sizing up the pretty heiress Irene Noel as a possible wife and mother to his children while relieving his sexual needs — if we are to believe his sister's account in *Jacob's Room* — with artists' models and typists, he advocates the simple ascetic life of the celibate huntsman, far from the snares of Aphrodite. He yearns in fact for the life sung by

Swinburne in the poem "Atalanta in Calydon," which he had bellowed forth in the Great Court at Trinity a few years before.

Thoby Stephen's jejune espousal of the life of the mythical, solitary male huntsman shows that "Cambridge" men, gay and straight, carried an atavistic hostility to women into the new Bloomsbury experiment. Can we wonder, thus, that Clive Bell never expanded upon his single sentence, attesting that, if Bloomsbury had two fathers — himself and Thoby — it also had two mothers — Thoby's two sisters, Vanessa and Virginia?

Virginia Woolf, of course, as a woman, and one who had never even been to school, much less university, was supremely "phenomenal," in Apostle jargon, and this fact became clear to her on a visit to Cambridge in 1909. Already an established journalist in London and a well-known wit, Virginia Stephen was staying with her old friends the Darwin sisters in their home on Silver Street in Cambridge, and was taken for tea at Trinity College. There she found herself in the rooms of James Strachey, the younger brother of her good friend Lytton Strachey. James had called in his fellow undergraduates Harry Norton and Rupert Brooke to help him cope with the female Darwin party.

Thanks to all the biographical minutiae that have been published about the men associated with the Bloomsbury group, we now know quite specifically that, at the time of the Darwin tea party, these three young men were embroiled in a complicated, absorbing gay triangle. Harry Norton was madly in love with James Strachey, who was passionately in love with Rupert Brooke, and Brooke, the gorgeous red-blond idol of Trinity men and Newnham women alike, was trying to figure out where his sexual inclinations might lie. It is unclear how far Woolf was aware that this trio of young men was seething with passion, but she saw that they were struggling to maintain even a surface politeness toward women visitors, and recorded this in her notebook:

The three young men sat in deep chairs; and gazed with soft intent eyes into the fire. Mr. Norton knew that he must talk, and he and I spoke laboriously. It was a very difficult duet; the other instruments keeping silent. I should like to account for their silence; but time presses and I am puzzled . . . these young men are evidently respectable; they are not only "able," but their views seem to me honest and simple. They lack all padding; so that one has convictions to disagree with, if one disagrees. Yet, we had nothing to say to each other; and I was conscious that not only my remarks but my presence was criticized. They wished for the truth and doubted whether a woman could speak it or be it.

Intuitively Virginia Woolf had put her finger on the philosophical version of misogyny that undergirded the ancient varsity world of her father, her brothers, and so many of her close friends in Bloomsbury. In Cambridge, women and the pursuit of truth were antithetical. It was that simple and that basic.

❧

Having, as the saying goes, "gone up" as freshmen, after a mere twenty-four or thirty weeks the men of "Cambridge" had to "go down," and when they did, they often fell hard. In a letter to his glorious new Oxford friend Bernard Swithinbank, Lytton Strachey described the horrid fate of his Trinity friend Saxon Sydney-Turner, who, upon leaving Cambridge, had been obliged to get a job.

> When I first knew [Sydney-Turner] he was a wild and most unrestrained freshman, who wrote poems, never went to bed, and declaimed Swinburne and Sir Thomas Browne till four o'clock in the morning in the Great Court at Trinity. He is now a Civil Servant at Somerset House, quite pale and inanimate, hardly more than an incompletely galvanized dead body . . . I feel that he'll be a tragic figure, if only he was aware of his tragedy. But then how can you be sure he *isn't*? *In appearance* he is small, bloodless, and effacé; he looks like some puzzled night animal blinking in the unaccustomed daylight.

Obliged to cede their comfy college sets to the incoming generation, the men of "Cambridge" hauled their trunks off to the far outskirts of the town, where the Victorian brick railway station seemed to symbolize the horrors facing them. Thus, Lytton wrote to Leonard Woolf in April 1905, "when Cambridge is over, when one is cast into the limbo of unintimacy, of business, of ugly antiquity — is there any hope?"

It was out of an unsatisfied longing for their alma mater, lodged in the hearts of Thoby Stephen, Clive Bell, Lytton Strachey, Saxon Sydney-Turner, and Desmond MacCarthy, that Bloomsbury grew. By 1904 all these men found themselves scattered about London, Stephen as a reluctant law student, Sydney-Turner as a resigned clerk at Somerset House, MacCarthy as a struggling journalist, Strachey licking his wounds after Trinity's rejection of his thesis on the statesman Warren Hastings. Bell was also back in London, having spent a year in Paris neglecting the Archives Nationales in favor of the bistros and ateliers of Montmartre. The huge, sprawling metropolis of London could not have been more unlike Cambridge, but it did at least have excellent public transport and, with the Royal Mail delivering three times a day on weekdays, the men of "Cambridge" had no trouble keeping in touch. Even those obliged to slave away for a living or live off their mothers could afford postage stamps, rides on the underground, and the occasional taxi. If all else failed, like their Victorian fathers, they walked. Even spidery Lytton thought nothing of walking ten miles across the city in the small hours of the night.

Thus, when Thoby Stephen announced that cocoa, whiskey, and biscuits (by which he meant something like arrowroot cookies) would be on hand for any friend who cared to call at 46 Gordon Square on Thursdays after dinner, his Cambridge friends, with a kind of desperate enthusiasm, headed for Bloomsbury. "Those Thursday evening parties," Virginia Woolf later recalled, "were, as far as I am concerned, the germ from which sprang all that has since been called — in newspapers and in novels, in Germany, in France — even, I daresay in Turkey and Timbuktu — by the name of Bloomsbury."

Lytton, Clive, Desmond, and Saxon, along with friends and relatives of theirs like James Strachey and Gerald Shove, were drawn to Gordon Square in the first place because "the Goth" had summoned them. By extension, the house in Gordon Square became, in Lytton parlance, "the gothic mansion" and Thoby's two sisters "the Visigoths." All the same, the Thursday night "at homes" were not an immediate success. When Vanessa and Virginia evinced an interest in meeting his friends, Thoby saw no way to keep them out of their own living room, and Lytton gloomily reported to Leonard on June 20, 1905:

"Later on MacCarthy and I went to the Gothic at home, which is now ruined by the presence of Vanessa and Virginia. Besides them and the Goth there were Gerald Duckworth, Turner and Bell. Very queer. The Goth and Turner have tea regularly in Bell's rooms in the Temple. The other day I went and it was purely Cambridge."

In her Memoir Club talk "Old Bloomsbury," Virginia Woolf explains why she was eager to be present at the "Thursdays." Her brother Thoby, she says, had "a great power of romanticizing his friends," and he had described Bell as "an astonishing fellow," "a perfect horseman," "a sort of mixture between Shelley and a sporting country squire." As for "Strache," he was a man who read Pope and had French pictures on his walls, "the essence of culture ... exotic, extreme in every way ... a prodigy of wit." Woolf, "a man who trembled all over," was as remarkable as Bell and Strachey yet quite different, "so violent, so savage; he despised the whole human race." Too bad he was in exile in Ceylon. As for Turner, he was "an absolute prodigy of learning ... who had the whole of Greek literature by heart."

When these demigods actually arrived at Gordon Square, however, shaking off their umbrellas and removing their galoshes, they proved to be rather a letdown to the two young women. Here were no handsome, suave old Etonians in Savile Row suits like George and Gerald Duckworth, but what Henry James memorably called "grubby poodles." "I had never seen young men so dingy, so lacking in physical splendor," Virginia Woolf remembered. Almost worse than the appearance of Thoby's friends were the long, tedious silences that prevailed at the beginning of each Thursday. These astonished Vanessa and Virginia, sitting quiet in the shadows and waiting. They had been trained by their mother to keep the conversational ball rolling. But then one man would raise the question of "good" and its relation to "art," and suddenly the talk flamed up and grew hot. Thoby's friends were back in "Cambridge" again, at a meeting of the Apostles or the Midnight Society, and they put down their cocoa and talked.

At first the two women held back, but soon Virginia especially felt able to put her oar in, and when she put her shoulders into the stroke, the men present forgot she was a woman. "It was some abstract question that drew out all our forces," Virginia recalled, and then never have I listened so intently to each step and half step in an argument. Never have I been to such pains to sharpen and launch my own little dart . . . It filled me with wonder to watch those who remained in the argument piling stone upon stone, cautiously, accurately, long after it had completely soared out of my sight . . . At last, rumpling his hair back, [Saxon] would pronounce very shortly some absolutely final summing up. The marvelous edifice was complete; one could stumble off to bed feeling that something very important had happened.

This was, in Virginia's memory, the miraculous thing she called "Old Bloomsbury." It was a place where she was suddenly judged on the quality of her ideas and her information, not her hats or her dress fabrics. Throughout her life, the people she met testified to the extraordinary effect Virginia Woolf had on them, but, especially before her marriage, the sharp brilliance of her mind and the wide range of her reading did not make social life easy for her. Even Virginia's father, while happy to share his love of ideas and books with her, would have much preferred Thoby to be the writer-scholar and Virginia a normal girl, obsessed with beaus and love letters. But now, in Gordon Square, dressed in her daytime skirt and shirtwaist, Virginia felt able to move out of the shadow, give voice to her ideas, and show what she knew. If someone contradicted her, she argued right back, and the words "I must say you made your point rather well" made her happier than any bouquet of flowers had done in the past.

To be treated as a mind by clever men, to be made a kind of honorary member of the Cambridge Conversazione Society, was a big step in Virginia Woolf's intellectual development. All the same, by 1907, when, as we shall see in the next chapter, her brother Thoby was dead, she began to realize that something had always been off kilter at the Thursday meetings. To be treated as a man was no longer enough for her; in fact, it rubbed her the wrong way.

In her 1922 account of "Old Bloomsbury" Woolf tried to grapple with the fact that, though she and her sister had been granted membership to an exclusive male club, it was only as Thoby Stephen's sisters, the "Visigoths." As independent persons, as women, as themselves, they were still, in some strange way, not present in "Old Bloomsbury."

I knew theoretically, from books, much more than I knew practically from life. I knew there were buggers in Plato's Greece; I suspected — it was not a question one could just ask Thoby — that there were buggers in Dr Butler's Trinity [College] Cambridge; but it never occurred to me that there were buggers even now in the Stephens' sitting room at Gordon Square. It never struck me that the abstractness, the simplicity which had been so great a relief after Hyde Park Gate was largely due to the fact that the majority of the young men who came there were not attracted by young women. I did not realize that love, far from being a thing they never mentioned, was in fact a thing which they seldom ceased to discuss . . . Those long sittings, those long silences, those long arguments . . . still excited me much more than any men I met with in the outer world of dinners and dances — and yet I was, dare I say it, intolerably bored. Why, I asked, did we have nothing to say to one another? Why were the most gifted of people so barren? Why were the most stimulating of friendships almost the most deadening? Why was it all so negative? Why did these young men make one feel that one could not honestly be anything? The answer to all my questions was, obviously — as you will have guessed — that there was no physical attraction between us.

I quote Woolf at length here because hers is an acute and important argument as American society, in the second decade of the twenty-first century, debates how men and women can interact in a professional and intellectual context for the benefit of all equally. Desire, Woolf is telling or reminding us, is the stimulus that sets our neurons sparking, that makes the meeting of minds so exciting, so productive. This does not mean that desire must lead inevitably to copulation — to use another favorite Bloomsbury word. But when the current of desire is shut off, things become barren, deadening.

In "Cambridge," men clear across the spectrum of sexuality were plugged into the circuit of desire, and this gave a passionate intensity to the brief weeks when they were "up" at university. Both Lytton Strachey, an active and ideologically committed homosexual, and Leonard Woolf, a shy, uncertain heterosexual, felt the current of desire, and each was in his own way transformed by it. But women had no part in "Cambridge," whether as a social structure or as a philosophy. To put it in the terms of twentieth-century feminist theory, women were the alien, the other, the negative to man's positive, matter to man's mind, chaos to man's order, night to man's day, "o" to man's "1," an empty hole fashioned to receive man's powerful member.

While the Goth lived, the current of desire ran beneath the Thursday meetings and passed through his two sisters. That Vanessa and Virginia both bore a strong physical resemblance to their brother Thoby was not incidental, and, as we shall see in the next chapter, the current of desire was already running silently between Vanessa Stephen and Clive Bell. But in November 1906, Thoby Stephen died, Vanessa and Virginia both emerged from the shadow of his dominance, and under their leadership the Bloomsbury group took a new social and sexual turn. By 1914 it was already splitting in two directions, which ran close to each other and even joined up at points, but were distinct. In remembrance of Proust, whose great novel was being published at precisely this time, I like to think of them as Vanessa's Way and Virginia's Way. How that division came about will be the subject of the next two chapters.

12

The Landmark Year

BY THE summer of 1906, cracks were developing in the façade of happy life for the four Stephens at 46 Gordon Square. As we saw in Chapter 4, his sale of the Thackeray manuscript had given Thoby Stephen some free money and with it a confidence in his ability to support a family on his fees as a barrister. His sisters knew that their elder brother was intent on finding a wife and that, once Thoby married and moved out, life would be more difficult. Living expenses would have to be divided by three, not four, and, even with Virginia now in good health and earning a little supplementary income, there would be an unwelcome tightening of the purse strings. Adrian appeared to have no plans beyond his next visit to the opera with Sydney-Turner and his next practical joke, and Vanessa found that she could not trust her younger brother with even simple things, like luggage. On the way to the big society wedding in Somerset of George Duckworth and Lady Margaret Herbert, at which Vanessa was to be bridesmaid, Adrian had managed to leave their bags at Swindon Station. Of course, arriving late by dint of losing track of the bridesmaid's dress could be interpreted as a Freudian error on the Stephens' part. They found the thirty-four-year-old bride, whose personal stock of information ran from fish forks to serving game in season, an incredible bore.

Virginia, savoring her new independent life and intent on her writing, was happier in Bloomsbury than she had been since her mother died, so she was alarmed when one day her sister remarked that she supposed that sometime they must all get married. Vanessa was three years older than Virginia, and once Thoby was gone, her status as a single woman would be exposed. Vanessa had been running a household for over ten years, and even the most fuddy-duddy aunties seemed not to expect Miss Stephen to ask an older female relative to live with her. On the other hand, once a woman was accepted by society as old enough to live by herself without a chaperone and take responsibility for her younger siblings, she looked to the world uncomfortably like an old maid.

Whereas the odds on Thoby's success in the marriage stakes improved as he got older, Vanessa's did not. She was closer to thirty than twenty and seems to have had no suitors since her disastrous relationship, at twenty, with Jack Hills, her sister Stella's widower. Vanessa loved to tease Virginia about the passion she inspired in women like Violet Dickinson, and Vanessa was quite aware that her artist friend Margery Snowden adored her, but a Boston marriage had no charms for her. After the move to Bloomsbury, Vanessa Stephen made herself very busy, going to lots of parties and attending a lot of meetings, but she did not get engaged. For a woman who looked in the mirror every day and saw herself beautiful, this was, to say the least, galling.

The ambition to become a painter, which Vanessa had long nursed, did not improve her marriage prospects. In England, being an artist was still not quite respectable even for men, and professional ambition of any kind in a woman was not considered attractive in 1906, or indeed in 1956. But there was also something about Vanessa Stephen that men found intimidating, and in the autobiography he wrote in old age, her brother-in-law, Leonard Woolf, was moved to analyze exactly what that was.

Vanessa was certainly handsome, Leonard tells us. He retained a clear memory of the effect that the "extraordinary beauty" of both the young Miss Stephens had had on men like him, and he says that most people considered Vanessa the more beautiful of the two Stephen sisters. And yet, he continues,

> to many people [Vanessa Bell] appeared frightening and formidable, for she was blended of three goddesses with slightly more of Athene and Artemis in her and her face than Aphrodite. I myself never found

her formidable, partly because she had the most beautiful speaking voice that I have ever heard, and partly because of her tranquility and quietude. (The tranquility was to some extent superficial; it did not extend deep down in her mind, for there in the depths there was also an extreme sensitivity, a nervous tension which had some resemblance to the mental instability of Virginia). There was something monumental, monolithic, granitic almost in most of the Stephens . . . There was a magnificent and monumental simplicity in Thoby which earned him his nickname of the Goth. Vanessa had the same quality expressed in feminine terms . . . There was often something adamantine in the content and language of her judgements. It was the strange combination of great beauty and feminine charm with a kind of lapidification of character and her caustic humour which made her such a fascinating person.

But then, in 1906, a highly eligible suitor presented himself to Vanessa Stephen, and an ardent one at that, a man who in honor of her beauty filled his flat with red roses when he was expecting her for a dinner party. Perhaps the ardor was the problem. The man was Clive Bell, but Vanessa did not return his passion, or so she said in 1906.

Vanessa had first gotten to know Bell (as she then called him) in Paris in 1904, at the end of the European trip she and her siblings took soon after their father's death. Clive Bell was then living in Paris, supposedly researching a book on the Congress of Verona but in fact enjoying *la vie de bohème* with members of the expatriate British artist colony. With great enthusiasm, Clive squired the Goth and his sisters around the studios of painter friends like Gerald Kelly and took them to deliciously louche establishments like the Chat Noir in Montmartre. Vanessa was enchanted, all her notions confirmed of how much more interesting life was outside Kensington.

Back in London, as we have seen, Thoby began his Thursday "at homes" in early 1905, and Clive Bell started turning up regularly at Gordon Square. Initially this was because he was Thoby Stephen's closest friend, but increasingly it was because he was fascinated by Vanessa. Clive's quick tongue and social adeptness rescued many of the Thursday sessions from tedium, and when he also began attending the Friday evenings, when Vanessa was at home to her friends in the art world, she was pleased. Bell had been introduced to the work of painters like Degas and Toulouse-Lautrec by his first lover, Anne Raven-Hill, so he came over as something of an expert on modern French painting. That he was starting an art collection of his own did not detract from his popularity with Vanessa's artist friends.

Clive Bell was a hunting man who enjoyed chasing women even more than foxes. The "adamantine," *noli me tangere* air of the beautiful Miss Stephen posed a challenge for him, but mere flirtation was out of the question at Gordon Square, with the young woman's two hulking brothers always at hand. Thoby Stephen, in particular, was well aware of his old friend's reputation as a womanizer, so Bell made it clear from the outset that his intentions toward Miss Stephen were strictly honorable. As an educated man of good family and independent means, Clive Bell was a most eligible suitor, and moreover, he and Vanessa Stephen had many interests in common. She clearly enjoyed his company, and their good friend Lytton Strachey was ready to swear that Bell was head over heels in love. Thus, when Bell duly proposed, he was confident of success, and when Miss Stephen refused, he was taken aback. After proposing a second time and receiving a second no, Bell went off to his family's lodge in the Highlands of Scotland to stalk stags, hook trout, and lick the wounds to his ego.

We have exact information on why Vanessa refused Clive's proposal of marriage since two letters containing her explanation have come down to us, one to Clive himself and a second to her closest friend, Margery Snowden. She liked Clive better than any of her friends, Vanessa wrote. She enjoyed his company enormously and would miss him terribly if he dropped out of her life. She wished him well and ventured to hope that he would soon find an occupation commensurate with his talents. But, to her great regret, she did not see herself married to him.

Let us pause here and pay attention to the fact that Vanessa Stephen — who had recently admitted to her sister that she wanted to be married and was receiving, as far as is recorded, her first marriage proposal in almost eight years — not once, but twice, turns down a highly eligible man she confesses to liking very much indeed. Hey presto, we are back in the Hyde Park Gate echo chamber again, with Vanessa weirdly reenacting her sister Stella's double refusal of

Jack Hills circa 1890. Both Stella and Vanessa expected and were expected to marry, and yet both, when initially faced with an actual, physical, passionately desiring suitor, were shy like young mares before their first stallions. Something deeper than mere Victorian maiden modesty is going on here.

Clive Bell had created an awkward situation at Gordon Square, and in August the four Stephens were happy to be off on an expedition to Greece and Turkey. Thoby, who had initiated the idea of the expedition and was paying most of the expenses from his Thackeray windfall, had made detailed plans for the trip. He and Adrian would depart London a couple of weeks ahead of their sisters, travel through France by train to Trieste, and then take a boat down the Dalmatian coast to Montenegro. From there they would set off on horseback, get the ferry to Patras, and then strike inland on mules to meet up with Vanessa, Virginia, and their friend Violet Dickinson. Thereafter the whole party would tour Athens and other great classical sites in the Peloponnese and make a side trip to the Euboean peninsula, where their friends the Noels had an estate at Achmetaga. Irene Noel, a vivacious girl and an heiress to boot, was spending the summer in Greece with her family, and Thoby was eager to press his suit with her.

Virginia looked forward to seeing Greece as eagerly as her older brother did. She was fascinated by classical civilization and had made great strides in her ability to read Greek under the enlightened tutoring of the Girton graduate Janet Case. After a frenzy of packing in the August heat, Vanessa too was eager to get away, but at some point on the sisters' long journey, she took ill. When she and Virginia were joined by their brothers in Olympia, Vanessa could not get out of bed.

In itself, Vanessa Bell's illness was unremarkable. In the early twentieth century there were any number of bugs eager to colonize immunologically unprepared tourists, and there were no good medications. Basically, an English traveler in foreign parts expected at some point in his holiday to come down with something, take to his bed and the chamber pot, and call in the local doctor. This person would hurry over, prescribe some vile concoction, and wait for his patient to get better so he could present his bill. On her honeymoon with Max Mallowan in 1929, Agatha Christie unwisely indulged in an orgy of shellfish in Athens and got very serious food poisoning. When her Greek-speaking husband told her he had to leave her on her sickbed since he was urgently expected at an archaeological dig in Syria, Agatha was not pleased. But she duly recovered, got herself back to England without fuss, and did not hold it against her Max. Just such a response might have been expected from the competent and independent Miss Stephen, who in Italy and France in 1904 had not allowed the bedbugs and primitive outhouses to spoil her pleasure. Yet now, apparently after coming down with a routine stomach ailment, she went to bed and stayed there.

If Thoby and Adrian Stephen had arrived in Olympia, Greece, on September 13, 1906, to find their sister Virginia being fussed over by a pack of doctors, they would have been worried but not surprised. The Goat, in their view, had always been jumpy and unpredictable — capricious, in fact. Vanessa, on the other hand, had always been the sturdy, sensible, let's-just-get-on-with-it sister, the one a brother could rely on to send him jolly food parcels at school or make sure he didn't leave his Latin crib sheet in his bedroom. In Father's hideous final years, while everyone else was tiptoeing around, Vanessa actually dared to stand up to the old man. Vanessa was strong, Vanessa was brave. When had Vanessa ever been ill? But now, quite suddenly the tables were turned, and it was Vanessa, not Virginia, whom Thoby and Adrian found lying upstairs in the shabby little Greek hotel, all weak and weepy.

And if Vanessa was, inexplicably, in bed, Virginia was full of fun and fizz, mopping the brow, swatting the flies, emptying the bedpan, the whole Florence Nightingale–Julia Stephen routine. She reveled in being the strong, protective sister at last and produced a side-splitting account, full of gastric and intestinal minutiae, of how Vanessa had been taken ill on the sea voyage from Brindisi to Patras. Recovering from their initial shock and assured by the local sawbones that Miss Stephen would be fit again in no time, Thoby and Adrian were happy to sit tight for a couple of days, soak their saddle sores in the tub, send out the dirty laundry, catch up with the letters from home, and get in a good tramp around the first of the ancient sites on their list.

Given the new tragedy lying in wait for the Stephen children, let me pause once again to note that Thoby and Adrian Stephen had not been close as children. They were separated by three years in age and by Virginia, an intervening sister whose sparkle stole the family show. Thoby had been sent away to prep school when his little brother was barely out of rompers, and Adrian, nicknamed "the Wombat" as a chubby, solemn child, had been Mother's special pet, her "Joy," and resented as such by the older children. But now, age twenty-three, six feet five inches tall, broad-shouldered, and handsome in the bony, big-nosed way of the Stephen male, Adrian could look his older brother in the eye, share an equestrian adventure in Montenegro, and jaw companionably of an evening about the excellences of Plato and Aristophanes and the unexpected horror of retsina. The expedition to Greece was a time for brotherly bonding, though it would never have occurred to these two conventional, taciturn young men to say so.

Thoby was cross about the way his sisters seemed to take it in turns to fall apart. Somehow women did not quite fit in Greece, Thoby felt, and all his precious plans for the great Greek adventure were threatened by Vanessa's illness. Adrian, whom one can picture freshly bathed, wearing a clean shirt and "Oxford bags" trousers held up by his old Trinity tie, saw things Thoby's way but refused to be downcast by Vanessa's illness. Adrian had not been sent away to school until he was eighteen, and he felt wiser in the ways of women. "Don't worry," let us imagine opera-loving Adrian telling Thoby. "Let's face it, *la donna è mobile,* and everyone gets a gyppy tummy on those Greek ferry boats. In no time Vanessa will be sitting on her camp stool under her silly green-lined umbrella, posing the local peasantry against picturesque ruins."

But instead of getting better, Vanessa got worse. On the train home from visiting the sites at Epidaurus, Mycenae, and Tiryns, she collapsed and had to be left behind with Violet while the other three Stephens went off to be feted by the Noels at Achmetaga. The fivesome then went to Athens, where Vanessa saw a doctor who recommended hot goat's milk. Virginia, still chirpy and intestinally unchallenged, recorded that she was so intent on reading Mérimée's *Lettres à une inconnue* (recommended to her by Lytton) that she kept letting the goat's milk boil over. With the women busy in the sickroom, the Stephen brothers took side trips, snoozed in the sun over their pocket Homers, and argued at length about a stretch of road from Portsmouth to Hindhead — "Definitely macadamized." "Definitely NOT!"

When the time came to depart by ferry to Istanbul, Vanessa was on a medical regimen of several bottles of champagne a day, no doubt an improvement over boiled goat's milk, but she still had to be carried to the boat on a litter. Soon after their arrival in Turkey, Thoby left for England, and the other three, along with Violet, did not prolong their stay. Islam had failed to enchant, and Vanessa was still barely ambulatory, so they took berths on the Orient Express and set out for home. By the time they were on the ferry from France to England, Violet Dickinson was complaining of feeling very ill, and when the party arrived at Victoria Station, George Duckworth was on hand, with a trained nurse. Thoby, George reported, had come down with something — the doctors said malaria — and having heard how ill Vanessa had been, George was taking no chances with the health of his beloved sister.

George need not have worried, at least not about Vanessa. Within days of arriving back in London she was writing letters, asking friends to come and cheer her up. Within two weeks she was not only well on the road to full recovery but, as we shall see, in radiant high spirits — which raises a question. What exactly was it that made Vanessa Stephen so horribly ill she had to be carried onto the ferry for Constantinople? This is a question that puzzled her doctors at the time and has puzzled biographers since. Hermione Lee reports that one Greek doctor diagnosed appendicitis, but it is not clear what Lee's evidence is for that diagnosis. The dangers of allowing an infected appendix to go untreated were clearly understood in 1906, appendectomies were both common and lucrative, and yet none of Vanessa's doctors offered to open her up. In fact, the new flock of doctors summoned to Gordon Square by George Duckworth to examine his sister came down on the side of "hysterics" — or, in modern Harley Street parlance, a nervous breakdown. For the Stephen-Duckworth family, that diagnosis was partly reassuring — but only partly. On the one hand, nine years earlier, Vanessa's half-sister, Stella Duckworth Hills, had died of what was very probably peritonitis. On the other hand, a nervous breakdown was not something the family took lightly, given Virginia's recent history.

To compare the life-threatening illness of Virginia in 1904 and Vanessa's version of Montezuma's revenge in 1906 seems spurious on the face of it. In fact, however, the comparison between the sisters is very much to the point. Let us remember what Leonard Woolf tells us about his sister-in-law: "The tranquility [of Vanessa Bell] was to some extent superficial; it did not extend deep down in her mind, for there in the depths there was also an extreme sensitivity, a nervous tension which had some resemblance to the mental instability of Virginia." Leonard's insight is confirmed by a letter Vanessa wrote to her painter friend Margery Snowden in which she refers to her "blue devils," periods of depression in her life that could, she wrote, last "for weeks or even months."

As I have noted earlier in this book, severe neuroticism and chronic depression were endemic in the Stephen family, but the question now becomes this: What did Vanessa Stephen have to be so neurotic and depressed about in 1906? The tragedies of her youth — her mother's rapid descent into death when she was fifteen, her sister Stella's tragic death when she was seventeen — were well in the past. When their father, Leslie Stephen, died, Vanessa was ready to confess that she had actually dreamed of killing the old man. What, after so many tears and tribulations, could reduce a stoic, strong-willed, pleasure-loving woman like Vanessa Stephen, with nothing wrong with her that the doctors could detect, to two months of inconvenient and expensive invalidism in Greece? Here, I think, the apparently casual diagnosis of "hysterics" by a Greek doctor deserves our attention.

"Hysterical" is a word long used to dismiss women with real problems, but hysteria ("womb sickness") is also an important mental disorder first recorded in the medical literature of the ancient Egyptians and Greeks. Until the early twentieth century it was viewed as a disease of virgin women and widows that was triggered by problems of sexuality and could be "cured" by sexual congress with a male. In the nineteenth century, Jean-Martin Charcot ran an intense clinical study of hysteria at La Salpêtrière, the public hospital in Paris, which had a rich supply of female paupers to experiment with and photograph in their picturesque madness. Meanwhile, an epidemic of hysteria had broken out among women of the affluent middle classes in Britain, Europe, and the United States, and since it proved gratifyingly difficult to cure, became an important source of income for medical men.

Thus, in 1893 the Viennese psychiatrist Josef Breuer and his younger colleague Sigmund Freud published *Studies in Hysteria,* notable mainly for Breuer's study of his patient "Anna O" (Bertha Pappenheim). In 1905 Freud wrote up a single case study of his patient "Dora" (Ida Bauer) that would become even more famous. The two young Austrian doctors theorized that the physical symptoms manifested by their hysterical patients — all female — revealed what was troubling the women psychologically. According to Freud and Breuer, the female patient's body symbolically enacts what she cannot speak, with the hysterical injury following the neurological path of some "real" injury. For example, a girl who is forbidden independent speech in her family and who once had suffered from laryngitis might develop hysterical aphonia, an inability to speak. Denied freedom of movement in her social group, a girl who had once broken an ankle might become unable to walk.

Vanessa Stephen's problems were far less serious than those of Pappenheim or Bauer, but she too was a hysteric, according to both the old "womb sickness" concept and the new Freudian theory. Her sudden collapse in the Peloponnese expressed both a helplessness she could not put into words and repressed sexual desire. Vanessa was facing a crucial life decision — whether or not to enter into marriage with Clive Bell — and for the first time in her life she felt unable to move forward. Struck down by an intestinal infection, and unconsciously taking on the role of invalid she had seen her sisters Stella and Virginia play, she could not get out of bed.

If one takes on the role of the Freudian analyst Vanessa Bell never consulted, one might conclude that the issue that preoccupied Vanessa Stephen in the summer of 1906 was whether to marry and take up a woman's traditional role or use her modest inheritance to pursue a career as an artist and remain single, like her friends Margery and Violet. One might advance further the idea that the abuse Vanessa had suffered at the hands of George Duckworth and the sting of having her proposed marriage to Jack Hills forbidden on the grounds of incest had made her wary of sex and unpersuaded that marriage was always in a woman's best interests.

As a sharply observant teenager, Vanessa Stephen had watched the way her mother and older sister Stella had lived and died. Leslie Stephen had burdened his darling Julia with four more children in quick succession and worn her down with his gloom and his unending demands. And he had then latched like an incubus onto Stella. Once her father was dead, Vanessa could at last act on the basis of her own needs and desires, and act she did. She took her Stephen brothers and sister abroad together for the first time and then moved them to unfashionable Bloomsbury, where she could color her walls green or tangerine, have friends in until three in the morning, and paint all the way through teatime if she liked. She was independent, with no one to wave an account book in her face and scream that chicken cost ten pence more a pound than mutton. She was free. Why would she want to tie herself to a husband?

But by the time Vanessa arrived in Olympia, she was no longer convinced that she had done the right thing in refusing Bell or sure of what she wanted. Her insides churned, and Greece turned out to be not nearly as nice as France or Italy. The buildings were shacks or piles of old stones, the people ragged, the beds full of fleas. As for the whole "Et in Arcadia ego" idea that her Hellenophile siblings kept rabbiting on about — well, classical literature was not Vanessa's thing, and landscape was not her genre. Nymphs and shepherds cavorting amid temple ruins under a radiant blue sky were so very G. F. Watts — her parents' favorite painter, but now in the twentieth century, Vanessa was happy to observe, thrown onto the aesthetic scrapheap.

Her beloved and deeply mourned sister Stella had once gone abroad on her honeymoon, fallen ill, and been rushed home. Now Vanessa was abroad and ill. Perhaps she had appendicitis like Stella. Perhaps she too was doomed to die young — who knew? But as she lay in bed, Vanessa found herself remembering Stella's shining joy after Jack Hills proposed for the third time and she allowed herself to accept. Stella had found the courage to reach out to happiness for herself, and in the year before her marriage, nothing, not even her stepfather's grotesque jealousy, had clouded Stella's radiance.

Now Vanessa was the same age Stella had been when she died, and she too was feeling the need to make her own choices, yield to her own desires, and tend to her own happiness. Hers was a sensual nature, and, as she would later confide in a letter, she had felt obscure sexual impulses as long as she could remember. Her recent tours of the big European museums had shown her that sexual desire and the female body were inseparable from great art. Perhaps, to be an artist, what Vanessa needed was knowledge of the male body and of her own.

And so, once comfortably installed in her own bed, petted and fussed over, Vanessa wrote to Clive Bell in the Highlands, urging him to return. And when he came into the room, there she was, propped up on the pillows, modestly décolleté, her forearms bare, reaching out her hand to him, tears in her huge dark eyes, a red rose tucked behind her ear.

∂❧

Meanwhile, Thoby Stephen, one floor below, was suffering something much worse than a malaria attack. Both he and Violet Dickinson, it turned out, had been infected with typhoid somewhere between Athens and Istanbul. To the London doctors of 1906, the symptoms of typhoid were indistinguishable from those of other tropical diseases — until the later stages, at which point diagnosis became irrelevant and prayer was medicine's best option. Slowly, agonizingly, the tall, robust Thoby gave ground to the *Salmonella typhi* bacterium, even as reassuring bulletins were issued by eminent physicians who expressed confidence that even if, regrettably, it was typhoid, such a healthy young man must surely recover.

But Thoby Stephen was born in an age before antibiotics, and like Prince Albert forty years earlier, he proved to be one of the unlucky 25 percent of patients for whom untreated typhoid proved fatal. In such cases, fever, sore throat, cough, and diarrhea give way to delirium, to a violent restlessness that defies opiates, and at last to intestinal hemorrhage. In desperation, Thoby Stephen's doctors put their exhausted, emaciated patient through a surgical procedure to "sew up the ulcer to prevent the pus from leaking ... a serious risk," as Virginia reported to Clive Bell, but on November 20, 1906, Thoby Stephen died. Two days later, Vanessa Stephen and Clive Bell announced their engagement.

In the days after her older brother's death, Virginia, racked with sorrow but refusing to give way, subjected herself to a peculiarly literary form of torture. Since Violet Dickinson had typhoid too and was fighting for her life, Virginia was advised that Violet must not know that Thoby had succumbed to the disease. For almost a month, Virginia sent off cheerful bulletins to her old friend, detailing the stages in Thoby's supposed recovery. These letters make for very creepy reading today. Miss Dickinson discovered the deception only when she was well enough to pick up a newspaper and find a reference to Thoby's death.

Virginia Woolf managed to overcome the sorrow and stress of her brother's death by keeping him alive, not just for Violet in the weeks just after his death, but for herself and the world, in perpetuity. She never forgot Thoby and recast him in her own version of a famous literary trope — the heroic, almost godlike beloved, killed in the flower of youth. In *Jacob's Room,* she mourned and celebrated her brother as Catullus did for his brother in "Ave atque vale," as Montaigne did for his friend La Boétie in "On Friendship," Shelley for Keats in "Adonais," and Tennyson for Hallam in *In Memoriam.* Through her art Virginia Woolf was able to weather a fourth family bereavement, changed, seasoned, but stronger.

Vanessa's reaction to Thoby's death could not have been more different, and it is at this point that the paths of the two sisters begin to diverge. Vanessa had not mourned the father she had grown to hate. Now she refused to mourn the brother she had loved very much — or at least she put her loss aside to mourn in secret and at leisure, away from prying eyes. As small children, Vanessa and Thoby had been knit exceptionally tight. When she was nine, Vanessa wept when Thoby was sent away to school, and for a time she took Jacko, her brother's favorite toy monkey, to bed with her. But that was then, and Clive was now. Among other lessons, Hyde Park Gate had taught Vanessa that buckets of tears and yards of black bombazine do not bring the dead back, so mourning was one of the conventional hypocrisies Vanessa Bell had left behind in Kensington. Clive declared his adoration of her and suddenly it was obvious that she adored him too. When Clive proposed again, only a day or so after his return to London, Vanessa accepted. She was ecstatically happy and made no attempt to hide it.

Overnight, or so it seemed, Vanessa and Clive became completely wrapped up in each other. A strong current of as-yet-unfulfilled desire ran between them, and they found themselves engaged in an endless and fascinating conversation *à deux* that even the first visit to his dispiriting family could not spoil. When her brother George Duckworth, oozing old-Etonian charm, negotiated a marriage settlement with Clive's colliery-owner father that was notably generous toward his beloved Vanessa and any eventual children of the match, Vanessa's joy was complete, her future suddenly secure. She wrote to her cousin Madge Vaughan, "I do feel that Thoby's life was not wasted. He was so splendidly happy, in these last two years especially . . . that sorrow does seem selfish and out of place . . . I as yet can hardly understand anything but the fact that I am happier than I ever thought people could be, and it goes on getting better every day."

As the immediate family hurtled headlong toward the wedding, Vanessa remained officially an invalid, and she delegated to her sister the task of informing people of her engagement. On November 24, for example, Virginia wrote to Madge Vaughan, "Dearest Madge, Nessa wants me to tell you that she is engaged to marry Mr. Clive Bell. It happened 2 days ago; he was a great friend of Thoby's and Adrian's at College — and we have seen a great deal of him. She is wonderfully happy and it is beautiful to see her. Yr loving AVS [Adeline Virginia Stephen]."

On December 17, writing again to cousin Madge, who had looked after her during her recent illness and was evidently fearing a relapse, Virginia wrote that she was well and moving on with her life. She had decided that she and Adrian must have their own separate establishment, perhaps ten minutes away from that of the Bells. "That does not mean that I expect to quarrel. I like him [Clive] very much — and you know what Nessa is — but the only chance is for us to start fresh again. They must have their lives, if we are to get any good from it — and I mean to." Virginia says that Clive's family has been most kind to her sister, that Clive makes Vanessa happy and she herself likes him: "He is clever and cultivated — more taste, I think, than genius; but he has the gift of making other people shine."

On December 18, in her second letter to Violet Dickinson after Violet learned of Thoby's death, Virginia strikes the same note. "Nessa became engaged 2 days after Thoby died; but she was really engaged I think the moment she saw Clive (as I call him!) . . . She went through those days in a kind of dream. I feel *perfectly happy* about her. He is very considerate and unselfish, and he is really interesting and clever besides. You know what she has in her, and all that seems now called out. She is a splendid creature — it seems so right and natural that she should marry Clive."

Madge Vaughan was a cousin by marriage and part of the family network, and Violet was something of a gossip, so there is a guarded, protective tone to these letters. Virginia's job was to keep at bay all potential criticism of Vanessa as unfeeling and to write in Vanessa's place, with the implication that Vanessa is still recovering from her own serious illness. But by the end of December, holed up for a miserably cold Christmas with her brother Adrian in a rented house in the New Forest and anticipating a visit to Clive's family at the New Year, which she rightly feared would be a nightmare, Virginia had a violent headache (headaches were the regular precursor to her breakdowns) and let the protective mask slip for her dearest friend Violet.

Violet had apparently been sending on friends' praise for the sweet, calm, and rational way Virginia has dealt with the tumultuous events of the past three months. Virginia responds bitterly: "I shall want all my sweetness to gild Vanessa's happiness. It does seem strange and intolerable sometimes. When I think of father and Thoby and then see that funny little creature [that is, Clive Bell] twitching his pink skin and jerking out his little spasm of laughter I wonder what odd freak there is in Nessa's eyesight. But I don't say this, and I won't say it, except to you."

On February 7, 1907, seven weeks after Thoby's death, Vanessa and Clive were married. On the strength of the twenty thousand pounds (almost a million, in today's pounds) that Clive received as his wedding present from his father, the happy couple decamped for a long, rapturous honeymoon, first in Pembrokeshire and then in Italy.

On the day of the wedding, stuck at Paddington Station after missing the train to Wales, Vanessa wrote a letter to Virginia, whom she had left barely an hour before. For her happiness to be complete, Vanessa needed Virginia, if not in person then at least by mail, and she was confident that in her new life she would always have both her sister and her husband. These letters between the sisters from early 1907, like the Kensington letters, have disappeared.

13

The Great Betrayal

IN EARLY February 1907, Clive and Vanessa were married at the St. Pancras town hall in the presence of a handful of friends and family that included George Duckworth and Virginia and Adrian Stephen. Still eager to show his love for Vanessa, George loaned the bridal couple his limousine for their getaway, but his chauffeur got lost in plebeian Paddington, and they missed their train to Pembroke.

Whether out of respect for the dead or out of embarrassment that a wedding should follow so quickly on a funeral, most people found out about the Bell nuptials only after they were over. This was the cause of much bad feeling, and, in a pattern that would harden over the years, Vanessa's response was to progressively sever ties with her extended family and with old friends of her parents. By 1908 Sir Richmond Ritchie, Anne Thackeray Ritchie's husband, was cutting the Bells at the opera in retaliation for the Bells' rudeness.

Virginia was both more conciliatory and affectionate, though she could do only so much to close the fault line between the old life and the new that her sister was opening. Thus, in July 1907, Virginia visited George Duckworth and his wife, Lady Margaret, and found it hard not to respond to their gestures of affection. "I see he [George] is much too hurt even to speak naturally of Nessa and Clive," Virginia wrote to Violet Dickinson. "But what my position is among them I don't know. I see what you call their kindness, and Margarets good feelings; and Georges odd relics of what was once affection — and then there is Nessa, like a wasteful child pulling the heads off flowers — beautiful as a goddess (at which you always smile) and Clive with his nice tastes, and kindness to me, and his slightness and acidity."

On their return from their honeymoon, the Bells moved into 46 Gordon Square and engaged in a flurry of redecoration. While abroad they had spent freely on pottery and pictures, but they kept their London reception rooms fashionably sparse, and Clive was observed hiding a matchbook that clashed with the color scheme. Jumping back a generation from the red velvet gloom of Hyde Park Gate, we can date two features of the Bell decor to the Pattle era of Vanessa's maternal grandmother and great-aunts. Vanessa hung Julia Cameron's photographs on her pale-colored walls, where they would arouse the admiration of Roger Fry, and she draped the antique shawls the Pattle women had brought with them from India over the backs of her chairs.

After much tedious house hunting and contentious consultations with friends, Virginia and Adrian Stephen took up housekeeping just around the corner from the Bells, in an elegant but rundown house at 29 Fitzroy Square. The annual rent was 120 pounds, but since Adrian still had only his investment income to live on, brother and sister eventually found it advantageous to move again, to a four-story house in nearby Brunswick Square, where they had ample room for paying housemates. Adrian occupied a set of rooms on the second floor and Virginia on the third. Maynard Keynes and, for a time, Duncan Grant took the ground floor. In 1911 Leonard Woolf came home on leave at last from Sri Lanka and, undaunted by stairs, took on a small set of rooms at the very top of the house. Today National Trust markers alert us to the fact that Gordon Square, Fitzroy Square, and Brunswick Square constituted the tight little London center of the Bloomsbury group, with, at different times, Clive Bell, Vanessa Bell, Maynard Keynes, Lytton Strachey, Duncan Grant, Roger Fry; Adrian Stephen and his wife, Karin; James Strachey and his wife, Alix; Dora Carrington, the artist who was Lytton's companion; and the Woolfs all renting or subletting different properties as prime residences, pieds-à-terre, and studios.

As Leonard Woolf later recalled, the Stephen lodgers got an excellent deal. For eleven or twelve pounds a month they had room service and all the meals they were at home for. Sophie Farrell, the Stephen family cook, along with her old friend Maud, had opted to move with "Miss Ginia" and Master Adrian rather than stay with the new Mrs. Bell. Sophie saw Virginia as a babe among wolves, and Virginia duly took Sophie along for practical advice when she went house hunting. Sophie was a first-class cook — I see the epic *boeuf en daube* that Mrs. Ramsay's unnamed cook serves the guests in *To the Lighthouse* as one of Sophie's recipes — so any deficiencies in the plumbing and heating chez Stephen were more than made up for by the food.

Virginia had been determined to keep a close eye on her surviving brother. She saw that Thoby's death had hit Adrian harder than anyone else and that Adrian was even less able than Vanessa to express grief in words. According to their nephew Quentin Bell, who had ample opportunity to observe them both, Adrian and Virginia had a great deal in common and loved each other very much but were never able to articulate their feelings. Certainly, during the years 1907–12, when they lived together, the relationship between sister and brother was often stormy, and visitors gleefully pointed to stains on the dining room walls where Virginia had shied food at Adrian. Virginia wrote to friends lamenting that she could not be a brother to Adrian while privately wishing he would just get on with life. The best times for brother and sister came when reminiscing about the happy family days in Kensington when Mother was alive, something both loved to do all their lives, according to their nephew. Together they felt able to speak of Stella, whose name no one in the family had dared to mention in ten years.

Over in Gordon Square, meanwhile, the Bells reveled in the creature comforts that Clive could now afford, and they radiated sensual happiness. To Lytton's joy, Clive and Vanessa began receiving him in the bedroom, lying next to each other, and it was no secret to their friends that Vanessa responded to her husband with ardor. According to Vanessa's daughter, Angelica Garnett, who seems to be repeating what her mother told her, during the year and a half in which she became engaged, married, and had her first son, Vanessa Bell was "supremely happy and fulfilled." "She was twenty-eight and had waited a long time for sexual experience. Now that it had come, she was transfigured; she was bowled over not only by the sex itself but by the intimacy it conferred on their relationship. All her tender, delicate and most endearing qualities came to the surface; she teased, joked, and laughed, enjoying the half-private, half-public parade of their feelings."

It was at this point, when a "transfigured" Vanessa was experiencing a happiness she had never known before and daring to open up to the world, that, as Angelica Garnett puts it, "Virginia took it into her head to flirt with Clive."

❧

The flirtation—for it was never an "affair" in the usual sense of the word—started while the Bells were in Italy on their honeymoon, or even before. The first extant letter from Virginia Woolf to Clive Bell dates to December 1906. Deciding which of the Stephen sisters they admired more had always been a dilemma for Thoby Stephen's friends, and even during the brief weeks of his engagement Clive lavished expressions of affection, admiration, and concern on Virginia. He, like his wife, wrote to Virginia regularly during the first weeks of their honeymoon, and Adrian and Virginia joined the Bells in Paris for the last weeks of the honeymoon.

Virginia had told friends before her sister married that she and Adrian saw themselves leading lives separate from the Bells, but this was not what happened. Clive was an extremely social animal, he now had ample funds to travel and entertain friends, and as the ardor he had confessed to Lytton before his wedding was sated, he was not inclined to spend much time alone with his new wife. Clive was aware that his Cambridge friends considered him an intellectual lightweight, and he remembered, if Vanessa had forgotten, that only months earlier she had not only turned down his proposals of marriage but dared to suggest he get a job. Paying conspicuous attention to his wife's sister helped Clive salve the wounds to his amour propre while enhancing the Casanova self-image he had been developing since his late teens.

Thus, right from the beginning of the Bell marriage, Virginia, at first accompanied by Adrian but soon alone, found herself spending many of her London days, and many holidays too, with the Bells. Seeing Clive and Vanessa together scratched a sore in Virginia's psyche, and this is when she began to flatter and flirt with her brother-in-law, drawing Clive's attention away from his wife and toward her. She was becoming Witcherina, the nickname her niece Angelica would later know her by.

As early as mid-February 1907, only weeks after the wedding, a flustered, flowery, quotation-packed letter from Virginia to Clive already sounds a note of hyperbolic intensity. The editors of her correspondence note that she actually wrote a draft of this letter. After amusingly relating her reaction to a telegram she has received about renting 29 Fitzroy Square, Virginia decides she must turn to Vanessa for real estate advice, and she then free-associates over her new pet name for her sister — Dolphin: "It contains all the beauty of the sky, and the melancholy of the sea, and the laughter of the Dolphin in its circumference, first in the mystic Van, spread like a mirror of grey glass to heaven. Next in the swishing tail of its successive esses, and finally in the grave pause and suspension of the ultimate. A breathing peace like the respiration of Earth itself."

In the next extant letter, Virginia writes to the honeymooning Clive on March 22 that she has quarreled with Walter Headlam — one of the men seeking to marry her — since he has dared give an opinion on "my own proper science: the theory of Vanessa." Virginia concludes her letter to Clive: "Give my love to my sister, and, if you like, kiss her on her left eye, with the eyelid smoothed over the curve, and just blue on the crest." In her letter to Clive of August 18, 1907, Virginia Woolf similarly ends her letter: "Both eyes are to be kissed, the tip of the right ear, and the snout if its wet."

By August 1907 it was apparent that Vanessa was pregnant and even happier than before. Virginia's adoration of her sister moved up a notch, but her attitude to Clive remained ambivalent at best. She reported to Violet: "Nessa is like a great child, more happy and serene than ever, draped in a long robe of crimson or raspberry coloured silk, with clear drops of amethyst . . . To be with her is to sit in autumn sunlight, but then there is Clive!"

Violet seems to have sensed that something was not quite right in Virginia's relationship with Clive since in a letter of October 1907, Virginia writes defensively, "Nessa and Clive came back yesterday — but I cant now go into his character; it will really be some time before I can separate him from her. I dont think I have spoken alone with him since they were married." Within six months, however, Clive and Virginia were speaking to each other alone quite a lot, as well as exchanging intimate letters when apart.

Julian Heward Bell was born on February 4, 1908, a large, strong, healthy child. Julian immediately bonded with his mother, but he had difficulties with feeding. The Bells hired a nanny and a nurse to take care of the baby, but when Julian cried in the night Vanessa got up to nurse him. This caused Clive, who hated his sleep to be disturbed, to move into his dressing room. When Vanessa's breast milk failed to satisfy, Julian was hungry and colicky, his howls echoing up and down the stairs at 46 Gordon Square, and things did not improve when the Bells, accompanied by Virginia and Julian's nurse, went away to St. Ives in Cornwall in chilly April. The owner of the rented house also had a fractious child, and every adult conversation seemed to be interrupted by a scream from upstairs. Clive refused even to pick up his child — not uncommon behavior for a father at this period — and Vanessa refused to enroll her sister's help in caring for Julian. Instead she was relieved when Clive and Virginia, who was a prodigious walker, went off for walks together with their dogs, Gurth and Hans. Clive Bell appreciated the brilliance of Virginia's mind even as he responded to the beauty of her long, slender body, unswollen by pregnancy and lactation. Virginia was struggling to write her first novel, then burdened with the title *Melymbrosia,* and Clive became her chosen reader.

When Virginia departed St. Ives for London, she left behind her copy of the book she was reviewing for the *Times Literary Supplement,* and in his hurry to retrieve the book and get it to Virginia before her train left, Clive fell and injured himself. Such extreme solicitude may have raised a tiny red flag in Vanessa's mind for, in her next letter — the first since those she had written in 1904 during Virginia's illness that Virginia kept hold of — she suggests to Virginia that they had all been suffering from boredom while in St. Ives. Vanessa composes a little monologue (a very Virginian fictional technique, I would note) of how Virginia might be viewing herself and Clive. "'Of course,'" Vanessa imagines Virginia telling their London friends, "'Nessa was quite taken up with the baby. Yes I'm afraid she is losing all her individuality and becoming the usual domestic mother and Clive — of course I like him very much, but his mind is of a peculiarly literal and prosaic type. However they seem perfectly happy and I expect it's a good thing I didn't stay longer. I was evidently beginning to bore them.' Now Billy [that is, Virginia] on your honour haven't you uttered one of these sentiments?"

In another letter, having seen some of Virginia's letters to Clive, Vanessa remarks that her sister was writing her the kind of love letters that her husband never wrote to her. On some level, Vanessa Bell was aware that she was one side of a love triangle being formed with her sister and her husband, and for a brief moment she came close to challenging them about it.

When Clive took his wife and new son to visit his parents at Cleeve House in Wiltshire, he fell back into the company of the Raven-Hills. Anne Raven-Hill was the neighbor's wife with whom Clive had enjoyed a passionate affair for several years. In 1908 Anne was striving to maintain a façade of respectability while nursing a child that, as the Wiltshire rumormongers had it, was not her husband's.

Three key letters written at the time of the Bells' visit to Cleeve House in 1908 — one from Clive to Virginia, one from Virginia to Clive, and one from Vanessa to Virginia — are evidence that the company of Anne Raven-Hill and her complaisant artist husband caused a turning point in the relationship between wife and husband, sister and husband, and sister and sister. Suddenly ex-urban Wiltshire starts to resemble the Vienna of Arthur Schnitzler and Freud or the Paris of Colette and Willy.

Clive wrote to Virginia,

Mrs Raven-Hill, Mrs Armour, Mrs Clive Bell, three young or youngish women; how beautiful do they sit, each in her own day nursery smiling down Madonna-like on a smiling child. Last night they dined with three men: Mr Raven-Hill, Mr Armour, Mr Clive Bell, artists, young members of the youngest Bohemian clubs, stained by drink and lust and too warm contact with the sin-besodden world . . . but Vanessa like some beautiful black velvet foil takes the measure of her peeresses and can judge their colour to a shade. Her appreciation is so sure that she is rarely descried, and yet she continues to get confidences. Explain me that.

Responding on April 15, Virginia sounded a new note of open flirtatiousness to Clive. While in St. Ives she had offered to let Clive kiss her, and now she concluded her letter to her brother-in-law in this provocative way:

> I have been writing Nessa's life; and I am going to send you 2 chapters in a day or so. It might have been so good! As it is, I am too near and too far; and it seems to be blurred, and I ask myself why write it at all seeing I never shall recapture what you have by your side this minute . . . I gather that you are going to a dance; and I believe you go because you think your wife the most beautiful woman in England, and she goes because she thinks so too. Kiss her, most passionately, in all my private places — neck — arm, an eyeball, and tell her — what new thing is there to tell her? How fond I am of her husband?

On April 19 Vanessa at Cleeve House wrote to Virginia about the astounding Mrs. Raven-Hill: "Talk about freedom of talk. She stops at nothing and the joys of married life were freely discussed and notes compared by her, Mrs Armour and myself, and I quite enjoyed myself as you will believe. Also I can see that I can get some useful tips from Mrs Raven-Hill as to the best means of checking one's family and I mean to make use of the dance at Devizes for the purpose, though as she is very deaf I shall probably cause a scandal."

Here we begin to see a new Vanessa, no longer uncertain, probing, and pleading, as in the letter from St. Ives, but gossiping salaciously about birth control to her naive unmarried sister and taking on the persona of the sophisticated, blasé woman of the world she was beginning to understand her husband expected her to be.

In 1909, according to Quentin Bell, the Bells, Virginia, Saxon Sydney-Turner, Adrian Stephen, and Walter Lamb, one of Virginia's suitors, began a letter-writing game that enabled Clive, in his fictional persona, to "renew his gallantries" to Virginia in her fictional persona, "with unusual openness and ardour." To taunt Virginia, who welcomed his letters but eluded his embraces, Clive would lavish caresses on his wife. It was all very sleazy, and Lytton Strachey chided Virginia for the pain she was causing her sister.

By 1909 Vanessa and Clive Bell were drifting apart, and in 1910, the year in which his second son, Quentin, was born, Clive Bell renewed his liaison with Anne Raven-Hill. Encouraged by his wife's *savoir vivre,* he no longer bothered to hide his fascination with her sister. He and Virginia were in regular correspondence when apart, and when together they walked and talked, arguing with gusto but quick to reconcile. This went on for more than two years. It took the arrival of Leonard Woolf from Sri Lanka in the summer of 1911 to stop the Clive-Virginia "thing" in its tracks.

ঌ

What was going on in the heads of those in this odd little amorous triangle? On Clive's side the answer is not hard to come up with, and when he described himself as an "artist" and a member "of the youngest Bohemian clubs, stained by drink and lust and too warm contact with the sin-besodden world," he offered us an important clue to his character and his motivation. Clive Bell had an active libido and a reliable cock, Anne Raven-Hill seems to have taught him how to give women pleasure in bed, and in Paris he fell under the spell of the belle époque, with its jeweled cocottes, purple-silk-cravated homosexuals, leather-booted lesbians, and wild-eyed opiomanes. As young men, Clive's artist friends, like Gerald Kelly and Duncan Grant, lived in that world, and throughout his life Clive would seek it out on yearly visits to France.

Clive knew that, as a married man, he would come into the kind of money that made the life of the Baudelairean flâneur possible. Back in England in 1905, he settled quickly on Vanessa Stephen as an agreeable woman likely to please his father, and when Vanessa responded to conjugal intimacy with unexpected passion, Clive was amused and ready to try the same trick on his sister-in-law. Clive had always found Virginia attractive, and the fascination with his wife's body that she revealed to him in her letters appealed to the libertine in him. To seduce Virginia would be delectably incestuous as well as adulterous, and Clive could persuade himself that Virginia would be glad to be relieved of her maidenhood at long last. Thus, what Clive Bell wanted from Virginia, his son Quentin bluntly tells us, was "no less . . . and not much more than a delightful little infidelity, ending up in bed." Lytton, who was always going on about Virginia's virginal nature, would definitely have approved when Clive told him about the seduction.

The deliciously French version of libertinism made fashionable circa 1900 by best-selling literary entrepreneurs like the author Colette's husband, Henry Gauthier-Villars, alias Willy, had immense allure for affluent heterosexual Englishmen weary of Victorianism. In one of the salacious little essays he may actually have penned himself, Willy advises the man about town to marry a rich, pretty girl, offer her an advanced course in eroticism in the manner of *Les liaisons dangereuses,* and then move on to his next mistress. This is pretty much exactly what Clive Bell did. With the new king, Edward VII, doing his best to make Sandringham more like Neuilly, men like Clive Bell were encouraged to see fidelity in marriage as not just absurdly Victorian but hideously lower-middle-class. Artists and aristocrats married, sired heirs, and then, duty done, moved on. Having friends in the art world allowed Clive Bell to see himself as an artist, and his family's money gave him aristocratic pretensions. Did he not shoot and ride to hounds with the county set and rent a trout stream in the Highlands — all, of course, thanks to the large fortune his grandfather had made out of the slag heaps and poisoned air of Merthyr Tydvil in Wales?

As for why Virginia let herself get entangled with Clive, she must have asked herself that question many times, but she never put her thoughts and feelings down on paper. The fraught relationship with her sister and brother-in-law before her own marriage was not something that could be communicated to a friend like Violet; neither was it the kind of thing she cared to record in her diary. One thing is clear. Virginia Woolf never, to put it crudely, had the hots for Clive Bell. As her comments to Violet Dickinson in the months following her brother Thoby's death indicate, she felt an ambivalence bordering on repulsion for her sister's husband — which makes it all the stranger that, within weeks of her sister's marriage, she embarked on a sexual game for which no one had yet given her the rule book.

In the period between her sister's marriage and her own, Virginia Woolf seesawed between frenzied activity and mental collapse, her mind too befogged to see sense or heed the advice of friends like Violet. Professionally, she had made great strides since her father's death in 1904, and if at times she craved solitude, holing up in rented rooms in Yorkshire and Cornwall to write, she always kept in constant touch by letter. When she emerged, her days were a whirl of social engagements mixed with serious writerly work. The modest fees she earned from her reviews added to her small but steady income from her various inheritances, allowed her in 1910 to rent a small house at Firle on the Sussex coast, an easy rail journey from London. This would be the first of a series of houses in rural Sussex (notably Asheham and Monk's House) where Virginia would work on her novels and her reviews, welcome chosen friends, and lead the healthy outdoor country life she thrived on.

Socially, Virginia continued to rely on the affection and support of female friends like Nelly Cecil and the Thynne sisters, but her flirtatious relationship with Violet Dickinson had cooled. Violet was doing more traveling with other female friends, and Virginia felt an increasing urge to be married. Despite her mental fragility, or perhaps because of it — so many men adore crazy women — Virginia, unlike Vanessa at the same age, attracted suitors. Walter Headlam, Edward Hilton Young, Walter Lamb, and Sydney Waterlow all wanted to marry her, and she enjoyed keeping them dangling.

When these gentlemen proposed, however, she gracefully and decisively said no. When it came right down to it, she could not imagine herself in bed with any of them and was not at all sure that they could actually imagine themselves in bed with her. She was a tall, athletic woman, and the Cambridge classicist Lamb was so small and so obsequious. As for Headlam, rumors had been floating around about his taste for small girls even when Julia Stephen was alive. The diplomat Sydney Waterlow, after Virginia turned him down in the fall of 1911, stalked off and found himself a prostitute, which at least shows that his preference was for women. Waterlow continued to socialize with the Bloomsbury group, and his later comment on Virginia and her sister is interesting: "Vanessa icy, cynical, artistic. Virginia much more emotional and interested in life rather than beauty."

Having yet to feel any desire for a man, Virginia gave serious thought to marrying Lytton Strachey. Of course, Lytton circa 1910 was, as Quentin Bell puts it, "the Bloomsbury arch-bugger," and — in comparison with his gay friends Duncan Grant and Maynard Keynes — an ugly, self-absorbed, tortured, unsuccessful bugger to boot. But in some odd way Lytton's lack of physical allure for Virginia, or hers for him, made the marriage conceivable to them both. Many gay men in this period married women, and both Lytton and Virginia longed for secure comfort and domestic companionship. Both were passionately engaged with literature, and there were times when they had a meeting of minds that was thrilling.

And so, one night, Lytton proposed and Virginia accepted, but then the next day, deciding he had made a colossal mistake, Lytton withdrew his proposal and Virginia said she understood. As he reported the very next day to Leonard in Sri Lanka, Lytton, overcome by this close brush with female chastity, hurtled back to Cambridge to have sex with the obliging Duncan. As for Virginia, she was not unhappy to put another of her flirtations behind her, and her heart was not broken. All the same, to have a man propose and withdraw in a matter of hours did nothing for her self-esteem, and she knew Lytton well enough to be sure the event would be all over Bloomsbury within the week. Lytton Strachey and Virginia Woolf would always care for each other, and there were moments over the next years when the old mental intimacy was revived, but their paths would diverge more and more from this point on.

Beneath the busy surface of life that Virginia brightly reported in letters to her various women friends, there were deep, unacknowledged currents of confusion, resentment, and anger that kept her hovering on the edge of a serious breakdown and needing to retreat regularly to a private clinic. The fundamental problem triggering these minor attacks was Vanessa. Ever since the deaths of their mother and older sister, no one had mattered to Virginia like Vanessa. She was the rock Virginia stood on as the successive storms of family deaths and mental breakdowns crashed over her. The relationship between the sisters, based on Virginia's need for care and craving for love, had never been simple, but it had seemed secure. And then, literally in a matter of days, it was, as Virginia saw it, torn up by the roots, and she lost Vanessa not to death, which, in a sad way, she had learned to deal with, but to a man, and a man she saw as unworthy. Quite suddenly, the sisters no longer looked to a shared future, as they had after all the other family deaths. They were almost never alone together. Clive was always there between them, taking his share of grief as Thoby's best friend, relieving Vanessa of the need to grieve.

In her diary on the eve of her sister's wedding Virginia addressed a tortured entry to Vanessa: "We have been your humble Beasts since we left our isles," wrote Virginia to Vanessa, referring to herself, according to their shared custom, as a plural entity, "the apes." "During that time we have wooed you and sung many songs . . . in the hope that thus enchanted you would condescend one day to marry us. But as we no longer expect this honour we entreat that you keep us still for your lovers should you have need of such."

This is the letter of a jilted lover, not a sister, and from this point Virginia became obsessed with Vanessa. While putting Vanessa on a pedestal and thus launching the Bloomsbury myth of Vanessa as a Greek goddess, she set out to undermine Vanessa's relationship with Clive. If she could prove to Vanessa, in the most shocking way possible, that Clive was unfaithful and unworthy of her love, then surely Vanessa would return to her. Or so, in her unhappiness and her delusion, Virginia Stephen thought.

And how did Vanessa react to the "thing" between her husband and her sister? We can only surmise what she was thinking and feeling from what she did, since she seems never to have put anything about this part of her early married life down on paper. It was probably in 1908, soon after Julian's birth, that she became aware that her husband was trying to get her sister into bed and that her sister was leading him on, but there is no record of a confrontation. Other women might have indulged in storms of tears or shied gravy boats across the dinner table, but dramatic scenes were not Vanessa Bell's style. She apparently watched the flirtation take its course as if it amused her, but as Lytton intuited when he taxed Virginia with causing her sister pain, Vanessa's smiling complicity was an act of bravado, designed to deflect attention from inner anguish.

As we have seen, after the storms and shoals of her youth, Vanessa had grave doubts about marriage and avoided it for some eight years after the emotional disarray caused by her wish to marry Jack Hills. But then, amid the fresh trauma of her brother Thoby's illness and death, she had gambled on finding, with his close friend Clive Bell, a place of intimacy where she could explore sexual pleasure, heal old wounds, and produce children to take the place of the beloved dead. She dared to envisage herself playing her own modern version of the role of adored wife and mother and domestic prodigy, which she remembered her mother playing so well. That dream lasted barely a year, and when she woke up and saw her husband both angling for Virginia and ogling Anne Raven-Hill, the wound to Vanessa's self-esteem went deep. Had her husband within months of marriage merely revealed himself to be an unrepentant serial philanderer, it would have been hard, but Vanessa Bell could at least have found love and support in her sister. Virginia would have understood what she was going through without needing to be told. But to have Virginia colluding in Clive's amorous projects was a betrayal worthy of a novel by the Stephens' old family friend Henry James.

As her biographer Frances Spalding notes, "despite her belief in honesty there were certain matters on which [Vanessa Bell] maintained a guarded reticence, an impenetrable privacy." But at Charleston in 1918, at a moment of high stress in the unstable love triangle between herself, Duncan Grant, and David Garnett, Vanessa made a revealing contribution to a heated discussion of whether "our more or less high opinion of a rival made us more or less jealous." In his diary, Grant recorded, "Nessa thought the higher opinion the greater the jealousy . . . She produced Virginia of whom she had been more jealous than anyone at a time when she admired her more than any woman she knew." I take this to be a reference to the "thing" between Virginia and Clive.

Virginia was even more circumspect, apparently referring to the events of 1907–11 only once in a letter to her friend Gwen Darwin Raverat, in March 1925. Raverat's husband, Jacques, had just died after a long battle with multiple sclerosis, but as newlyweds, the Raverats had been very happy when subletting from the Stephens in Fitzroy Square. Comparing their experience to her own in the same place, Woolf wrote: "Yes I will tell you the whole of my life history one day, but I think it was my affair with Clive and Nessa I was thinking of when I said I envied you and Jacques at Fitzroy Square. For some reason that turned more of a knife in me than anything else has done."

The remark applies equally or more, I think, to Vanessa.

Faced with a double treachery, Vanessa took stock of the man she had married and concluded that rebuking her husband in 1909 was as useless as mourning her brother had been in 1906. She had made her bed and she chose to lie in it, however crowded. The real traitor, as Vanessa saw it, was Virginia, and punishing her sister was easy. Vanessa had had occasion to see the sharp side to Virginia's shy, dreamy, withdrawn nature. When she found herself the target of some perceived injustice, Virginia would lash out, turn turkey-cock red in the face, and use her emotional intelligence and verbal skills to wound. But once Virginia had cooled down and come to see that she had vented her anger at the expense of people she loved, she was all remorse and desperate to make it up. What she then hated most was not rebuke, but silence and a withdrawal of confidence.

So Vanessa's revenge was to allow Virginia to know that she knew about what was going on between her and Clive, and say nothing. To admonish is to call attention and seek acknowledgment and confession. To confess is to ask for forgiveness. Virginia was not allowed to confess and thus was offered no forgiveness. Turning weakness into power, Vanessa silently inserted a knife and twisted it, thereby becoming, in Sydney Waterlow's words, "icy and cynical."

In a seeming paradox, the relationship between Virginia Woolf and Vanessa Bell opens up for us to see at the very time it came under great stress. The letters the two sisters kept after 1908 and that we can read today offer a simulacrum of the old, unselfconscious intimacy that we can assume was recorded in the lost pre-1904 correspondence. Funny, intimate, and perceptive, the published correspondence of Virginia Woolf and Vanessa Bell is a joy to read. It is also deceptive. Like Lytton, with his letters to Leonard in Sri Lanka, the sisters intended that their letters should survive them. The record they offer us is, thus, both communication and performance. Like a thighbone that is snapped and never properly set, the relationship between the sisters was broken, and they would hobble on together for the rest of their lives.

That a strain of resistance, even hostility, ran beneath the affectionate surface when her mother, Vanessa Bell, and her aunt Virginia Woolf were alone together was apparent twenty years later to Vanessa's teenage daughter, Angelica. In *Deceived with Kindness,* the first volume of her memoir, Angelica Bell Garnett remembered Charleston, her mother's personal domain in Sussex, as a combination of secret garden, full of ripe fruit and errant chickens, and a fortress, guns loaded and ready to repel invasion. During its heyday in the 1930s, according to Bell Garnett, Virginia Woolf and her husband, Leonard, mainly came to Charleston when invited for group celebrations. On occasion, however, Virginia would make an unannounced sortie from nearby Monk's House, only to be confronted with an invisible wall, which she needed all her wit and whimsy to climb over.

Enacting a ritual rooted in the Kensington past, Virginia would demand that Pixerina (Angelica) should kiss Witcherina (herself) from wrist to elbow — all this in an effort to extract one embarrassed, reluctant kiss from Vanessa.

Once this strange little exercise was over, Vanessa would feel able to relax, smile, and order tea. She and Virginia would sit in deck chairs and gossip, the picture of sisterly love and understanding, and yet, Angelica concludes, "seeing them together, in spite of their habitual ironic affection and without any idea of the cause, I could see a wariness on the part of Vanessa and on Virginia's side a desperate plea for forgiveness."

ॐ

That Vanessa Bell destroyed the correspondence with her sister from their last years in Hyde Park Gate is only my hypothesis. That Clive Bell did the opposite is a fact. He kept Virginia's letters from 1907–11, and, later on, would occasionally produce them to amuse his mistresses who found Virginia Woolf intimidating. Here in the writer's own hand was proud testimony that Clive Bell had been the man who came closest to conquering the frigidity Bloomsbury loved to gossip about.

Clive Bell never got close to getting into bed with Virginia Woolf. Many years later, when Virginia accused Clive of being "a cuckoo who lays eggs in other birds' nests," Clive jovially responded, "My dear Virginia, you would never let me lay an egg in your nest." But the existence of the letters documenting their "affair" was an act of treachery that would haunt their relationship. For the rest of her life, Virginia would go to the same parties and take part in the same country house weekends as Clive, observing him, judging him, pinning him down like a dead moth in the pages of her diary, all the while knowing that he had her letters.

Thanks to Clive Bell, those early, disturbed, inchoate letters Woolf wrote to him are part of the collected edition of her correspondence. They can be cited as an example of Bloomsbury's sexual perversity. We too, like Clive's mistress Mary Hutchinson, can read titillating sentences like "kiss my sister on the tip of the left ear and the snout if wet." But then this question arises: Is this frankness and a lack of sexual prejudice, or is it the posthumous revenge of a thwarted cad?

PART V

A Tale of
Two Sisters

14

Vanessa's Way, Part 1

ASKED WHAT they associate with the Bloomsbury group, people tend to reply with a word — SEX! — and kinky, complicated sex it was, fodder for a tall, growing heap of books and memoirs. We have Duncan Grant sleeping with Lytton Strachey and Maynard Keynes and Adrian Stephen and Vanessa Bell and David "Bunny" Garnett. We have gay Lytton relieving the sex-averse artist Dora Carrington of her hymen and Carrington (as she preferred to be called) bedding the muscular army veteran Ralph Partridge because her adored Lytton liked to have a hot he-male in charge of his house. Then there is gorgeous hetero Bunny shagging Duncan and trying to shag Vanessa and ending up twenty years later as the husband of Duncan and Vanessa's daughter, Angelica. Julian Bell, Angelica's older brother, has a quick fling with Anthony Blunt — the future Cambridge spy — while her other brother, the self-described "old Bloomsbury bugger" Quentin, does his best to stop his father, Clive, from jumping his young women friends. If just reading this makes your head reel, imagine how it was to live through it, as Virginia Woolf did!

As the books appear — a new biography of Morgan Forster, very gay, a new biography of David Garnett, very straight — questions of psychology and motivation continue to be raised, especially with regard to the women associated with Bloomsbury. Did Lytton save or enslave Carrington? When Vanessa Bell dedicated her life to the comfort and happiness of Duncan Grant, was she rebelling against Victorian convention or inventing a new model of female self-sacrifice? Was Angelica the instrument of David Garnett's revenge or a frisky young thing weirdly encouraged by her mother to explore sex in the arms of an attractive older man?

All these complex scenarios were spun around and by Virginia Woolf's sister Vanessa Stephen Bell, and as one surveys the accumulating evidence, it becomes clear that, if indeed Vanessa Bell and Virginia Woolf together were the founding mothers of Bloomsbury, they occupied different spaces and played different roles. Vanessa was, as we shall see in this chapter, the heart of Bloomsbury, and her Charleston farm near Lewes in Sussex was the group's archetypal place. In her thousands of paintings and her dozens of photographs, Vanessa Bell offers us a pictorial record of Bloomsbury, while also contributing a trove of letters and autobiographical fragments. Virginia meanwhile was the Boswell of Bloomsbury, and to her we owe six fat, tightly packed volumes of letters, and five equally fat volumes of diaries, all in small print and supplemented by juvenilia and the many volumes of her fiction and her essays.

One of the conceits of Bloomsbury was that Vanessa and Virginia were compounded of ancient Greek goddesses. Virginia was both Artemis, virgin goddess of the chase and the moon, and Athena, goddess of wisdom, more mind than woman, springing whole out of the head of her father, Zeus. Vanessa was both Aphrodite, goddess of sexual love, and Demeter, goddess of fertility, who made the earth dark when her daughter Persephone was stolen from her.

Both images are a partial truth at best. As her letters and essays prove, Vanessa wrote with clarity and elegance and probably inherited a bigger share of the Stephen intellect than her two brothers did. She had only three children, whereas her mother had had seven, and she was sexually active from age twenty-eight to thirty-nine, and only intermittently even during that period. Virginia did not desire men, it is true, but she was as sensuous as the furry animals she habitually compared herself to. As girl and woman, she was attracted to women, and she was as eager for motherhood as her sister was.

But if Vanessa had a lot of Athena in her, and Virginia yearned to be a Demeter, when it came to the sexual antics of their friends, each Stephen sister followed her own course. Vanessa at the center stage-managed, designed, and oversaw the script for many of the Bloomsbury dramas. Some were farce, like Maynard arriving for the weekend with his plebeian Ganymede, Mr. Atkins. Some were tragedy, like the commitment to an asylum of Harry Norton, a distinguished Cambridge University mathematician and a close friend of both Clive and Vanessa Bell. Virginia moved in and out of Bloomsbury, now active participant mesmerizing her friends with her whimsical fantasy and mordant wit, now detached, critical observer.

When Leonard Woolf became Virginia's husband, he became the most important person shaping her world, but Vanessa was always the second sun in Virginia Woolf's sky, and to understand her we need to see the evolution of their relationship and the contrast between their lives. Even as she weaned herself off the adoring, erotic dependence on Vanessa of the period 1907–11, Woolf followed the idiosyncratic trajectory of her sister's life with passionate concern and a deep longing for the harmonious intimacy they had once known. As late as June 1929, Woolf was adding a desolate little postscript to a letter to Vanessa, her "Dearest Dolphin": "I almost wrote you, by the way, ten pages of adoration and deification of motherhood — but refrained, thinking you wd think it sentimental. Now if you sometimes kissed me *voluntarily* I wd. not be afraid." Woolf signs herself "B" — Billy, the Goat of the happy old Kensington days.

Through her flirtation with Clive Bell, Virginia had, without thinking it through, sought to take control of her sister's life and reclaim Vanessa for herself. She would never make that mistake again. Vanessa had declared herself a woman intent on living her own life and controlling her own destiny, and Virginia's role was to support, if not endorse, the choices her sister made. Unfailing loyalty was Virginia's way of atoning for the great betrayal.

In the next four chapters, we will be interweaving the lives of the two sisters and contrasting the different communities that gathered around them within the general social entity known as the Bloomsbury group.

Vanessa's Bloomsbury was small, well-defined, male-oriented, self-absorbed, financed largely by unearned income, hostile to the world outside, very gay in both senses of that word, the epitome of what people admired and loathed about the group. As we shall see, Vanessa Bell's Bloomsbury declined when Carrington became Lytton Strachey's companion and housekeeper and Lytton and

Carrington's homes at Tidmarsh and Hamspray competed with Charleston for visitors. It suffered even more when John Maynard Keynes married the Russian dancer Lydia Lopokova, and the Keynes estate at Tilton in Sussex again turned into an alternative mecca for the group. Vanessa Bell's Bloomsbury swelled again as her sons came of age and her daughter blossomed.

Virginia Woolf's Bloomsbury was larger, fuzzier, busier, less sybaritic, more porous, more integrated, more down-to-earth. After World War I, unlike her sister's, it blossomed with stimulating and supportive friendships with women while remaining rooted in the love of one man, her husband and partner, Leonard Woolf.

&

If Virginia had hoped to show her sister that Vanessa had married a man far inferior to their father or their older brother Thoby, she succeeded. If Virginia had hoped to separate the Bells, she failed. It suited Vanessa far better to be a Mrs. Bell, with a husband in tow — at least on odd weekends — than a Miss Stephen or a divorcée. In some ways Clive Bell was a model husband — affluent, socially adept, even-tempered, and generous, a pampered man and inclined to pomposity, certainly, but not hard for a clever woman to manage. Even after they went their separate ways, the Bells continued for some years to find pleasure in bed when under the same roof, and as late as 1912 Vanessa still saw her husband as a prime candidate to give her the third child she wanted. "Do you miss your Dolph, my legitimate Male?" she coyly wrote to Clive.

Children had come to be even more important than painting to Vanessa Bell, in part because they were her trump card in the lifelong game of one-upwomanship she played with her sister. Virginia was the first to admit that, however well her books and articles might sell, she would always feel inferior to Vanessa because she had no children. Vanessa Bell was in no way a modern "helicopter"-style mother, and she often went off on long vacations without her children when they were young. That said, she was as committed as her mother, Julia Stephen, had been to ensuring that her children assumed their proper place in English society. That commitment will, as we shall see, take especial importance for her third child, Angelica.

For her children's sake, it was essential for Vanessa Bell to secure the support not only of her "legitimate Male" Clive Bell but also of his wealthy father. In this she succeeded. She made the children an enjoyable joint enterprise in which Clive and his family supplied the money and she did the parenting. Clive took pride in his paternity and was ready to enjoy his sons as soon as they changed from howling banshees to articulate charmers. As for Clive's father, William Heward Bell, an ill-tempered man with strong patriarchal instincts, he was gratified by his "artistic" younger son's ability to sire two healthy male offspring in as many years. As part of the generous settlement George Duckworth had negotiated for her at the time of her marriage, Vanessa personally received Mr. Bell's check for one thousand pounds for each child she produced — some fifty thousand in today's pounds. Hence, although Vanessa dreaded her visits to the home of her parents-in-law and wrote vivid accounts to her sister of the horrors of life at Cleeve House, she continued to make the annual pilgrimage to Wiltshire, dragging her increasingly reluctant children with her.

Socially, Vanessa's mask of serenity, her policy of non-confrontation, her silent but steely determination to do what suited her best paid dividends for many years. It made a sister-husband affair that smoldered for over three years into something incidental, unworthy of gossip even in gossip-addicted Bloomsbury. She accepted without demur the fact that her husband was a serial philanderer whose mistresses grew younger and younger as he himself grew old. As the years went by, Vanessa would chuckle over stories of Clive's sexual adventures, entertain his mistresses in her home, flatter his ego, and smile at his prejudices. She was his reliable ally in the social battles he chose to engage, notably the one with Lady Ottoline Morrell, the flamboyant socialite and generous patron of the arts whom Clive could not forgive for saving him from the army by offering him employment on her estate at Garsington during World War I and requiring him to do no actual work. For Clive Bell such aristocratic patronage was insupportable, so Clive and Vanessa and their friend Lytton Strachey, another major beneficiary of Lady Ottoline's largesse, were very nasty indeed about her behind her back.

Clive hated unpleasantness and mess, and since divorce in those times was inevitably messy and unpleasant, the question of divorce seems rarely to have arisen in the sixty-three years of the Bell marriage. By lavishing on her husband the charm and tolerance for which she would become famous in the Bloomsbury group, Vanessa kept Clive tied to her by a long, flexible leash. But if, deep down, Vanessa Stephen had hoped to find with Clive Bell the passionate devotion that her adored mother, Julia Stephen, had secured in both her marriages, she had failed. Cynicism, disillusion, and unfulfilled sexual needs would henceforth color Vanessa Bell's worldview.

Another woman faced with the dual challenge of both Virginia and Mrs. Raven-Hill would have looked at once for a lover of her own, but instead, Vanessa found support and solace in the company of her husband's most amusing friends, first Lytton Strachey and then Maynard Keynes. That both men were outrageously gay was part of the complicated appeal they had for her.

Lytton Strachey, as we have seen, enters our story as a close "Cambridge" friend of both Thoby Stephen and Clive Bell, as Leonard Woolf's loyal correspondent during Woolf's years in Sri Lanka, and as an influential member of both the Cambridge Conversazione Society and the play-reading Midnight Society. Delighting in gossip and fascinated by the way heterosexuals fell in love and got married, Lytton in 1906 had helped stoke the fire of Clive Bell's passion for Vanessa Stephen even as he was trying to convince Leonard Woolf to come back to England and woo Virginia. Now, in the early, confusing, and distressing years of the Bell marriage, Lytton Strachey became Vanessa's most intimate friend and closest ally.

If Vanessa had personal reasons to cut connections with the Kensington world of her parents, Lytton was by her side to tell her enthusiastically that she was right to do it. The Victorian world had finally gone unlamented into its grave, crowed Lytton. He and Vanessa were part of a new and wonderful generation of artists and rebels. "I sometimes feel," Lytton had written to Leonard as early as 1904, "as if it were not ourselves who are concerned but that the destinies of the whole world are somehow involved in ours. We are — oh! — in more ways than one — like the Athenians of the Periclean Age. We are the mysterious priests of a new and amazing civilization. We are greater than our fathers; we are greater than Shelley; we are greater than the eighteenth century; we are greater than the Renaissance; we are greater than the Romans and the Greeks."

In an autobiographical fragment, Vanessa Bell identifies Lytton Strachey as the catalyst for transforming the "Old Bloomsbury" of her conventional brother Thoby into a group that rebelled against the parental generation. "Only those just getting to know [Lytton] well," she wrote, "in those days when complete freedom of mind and expression were almost unknown, can understand what an exciting world of explorations of thought and feelings [Lytton] seemed to reveal. His great honesty of mind and remorseless poking fun at any sham forced others to be honest and showed a world in which one need no longer be afraid of saying what one thought, surely the first step to anything that would be of interest and value."

In the new Bloomsbury that formed after the death of Thoby Stephen under the influence of Lytton Strachey, by common consent and in personal statements that amounted almost to a manifesto, morality was to be divorced from sex, and ethics was displaced in favor of aesthetics. Heterosexuals in the group, especially male heterosexuals, were authorized to observe a code of conduct common among homosexual men. Every man had the right, amounting to a duty, to follow the dictates of his heart — or, to put it less delicately, go where his dick led him, and if a man desired the lover or spouse of a dear friend, he would have him or her if he could. Spouses and lovers and friends would, of course, let out howls of pain and hurl accusations after such betrayals, but they were expected to get a grip in short order and harbor no hard feelings.

Given the dangers of sex with professionals (this was the era when venereal diseases flourished unchecked in brothels that catered to heterosexual men and before AIDS wreaked havoc in the gay community), Bloomsberries (a name coined by Molly MacCarthy) sought where possible to find sex partners in their own set. Thus, though knowing his dear friend Lytton Strachey was passionately attached to Duncan Grant, Maynard Keynes had no real compunction about securing Duncan as his own lover. When Duncan moved on, he and Lytton and Maynard all remained friends. Similarly, Clive Bell switched from Anne Raven-Hill to Mary Hutchinson and then Gwen St. Aubyn, Christabel Aberconway, and so on, while pursuing Molly MacCarthy, the wife of his dear, charmingly adulterous friend Desmond, and later, Frances Marshall, the lover and eventually the wife of his friend Ralph Partridge.

In the brave new world of Gordon Square, women would enjoy, or at least have, the same right to complete sexual freedom as men. This was the doctrine preached by Lytton Strachey, the doctrine accepted, with tragic results, by his female companion, Carrington. Basking in Lytton's praise and extrapolating from Lytton's ideas, Vanessa Bell was not yet ready to take a male lover of her own, but she embraced the idea of a society in which a woman, or at least a woman like herself, could exercise autonomy, own her body, consult her own interests, follow her desire, paint a nude picture, or pose for one, as she chose.

Social revolution à la Lytton began with names. Upper-middle-class Englishmen before World War I habitually referred to one another by their surnames, and women were Miss X or Mrs. Y, but the denizens of Bloomsbury used first names. Bell became Clive, Strachey became Lytton, Forster became Morgan, Miss Stephen/Mrs. Bell became Vanessa, or even Nessa. Bloomsbury men and women also had the same esoteric vocabulary, from "catachresis" to "catamite," from "Coptic" to "copulate," and together they acted out bawdy Restoration comedies and discussed anything from Beethoven to Botticelli to Bolshevism to buggery. As her letters amply prove, Vanessa Bell had, in the words of her biographer Frances Spalding, "entered the smoking room and she . . . began to produce bawdy words with all the glee of a spoiled child."

Both Virginia and Vanessa recorded how excited they had been to talk like the men. "The word bugger was never far from our lips," wrote Virginia Woolf proudly in "Old Bloomsbury." "We discussed copulation with the same excitement and openness with which we had discussed the nature of good." For women to be made privy to things that men habitually said only to one another was new in middle-class English society, and this inclusiveness has been heralded in Bloomsbury literature as an "antidote to Victorian Puritanism." "Vanessa by her behavior was making social history," writes Spalding. "Not only was she using words that her mother would have pretended not to understand, but she was doing so in conversation with men, thereby insisting on an equality rare even among feminists." (Spalding is, I think, right on the money when she says that Victorian women "pretended not to understand" certain words, not that they did not know them. In her frequent visits to the London slums, Julia Stephen Duckworth certainly heard words like "cunt," but, unlike her daughter Vanessa, she never used them in her correspondence.)

It was Lytton who, in an incident that would go down in Bloomsbury mythology, entered the Bell drawing room, spotted a white stain on Vanessa's dress, and remarked, "Semen?" It was Lytton who instructed Vanessa to read *Les liaisons dangereuses,* an eighteenth-century novel of subtle and delicious perversity that was written, not incidentally, given the later importance of Bloomsbury correspondence, entirely in letters. It was Lytton who lent Vanessa his "most indecent poems," as an astonished and delighted Maynard Keynes reported to Duncan Grant, and gave her permission to type them up and circulate them.

Given the exalted claims Lytton in 1904 was making for Bloomsbury as the new "Periclean Age," it is fun to look at one of the poems that Vanessa Bell found so liberating. As an appendix to the second volume of his biography, which is devoted to celebrating Lytton Strachey's literary legacy, Sir Michael Holroyd reproduces Lytton's 1904 long narrative poem "The Death of Milo." If I may summarize, the "mighty boxer" Milo decides on a trial of strength with an oak tree and becomes inextricably caught in its fork. (I am not making this up!) Milo dies in the tree's grasp but defies his fate in an orgasmic act of what, in the argot of the Strachey clan, was known as "forthing" — excretion and micturition. "From the opening gut," begins one stanza, "slow as the child of anxious birth it voyaged . . . then hung one trembling moment, and to earth."

Reportedly, when Vanessa passed her poems like this, Virginia Woolf laughed. I think Woolf was right. As a piece of second-grade humor or adult male rodomontade, if I may borrow from Lytton's French vocabulary, "The Death of Milo" is very funny in ways that its young author probably did not intend.

Apart from his literary work, Vanessa took a friendly interest in Lytton's amatory pursuits, and by April 28, 1909, she was writing to him from Florence, noting that the *pensione* where she and Clive were staying "has some awful females, but two young men who sing you might flirt with. They walk past our windows on their way to the baths every morning and there are strange goings on on the veranda at all hours of the night. There might be still stranger if you were here."

She also notes as a feature of the landscape bound to interest Lytton that "as we came along in the train a row of naked boys saluted us." To judge by

Lytton's correspondence, Vanessa Bell here is echoing comments about small naked foreign boys she had heard from her gay male friends. One particularly egregious example can be found in an August 1931 letter Lytton wrote to his lover Roger Senhouse, offering news of a recent trip taken in Spain and Morocco by their mutual friends Raymond Mortimer and George "Dadie" Rylands. "Dearest dearest creature," wrote Lytton to Roger, "a letter from Dadie at Tocklington contained the following—'The Spaniards do not quite see eye to eye with us in affairs of the body, but there was a guide at Marrakech — and R[aymond] bargained (in vain) for a child of five summers. I was most distressed.'" Presumably owing to the bargain being attempted, rather than its failure.

Vanessa Bell, it seems, in an attempt at urbane sophistication, was picking up on a particular kind of cultural blindness among these men at this time, which would become a problem she had to solve as the mother of two boys. Was it possible that friends whom she welcomed in her home, like Senhouse and Mortimer, might pose a threat not just to anonymous little boys in Spain or Morocco, but to her darling Julian and his brother? When is a boy old enough to engage in a sexual relationship with an adult male? In England between the world wars, people like the Bells, who enjoyed sexual freedom, practiced tolerance, and scorned conventional morality, were content to leave that question to classical scholars. They had been reliably informed that in the original, unexpurgated text of the *Phaedrus,* Socrates extolled the love of a man and a boy as the highest form of human love. What was good enough for Plato was surely good enough for Bloomsbury.

ॐ

It was Lytton Strachey who brought John Maynard Keynes into the Bloomsbury group, and he may have come to regret it, since Maynard struck almost everyone but Carrington, who worshiped Lytton, as Lytton to the power of ten. All his life, Keynes could get more done in a day than other able men in three, and once installed in the ranks of academia and government, he moved smoothly up the ladder of power. Even Bertrand Russell, the famous philosopher, pacifist, and Nobel Prize winner, acknowledged the diamond brilliance of Keynes's mind even though he could not stand to be with Keynes the man.

Keynes knew from boyhood that he was homosexual. At Eton, where he won all the prizes while excelling at the notoriously bloody Wall Game and was elected to Pop, the elite social club, Keynes had at least one male lover, Dillwyn Knox, and several of those passionate friendships that at public schools were allowed to hover deliciously on the very edge of orgasm. At Trinity College as an undergraduate and at King's College as a fellow, Keynes felt both sexually and intellectually at home — love affairs between men were too common to provoke comment, much less punishment. Homosexuality was central to Keynes's self-identity, and right up to the time of his marriage, in 1925, he pursued love and lovers with the same energy, pragmatism, and success that he applied to economic theory, international finance, and the stock market.

Once Keynes moved to London, he became close to the members of the Bloomsbury group. In 1909, Vanessa and her husband, Clive, were staying in Cambridge, and Maynard had them to tea at King's. While Vanessa poured and passed the scones in her best Kensington manner, Maynard regaled her and Clive with the latest homosexual gossip. Harry Norton, they learned, was despairingly in love with James Strachey, who was madly in love with Rupert Brooke, who had an endearing way of diving nude into a lake and emerging with a full erection. Maynard himself was successfully competing with Lytton Strachey for the favors of Duncan Grant. Maynard wrote of his meeting with the Bells to Duncan: "Vanessa explained how interesting it was for her to come up and have a look at us, Lytton having explained every one of our secrets. She was perfectly lovely — I've never seen her so beautiful — and very conversational . . . She seemed to hold the floor." This scene of shared conviviality between men and women at King's College contrasts strongly with the scene of silence and intellectual dismissal described, as we saw in Chapter 11, by Virginia Woolf at Trinity College at around the same time.

As Lytton became increasingly entangled with Lady Ottoline Morrell and Carrington and absorbed in the writing of his great book *Eminent Victorians,* Maynard Keynes replaced him as Vanessa Bell's closest friend. Maynard was deeply attached to both his mother and his sister and partial to the company of women as long as they didn't try to be clever, and he savored Vanessa's charm, bohemian style, devotion to painting, and scabrous conversation. Thus, in April 1914, following an enjoyable weekend at Asheham, the Sussex house that she and Virginia had subleased to Maynard, Vanessa was on sufficiently intimate terms to open a thank-you letter as follows:

> Dear Maynard, it is plainly quite superfluous for me to write and tell you how much we [she and Clive] had enjoyed ourselves at Asheham and so the only thing I can do, since you insist upon my writing, is to make my letter so bawdy that you will have to destroy it at once for fear of Lily's [the maid at Asheham] seeing it. Did you have a pleasant afternoon buggering one or more of the young men we left for you? It must have been delicious out on the downs in that afternoon sun, a thing I have often wanted to do, but one never gets the opportunity and the desire at the right moment. I imagine you, however, with your bare limbs intertwined with him and all the ecstatic preliminaries of Sucking Sodomy.

From 1911 to 1925, there were four key men revolving around Vanessa Bell — Clive Bell, Duncan Grant, Roger Fry, and John Maynard Keynes. The testimony of Quentin Bell in 1995 and the research of Robert Skidelsky, in his groundbreaking 2003 biography of Keynes, establish that, though Maynard was never Vanessa's lover, he was something almost more important, a loving, generous, reliable friend. In 1916 it was Keynes — arriving at the decisive hearing with his official red attaché case, embossed with the royal crest, to impress the hell out of the local worthies — who managed to get Duncan Grant and Bunny Garnett registered as conscientious objectors and thus kept them out of jail. Then, for the two years when Duncan and Bunny worked as agricultural laborers in lieu of military service and kept on hold their careers as painter and writer, Maynard supported them, paying both men an annuity.

As Quentin Bell makes clear in *Bloomsbury Recalled*, when Vanessa was living at the Charleston farmhouse with her lover Duncan Grant and his lover Bunny Garnett between 1916 and 1919, Maynard was present more often than Clive and Roger and, as a member of the English homosexual community, fitted in more easily. The arrival of Maynard from Whitehall in his chauffeur-driven car, bearing gifts, was always a joyful event for all five members of Vanessa's wartime household. The fact that Maynard never really hit it off personally with Virginia — who found his self-importance grating and pompous — or politically with Leonard made his friendship even more precious to Vanessa.

As he advanced in power and influence, Maynard continued to use them on behalf of his Bloomsbury chums. He obligingly paid Duncan and Vanessa to decorate his King's College rooms, bought pictures at his artist friends' recommendation, and served on art committees to aid struggling British artists. To be close to his friends, Keynes first sublet a large suite of rooms from Virginia and Adrian Stephen in Fitzroy Square and then took over the lease on that whole property, subletting it in turn to Clive Bell and a flock of other Bloomsbury characters before making it his main London residence. Growing fond of the Sussex countryside, he bought the Tilton estate that abutted the Bells' Charleston farm.

After World War I, Maynard took over the investment portfolios of Clive, Vanessa, and Duncan. Given that Keynes was the man famous in university annals for turning King's into one of the richest Cambridge colleges, this was a rather considerable advantage. It was in no small part thanks to Keynes that after 1918 Vanessa Bell was able to rent agreeable homes not only in London and Sussex but in France, and keep up a household staff that allowed her to entertain her friends and at the same time devote hours of every day to her painting.

Part of the fame enjoyed today by Vanessa Bell is the result of her art — the little exhibit of her photographs at the Dulwich College Picture Gallery organized by the singer and writer Patti Smith, in 2017, is a good example — but much of it also comes from the central role she played in the life of the Bloomsbury group. As Bloomsbury came into its glory days between the two world wars, Vanessa Bell became the Bloomsbury hostess par excellence, even as her sister became the recording angel. In her various homes, Vanessa developed a style of housekeeping whose mix of the Spartan and the sybaritic, of tolerance and tact, taste and intellect, charm and erudition, fresh air and fresh vegetables drew a select group of friends like a magnet. Visitors to Charleston after the end of World War I could rely on quiet mornings of solitary work followed by long walks on the Sussex downs, and then, after a splash of water on the face and under the armpits, there were boozy evenings full of gourmet food, society smut from Clive Bell, inside-Whitehall revelations from Maynard Keynes, and killing impersonations from Duncan Grant.

It was not by chance that in 1918 John Maynard Keynes drafted much of his famous pamphlet "The Economic Consequences of the Peace" in a deck chair in the sunny walled garden at Charleston. Soon to be recognized as the greatest economist of his time, Keynes foresaw terrible consequences should the victorious allies decide to bring Germany to its knees in retribution. Keynes would be proved right. Adolf Hitler was one of the men who never forgave the vindictive terms of the 1919 Treaty of Versailles. But as he sat envisaging a second armageddon in his lifetime, Keynes could find a kind of elemental comfort in the pandemonium of children and chickens and wet canvases that surrounded queenly Vanessa Bell.

Between 1918 and 1925 — the year when Maynard married Lydia Lopokova — he, Vanessa Bell, and Duncan Grant were what Quentin Bell describes as a happy, carefree "triumvirate." Largely at Maynard's expense, the trio dined out at the top London restaurants and took lavish trips to the Continent in Keynes's limousine. One gets the impression from the memoirs of Quentin Bell that in some ways Maynard Keynes was more of a father to him than either his actual father, Clive Bell, or his mother's chosen partner, Duncan Grant. Both Vanessa and Virginia found Keynes's wife, Lydia Lopokova Keynes, impossible, but Quentin as a boy had the run of the Keyneses' house in Bloomsbury, and he calls the Maynard-Lydia marriage "a vast success." Quentin Bell concludes that, when Keynes dropped out of their lives, or was forced out by Vanessa's hostility to Lydia, life for his mother and Duncan Grant "was permanently impoverished."

❧

By 1911, using words that would have shocked her mother, reading salacious literature, partaking of the latest gay gossip, and enjoying Maynard's largesse were no longer enough for thirty-two-year-old Vanessa Bell, and she began a love affair with the art critic Roger Fry. The affair came to a shuddering halt in 1914, but while it lasted it was immensely exciting not just for Vanessa but for all the Bloomsbury group.

Vanessa had briefly met Fry back in 1906 after one of his art lectures, and when she spotted him at the Cambridge railway station in January 1910, she claimed an acquaintance. In the train compartment on the way back to London, the busy Fry put his papers aside and soon showed that he was not only an excellent lecturer but a good listener and a wonderful conversationalist. Fry, Vanessa remarked as she sat back and let her husband and Fry talk, was the rare Cambridge bird who seemed to both like and desire women, especially intelligent, art-loving women. Now in his mid-forties and famous, if not rich and titled, Fry had a flock of art groupies, including Lady Ottoline Morrell.

That initial favorable impression of Fry was confirmed in late 1910 after Vanessa gave birth to her second child. The baby came three weeks later than expected and was a second son. Vanessa was disappointed. She had been sure that the second child she was bearing was a daughter and had a name ready for "her" — Clarissa, a name that lives on in two of Virginia Woolf's novels. Revealing a lack of interest in her second son that he himself felt persisted all his life, Vanessa begged friends like Saxon Sydney-Turner to come up with a name for the baby. Gratian? Or perhaps Claudian? She did not settle on the name Quentin for more than a year and, as an auntly joke, Virginia Woolf would still be referring to Quentin as Claudian when he was twenty.

When the new baby failed to thrive even more dramatically than her first child, Julian, had done, Vanessa was distraught, and when it came to howling babies, Clive was, of course, nowhere to be seen. Following this difficult postpartum period, Clive invited Roger Fry to dinner, and the interest Vanessa had in Fry's ideas on painting turned into something much warmer. Somehow, while Clive went off to fetch some wine, she felt able to confide her worries about her baby to their guest. Fry listened and said he and his wife, Helen, had also had "fearful times" with their newborn son. "I had a sort of inkling then," wrote Vanessa to Roger in October 1912, "that you would be sympathetic and understand. No one else that I cared about had been and I had had to keep most of my worries to myself." When the Bells invited Roger to join them and Harry Norton, an old Cambridge friend of Clive's who now formed part of Vanessa's gay coterie, on a trip to Turkey, Fry happily agreed.

Roger Fry stood out from the old Cambridge pack by being a scientist by training, an art critic by vocation, and a straight man who — like Thackeray —

had a mad wife. Fry had graduated from Cambridge some twelve years before Clive Bell, and unlike him, had been elected an Apostle. After getting a first-class degree in the natural sciences Tripos, Fry, unlike Lytton Strachey, was immediately offered a fellowship at Cambridge but refused it to follow his interest in the fine arts. That decision incurred the wrath of his wealthy father, who cut off all future economic support. Undeterred by the need to earn his own living, Fry not only followed his passion for art but married a fortuneless fellow artist, Helen Coombe, and quickly had two children with her. A man of astonishing brilliance, inexhaustible curiosity, and restless energy, Fry quickly established himself as an expert on early Italian painting and a great art critic.

Fry seemed destined for England's highest academic honors and an eventual knighthood until his attention was drawn away from Duccio and Guido Reni to Cézanne, Degas, and young living artists like Picasso and Matisse. Roger Fry came from an illustrious Quaker family, and though he had given up the faith, he had the strong backbone and the nonconformist instincts of his ancestors. Refusing to trim his ideas and interests to fit his professional prospects and financial needs, Fry in lectures and essays began to advance revolutionary ideas on art. These so set the teeth of the English art establishment on edge that he was blackballed for top academic posts. He was then obliged to take on an exhausting schedule of writing and lecturing in order to support his family, especially after his wife was admitted to a private clinic for the insane. Helen Fry had become unmanageably crazy, a danger to her children as well as herself: after her death, an autopsy revealed that the bone of her skull was progressively thickening, crushing her brain. Roger had felt he had no choice but to commit his wife, but her pathetic pleas to be allowed to return home to him and the children weighed heavily on him.

When planning the expedition to Turkey, Clive had expected Vanessa to cope with Harry Norton while he went around the cultural sites with Roger. Clive was setting himself up as an expert on contemporary French painting, and Roger's rejection of storytelling art and his theory of "significant form" fascinated him. Once they arrived in Istanbul, however, the foursome began to split up in an unexpected way. Fry was soon speaking passable Turkish, scouring the bazaars for local arts and crafts, and generally taking on the role of guide, companion, and interpreter. He also proved to be an enthusiastic painter, and he and Vanessa began setting up their easels side by side before some picturesque landscape.

When the quartet of English tourists moved on to the provincial city of Broussa (or Brusa), Vanessa suddenly suffered a major breakdown. She became terrified that, like her sister Virginia, she was losing her mind. This collapse proved too much for Clive, who went off with Norton to tour the city's famous mosques, and it was left to Roger to keep Vanessa's spirits up. When she was haunted by nightmares and unable to sleep, he watched through the night with her, listening to her fears, keeping her back from insanity as he had tried in vain to do for his wife. It was now to Roger Fry, not Clive Bell, that Vanessa reached out a bare, shapely arm, and the two spent hours in absorbed conversation. Forgetting Lady Ottoline Morrell, who had quite unexpectedly taken him into her bed the night before his departure for Turkey, Roger Fry was soon madly in love with Vanessa Bell, and she showed herself more than receptive to his feelings.

Meanwhile, back in England, Virginia, after another stay in Jean Thomas's private clinic, was in good health but increasingly concerned about her sister, who had been suffering from unexplained fainting spells. Despite reassuring telegrams and letters from Clive, Virginia became more and more convinced that something bad was going on in Turkey, and her fears were confirmed when, as she was en route for a holiday in Greece with her friend Ka Cox, she learned that Vanessa had suffered a miscarriage in Broussa and was now bedridden. Seizing on the role of the strong, capable sister, Virginia set off alone at once to help bring Vanessa home. In a letter to Violet Dickinson she wrote after returning to London, in May 1911, Virginia described what had happened:

> Did you hear of our adventures in the East? Nessa managed to bring off a miscarriage in Broussa a days journey from Constantinople. I went out and found her surrounded with males and with a chemist for a doctor. We had to have a litter made to carry her stretched on it, through Constantinople and home by the Orient Express. *It was the oddest parody of what we [Virginia and Violet] did five years ago in Greece . . .* We had the oddest time abroad. I was there for a week. *Roger put everything down to insanity, which was puzzling at first.* [my emphasis]

As this passage shows, Virginia Woolf and Roger Fry, who both had experience of mental illness, diagnosed Vanessa's problems as more psychological than gynecological. In fact, when Vanessa Bell got back to London and indignantly confronted the doctor who had given her permission to embark for Turkey, he denied that she had suffered a miscarriage. Be that as it may — and there were no quick tests for pregnancy back in 1911 — there was a pattern in Vanessa's behavior that her sister picked up on. Just as in 1906, Vanessa was unconsciously staging a bout of invalidism in order to make a difficult transition in her life. That transition again had to do with a potential sex partner — not a prospective husband, this time, but a prospective lover whom she had identified as Roger Fry. Given how hesitant both Clive and Vanessa had been to give Virginia a clear picture of the situation in Broussa, it is possible neither of them exactly welcomed her arrival in Turkey.

Certainly, within weeks of her dramatic return to London on a stretcher, Vanessa had found a sympathetic psychiatrist and, under the cover of a yearlong recovery from her supposed miscarriage, she and Roger engaged in a passionate love affair. Vanessa was anxious to keep her affair secret from both her husband — whose desire revived as soon as he saw a heterosexual male closing in on his wife — and her sister, whom she saw as a rival. When introduced, Virginia and Roger had immediately become fast friends.

Vanessa Bell and Roger Fry were lovers for less than two years, but that brief period was immensely stimulating and huge fun. Fry was intent on stirring up the stodgy English art scene, and in the fall of 1911 and 1912, with the enthusiastic collaboration of his new Bloomsbury friends, he put on two exhibitions of paintings at the Grafton Galleries for which he coined the term "post-impressionist." These exhibitions were greeted with howls of outrage and accusations of obscenity by press and public alike, but to British artists like Duncan Grant and Vanessa Bell, the paintings that Fry had personally identified, shipped, and hung were a revelation. The Grafton exhibitions did nothing for Fry's reputation in the English art world, but undeterred, he raised a little money from friends and launched the Omega Workshops. An homage to the Arts and Crafts movement of the late nineteenth century and a precursor of the Bauhaus movement, the Omega Workshops were conceived as an artists' cooperative that would foster, collect, and market the latest in British design.

The sexual passion that flamed up in Vanessa soon died down. One gathers from Frances Spalding's twin biographies of Bell and Fry that Roger Fry was too straightforward, too idealistic, too energetic, too intellectual, too poor, too old, too nice, and too Quaker for Vanessa. Worst of all, perhaps, as a painter, he seemed to have learned nothing from the Picassos or Matisses he had transported to London. Fry could turn his hand to almost anything — mending a broken water pump at Asheham, turning a pot on a wheel on his first try, translating the obscurantist French poet Mallarmé — but the paintings he produced in such profusion and with such enthusiasm seemed to Vanessa pedestrian, fuddy-duddy.

For Roger Fry, Vanessa Bell was the ideal woman. He listened to her, sympathized with her, adored her unconditionally, and desired her passionately, but he failed to understand her. In the end, what he wanted from their relationship was what all too briefly he had had with Helen Coombe — a wife who would keep his hearth burning and welcome him with open arms when he returned from his forays into world art. But Vanessa Bell was not interested in ordinary domesticity, and the husband she had suited her in many ways. Clive had given her orgasms as well as sons, still supported her in agreeable affluence, and, unlike Roger, never felt compelled to get up immediately after a good lunch, jump on his bike, and do six more things before dinner. As Virginia Woolf wrote to John Lehmann after she, Leonard, Roger, and Fry's sister went on a trip to Greece, "Roger is the greatest fun — as mild as milk, but if you have seen milk that is also quicksilver . . . He disposes of whole museums with one brush of his tail. He plays chess when the dust is sweeping the pawns from the board. He writes articles with one hand & carries on violent arguments with the other."

And then there was Duncan Grant, the old family friend whom Vanessa now, thanks to Roger Fry, met almost every day in the galleries and in the Omega Workshops for which both artists worked and served as trustees.

ॐ

From the very first, Vanessa Bell's letters to Roger Fry are fatefully peppered with the name Duncan, and it is fascinating to trace the way she unconsciously transferred her erotic fantasies from one man to the other. In the very first letter we have from her to Fry, she wrote on June 23, 1911, "[Duncan] and I have decided to emulate Gill and paint really indecent subjects. I suggest a series of copulations in strange attitudes and have offered to pose. Will you join? I mean in the painting. We think there ought to be more indecent pictures painted, and you shall show them in your show."

Here again we can see Vanessa attempting the combination of sexual vocabulary and arch sophistication that Lytton Strachey had perfected in his letters and in his conversation.

On November 23, Vanessa Bell was again striving to arouse the ardor of Roger Fry by narrating a recent event that had obviously aroused her. Duncan Grant had been invited to dinner by Clive Bell and was for some reason shaving in the bathroom at the Bell residence at 49 Fitzroy Square. "And then — what do you think happened?" wrote Vanessa to Roger. "I had my bath in his [Duncan's] presence . . . and he wanted to shave and didn't see why he should move . . . and I didn't see why I should remain dirty, and Clive was there, and didn't object — and so! But I'm afraid he [Duncan] remained quite unmoved and I was really very decent. I felt no embarrassment and I think perhaps it was a useful precedent."

A precedent, useful or not, the bathroom scene certainly was, and we can hear the knell of Vanessa Bell's passion for Roger Fry sounding in a letter she wrote to her husband, Clive, while she and Roger were on holiday in the French countryside in May 1914. Roger Fry, let it be noted, was a very thin, white-haired man closing on fifty, Vanessa an increasingly voluptuous thirty-five. "Dearest," wrote Vanessa to Clive in Paris,

> We [she and Roger] have been very lucky so far . . . having had dinner on the train and found a most comfortable inn . . . and the best bed I have ever slept in. I went in to a solitary, soft couch with no hint of bony attenuated legs to spoil its down, and slept the sleep of the virtuous . . . We started out about 10 and bicycled slowly about four miles to

the village where we had lunch. I am now quite at home on my bicycle and am said (by R) to have a very neat figure. My ankle of course is seen to advantage. The attitude is one of prim decorum and a little strange to me at first, also a little hard on the cunt and on the muscles of my soft legs . . . Our tour as you see is being conducted on terms of modesty and propriety — how unlike your bachelor existence. In Paris. I suppose you are at this moment being fondled under the table by some whore and presently will go off with her . . . Do you think you or Duncan or both will meet us anywhere?

Within a year of writing that letter, Vanessa had taken a leaf from her gay friends' playbook and told Fry, with brutal frankness, that she could henceforth be only a friend to him.

For several years, Fry poured out his despair and frustration and incomprehension in letters to Vanessa, but she was already steering the treacherous shoals of her new affair with Duncan Grant. Vanessa confided her love troubles with Duncan to Roger as Maynard had confided his troubles with Duncan to Lytton years earlier, and Fry responded with affection and understanding, just as he had years earlier when she told him about Quentin's feeding difficulties. Roger Fry remained a loving, trustworthy friend to Vanessa Bell and to her sons and was a key member of the Charleston set. When Fry died in 1934, after what was supposed to be routine surgery, the grief, shock, and admiration for Fry that Vanessa expressed were heartfelt.

Vanessa's younger son, Quentin Bell, was profoundly influenced by Roger Fry. He loved and revered Roger the man and, like Fry, became an artist, art critic, and art historian. All the same, in the book of essays *Bloomsbury Recalled,* which he wrote shortly before his death, Bell scrupulously refuses to blame his mother for rejecting Fry's love. He merely remarks that "the period when Vanessa discovered Roger Fry was, perhaps, the happiest in her life," the time when his mother — so "grave and sad" in later life — was always laughing.

But if Vanessa Bell managed to keep Roger Fry spinning in her orbit even after she had rejected him as a lover, Virginia Woolf was Fry's delighted and devoted friend from the outset, and in the last years of her life, Virginia Woolf undertook a biography of Fry. In some ways, I think, Woolf sought to atone for all that Fry had suffered at the hands of her sister, that "wasteful child pulling the heads off flowers — beautiful as a goddess," as Woolf had once written to Violet Dickinson.

The Fry biography, to be published by her own Hogarth Press, was a labor of love, but as she wrestled with it, Woolf was increasingly sure the book was doomed to fail. "Discretion is not the better part of biography," Lytton Strachey had wittily remarked, and her *Roger Fry,* Woolf could see, was much closer to her father's *Dictionary of National Biography* than to Lytton Strachey's *Eminent Victorians,* offering none of the catnip of sexual innuendo that English readers had by this time come to expect from their literary historians as well as their novelists.

Anyone privileged to know Roger Fry knew that, while his tragically insane wife, Helen, was still alive, he had several women lovers and had conducted a brief but passionate affair with the wife of his friend and collaborator Clive Bell. Those in the know were also aware that "Goldie" Dickinson, Fry's oldest friend from Cambridge, was for many years passionately, hopelessly in love with Fry, and that many of Fry's other close friends were homosexual. Woolf knew that Fry's relationships were as important to an understanding of Fry the man as his expertise in the Italian quattrocento was to Fry the art critic, but nonetheless in her book she declined to offer even the coded hints Lytton specialized in. Vanessa, Goldie, and Helen Anrep, Fry's final partner, as well as Fry's sisters and his children, were still alive and would feel wounded by any revelations about his private life. Virginia Woolf was a professional writer and publisher to her fingertips. All the same, consideration for the feelings of others mattered more to her, and to Leonard, her co-publisher, than the number of copies sold. Hence, what might be called the sex life of Roger Fry finds no space in her book, which was greeted with muted praise when published and is today little read, even by Woolf's admirers.

What we have in Woolf's biography of Fry, the last thing she completed for publication before her suicide, is careful discussion of issues such as the influence on Fry of his Quaker heritage and the outrage he felt at the sometimes bloody canings that masters inflicted on little boys every week at his renowned prep school. Woolf was always on the lookout for documented examples of child sexual abuse. First and foremost, however, the book is the tribute to an important man from a great writer who had known and loved him well and could attest to both his greatnesses and his oddities.

With all her wide experience of biography, Woolf knew that, as a genre, it works by accretion over time, with each generation finding its point of interest, doing its own research, and directing its spin. Sure enough, biographers like Frances Spalding in the 1980s, free of legal concerns and social shibboleths, would be able to build on Woolf's material and use Woolf's personal testimony to offer the public fuller, more comprehensive, and more objective biographies of Roger Fry.

15

Virginia's Way, Part 1

VANESSA BELL need not have worried that her sister would steal Roger Fry. By the late summer of 1911, Virginia was going through a revolution of her own. It came in the tall, gaunt, sunburned shape of Leonard Woolf, back in England on leave after seven years as a rising officer in the colonial administration of Sri Lanka. In her Memoir Club paper "Old Bloomsbury," Virginia Woolf remembered that her brother Thoby had described his Trinity friend Leonard Woolf to her as "a man who trembled all over . . . so violent, so savage; he despised the whole human race." Whether or not Thoby Stephen actually uttered them, those words capture a lot about Virginia Woolf's husband. That she chose this man to be her husband, and remained his partner for life, tells us a lot about Virginia Woolf.

As early as 1908 Lytton Strachey was actively promoting the marriage of his friends Virginia and Leonard, arguing in his letters that Leonard alone was worthy of Virginia and that their marriage would succeed because Leonard was physically attracted to Virginia. Lytton was right. Leonard tells us in his autobiography that he fell in love with Virginia the first time he saw her. He also says, with characteristic straightforwardness, that though Virginia's ethereal personality and diamond-sharp intellect drew him to her, he expected sexual pleasure to become part of their love.

When Leonard Woolf at last made his mind up to come back home, Virginia Stephen was an almost thirty-year-old virgin and not happy about it. Vanessa, Clive, and Lytton had made the state of Virginia's hymen a subject of open discussion in Bloomsbury and Sussex. The same would happen to Carrington some years later.

According to the expanding LGBTQA spectrum we have developed in the twenty-first century, Virginia Woolf might, I think, best be described as very sensuous but sexually inhibited, unhappy in her own body, and more physically attracted to women than men. Virginia's attraction to lesbians is a kind of running joke between her and Vanessa, and in the letters Virginia wrote to Violet Dickinson before marrying Leonard Woolf, she is quite open about her "Sapphic" feelings. To Dickinson, she presents herself as a fragile sparrow or kangaroo or wallaby longing to jump back into the pouch. "I feel all my heart drawn to you," she wrote to Dickinson. "Upon that, I cuddle on my mat, and roll over and let you look for fleas." Based on my reading of the early letters, for men Woolf shows not a flicker of desire. Where Charlotte Brontë, Elizabeth Barrett Browning, and George Eliot had been plain women who were passionately attracted to men who often failed to reciprocate their feelings, Virginia Woolf was a beautiful woman who attracted men and, as we have seen in Chapter 13, kept them at bay.

When Leonard first proposed, Virginia asked for time to consider, and in a remarkable letter, on May 1, 1912, she strove to be as open and straightforward as possible about her most intimate needs and desires — "I want everything — love, intimacy, adventure, work" she writes — but also about her lack of sexual desire. "As I told you brutally the other day, I feel no physical attraction in you. There are moments — when you kissed me the other day was one — when I feel no more than a rock." In her willingness to confront her sexual issues and put them into her own words, Virginia was very different from her sister, and Leonard's passion burned through her defenses; she had never met a man she liked, admired, and trusted so much. With Leonard Woolf, Virginia Stephen was willing to give sex a try, and in May 1912 they were married at St. Pancras town hall.

The short ceremony was interrupted when Vanessa Bell, out of the blue, broke in to request information from the civic official as to how she could

Virginia and Leonard Woolf on their wedding day

change the name of her second son. Such casual interference from the Bells would mark the early years of the Woolf marriage.

On her honeymoon, Virginia tried hard to respond to her husband, and in one letter from Italy she laughingly remarks that really, making love is not so hard. But this was wishful thinking on her part, and her husband, an inexperienced and over-eager lover, was feeling a kind of despair. After a particularly bad night, he sent a letter of appeal to his wife's sister, the act of a practical, well-meaning man who had successfully governed a large province in Sri Lanka but had no idea as yet of how to handle the socio-sexual dynamics of Bloomsbury. Leonard may have realized he had in good faith made a bad move when he got Vanessa's reply.

You and Virginia have been very naughty not keeping us filled in on all your doings, Vanessa begins, but

> after your awful description of a night with the apes [Virginia's weirdly plural pet name] I can imagine why *you* don't write to me. I am happy to say it's years since I spent a night in their [Virginia's] company, and I can't conceive anything more wretched than it sounds. It would be bad enough to know they were in the next bed with all their smells and their whines and their wettings, but to have to change beds with them and all the rest of it — a coal hole would be more to my taste.

Vanessa was, perhaps, making a ham-fisted attempt at honeymoon humor, but if Leonard shared the letter with Virginia, as he most probably did, one doubts that she found it funny.

Back in England, Leonard and Virginia consulted specialists, and word of the Woolfs' sexual incompatibility spread around Bloomsbury. All parties, including Virginia, believed that the marital difficulties were her fault. She was not only deemed "frigid," in the vocabulary of the day, but unlike other women (surprisingly, the sex goddesses Madame de Pompadour and Marilyn Monroe come to mind), she was unable to fake pleasure or even just close her eyes and think of England, as per the old Victorian saying.

From a modern perspective, the one-sidedness of the medical consensus on the Woolfs' sexual issues is rather glaring. Leonard Woolf was certainly no sexual athlete like Clive or Maynard, and at least one close friend with a lot of expertise in the matter thought Leonard was gay. In his 1978 book *Thrown to the Woolfs,* John Lehmann, for some years a partner in the Hogarth Press, opined that Leonard was a closeted homosexual, his manifest neuroses rooted in frustrated sexuality. Lehmann saw Woolf pay serious money for a nude male statue for his garden and react with pleasure to an especially attractive young man. Lehmann says Leonard once admitted that he had been in love with Thoby Stephen, which casts more light on the circle of Cambridge men in "Old Bloomsbury" that I discussed in Chapter 11.

Conjecture aside, we know that Leonard was the product of a prep school–public school system in which Jewish boys were routinely bullied, and abuse could easily take a sexual turn. In the Cambridge of his day, gay life flourished, and after university Woolf spent years in the kind of colonial outpost where white women were scarce and the exploitation of local boys was common. The single affair in Sri Lanka, which Woolf briefly alludes to in his autobiography, was, however, with a woman. After his marriage to Virginia, Leonard had no mistresses. Bloomsbury letters and memoirs would have mentioned it if he had. According to Virginia's biographer Hermione Lee, Leonard Woolf never had sex with his second wife, Trekkie Parsons.

Vanessa Bell was included in the Woolfs' medical and private consultations in 1912 and was pleased to be able to pass details on to her husband. Clive was no longer hoping to get Virginia into bed, but he was jealous of any man who might, and he didn't much like the post–Sri Lanka Leonard. Clive would be glad, Vanessa knew, that things were not working out well between the newlyweds, so on December 27, 1912, she wrote to him that the "Woolves," as she was beginning to call them,

> are evidently both a little exercised in their minds on the subject of the Goat's [that is, Virginia's] coldness. I think I may have annoyed her but consoled him by saying that I thought she had never understood or sympathized with sexual passion in men. Apparently she still gets no pleasure at all from the act, which I think is curious. They were very anxious to know when I first had an orgasm. I couldn't remember. Do you? But no doubt I sympathized with such things if I didn't have them from the time I was 2.

Ah — here we have Bloomsbury's legendary "frankness" and "honesty" on the page. A woman of the respectable higher professional classes, daring as early as 1912 to use the word "orgasm" in a letter to a man and admitting to having felt sexual tingles since infancy. Perhaps, as Bell's biographer Spalding claims, a letter like this marks an important step toward equality between the sexes — or perhaps it was a twisted kind of revenge from a woman whose own sexuality was far from straightforward and has been publicly betrayed in her own marriage. Certainly, Vanessa's new frankness in matters sexual was of no help to Virginia, who in 1913 plunged into a yet more serious mental breakdown, taking a massive dose of the barbiturate Veronal to try to kill herself.

The word "genius" had been used about Virginia Woolf since her teens, notably by Violet Dickinson and Madge Vaughan, and her new husband passionately endorsed this. Virginia, Leonard tells us in his autobiography, was the only real genius he had ever known, but according to his analysis, hers was a genius periodically riven by self-doubt. Whereas the poet Robert Lowell became physically aggressive and hypersexual when manic and manifested a Napoleonic, "I can conquer the world" complex, Virginia Woolf turned her aggression on herself, convinced of her own laziness, unearned privilege, and inability to achieve anything important. "I am obsessed at night with the idea of my own worthlessness," she told her composer friend Ethel Smyth in 1929. While manic, Woolf turned violently against those she loved best, screaming vituperations against her sister and refusing for some time to even be in the same room as her husband. Leonard had never seen his wife like this, and he was overcome with shock and horror. Virginia was, by any standard, raving mad and lucky to be able (just!) to afford a private asylum. And yet, there was a truth in her mania and an inspiration.

The truth related to her as a woman. If Virginia Woolf in 1913 felt obscurely that it was not her fault that she could not feel orgasm, that faking sexual pleasure was an elemental form of deception that no woman should be forced into, and that both her husband and sister were now colluding against her behind her back, was this madness or a higher kind of sanity?

The inspiration related to her aspiration to be a novelist. "In the lava of my madness," she once wrote to Ethel Smyth, "I still find most of the things I write about." To the same confidant, she wrote in October 1930: "After being ill and suffering every form and variety of nightmare and extravagant intensity of perception — for I used to make up poems, stories, profound to me and inspired phrases all day long, as I lay in bed, and thus sketched, I think, all that I now by the light of reason try to put into prose."

⁊❧

The first three years of the Woolfs' marriage were traumatic and would have broken most couples. Virginia had one breakdown after another. Her fertility, not her frigidity, came to be the main issue, since she professed herself willing, even eager, to continue "normal" marital relations regardless of her "pleasure in the act." Leonard felt passion as well as love for his wife, and he had a legal right to sexual congress, but if he chose to exercise it, he would put Virginia at risk of becoming pregnant. As everyone close to her knew, Virginia loved children and had always seen herself as a mother. One of the most poignant things she received as a wedding gift was an antique cradle, presented to her by her beloved old friend Violet Dickinson.

On the issue of children, Vanessa rallied to her sister's side, urging that Virginia should be allowed to have children if she could, since that was what she wanted. Only four years earlier, soon after she had given birth to her first child and Virginia was expected to marry Lytton Strachey, Vanessa had written to Virginia,

> Can't you imagine us in 20 years' time, you and I two celebrated ladies, with our families about us, yours very odd and small and you with a growing reputation for your works, I with nothing but my capacities as a hostess and my husband's value to live on? Your husband will probably be dead, I think, for you won't have boiled his milk enough, but you will be quite happy and enjoy sparring with your clever and cranky daughter. I'm afraid she'll be more beautiful than mine, who I know will take after the Bells. When mine is on the road [that is, in utero] I shall refuse to come here [Scotland] and shall see you every day and gaze at the most beautiful of Aunt Julia's photographs incessantly.

Virginia's doctors, on the other hand — including Sir Charles Savage, the man who had once advised the family about Laura Stephen — were of the opinion that their patient was too mentally unstable to withstand the stresses of pregnancy and motherhood. The love of children was deep within Leonard also, but he not only loved Virginia more than anything else in the world; he felt he was responsible for her. Wary now of advice from Vanessa and Clive, respecting the authority of psychiatric experts, fearing that a pregnancy would lead his wife to commit suicide or, even worse, spend the rest of her life in an asylum like her sister Laura and Helen Fry, Leonard decided that he and Virginia would no longer have vaginal intercourse.

Was it the right decision? Many women with severe mental disorders have had children and have thereby both derived and given great joy. Virginia saw childlessness as a personal tragedy and once again blamed herself. Years later she wrote to her friend the artist Ethel Sands, "I'm always angry with myself for not having forced Leonard to take the risk [of her getting pregnant] in spite of doctors; he was afraid for me and wouldn't; but if I'd had more self-control no doubt it would have been all right." We now know that serious mood disorders like Woolf's are not notably amenable to "self-control," and Woolf is forgetting how extremely ill she had been. Moreover, from the point of view of her work and our pleasure in it, if Virginia Woolf had had children, would she have been able to write *To the Lighthouse* or *Orlando*? As she herself remarked in a 1930 letter to her nephew Quentin, after a particularly exhausting and infuriating week of small domestic dramas, "How any woman with a family ever put pen to paper I cannot fathom."

In January 1915, seeing how profoundly her mental condition threatened her relationship with Leonard and facing a future that might, if she had the strength, include novels but no children, Woolf fell into yet another terrifying psychotic crisis. The breakdown was indirectly presaged in the final diary entry of 1915, where Virginia recorded a walk along the river on January 9 during which she and Leonard met a party of what she calls "imbeciles": "Every one in that long line a miserable ineffective shuffling idiotic creature with no forehead and no chin & an imbecile grin, or a wild suspicious stare. It was perfectly horrible. They should certainly be killed."

This is a cruel remark made by a woman who was terrifyingly sure that she was about to reenter the world of the mad.

After leaving the clinic in 1915, Woolf was for more than a year placed once again under constant surveillance lest she jump out a window or take an overdose. No effective antidepressant drugs were available at this point in time, so Woolf's doctors administered opiates and sleeping pills and instructed their patient to stay in bed, drink lots of milk — a remedy beloved of doctors since the ancient Egyptians — and gain weight. A respected literary journalist and avid reader, she was forbidden to do any serious reading or writing. A tall, athletic woman who loved to walk for hours through the countryside or the streets of London, she was forced for many months to take a human companion with her whenever she went outside. A woman who savored solitude, she was never permitted to be alone. She became, in effect, a dumb, somnolent, force-fed beast in a padded stall with no windows. As she confided in 1930 to Ethel Smyth, "Think — not one moment's freedom from doctor discipline — perfectly strange, conventional men; 'you shan't read this' and 'you shan't write a word' and 'you shall lie still and drink milk' for six months."

The treatment meted out to Virginia Woolf in a private British clinic during World War I was essentially the popular Weir Mitchell system used on Charlotte Perkins Gilman in the United States in the 1880s. It was, of course, a treatment for the affluent and a great advance over such "treatments" as the clitoridectomies performed on indigent women by the great Jean-Martin Charcot, Silas Weir Mitchell's nineteenth-century competitor. Worse things were in the offing. What woman with mental health issues would not prefer milk and bed rest to the radical therapies of the mid-twentieth century such as the lobotomy inflicted on Rosemary Kennedy or the massive electric shocks administered to Sylvia Plath?

All the same, one can see how Virginia Woolf, in her novel *Mrs. Dalloway,* came to make a villain of the rich, unctuous, socialite psychiatrist Sir William Bradshaw, modeled, one can assume, on men like Savage. In the novel, Bradshaw's patient Septimus Smith, a war veteran suffering from shell shock, is feeling a moment of renewed hope and sanity, thanks to the loving care of his Italian wife. But then his doctor arrives unheralded at his door, and Septimus's response is to jump out the nearest window to his death. When Bradshaw arrives late at Mrs. Dalloway's party, explaining that he has been delayed by the suicide of one of his patients, Clarissa thinks to herself, "if this young man had gone to him, and Sir William had impressed him like that with his power, might he not have said ... they make life intolerable, men like that." Clarissa Dalloway senses in Bradshaw a man "obscurely evil, without sex or lust, extremely polite to women, but capable of some indescribable outrage, forcing your soul."

Woolf emerged from her long struggle with illness in 1917 to be confronted with the insanity of trench warfare, but it did not tax her mental equilibrium as it did that of her husband and men friends. As they testify in their autobiographies, Bertrand Russell, John Maynard Keynes, and Leonard Woolf were constantly on the brink of nervous breakdown at that time. These exceptionally intelligent, rational, and capable men were taken off guard by the declaration of war. In the summer of 1914, only months before war broke out, Leonard Woolf records that he experienced "unmitigated, pure, often acute pleasure, such as I had never before had and have never had again. For the first time in the history of the world the rights of Jews, cobblers, and coloured men not to be beaten, hanged, or judicially murdered by officers, Junkers, or white men were publicly admitted; it looked for a moment as if militarism, imperialism, and antisemitism were on the run."

Comfortably convinced that the world was moving toward peace, enlightenment, and prosperity, men like Leonard Woolf suddenly found themselves up to their eyeballs in the stupidity, ignorance, and waste of the greatest war the world had ever seen. Nothing they could do to protest the course of international affairs made any difference, and every day, as they sat out the war in England, they saw other men go off in their place to die or to return horribly maimed in body and mind.

Virginia missed and mourned the men like her friend Rupert Brooke and her husband's brother Cecil Woolf who were killed in battle. But, as she was to say so forcefully years later in *Three Guineas,* war is neither the work nor the sport of women, so she did not bear the burden of responsibility, guilt, and helplessness that weighed on her husband.

And when the sky was clear and the moon high and the air-raid sirens wailed and the German bombers passed over her home in Richmond on their way to central London, Woolf did not give way to fear or even depression. She and Leonard and their live-in maids calmly dressed warm and took their bedding down to the basement. There, in her diary, Virginia recorded not terror, not even fatigue, but boredom and the imperative to get back to work as soon as the "all clear" sounded.

As long as her husband was there, facing death by her side, she felt, oddly, secure. When he was forced to be away, earning money with his lecture tours, she missed him and they wrote almost every day. "My Darling Goose M," wrote Virginia to Leonard on October 29, 1917, "I promise to do everything as if you were there, but you won't be there, and I shall find Saxon [Sydney-Turner] such a stick and such a pussy cat after my own passionate and ferocious and entirely adorable M[ongoose]."

જ

Part of the work that occupied Woolf every day was writing in her diary. She had kept diaries and notebooks since her girlhood — they were "five-finger exercises for future excellence," in the words of fellow writer Doris Lessing. When she took her diary up again in July 1917 after an eighteen-month gap, it was not to mull over her recent encounters with psychiatry or to conduct a Freudian self-analysis. Indeed, if we turn to *The Diary of Virginia Woolf* — all five thick, brilliantly and exhaustively edited volumes of it — expecting to dive deep into the inner turmoil of a famously mad writer — as we do, for example, with Sylvia Plath in *The Bell Jar* or Charlotte Perkins Gilman in *The Yellow Wallpaper* or Anne Sexton in her poems — we shall be disappointed.

Woolf wrote her diary in a state of high rationality, conceiving it as a writerly tool and an aesthetic artifact. The diarist would record the doings of her external world and hone her craft as a novelist, with snatches of dialogue, character sketches, nature notes, and social vignettes. Her goal in writing the diary, Woolf wrote in the entry of April 20, 1919, was to capture the "loose drifting material of life" in a prose "loose knit & yet not slovenly, so elastic that it will embrace anything . . . like some deep old desk or capacious hold-all, in which one flings a mass of odds & ends." Over the years the diary would become, she hoped, "a mould, transparent enough to reflect the light of our life & yet steady & tranquil, composed with the aloofness of a work of art."

Well, here we are a hundred years later, reading *The Diary of Virginia Woolf* alongside *To the Lighthouse* and *A Room of One's Own,* so Woolf obviously succeeded in her lofty aesthetic goal. Moreover, if we plot the diary entries against Woolf's battles with incipient psychosis, we can see that writing a diary was in fact a direct but undisclosed response to her mental illness. It was a form of disciplined self-therapy, and one more effective than anything prescribed by her doctors. In her diary, Woolf eliminates the menacing turmoil of her inner life and sticks fast to the often grim but reassuring nitty-gritty of the external world.

Woolf's diary, in contrast to her often experimental fiction, is very much in the tradition of English diarists, observant and down-to-earth, at times lyrical, often caustic. It is also quintessentially a woman's diary. It lets us know, for example, that Virginia Woolf, like her sister Vanessa and many other middle-class women with home help, always stayed in bed on the first day of her period. The bulky cotton pads on sale offered spotty (!) protection and were quite expensive, and Virginia once boasts in a letter to Vanessa that she has saved several shillings a month by fabricating her own pads.

Woolf the diarist is willing to admit that she has rotting, crumbly teeth and that she comes down with flu several times every winter — but there was nothing unusual about that. In chilly, damp, sugar-addicted Britain, colds and flu were commonplace, and in the Woolfs' social set, only the Sinhalese, the Americans, and Clive's mistress Mary Hutchinson flashed a gleaming smile. Leonard too had bad teeth and got a lot of colds. He also had regular bouts of malaria and had suffered since adolescence from a chronic nervous tremor of the hands serious enough to disqualify him for military service. But Leonard kept going and refused to complain, and so did Virginia. Illness, if we believe the diarist, is just a fact of life, to be slotted into a busy schedule with humor and without complaint.

That Virginia had an illness that, unlike Leonard's malaria, could be terrifyingly unmanageable was the diary's secret. Woolf the diarist is not weak and not helpless, neither defined nor confined by mental illness. And for over twenty years the physical record of daily events and ideas that the diarist not only wrote but regularly read and reread for confirmation and encouragement, helped keep the woman on the right side of madness.

Virginia's Bloomsbury friends knew about her diary, knew that she was busy recording the world around her, and this knowledge induced a distinct wariness. Highly self-conscious and already obsessed with its legacy, Bloomsbury could sense that in Virginia Woolf it had found its Pepys or its Boswell. Already by the end of World War I, Woolf's published reviews and literary essays had an easy brilliance and casual erudition that commanded respect and helped sell copies on the newsstand. She was also crafting a new kind of novel and finding readers on both sides of the Atlantic. In person, her combination of *whizz-bang-pop* social critique and dreamy fantasy held her friends spellbound at Garsington or Charleston. Her letters, as anyone today can attest who reads them in chronological order, grew more marvelously witty each year.

But for her friends, the question arose as to what Virginia — fervent and flighty, her outworn bloomers sometimes slipping to her ankles in public, the woman who was institutionalized in 1905, took a massive overdose of Veronal in 1913, and in 1915 was vituperatively, bouncing-off-the-asylum-walls MAD — was saying about everyone in the diary. Some in Bloomsbury, Clive Bell, for example, had cause to be worried.

Clive Bell was always welcome in the home of Virginia and Leonard Woolf, not because he and Leonard were old Cambridge friends, though they had been, but because Clive had married Vanessa, Virginia's sister. Their open door did not mean, however, that the Woolfs actually liked him or appreciated him much, to judge from the diary entry in which Virginia recounts a pleasant tea party she had on January 13, 1918.

Clive Bell, his Cambridge friend Gerald Shove, and Shove's young Newnham-educated wife, Fredegond — one of Virginia's Fisher first cousins once removed — had unexpectedly dropped in on the Woolfs at Hogarth House, their home in Richmond, a London suburb. Virginia Woolf was happy to see them that dark January afternoon and was able to manage tea with milk and even sugar, despite the wartime food shortages. Marooned in the outer boroughs for much of the time, she was thirsty for news of all her friends in central London, and Clive Bell had an avocation for collecting and disseminating gossip. It was his strategy for deflecting, forestalling, and controlling what people said about him.

Whenever her brother-in-law turned up on her doorstep, Virginia would sit him down next to her, and smoke and chat and giggle with him over the teacups. Leonard meanwhile would take himself off to type another article for the international journal he edited or to compose a lecture for his next Cooperative Society tour of "The North." Leonard, as his wife once laughingly recorded, was like a mowing machine, relentlessly cutting his way through the work, week after week. Clive, hopping between braggadocio and schadenfreude, played grasshopper to Leonard's ant, and the entry in Woolf's diary uncovers the deep currents of hostility that, beneath the surface amity, ran between Virginia and Clive. "When one sees Clive fairly often, his devices for keeping up to the mark in the way of success & brilliance become rather obvious . . . His habits are like those of some faded beauty; a touch of rouge, a lock of yellow hair, lips crimsoned!"

The male butterfly has fluttered his wings, approached the flame, and *zap, sizzle, splatter.*

16

Vanessa's Way, Part 2

WHILE VIRGINIA between 1913 and 1917 was fighting for her marriage and her sanity, Vanessa was undergoing a crisis of her own making. She had found her ideal man and was marshaling all the charm, intelligence, energy, determination, and tolerance for which she was famous in her social set to make their relationship work. The man was Duncan Grant and he would be Vanessa's beloved companion until her death in 1964.

Duncan Grant entered Vanessa Bell's life as a family friend in 1907 when she was on her honeymoon in Paris. Lytton Strachey had urged the Bells to look up his young cousin Duncan who, thanks to a gift from a maternal aunt, was enrolled in the art school of the noted French painter Jacques-Émile Blanche. When Maynard Keynes became a part of Bloomsbury, renting rooms from Virginia and Adrian Stephen, he brought Duncan, who was then his lover, along with him. By 1911, Duncan was such an integral part of the Bloomsbury group that, as we have seen in Chapter 14, he was not only dining at home with the Bells but shaving in their bathroom at the hour when Vanessa Bell was accustomed to taking her bath.

Duncan, along with Vanessa, was one of the British artists whose paintings Roger Fry chose to hang in the second post-impressionist exhibition at the Grafton Galleries, and he became one of the most enthusiastic and active members of the Omega Workshops. With Roger so often abroad and her husband bent on the pursuit of other women, Vanessa and Duncan spent more and more time together and began to collaborate on projects. After harshly and inexorably breaking off her affair with Roger Fry, Vanessa, in a storm of tears, astonished her sister Virginia by blurting out that she was in love with Duncan Grant.

Vanessa Bell, as we have seen, was not prone to shed tears, indulge in dramatic scenes, or tell love secrets to her sister, but her loss of control at that moment is more than understandable. Duncan Grant, according to the testimony of just about everyone who knew him, was an unusually attractive man. In 1915, he was just thirty years old, slim, well-muscled, the very kind of man he himself loved to sketch and photograph. He cared nothing for money, usually needing to borrow a few pennies from Clive Bell to get the bus home after dinner, but he was already being heralded as one of England's most promising young painters. He was good-natured, even-tempered, marvelous company, a practical joker and impersonator, the life and soul of every party. His mother and his aunts adored him, and he rarely had a bad word to say about anyone. He was charm personified. And — for it was never a "but" with Duncan Grant — he was actively, unrepentantly gay. Asked, as a very old man, by the journalist Paul Levy if the men of Bloomsbury actually had all that sex with one another, or just talked about it, Grant shrugged and replied that he couldn't speak for the rest, but he personally had been happy to have sex with anyone who wanted to have sex with him.

When exactly Vanessa Bell and Duncan Grant became lovers is unclear, though we know from Vanessa's letter to Roger that in 1911 her naked body, newly reminiscent of a Rubens or Renoir woman after two pregnancies, had failed to "move" Duncan. What is certain is that, when she fell in love with him, she knew with absolute certainty that, whereas he liked women and felt comfortable in their company, it was men he desired.

As we have seen, Vanessa had been made privy to intimate details about the sex lives of Lytton Strachey and Maynard Keynes, two of Duncan's several lovers among the old "Cambridge" set. More pertinent to her situation circa 1915, she knew that Duncan was in love with her brother, and the two were sleeping together. Adrian Stephen, however, while willing to try sex with a man, was pursuing Karin Costelloe with a view to marriage, and this was making relations between him and Duncan difficult. It was well known in Bloomsbury that when Duncan fell madly in love with a man, and that man left him for a woman, he would lose all his sunny good humor and look, quite literally, for a shoulder to cry on. Informed that the Adrian-Karin engagement was about to be announced, Vanessa may have seized the moment to invite Duncan into her bed.

We do not expect people in love to be rational, and temperamentally, as their forty-year partnership would prove, Duncan Grant and Vanessa Bell suited each other very well. Unlike Leslie Stephen, Duncan was never "ill to live with." When not absorbed in his painting and drawing, Duncan, unlike the supercharged Roger, was always ready to kick back and enjoy the *dolce far niente*. Unlike Clive, Duncan was not pompous, and any social climbing he did (in later life he was a favorite painter of the Queen Mother and a valued friend of Deborah, Duchess of Devonshire) came naturally from his family's roots in the Scottish nobility. Like Vanessa, Duncan was intelligent but not intellectual, cultured but not erudite. Like Vanessa's, Duncan's bohemianism rested on a solid support of unearned income. He lived on the assumption that it was the world's duty as well as its pleasure to support its artists, and that money would come to those who were charmingly eccentric (but not mad, like poor Blake or van Gogh!) and knew how to ask nicely.

All that said, let us pause and digest the fact that Vanessa Bell, an object of worship for the remarkable and steadfastly heterosexual Roger Fry, fell in love with the man she had just seen taking her younger brother into his bed. The faint motif of incest in Vanessa Bell's life and the repetition compulsion emerge here once again. The relationship of Vanessa Bell and Duncan Grant offers, in fact, prima facie evidence that the resentment she had harbored toward her father had soured her on conventional marriage and that her relationships with George Duckworth and Jack Hills had shaped her sexuality, quite as much as the unsolicited fumblings of George and his brother Gerald had shaped Virginia's.

As one reads the letters and biographies of Vanessa Bell, it is hard not to wonder how many nights the beautiful, voluptuous, sensual Aphrodite of Bloomsbury mythology actually wanted to share her bed with a man. Agreeable heterosexual men were, after all, not impossible to find even among the upper classes in central London circa 1914, and Desmond MacCarthy, to choose one, might have volunteered to do for Vanessa what Clive was doing for Mary Hutchinson. As we follow the strange course of Vanessa and Duncan's early relationship, it becomes apparent that her desire for him was fueled not so much by sexual need but by her passion for painting and children.

By painting alongside him, Vanessa had become convinced that Duncan Grant was what she herself would like to be — a great painter. She was also in a hurry to have a third child, hoping it would be a girl. In comparison with Duncan, Roger Fry, for all his avant-garde theories, was more George Frederick Watts than Matisse. As an elderly, bony man very content with his two children and yet sexually demanding, Fry was not the man Vanessa Bell fancied conceiving a child with. In comparison the beautiful gay genius Duncan Grant seemed perfect as partner and sire.

From the outset, the sexual compact between Duncan and Vanessa was very odd. Grant never hid the fact that, when he had sexual intercourse with Vanessa, he was doing it as a favor to a friend. Informed at the outset of how much it would mean to her to have another child, he was ready to service Vanessa as a stallion might a mare. In return, he would enjoy the pleasing home, good food, and good company she excelled in providing, and feel free to use her body for comfort and release on the odd occasions when something was going wrong with his love affairs with men. In the 1918 diary he wrote for his resident lover, David Garnett, Duncan admits, "I am so uncertain of my real feeling to V. I am utterly unable to feign more than I feel when called upon to feel much, with the consequence that I seem to feel less than I do. I suppose the only thing lacking in my feelings to her is passion. What of that there might be seems crushed out of me, by a bewildering suffering expectation of it (hardly conscious) by her. I think I feel that if I showed any, it would be met by such an avalanche that I should be crushed."

Duncan Grant was famous for his frankness, for his lack of pretense, and he set the terms of his relationship with Vanessa at the start, never deceiving her or promising more than he was willing to give. Nonetheless, by the end of 1914, Vanessa had decided that she could not live without him.

A key turn in the relationship between Vanessa Bell and Duncan Grant oc-curred at a dinner party in a swank London restaurant hosted by Maynard Keynes in January 1915. In an act of Mephistophelian mischief, Maynard, who had no doubt got wind of Vanessa's passion for Duncan, placed Duncan be-tween Vanessa and a newcomer to the group, David Garnett, usually known as Bunny.

Garnett, twenty-three, tall, blond, athletic, heavily muscled, was, as May-nard knew full well, exactly the kind of man Duncan found irresistible. Indeed, after the dinner, Bunny and Duncan went off into the night together and had sex, and Duncan quickly forgot about Adrian Stephen. Garnett could (and later did) boast of a phallic potency that was a match even for Grant's and, having recently heard Lytton Strachey deliver a panegyric to libertinism, he was eager to experiment with sex with a male, especially an attractive and in-fluential older man like Grant. All the same, as Duncan was well aware, Bunny never thought of himself as anything other than heterosexual.

As soon as she saw Bunny Garnett seated next to Duncan at the restau-rant, Vanessa knew that she had a rival, and a formidable one. Duncan did not repine for long when a lover dumped him, and Maynard had put gor-geous Bunny almost literally in his lap. Ever the pragmatist, Vanessa came to the rapid conclusion that she would have to have Bunny, or some version of Bunny, if she was to keep Duncan in her life. So she made her own move, and it seemed to work marvelously.

At Maynard's dinner party, Bunny had not been insensible to the charms of the woman seated next to Duncan. Bunny liked experienced older women and had already taken a couple of them into his bed. When the delightfully full-bodied Mrs. Bell asked when they might meet again, he asked her to tea the next week. She duly came to his flat and was entertained with tea and, in a deliciously Freudian move, sticky chocolate éclairs, and the two of them seemed to hit it off. Bunny happily confided in his diary that he and Vanessa Bell, Lytton's intimate friend and the doyenne of Bloomsbury society, were on the same libertine page.

For the next year or so, while her sister was once again in a clinic, and friends like Rupert Brooke and Cecil Woolf died on the battlefield along with millions of other young men, Vanessa Bell was living with her Duncan and his

Bunny at Wissett Lodge, a rundown property in Suffolk belonging to Duncan's family. Vanessa arrived there with her two young sons and a cartful of trunks, plus Trissie and Flossie, her nurse and cook, and she refused to be dismayed by the lack of running water and electricity. With her boys occupied with exploring their new rural domain under the nominal supervision of Trissie, Vanessa had her mornings to herself for painting projects. Meanwhile Duncan and Bunny made desultory attempts to get the market garden and orchard in shape and thus satisfy the conditions of their exemption from military service.

Vanessa Bell took a number of photographs of her family and guests at Wissett Lodge, and several of them show her sons running happily around the estate without any clothes on. In *Vanessa Bell's Family Album,* the collection of his mother's pictures that he and his sister, Angelica, published in 1981, Quentin Bell claims that these shots of him and his older brother as little chubby, curly children are some of the best examples of his mother's skill at photographic composition. He also says that the pictures were by way of being studies of "putti" — the naked cherubs often featured in baroque paintings. Today, the Tate Gallery, which is the repository of Vanessa Bell's photographs, has withdrawn all these nude images of the Bell children from their catalog, and refuses to allow them to be reproduced unless they are of central importance to an artist's or scholar's work. One photograph that appeared as recently as 2003 in Robert Skidelsky's biography of John Maynard Keynes indicates that even Vanessa's friends may have been unsettled by her love of taking rolls of film of her naked sons. Keynes, seated in a garden chair, has the two Bell boys on his lap, one facing in and one facing out, and he raises his knee to conceal the outer child's genitalia.

A series of visitors descended on Wissett on weekends, including the extraordinarily attired Lady Ottoline, who appreciated neither the fleas in her bed nor the firecracker with which Julian Bell lit her cigarette. Julian, one gathers, was the proverbial imp of Satan and, though the focus of Vanessa's maternal attention, not a very happy little nine-year-old. Julian had inherited a large measure of what Virginia Woolf called "the Stephen integrity" and, unlike his mother, was very worried about the war. When staying with the Woolfs one night, he woke up his aunt Virginia to discuss what was happening on the battlefield. Chubby, wheezy Quentin (he would suffer from serious bouts of lung disease as an adolescent and young man), barely seven, just tried to keep up with his big brother.

ॐ

When Bunny went off to work with a Quaker ambulance corps in France, Vanessa had Duncan to herself, and they both sent Bunny affectionate little letters. When he came back after a few months, having seen more than enough of war, and fell once again into Duncan's welcoming arms, Vanessa slipped the jobless Bunny the odd five-pound note. This was unusual generosity for a woman whose domestic budget was perennially stretched, but Vanessa still needed Duncan, and to Duncan, Bunny still managed to be indispensable. Questioned by her husband, Clive, on the progress of her love affair with Duncan, Vanessa admitted in a letter that "no little Grant has yet had a chance to come into existence."

This remark offers interesting insight into an unusual marriage. Clive Bell had been grumpy and jealous when his wife took up with Roger Fry, but then Fry was everything Clive wished he could be — except poor. Clive and Duncan, on the other hand, hit it off perfectly: as old men, after the death of Vanessa, they would continue to live together at Charleston for some years. Clive saw Duncan as a social asset, not a threat to his manhood, and was perfectly happy, if I may attempt a cricket metaphor, to have Duncan and his googlies join the side and take the occasional over.

But by the beginning of 1916, even Vanessa could not keep her head in the sand about the war, and it was harder than ever for "conchies" like Duncan and Bunny to walk in the streets. The local authorities in Suffolk decreed, not unreasonably, that the men at Wissett Lodge were doing nothing to nourish the nation. At the beginning of 1916 universal conscription was declared for all British males between eighteen and forty, so the status as conscientious objectors of Morgan Forster, Lytton Strachey, Clive Bell, Adrian Stephen, Duncan Grant, and David Garnett came under official reexamination. The mandatory medical examination eliminated Lytton, a man whom even the most jingoistic of doctors could not imagine hefting a pack, as well as Leonard, with his uncontrollable hand tremor, and Adrian, who was discovered to have a chronic heart ailment. Clive, Duncan, and Bunny, however, were all deemed fit for service in an army that had already lost a million men, and they were summoned to appear before their local draft board — a group of men selected for their patriotism and known to take a very poor view of "conchies," especially rugged young ones like Garnett.

It was at this point that Vanessa Bell took matters into her own hands. She prevailed on her friend Maynard Keynes, a big wheel at the Treasury, to use his influence at the appeal hearing to get conscientious objector status approved for both Grant and Garnett. She charmed a farmer close to Asheham, her former rental in Sussex, to take both men on as agricultural workers and thus fulfill their commitment to support the war effort. And she discovered Charleston, a large, elegant, remote, and dilapidated farmhouse from which Grant and Garnett could cycle to work, and she moved her household and her children there.

Life in the Charleston farmhouse between the spring of 1916 and the end of 1918 was not a picnic in the park with ants in the smoked salmon sandwiches, as it had been at Wissett Lodge. As the war dragged on, food became increasingly difficult to obtain even in the countryside, and Vanessa Bell had to scramble to find women servants willing to move to a dilapidated farm ten miles from the nearest railway station. One of the jobs Virginia Woolf took on when she returned to health after her breakdown was visiting domestic employment agencies, writing letters, and interviewing maids and governesses on her sister's behalf. The women Woolf found were, unsurprisingly, a rather odd bunch, and they tended to leave as soon as a better position came up.

No longer standing rapt before her easel each morning while waiting for cook to give the signal for lunch, Vanessa grimly turned her hand to things her mother had left to the servants or ordered in from the shops. She kept ducks and chickens, planted and weeded and harvested a large vegetable garden and a fruit orchard, made bread and cake and jam and pickles, sewed clothes, kept her free-ranging sons from killing themselves, and taught them Latin when it rained. When the two men returned at night, weary and numb from farm work, they found a fire in the hearth, a pot of water heating to wash and shave with, and some sort of dinner simmering on the hob. On weekends, Vanessa and Duncan still set up their easels side by side, and the dull surfaces and battered furniture of the old house also began to glow with brilliantly colored designs.

When, in mid-August 1918, Virginia Woolf was at last well enough to come to Charleston and see how her sister was doing, she recorded how deeply impressed she was by the burden of domestic care Vanessa had shouldered. She was also astonished by the meagerness of the meals. For a very thin woman inclined to anorexia, it was rather a new experience for Virginia Woolf to find herself wishing for second helpings. The pump supplying well water for the household was very temperamental, so Vanessa, Virginia noticed, had given up bathing, and her clothing was barely decent. Attempting to write a letter, Woolf dipped her pen into an inkpot and found it clogged with dead flies. "My visit to Charleston," Virginia wrote in her diary, "was spent mostly in sitting in the drawing [room] & talking to N [Nessa] while she made herself a small brown coat. Duncan wandered in & out, sometimes digging a vegetable bed, sometimes painting a water colour of bedroom china, pinned to a door. In the evening there was the lumpish Bunny inclined to be surly & N [Nessa] inclined to take him up sharply."

That night in the farmhouse kitchen there was a discussion of money, "which is not any longer a distant speculative sort of commodity," Virginia wrote. She was outraged to hear Bunny spout a socialist ideology, which seemed to mean in practice that a woman like Mrs. Clive Bell should be glad to spend her unearned income maintaining an artist like him. The famous Bunny Garnett charm had no effect on Virginia Woolf, who describes him as a tongue-tied, socially inept young man, "caked with earth, stiff as a clod, you can almost see the docks & nettles sprouting from his mind; his sentences creak with rust."

Here Woolf is being unfair. Garnett was far from stupid: he had a first-class degree in science from London University, and after the war he would quickly make his name as a writer, editor, and publisher. Eager to maintain his superb physique, Bunny did not mind manual labor, and he was the one who did most of the farm work while Duncan smoked and looked on. He was a real help in the vegetable garden and the orchard at Charleston, and the honey from the hives he kept was precious. Virginia felt able to criticize Bunny in her diary because she heard Vanessa "taking him up sharply" and saw that her sister was at odds with the man. Bunny was a subject on which the sisters could agree and unite. Duncan, on the other hand, who was also depending on Vanessa's largesse and allowing the domestic burden to fall mainly on her shoulders, enjoyed immunity from Virginia's Woolf's famous putdowns.

There was no way for Vanessa Bell to hide from her sister the practical problems she faced at Charleston. What Vanessa kept to herself, because it reflected on her own judgment, was the emotional powder keg she had chosen to sit on. The relationship between Duncan and Bunny was stormy, and all too often the men came to blows, making the oil lamps flicker and threatening to wake the sleeping boys upstairs. They openly shared a bedroom but would also go off to London from time to time to find other sex partners. Whereas Bunny didn't care how many men Duncan slept with, Duncan was violently jealous about Bunny's women, notably his dalliances with Barbara Hiles and his hot pursuit of Alix Sargant-Florence. When Duncan got wind of Bunny's London adventures, he turned both tearful and violent.

The situation was further complicated when once, in Duncan's absence, Bunny told Vanessa "that he had for a long time wanted to sleep with her and that if she did she would find he got less on her nerves." Vanessa's response was to look at him with "those childlike blue eyes" and say it was impossible for them to have sex because Duncan was bound to find out "and it would upset him dreadfully."

When Bunny went off for several days in February 1918, the distraught Duncan turned to Vanessa for advice and comfort. In the self-analytic diary he wrote intending that Bunny should read it, Duncan wrote, "I copulated on Saturday with her [Vanessa] with great satisfaction to myself physically. It is a convenient way females have of letting off one's spunk and comfortable. Also the pleasure it gives is reassuring. You don't get this dumb misunderstanding body of a person who isn't a bugger. That's one for you Bunny!"

It was as a result of this unromantic release of spunk that Vanessa Bell finally got pregnant by Duncan Grant. Once the pregnancy was confirmed, having fulfilled this peculiar obligation to the woman for whom he felt deep affection and to whom he was so indebted, Duncan Grant politely but firmly declined to ever seek physical comfort with her again. That February night in 1918 was probably the last time Vanessa Bell, then a month short of her thirty-ninth birthday, took a man into her bed. Henceforth she would be more Artemis than Aphrodite — but, like Demeter, she would have a daughter.

ॐ

On Wednesday, July 27, 1918, Virginia Woolf recorded in her diary how she had sallied forth from Richmond on the train for one of her "field days" in central London. After lunching at the 1917 Club, where younger women like Fredegond Shove, Alix Sargant-Florence (not yet Strachey), and Carrington were often stimulating to the point of abrasion, Woolf walked over to 46 Gordon Square, expecting a warm welcome. This was the house that the four Stephens had leased after the death of their father in 1904, the house that Vanessa and Clive Bell took over for themselves after Thoby Stephen's death and their marriage, and that Clive sold to his friend Maynard Keynes in 1916. At number 46, Virginia Woolf found her sister Vanessa Bell, as well as Clive Bell and his current *maîtresse en titre,* Mary Hutchinson. Vanessa was supervising the packing and removal of furniture and other personal belongings to Charleston.

Vanessa Bell was visibly enceinte, the moving of her stuff out of Gordon Square under the eyes of her husband and his lover was stressful, and the arrival of her sister was at best inopportune. What might Virginia in her diary be recording about the complex negotiations between Vanessa and her husband and his mistress, on the one hand, and her sort-of lover Duncan and his on-and-off lover Bunny on the other? What might Virginia blurt out to some random person when she next spent the weekend as Lady Ottoline Morrell's guest at Garsington? Apart from anything else, Clive, registered as a conscientious objector, was supposed to be doing manual labor on the Morrell estate near Oxford, not flitting about London with his inamorata.

And Virginia did sometimes get carried away when in lively conversation. A few months after her encounter with Vanessa and Clive and Mary at Gordon Square, Virginia, on a visit to Lady Ottoline at Garsington, let slip to the young painter Mark Gertler that her sister Vanessa did not much care for

Mary Hutchinson. Vanessa didn't, of course — and who could really blame her? — but Virginia's remark got echoed back, annoying Clive, upsetting Mary, and threatening to upset the apple cart at Charleston. "A fortnight ago all Bloomsbury rang with my crimes," wrote Virginia on October 26. "MH [Mary Hutchinson] was conveyed about London in a fainting condition in taxi cabs; Lytton [Mary's cousin and confidant] was appealed to come to her rescue; Duncan, Clive, Vanessa — all were in agonies & desperations . . . I'm beginning to think that friendships maintained in this atmosphere are altogether too sharp, brittle & painful."

Keeping things from Virginia, lest she blab, was thus standard procedure for the Charleston set, and in the summer of 1918, Virginia knew far too much about what was going on in the Sussex farmhouse. Virginia knew that the child her sister was carrying was Duncan Grant's and that the pregnancy was something Vanessa had long wanted. She knew that Vanessa was fiercely determined to keep the paternity of her third child a secret. She knew that Vanessa would face serious social and financial problems if she were widely known to be the mother of an illegitimate child.

As we have seen, divorce from Clive was never an option Vanessa considered, and marriage to Duncan was never even on the table. At a time when homosexual men frequently married for the domestic comfort, social cover, and children that wives offered, Duncan Grant was an exception. He was emphatically, immovably not a marrying man. Unlike Maynard, he was not in the public eye and the corridors of power, so he would never need a Lady Keynes to stand by his side in a nice fur coat and ram the lid down on all rumors of his homosexual past. And Duncan had never shown any interest in having children. He found Vanessa to be a charming companion. She offered, without fuss or complaint, the material comforts that mattered to him. When she painted by his side, she did not chat. But since she gave all this freely, out of love, what reason would he have to marry her?

The stirring of the baby in her womb made Vanessa happy, and it confirmed the image of her as beautiful, fertile mother goddess, which held such appeal for her gay chums like Lytton, Maynard, and Harry Norton. At the same time, however, the pregnancy put her very much at her husband's mercy.

If Clive Bell should choose to deny paternity of the child in her womb or, worse still, sue for divorce, Vanessa Bell could, of course, countersue on the grounds of his infidelity with, say, Mrs. St. John Hutchinson, but it would do her little good. Vanessa Bell liked to see herself as a bohemian rebel against the stuffy conventionality of her Kensington past, but divorce was a step too far. It would put her in the class of notoriously promiscuous women like the wives of the artists Augustus John and Henry Lamb, or worse still, Frieda Lawrence. When she and D. H. Lawrence fell in love, Frieda von Richthofen Weekley had abandoned her first husband and her children, and now Lawrence was celebrating her tempestuous nature and sexual abandon in one scandalous novel after another. To Vanessa Bell such public displays of promiscuity were abhorrent, and given how avidly the British public read the divorce columns, she risked seeing the affairs of her Charleston household breathlessly reported in tabloids like the *Daily Mail* if she divorced.

Worse yet, divorce would ruin her financially and damage the prospects of all three of her children. Even after he and his wife ceased to sleep together, Clive Bell continued to pay his wife an allowance and kick in occasional money for her and their sons. Once, for example, seeing his wife so dirty and unkempt, he paid to hire an extra man at Charleston to operate the pump that kept the household supplied with water. If her new baby was accepted as a Bell, Vanessa would get that lovely check for a thousand pounds from her father-in-law, and all the Bell grandchildren were slated to come into a modest inheritance when their grandfather died.

Without the Bell money, Vanessa would have to fall back on income from the legacies she had received from her father, her sister Stella, and her brother Thoby, plus any art commissions she could secure. In 1912 Vanessa Bell had been delighted to sell her first canvas for five pounds, and now, with the patronage of dear Maynard, she was getting forty or fifty pounds, but her painting could not be counted on for reliable income, and to paint she needed free time. Before the war, Vanessa Bell had enjoyed the services of a reliable domestic staff of four or five, and once the world got back to normal, she expected to do the same. When Vanessa Bell got word that one of the Olivier sisters was not only bringing a bastard child into the world but also planning to look after the baby herself, Vanessa was appalled. The care of children was something she had always delegated to women servants. So Vanessa Bell saw an imperative need to keep Clive lined up as the prospective father, and if that meant being very nice indeed to Mary Hutchinson, then so be it.

Virginia Woolf understood all of this, and as we can all now attest with the volumes in front of us, she put none of it into her diary and not very much in her letters. Virginia loved gossip almost as much as Clive and Lytton did, but, viewing her diary as a literary document that would someday appear in print, Woolf offers only that version of Vanessa that Vanessa herself would enjoy reading. What posterity will know of Vanessa Stephen Bell from Virginia Stephen Woolf will be praise, even adulation. The diarist may note on a visit to Charleston that Vanessa is busy making herself "a small brown coat," but the sister refrains from pointing out that Vanessa needs a new coat to stretch over the illegitimate child in her belly.

But when, on her arrival at Gordon Square in July, loyal Virginia found herself under combined attack from Vanessa, Clive, and Mary, she was indignant and could not resist fighting back just a little by recording a snatch of dialogue. She relies on Leonard (whom she allowed to read her diary and who didn't have much use for the Bells) and her prospective reader (that is, us) to work out what is going on and to get the joke.

[Clive Bell to Virginia Woolf] "You've wrecked one of my best friendships . . . by your habit of describing facts from your standpoint . . ."

"What you call God's Truth," said Nessa. "One couldn't have an intimacy with you & anyone else at the same time — You describe people as I paint pots."

"You put things in curl, & they come out afterwards" Mary murmured from the shadow of her sympathetic silence.

For preeminent gossips and self-declared tellers of the "honest" truth like Clive and Vanessa, this was, to use an old English expression, a bit rich.

៖

During the late summer and fall of 1918, Virginia Woolf was in frequent correspondence with her sister about securing a reliable domestic staff for Charleston. At a time when many young women could earn decent wages in the munitions factories, this was a difficult assignment, and in despair at one point, Virginia volunteered to dispatch both of her own resident servants, Nelly and Lottie Boxall, to help out at Charleston. At this suggestion, however, the Boxall sisters, who had been to Charleston before, refused to move to Sussex, and Vanessa got testy.

Virginia was not being wholly self-sacrificing in offering to dispatch the Boxalls. She could see that it was iniquitous to have two young women "chained in a kitchen to laze & work & suck their life from the two in the drawing room," but social conscience did not make her actually like the Boxalls, who exercised an insidious form of control over her. While claiming devotion to their employers, Nelly and Lottie took advantage of their mistress's guilt by going off on personal business whenever it suited them. They also engaged in acts of carelessness that verged on passive aggression, on one occasion upsetting onto the floor a whole charge of type for the Hogarth Press that Virginia had laboriously sorted. When Nelly was hospitalized in 1929, Virginia was able to secure the services of a sensible middle-class woman who, though refusing to scrub, was a good cook and spoke, as it were, the same language. Virginia was overjoyed — but Nelly recovered from her operation and insisted on coming back!

Virginia Woolf liked to feel that she could cope with just a regular charwoman, and when a new kitchen stove was installed at Monk's House, her final home in Sussex, she happily cooked for herself and Leonard. But when guests descended on the Woolfs, which they did on many weekends, when Virginia was working to deadline or confined to bed for days, which happened a lot, Leonard needed someone to run the house, however imperfectly. Having once been sovereign of a small province in Sri Lanka, he, unlike his wife, had no difficulty dealing with a few fractious domestics.

In September 1918, Virginia and Leonard were at Asheham, the Sussex country property they were then renting, and Virginia biked the eight miles over to Charleston, hoping to have a bit of her busy sister to herself. Virginia was eager to make plans with Vanessa for the birth of the new baby, due around the turn of the year, and assess the situation at Charleston. Had Clive definitely undertaken to claim the new baby as his? How was Duncan reacting to the whole paternity issue? With the war finally coming to an end, when was Bunny planning to move out?

These were the kinds of intimate matters that Vanessa and Virginia hated to put in letters since they knew that their domestic staff took time off, between the dusting and scrubbing, to read any diaries and correspondence left lying about. It was easier, the sisters found, to keep secrets from one's dearest friends than from one's parlor maid or governess. Vanessa and Virginia could discuss the things that mattered most in their lives only when face-to-face and alone, which was almost never.

Indeed, in September 1918, Vanessa had barely sent the boys out to play, seen Duncan off with his easel and palette, and settled some pressing housekeeping matters when Clive Bell and Mary Hutchinson arrived at Charleston unannounced. They did not come on foot from the station like most guests, but in a hired motorcar. In her diary Woolf wrote, "Mary produced chocolates, cakes & sweets in abundance. I'm ashamed to say that that is my chief impression, but I left soon after, so that I left unsaid and unasked all my ideas and questions. She [Mary] was, as usual, mute as a trout — I say trout because of her spotted dress, & also because, though silent, she has the swift composure of a fish. I walked home, shoving my bicycle, too badly punctured to ride."

The contrast between the affluent couple with their motorcar and confectionary delights and the disappointed sister pushing her bike the eight miles home is poignant — as the novelist Woolf understood very well.

On December 13, Vanessa Bell wrote to Virginia Woolf, thanking her for agreeing to look after Julian and Quentin during the fast-approaching confinement and giving very precise information on how to feed and entertain her sons. "I see that it is after all a great thing so to bring up an Ape," wrote Vanessa to Virginia, "that he'll come to your rescue in time of need." Had I been Virginia Woolf, I would have been offended by that.

On December 25, a month or so after the armistice ended almost five years of war, in the icy upstairs bedroom at Charleston, Vanessa Bell gave birth to a baby girl. The baby weighed in at seven and a half pounds, and was laid in a shoebox. She would eventually be known as Angelica.

316 • VIRGINIA WOOLF

Virginia and Leonard had made sure to be at Asheham over Christmas, and Julian and Quentin were driven over to the Woolfs when the birth seemed imminent. The agreement reached between the sisters was that the boys would return from Sussex to Richmond with their aunt and uncle and stay there for some weeks until their mother was able to have them home again. As it turned out, Virginia came down with a very bad case of flu in early January, her illness exacerbated by acute pain in her jaw from an abscessed tooth, so the boys were obliged to spend some time in the care of servants at their father's flat in Bloomsbury.

Clive Bell himself was away, that is to say not in London with his sons, not in Sussex with his wife, and not in Wiltshire with the Bell family. By prearrangement, Duncan Grant sent a telegram in Clive's name to Clive's parents, announcing the safe arrival of a third grandchild. The new baby would be a Bell, and legitimate, and Vanessa's mind was at ease, with everything going according to plan.

Clive Bell was willing to do what his wife wanted and accept the child sired by his good friend Duncan as his own. Clive felt no animosity toward his wife, and for a wife to have a child out of wedlock and for a husband to give that child his name and his standing in society was definitely *grand seigneur*. Clive the avid historian might have cited the 1st Lord Melbourne, who had done as much for the second son of his wife, Elisabeth; this child rose to be Queen Victoria's first prime minister.

To put it crudely, Duncan Grant had, for his part, signed on to be a sperm donor and nothing else. Though only six years younger, he was treated as a teenager by Vanessa, and that suited him very well. Infidelities and illegitimate children were not unknown in Duncan's upper-class Scottish family (his mother had had a rather frisky youth), but such things had always been kept under wraps. A divorce and an implicit claim of paternity might threaten his promising career, and it was not what his family, especially his mother, wanted for him. Relations between Mrs. Grant and Vanessa were courteous but cool, and even though the Grant clan, unlike the Bell parents, was perfectly aware of Angelica's parentage — the child bore a distinct resemblance to her father — it was not something they cared to remark on, then or later.

The only person who raised objections to the Clive-Vanessa-Duncan pact to make Clive the new baby's official father was, surprisingly, David Garnett. His own parents, to whom he was deeply attached, were left-wing intellectuals, and he saw Vanessa's reasons for claiming her child as a Bell as bourgeois money-grubbing. Bunny himself was eager to be a father — he would eventually have six children by his two wives — and at night in bed with Duncan, Bunny argued that Duncan was wrong to sign away his paternal rights at the behest of others. Bunny felt that it was time Duncan stopped acting like a teenager and accepted the responsibilities of a man, and after all Vanessa might be giving him the only child he would ever have. How would it feel to see another man act the father to his child?

In the bitterly cold January of 1919, however, with the telegrams sent and the newspapers informed, the official paternity of the unnamed baby girl was on the record and definitively off the agenda at Charleston. Vanessa Bell and Duncan Grant were facing their first parenting problem, and it was an urgent one. The baby could not keep her food down and lost weight instead of gaining. As we saw in earlier chapters, Vanessa had experienced difficulties with feeding in the first weeks of the lives of both her older children. Probably she hoped to nurse her third child, but when her breast milk did not come in, no wet-nurse was available. When Angelica failed to thrive, the woman hired to take care of the baby proved less than useless, and the local doctor prescribed "orange juice and dilute carbolic." Unsurprisingly, this treatment almost killed the patient.

With Vanessa frantic with anxiety, Bunny, a practical chap with a solid science background, had the happy idea of calling in a woman expert in the person of his old friend Noël Olivier. The two had known each other in the old neo-pagan days (he had slept with her sister Daphne) and Noël, a member of a notable generation of Newnhamites, was now in practice as a doctor. Unable to come down to Sussex herself, Dr. Olivier dispatched her colleague Dr. Marie Moralt to Charleston, and despite stalwart opposition from the local man, who had no use for women doctors, Moralt put the baby on cow's milk and "Grey's Powders." Within days the Bell baby was feeding greedily from a bottle and putting on nine ounces a day.

318 • VIRGINIA WOOLF

How much of this nutritional drama in Sussex reached the ears of the Woolfs in Richmond is unclear. Regina Marler, in her volume of Vanessa Bell's letters, includes no letters between the sisters in the first months of 1919, and Virginia Woolf's diary contains no account of her baby niece's perilous first months. It is possible that Vanessa and Duncan did not want news of their problem to spread through the Bloomsbury community. Certainly, it was not until March 4 that Virginia Woolf had recovered enough from her flu and the extraction of her abscessed tooth to get over from Asheham to see for herself how things were going with Vanessa and the baby. She and Leonard now owned a reliable car, but having had a couple of accidents, Virginia did not drive. Instead she bicycled the eight miles in cold, driving rain, an escapade that must have reduced Leonard to a quivering heap of anger and anxiety.

Woolf records in her diary that she found the situation at Charleston an odd mixture of chaos and calm. Vanessa's domestic service had been reduced to a man of all work, a governess for the boys, and a "sharp Jewish-looking cook," and the cook took to her bed as soon as Woolf arrived. It was Duncan, therefore, who went upstairs to make up a bed for Virginia, and between them, Vanessa and Duncan and Bunny got dinner on the table and heated water on the hearth for diaper washing and hot-water bottles. None of this sounds especially heroic. A ratio of six able-bodied adults to one small baby, two boys quite old enough to lend a hand, and one guest happy to help might surely be considered adequate, even in an old farmhouse without electricity or plumbing or running water. Virginia's reaction is, as usual, to praise how marvelously her sister manages.

Vanessa may have been less than delighted to see her sister arrive. Woolf says she was able to have only about a half an hour with Vanessa, who stayed behind the door of the baby's room, and it seems Woolf's only glimpse of Angelica came when the baby was being changed before the fire in the kitchen. Only at the end of her diary entry does Virginia, as if reluctantly, describe her niece, but what she says speaks volumes: "She is a wistful, patient, contemplative little creature, examining the fire very meditatively, with a resigned expression & very large blue eyes. I suppose not much larger than a big hare, though perfectly formed — legs, thighs, fingers, toes — both fingers and toes very long & sensitive."

Woolf could see how weak Angelica still was at eleven weeks, such a contrast to her brother Julian who, at the same age, had let howls of outrage ring through the house when he didn't get enough to eat.

あ

The birth of Angelica Bell is one of the most scandalous events in the history of Bloomsbury, though not because she almost died from malnutrition and male medical malpractice. Bunny Garnett was in the farmhouse when Vanessa went into labor, and after the birth he and Duncan went upstairs together to congratulate the mother and take a first look at the newborn. That same evening, Bunny Garnett wrote of her to Lytton Strachey: "Its beauty is the remarkable thing about it. I think of marrying it; when she is twenty, I shall be 46 — will it be scandalous?"

Well, scandalous it duly became, and though his biographer Sarah Knights has recently mounted a stalwart defense of Garnett as a writer, editor, publisher, husband, family man, and lover of women, it still seems hard to condone a young man who looks down at his male lover's offspring in a shoebox and imagines, even as a joke, having "it" in his bed instead of "its" father twenty years on.

Did Duncan know what Bunny had written to Lytton? That is possible, for the two men seem to have had few secrets from each other. Could Garnett have possibly predicted that a few lines hastily dashed off by oil lamp one night would cast a shadow over his long, productive, and successful life? Obviously not. What percentage of the letters even the Bloomsberries wrote in 1918 survive? Did Garnett remember what he had written? He claimed later that he did not, and his denial is plausible. Who among us has not been reminded of some stupid thing we said or wrote in the heat of the moment many years ago, and forgot? Did Garnett for twenty years nurture plans to take revenge on Vanessa Bell and Duncan Grant, as Angelica Bell Garnett sought to convince the world in her best-selling, prize-winning memoir *Deceived with Kindness*? Probably not. As Sarah Knights amply documents, between the two world wars David Garnett was a very busy man, with books to write, businesses to run, a sick wife and two sons to provide for, and a farm to manage. When did he have time to brood and plot?

But if David Garnett was neither a man armed with a reliable crystal ball nor a man set on a twenty-year seduction strategy, his notorious message to Lytton was nonetheless a calculated act of revenge and a first salvo in a long campaign. With World War I over, with Duncan already on the hunt for his next *grande passion,* and with Vanessa finally free to show just how much she disliked the old one, Bunny knew his time at Charleston was nearing its end and was already trying to secure his own position in London. He had seen and heard enough of Lytton Strachey to know that the man specialized in gossip and had almost a fetish about his correspondence. So Bunny, intelligently, supplied the Bloomsbury rumor mill with a hot item and made himself a player, not a victim.

And the fact is that, some twenty years later, David Garnett did, as he had predicted, become not just Angelica Bell's lover but her husband, and the father of her four children. By becoming the son-in-law of Vanessa and Clive and Duncan, he moved into the heart of the Bloomsbury group, which still had a kind of cachet after the war, and he used it for his purposes. Luck played its part in Garnett's triumph — notably the death of his friend Julian Bell in 1937, which brought him back into the Charleston set, and the death of his wife, which left him free to marry — but he also played a savvy game. When the teenage Angelica jumped into his lap, he treated her as a woman, not a child. When she confided in him, he listened. He patiently groomed her until, after a few years of coy flirtation, in another moment famous in Bloomsbury history, they at last became lovers in H. G. Wells's back room.

Bloomsbury watched Bunny Garnett's seduction of Angelica Bell with appalled fascination. Duncan, motivated more by sexual jealousy than paternal concern, actually tried to warn Bunny off Angelica. In response, Bunny remarked that it was a bit late in the day for Duncan to play the Victorian paterfamilias, and he then walked off. Vanessa, who knew that Angelica had to take a lover sooner or later, seems to have decided, with a twisted reasoning all her own, that Bunny was at least a known quantity and that his wealth of sexual expertise would make initiation pleasurable for her daughter. Quentin Bell, still reeling from the death of his older brother, thought the affair a joke and went on vacation with the couple.

But when it became clear that Bunny intended to marry Angelica, not just sleep with her, Bloomsbury was horrified. Leonard Woolf and Maynard

Keynes both took Angelica aside and tried to persuade her that marriage to David Garnett was a bad idea. They probably pointed out that the man was a known serial philanderer whose affairs had caused his adoring wife, Rachel Marshall Garnett, great anguish for the last ten or more years of her tragically short life. Garnett's farm near Cambridge was a place he loved to return to on weekends to work off the flab and entertain his friends, but as his wife, Angelica, like Rachel, would find living there very lonely and cold and very hard work. But Angelica knew all this already, so she ignored the advice.

The one thing the kindly old men of Bloomsbury could not bring themselves to do was tell Angelica that, to their certain knowledge, at the time of her conception and birth, the man she was about to marry had been her father's lover for over two years and had also lusted after her mother. These were things that Vanessa could not bring herself to tell her daughter, and they were the things, Angelica tells us in her memoir, that would have prevented her from marrying David Garnett.

Why were Maynard and Leonard silent about these things despite the clear danger they saw facing a young woman they loved? Angelica has an answer. Vanessa was determined that her daughter should not know, and both men yielded to her indomitable will. "They recognised in [Vanessa] a force that was more full-blooded and more intransigent than their own, an emotional power that had to be reckoned with even though it was seldom expressed directly. If Vanessa adopted them with all the strength of her nature as a sort of extended family, she required from them an allegiance, almost an obedience."

With Julian Bell dead on a battleground in Spain, there was one person who, in the period 1938 to 1940 when Bunny and Angelica were having their affair, might have felt not just authorized but impelled to use her eyewitness testimony and her narrative skills to convey to Angelica the complex web of emotions and memories that bound her mother, Vanessa, her father, Duncan, and her lover, Bunny. That person was Virginia Woolf, who cared very much for Angelica and, though she had learned to have smooth professional relations as a publisher with David Garnett, had clear memories of how both she and Vanessa had hated and resented him back in 1918.

But as Britain lurched toward war with Germany, Virginia was in a troubled state of mind. She feared that her biography of Roger Fry would flop and that her new novel *Between the Acts* would never get finished. She was reading Freud and diving deep into her memories of Hyde Park Gate. The memory of Gerald lifting her onto the hall table at Talland House and fingering her genitals had come back to her. By 1940, the so-called phony war was over, and everything pointed to a swift German victory. Through her brother Adrian Stephen, now a prominent psychiatrist, Virginia and Leonard secured a prescription that would allow them to commit suicide before the Gestapo came for them.

Living at Monk's House since her London home had been destroyed by German bombers, and seeing little of her sister and her family, Virginia had been kept from knowledge of the Angelica-Bunny affair. When she finally got wind of it, she was extremely upset. At the first opportunity, she took her niece aside and asked Angelica if she intended to marry Bunny. Angelica said she did not, which was possibly true at the time. By early 1941, however, Virginia Woolf was dead, drowned. And it was then, as the bombs rained down on London, that Angelica finally yielded to Bunny, became his wife, and retreated to the safety of his farm.

The marriage of Angelica and Bunny was not a happy one, but it lasted for over twenty years. In 1955, hard up for money as always, David Garnett published a slimy *apologia pro matrimonio suo* in the form of a novel, which he titled *Aspects of Love*. The novel's dedication to "Angelica Vanessa Garnett" (from whom Garnett was then estranged) made it clear to Bloomsbury aficionados that *Aspects of Love* was a roman à clef. Garnett, however, who was strenuously erasing any record of his love affair with Duncan Grant from the annals of his life, changed the sex and the age of the characters in his book so as to eliminate even the tiniest taste of homosexuality.

In the novel, Garnett splits himself into two protagonists, young Alexis and his rich uncle George, two well-born studs who are irresistible to women. Both Alexis and George have sex with Rose, a talented actor at the beginning of what will be a successful career, but it is the older man, George, who carries Rose off. Uncle George finally marries Rose and gives her one child, a girl, Jenny. Twenty years on — the very time frame Garnett had envisaged in his letter to Lytton — forty-something Alexis has been invited into the home of Rose and George and becomes a friend of Jenny's. Though barely a teenager, Jenny falls madly in love with Alexis and begs him to possess her. Angelica Bell, let it be noted, was about eighteen when she and Garnett first became involved, and about twenty-two when they first had sex, but in Garnett's novel, the young girl becomes the seducer and the middle-aged man the seduced. Alexis nobly pushes Jenny away and tells her they must wait until she is older — and then goes off to sleep with another of Uncle George's hotties.

By narrative magic, Duncan Grant has been metamorphosed into the highly sexed artist Rose, the mother, not the father, of Jenny, and then, in a cameo, into Uncle George in extreme old age. Take that, Duncan, you old goat, one imagines Garnett saying to himself as he dashed off his novel. Take that for reducing me to tears back in February 1919 when I returned to Charleston from London to find another young man already, literally, in my bed. *Aspects of Love,* with its setting in a French chateau, a delicious villa in the Midi, and a chic apartment on Île Saint-Louis, is a slickly produced piece of high-class heterosexual soft porn. The scene when Jenny, in a diaphanous nightgown, throws herself at Alexis is especially troubling. A lot of people in England, however, loved the book, and Andrew Lloyd Webber, whose wives were getting progressively younger, acquired the rights and in 1989 launched it as his latest hit musical, with a hit ballad — "Love Changes Everything."

વ્જ

Had Vanessa Bell's third child been a boy, the awkward truth about his paternity could have been easily finessed. Like Julian and Quentin, Bell son number three would have found his place in the Bloomsbury constellation as he grew up. He would have learned, as if by osmosis, that Duncan, not Clive, had sired him, and been more pleased than sorry. Discovering that one is not the son of the unlikable man you call Father is a romantic trope for young men, as André Gide was remarking around that time in his great novel *Les faux-monnayeurs.* Bell son number three would have been cognizant of the status and material advantages accruing to him as a Bell, while feeling pride that he was a mixture of the more distinguished Stephens and Grants. But Vanessa's third child was a girl, and that changed everything.

As things would turn out, Garnett's objections to the fiction of Clive Bell's paternity were well founded. The initial lie seemed as harmless as it was expedient, but the lie would become a seventeen-year exercise in deception and hypocrisy, in which Vanessa required all who loved her to play parts. Making a happy and safe life for the daughter she loved, keeping her away from men like Jem Stephen, Jack Hills, and George Duckworth, became a primary goal for Vanessa Bell. She set out to create for her daughter a fairy-tale world in which, unlike the girls at Hyde Park Gate, she would be loved, valued, doted upon, indulged, and vigilantly kept from harm. And, given that so many of the males she surrounded herself with were homosexual, Vanessa Bell felt sure that Angelica would grow up safe. Roger Fry, born in 1866, was the least predatory of men, and he died when Angelica was sixteen. Of course, there was Clive, who was certainly predatory, and his mistresses got younger as he grew older, but Vanessa Bell was confident that she could manage her husband.

In practice, keeping her daughter safe and happy meant spoiling Angelica — telling her how pretty she was, how artistic, how delicious — while curbing her freedom and exerting constant control. By the age of five Angelica was already, she tells us in her memoir, aware that, whereas her brothers were given a long leash, permitted to take risks and make mistakes, she was petted and watched and caged. Even as she describes idyllic moments from her life at Charleston, Bell Garnett makes disquieting references to her fear of falling ill since illness gave "all kinds of people besides Vanessa disconcerting and intimate access to my body." On the next page she describes a photograph in which she is held in the arms of "a Madonna-like Vanessa, whose long straight fingers are too apt to find their way into every crevice of my body."

Vanessa was insistent that Angelica know nothing about the free-loving life Vanessa herself had lived between thirty and forty, and, remarkably, she had the power to keep other tongues from wagging. Since 1908, Bloomsbury had prided itself on its refusal of sexual restraint and its happy freedom to, for example, point to "semen" on a lady's dress, but none of the people who lived through those libertine times with Vanessa — not her former lover Roger, not her husband, Clive, not her sons, who had lived in the farmhouse where Duncan and Bunny fucked and fought — felt authorized to speak of them to Angelica. As the girl grew up, Charleston ceased to be a place where Clive, Duncan, and Maynard could openly conduct their amours. Duncan and Vanessa had separate rooms and were never seen to embrace. *"Pas devant les enfants,"* Vanessa would murmur if her guests threatened to revert to the old vocabulary of "cunt" and "catamite" and "buggery," and Angelica would be sent off with a governess or a friend.

Vanessa Bell had once championed women's right to sexual freedom, but she found it impossible to talk to her daughter about sex and refused to allow anyone else to do so. It was only when seventeen-year-old Angelica was about to leave for London to attend drama school that, on her older brother Julian's insistence, she was sent to a woman doctor charged by Vanessa with supplying the information about sex and reproduction. The doctor was astonished to find this child of Bloomsbury so totally uninformed.

To summarize, no one in the Charleston set that clustered around Vanessa Bell felt authorized, as it were, to include Angelica in the Bloomsbury group as they had included her two brothers. David Garnett did include her, and that, I think, is why she married him. At forty-six Garnett was still a very attractive man, but the secret of his appeal to Angelica Bell was that he was the first to see her as a mature woman and treat her as an adult.

Angelica Bell did not learn the truth of her parentage until she was eighteen. In an agony of grief over the death in Spain of her son Julian, Vanessa Bell let the truth slip out almost by accident. Angelica received the information in silence, apparently unmoved. She agreed to her mother's request that she not "upset" Duncan or Clive — Vanessa could not bear for people to be "upset" — by revealing that she knew the truth, and she kept that agreement to the end of both men's lives. But beneath a surface serenity she modeled on her mother's, Angelica Bell was very upset indeed. She felt that her world had been undermined, turned upside-down. Some six years later, as David Garnett's wife and the mother of his child, her mental disarray only intensified when, she claims, she finally learned that Bunny and Duncan, to Vanessa's knowledge and with her consent, had been lovers at the time of her birth.

Corrosive to Angelica's peace of mind as she came into adulthood was the perception that the fairy-tale world her mother had created around her had been an elaborate charade. The worst part was not the knowledge of her illegitimacy but the fact that everyone had been in on the secret except herself.

The sociable man who had taken her on his knee, spoiled her as a girl, and now wore her proudly on his arm at London parties was not her father. The charming man who made his home with her mother and was so unfailingly funny and nice to everyone was her father, but neither he nor his clan had ever shown her the slightest preference. Her brothers loved her and often looked out for her, but they had been allowed to know from adolescence that they were Bells, and she was somehow neither Bell nor Grant.

In our century, we have come to see that knowing who one's biological parents are is a basic human desire and perhaps a basic human right. Vanessa denied that right to her daughter, preferring silence to candor, deception to honesty, and that seems to have sabotaged their relationship very early on. Once Angelica understood that her mother had constructed a beautiful cage for her as a girl, she began to set up invisible barriers to intimacy that even her daughters, who found Vanessa a magical grandmother, could not break down.

Angelica yearned in vain for Duncan Grant to treat her as his child, especially when in his last years he began displaying so much interest and grandfatherly affection for the children of his former lover Paul Roche. All the same Angelica loved her father while reserving for her mother a bitterness that came close to hatred. Years after Vanessa's death and after hours of therapy, Angelica Bell tells us, she still felt the power of her mother, adoring, protective, secretive, blocking out her sun.

It is chilling to read Angelica Bell Garnett's bitter account of her relationship with her mother alongside a 1936 letter in which Vanessa Bell confided how much having a daughter had meant to her. The letter is to Julian, who, inexplicably to his mother, had gone off to China. Julian worried about his sister and, confident in his mother's love for him, felt able to say from afar what many near at hand believed — that Vanessa should set Angelica free and allow her to get on with her life. Vanessa refused to believe that she was a possessive mother, but she was eager to say how much Angelica meant to her. To her elder son, Vanessa was willing to explore her inner world on paper as she had never done with anyone else, even Virginia.

When Julian, her first child, was born, Vanessa wrote, he "entirely revolutionized existence for me, starting all the feelings that had slept all my life till then." Then, as if Quentin, who would become her rock and stay in later life, did not even exist for her, Vanessa goes on to describe her feelings for Angelica:

> ... but Angelica being of my own sex ... suddenly gave me a feeling of complete intimacy with someone who had something so much in common with me fundamentally that it was like a revelation ... it was different from any relationship I'd ever experienced except perhaps at moments with my mother and Stella — I don't think I've ever had that peculiar thing even with Virginia. Well, that looks rather bad, doesn't it? But I didn't try to keep her [Angelica], did I? ... I wanted her to be independent *au fond*. For one thing I'd had a tremendous lesson as to that particular thing with my mother and Stella, who were so devoted and inseparable that Stella never had any real life of her own.

The life at 22 Hyde Park Gate, Kensington, cast a very long shadow.

How did Virginia Woolf, who explored mother-daughter relationships in so many novels and in her essays fiercely championed a girl child's right to freedom, education, and opportunity, feel about the way Vanessa chose to rear her daughter? Virginia too had seen how the relationship between Julia and Stella played out, so how did she feel about the power Vanessa exerted over Angelica? Remembering what had secretly happened to her as a small child, how did she react to seeing, in Vanessa's family album, photos of a small, skinny, straight-haired naked Angelica staring stiff and unsmiling straight into her mother's camera, or sitting between two adult males who seem to feel no need to remove so much as a tweed jacket or a tie despite the summer heat?

In *Vanessa Bell's Family Album,* the coffee table book that she and her brother Quentin published in 1981, Angelica Bell chose to include several of these nude studies of herself as a little girl. One assumes that she saw no problem with them and endorsed her brother's contention that they showcased their mother's talent for photography. For my part, as I look at my copy of what is today a rare book, I completely endorse the decision of the Tate Gallery, the repository for Vanessa Bell's photographs, to take them out of its catalog and carefully weigh all requests for permission to reproduce them. The fear that these images could circulate unchecked on the internet as child pornography seems all too real.

But to return to the question of what Virginia Woolf thought of her niece Angelica's upbringing, the answer is that we have little hard information, just a few indirect hints, since Virginia knew that Vanessa would brook no interference with any of her children. The following little piece from a letter of April 24, 1929, is as close as Virginia ever got to hinting at what she saw as a problem with Vanessa's relationship with her children. Recounting a visit she and Leonard had had from Julian, Virginia writes, "Julian . . . is growing like a crab, I mean only half covered with shell . . . The Bell sociability is so odd, mixed with the Stephen integrity. I daresay he'll give you a lot of trouble before he's done . . . he's too charming and violent and gifted altogether, and *in love with you in the bargain*" [my emphasis].

This is remarkably prescient. Within four years of this letter, Julian Bell had taken a teaching position in Wuhan, China, about as far from Bloomsbury and his mother as he could get. On his return from the East in 1935, driven by his passionate opposition to fascism and eager to put his life on the line, Julian joined an ambulance corps on the battlefront during the Spanish Civil War and was killed within days of his arrival. Caught in a bombing raid, Julian threw his body over his companion in the ambulance to protect him.

With Angelica, Virginia was even more careful than with her nephews not to say anything that could be construed as criticism. She knew how important Angelica was to her sister, and in her diary she refrained from exploring the relationship of her sister and her niece. Though women friends like Ethel Smyth and Ethel Sands would have had treasures of memories and advice to offer, Angelica was not something Virginia could discuss with them in letters.

Thus, the little we know about the relationship of Virginia and Angelica comes mainly from Angelica's 1984 memoir. Angelica Garnett says that her uncle Leonard sternly disapproved of the way she was being brought up and shocked her on two occasions by demanding that she acknowledge an act of serious carelessness. "These contacts with a sterner reality impressed me," writes Angelica Garnett, since they formed a contrast with "Vanessa's tendency to compound and procrastinate in favor of those she loved, and Duncan's ability to laugh away and ignore things he didn't like." Virginia Woolf probably endorsed her husband's sternness to Angelica but refrained from saying so, lest it be reported back.

Vanessa always organized a gala party for her daughter's birthday. When Angelica turned eleven, the party had an Alice in Wonderland theme, and Virginia Woolf turned up with ears and paws, as the March Hare. Returning home after the party, Leonard, dressed up as the Carpenter, "came in conflict with the police on behalf of a drunken prostitute who, being insulted by three tipsy men, answered them in their own coin. 'Why don't you go for the men who began it? My name's Woolf and I can take my oath the woman's not to blame.'" Virginia reported all this to Clive Bell, while also noting that Angelica at her party had been "ravishing, flirtatious, commanding and seductive." That sounds more like Virginia Woolf the caustic social critic than Virginia the affectionate auntie.

In the final year or so of her life, Virginia Woolf was happy to note that Angelica was showing an interest in books and ideas at last and was beginning, like her brothers, to take a part in adult conversation. Woolf gave Angelica a copy of the letters of Madame du Deffand, the great eighteenth-century writer and scientist, which she herself had been given by Lytton Strachey. She encouraged Angelica to give a talk at the Rodmell Women's Institute. "[Virginia] tried to probe and loosen my ideas," writes Angelica, "and, when she forgot to be brilliant and amusing, showed a capacity for intimacy which I found illuminating." The youngest of the three Bell children, Angelica had much less time to get to interact as an adult with Virginia Woolf. As a girl, she says, she was aware of being somehow a disappointment to her aunt. It is all very sad.

17

Virginia's Way, Part 2

AFTER THE end of World War I, Virginia and Leonard carefully put together a life based on a commonality of work, ideas, and values, which was there for all to see, and on intimate pleasures they kept hidden, not just from the world but from the diaries and memoirs they planned to leave to posterity. The past six years had been an education in group living for them both, and Leonard was now an expert in Bloomsbury politics as well as international socialism. They made no secret of keeping separate bedrooms, yet what Mongoose [Leonard] did to make Mandril [Virginia] so rapturously happy when they found themselves alone and unobserved — that they kept to themselves.

In their financial arrangements as well as their intimate relations, the Woolfs were different from Vanessa's Charleston set, working toward an economic parity that is far more common in our day than it was in theirs. Leonard in Sri Lanka had probably been sending money home to his widowed mother, so, despite his steady rise up the ranks of the colonial service, he came back to England in 1911 with only the few hundred pounds he had won in a raffle. When he made the decision to marry Virginia and stay in England, he had no job. Virginia, on the other hand, had a steady stream of investment income from various legacies and was also earning modest but regular fees from her reviews.

Living on his wife's money was not what Leonard wanted, and after their wedding, the Woolfs moved out of Bloomsbury, took cheap rooms in the Inns of Court, and, to the indignation of their old cook, Sophie Farrell, and her friend Maud, ate their meals at a nearby chophouse and employed a charwoman. Following Virginia's major breakdowns of 1913 and 1915, money got really tight as Virginia incurred medical bills that ate up her private income and her doctors forbade her to write. But over the next years both Woolfs put their pens and typewriters seriously to work and earned enough to live on, she as a reviewer, essayist, and novelist, he as an editor, lecturer, and journalist.

Along with her private happiness, the years between 1919 and 1939 were the period of Virginia Woolf's greatest creativity, with the publication of *Night and Day* (1919), *Jacob's Room* (1922), *The Common Reader* (1922 and 1932), *Mrs. Dalloway* (1925), *To the Lighthouse* (1927), *Orlando* (1928), *A Room of One's Own* (1929), *The Waves* (1932), *Flush* (1933), *The Years* (1937), and *Three Guineas* (1938). The first two were published by Duckworth, the publishing house founded by her brother Gerald, but the rest were published by the Hogarth Press, founded and owned by her and her husband.

At the outset, the Hogarth Press (named after the house they occupied in Richmond for some years) was a hobby, something to do together on weekends, something to keep Virginia's hands active and her mind at rest. Virginia as a young woman had taken a course in bookbinding, and she was delighted to locate a little printing press they could afford. The machine was barely functional, but the Woolfs persisted and began to turn out a few copies of short pieces by themselves and their friends. Virginia, with her steady hands, set the type, while Leonard, who was thin but wiry, pulled the handle. Together, they glued the pages, covered them in bits of wallpaper, and carried them down to the post office.

In May the new press published *The Critic in Judgement,* an essay by the well-known writer J. Middleton Murry; *Kew Gardens,* a short story by Virginia; and *Poems,* by T. S. Eliot. Tom Eliot was a young American working at Lloyds of London who had recently come into the Woolfs' orbit. At first, to Virginia's dismay, *Kew Gardens* got few orders, and that dismay deepened when Vanessa, whom she had asked to illustrate the story, complained bitterly at the amateurish way her illustrations had been printed. "She says she will not do any more art work for the HP which is a failure," wrote Virginia in her diary. "This both stung and chilled me."

But Leonard was an experienced editor who had wide connections with left-wing writers throughout Europe, while Virginia was an experienced reviewer with a nose for literary talent. Thus, it was not by chance that the Woolfs put their precious time, ink, and glue into publishing early poems by T. S. Eliot. Little by little, the Hogarth Press found readers, a bigger press was bought, and then a contract was signed with a commercial printer, leaving the owners to scout for talent, read submissions, secure reviews, and communicate with bookshops. Nothing came easily. In the early 1930s, Virginia could still be found in the basement of the Hogarth Press's new premises at Tavistock Square, dressed in dusty overalls and making up parcels of newly printed books.

By the mid-1930s, the Hogarth Press had a wide range of interesting publications, and its owners were able to buy and rent out the duplex in Richmond, establish their home and their business at two successive properties in Bloomsbury, and buy Monk's House, a tiny, rundown building in a magnificent garden that Virginia had come upon in her rovings through Sussex. Virginia delighted in having money to spend at last, and she happily paid for the extension, renovation, and furnishing of Monk's House. She commissioned Vanessa to design furniture and upholstery and, as a birthday gift, paid for live women models to pose for Vanessa.

Whereas, at least to my eye, Vanessa and Duncan essentially halted their artists' rebellion with Matisse, Virginia, on a steady diet of reading for the press, kept abreast of the challenges posed by the new generation of writers around the world. Virginia disliked James Joyce's *Ulysses,* but she and Leonard would have published it if they had been able to persuade their printers to take the risk of prosecution. Through her psychoanalyst brother and sister-in-law and her friends James and Alix Strachey, Virginia read deeply in the new field of Freudian psychoanalysis, and the Hogarth Press was by the 1930s able to take on the challenge of publishing the Stracheys' translation of *The Complete Works of Sigmund Freud.*

Through her socialist husband, Virginia was connected to the world of international politics and left-wing radicalism. That connection helped her see that inherited money is the privilege of the few, like herself, but also that creativity needs a few hundred a year and a room of one's own. Virginia Woolf always tuned in to the political scene with reluctance. All the same, if she, like her sister, had once found herself in conversation at a party with a gentleman called Asquith, she would have recognized the prime minister and refrained from asking if he was interested in politics—a memorable gaffe by Vanessa that went the rounds among Bloomsbury's enemies.

Reading the diaries and letters and memoirs of Virginia Woolf and Leonard Woolf, one is impressed by the amount of work they got through while still being sociable on weekends, taking Continental holidays with friends like the Frys, having dinner at Clive's favorite little Italian restaurant in town, maintaining a very large garden, and making their own jam from local strawberries. But at the end of a busy week in London, lunching with prospective contributors, reading submissions, editing copy, talking to press representatives in the field, writing articles and novels and essays and innumerable letters both professional and private, what Virginia wanted to do was go down to Sussex, troll the local shops for fish and buns and toffee, walk the moors to see the hares and the butterflies, feed the dogs (neither Virginia nor Leonard could bear to live without a dog), and then close the door—just Mongoose and Mandril.

Vanessa was still indispensable to Virginia, and relations between the sisters had settled into a more comfortable pattern by the early 1930s, when both Vanessa and Duncan were achieving a success in the art world that equaled the success of Virginia and Leonard in the publishing world. The influence of Vanessa's circle of working painters on Virginia as a novelist was considerable, and as Woolf learned to see paintings with her sister's expert eye, she carried those insights into words on the page. *The Waves,* Woolf's most experimental and poetic novel, is also highly pictorial, structured around descriptions of a seascape as it changes from season to season. In *To the Lighthouse,* Lily Briscoe and the painting whose finishing touch is a blurred shape representing the Madonna-like Mrs. Ramsay are keys to the meaning of the book.

Virginia learned to rein in the passion for Vanessa she had once let loose in her letters to Clive, but amid the social updates and family chat she supplies in her letters, Virginia still occasionally sounds the old note of abandonment. She needed Vanessa and always wanted more of her while knowing that Vanessa did not need her and wanted rather less than more. Writing to her sister, who was in the French village of Cassis, where Vanessa and her household had taken root during the winters, Woolf in London wrote on April 12, 1929, "I can't tell you how bitter and autumnal it is; not a leaf out, many indeed have gone in. And the snow falls in my heart too, slow, soft flakes salt-tasting with tears. Why? Ah Hah! Dolphin being a beast covered with brine who never shed a tear don't know the meaning of that pleasure. And Duncan, whom I adore, is cased in oil silk from the assault of the waves."

Even without their very particular and deeply rooted psychological issues and Vanessa's decision to spend more of the year in France, two social factors kept Virginia and Vanessa apart more and more in the interwar years — Virginia's husband and her precarious health. If Vanessa stood at the heart of the Bloomsbury group because she was Clive's wife, Lytton and Maynard's friend, and Duncan's partner, Virginia often stood outside the Bloomsbury group because she was Leonard's wife. Leonard made it increasingly clear that he did not enjoy being with the Charleston set and felt at odds with their sybaritic way of life, their indifference to the course of European politics and the effects of the economic depression on ordinary people who did not have Maynard Keynes to manage their stock portfolio.

Where Clive was independently affluent and increasingly jingoistic in his views, Leonard had to earn his living and was a committed socialist. Where Lytton was a gay butterfly, earning fat American publishing contracts with his books on Queen Victoria and Queen Elizabeth, Leonard was an industrious ant, publishing the poetry of Rilke, the stories of Christopher Isherwood, and *The Notebooks* of Anton Chekhov, which Leonard translated himself, with his friend Samuel S. Koteliansky. Where Maynard moved smoothly up the British power hierarchy in politics, diplomacy, and economics, Leonard was a worker for world peace, watching with alarm as totalitarianism gained ground in Russia, in Italy, in Spain, in Germany. Where Duncan was happy as long as he could paint and have sex with beautiful men, Leonard was as celibate as a monk. That the highly cultured, polylingual Leonard Woolf never traded in his social conscience for aesthetic sensibility or put poetry over politics set him apart from the people Vanessa Bell welcomed in her homes.

Leonard Woolf was also, as his name declared without ambiguity, a Jew, a non-observant Jew who nonetheless could chant the Torah in Hebrew as

readily as he could recite the choruses of Sophocles in Greek or cite the Ma-
haramsa in Pali. Leonard Woolf did not need the rise of Hitler to know that
the centuries-old perception of Jews as a poisonous threat to European society
was flaming up, not dying down. In tolerant, cultured, well-traveled Bloomsbury, Leonard was always the outsider, the butt of casual anti-Semitic slurs
from close companions such as Clive Bell and Maynard Keynes and even, at
moments, from his wife. As he explains in his autobiography, Leonard had
learned to operate successfully in the high professional class, linked to the aristocracy, into which his wife had been born, but he always felt himself an
outsider, welcomed to the old boys' club as a guest but never eligible for membership.

Anti-Semitism was something Virginia Woolf breathed like air all her life.
She was also, she would admit, a huge snob, and both prejudices were aroused
by members of her husband's family, especially the women. "How I hated marrying a Jew," she wrote to Ethel Smyth in August 1930. "How I hated their nasal voices, and their oriental jewelry, and their noses and their wattles — what
a snob I was for they have immense vitality, and I think I like that quality best
of all." And, after that grudging compliment, she goes on to say that "Jews can't
die . . . they pullulate, copulate, and amass . . . millions of money."

Such remarks are, to say the least, disquieting, but putting one's prejudices
down in black and white can be a step toward overcoming them, and heaven
knows, many of us have problems with our in-laws. The mass of documentation the Woolfs left proves that, throughout their marriage, both Virginia
and Leonard regularly visited and hosted members of his family, notably his
brothers. When his mother moved to Hove, which they felt was uncomfortably close to their Sussex getaway, the Leonard Woolfs were nonetheless attentive to her care. As we can see from the portrait of suburban English-Jewish
society he gives in his 1914 novel *The Wise Virgins,* Leonard had more than
a touch of anti-Semitic snobbery himself, and I think he gave his wife credit
for at least striving to rise above vulgar prejudice. By 1940, faced with the imminent prospect of invasion, and better informed than most about what was
happening to Jews in Hitler's Germany, Virginia and Leonard were sure that
their names would both be on the Gestapo's list of arrests. According to Isaiah
Berlin, Virginia Woolf then spoke of herself and Leonard as "we Jews."

As to Virginia Woolf's health, Michael Cunningham's best-selling 1998 novel *The Hours* and the subsequent 2002 movie starring the Oscar-winning Nicole Kidman have made a strong case that Leonard Woolf's paternalist efforts at protection narrowed his wife's social horizons and hobbled her creativity. I found that case persuasive until I began to immerse myself in Virginia Woolf's own letters and journals. Then I could count how many times after 1904 she fell into a catastrophic mental breakdown, how constantly she hovered on the edge of mania, and how rationally terrified she was of falling again. Within a few years of marriage, she and Leonard had enough experience of her illness to know that small things — a series of late nights, a severe cold that prevented her from working, a social event that turned unpleasant, a hectic trip abroad — could trigger a manic-depressive episode. A vague headache, a refusal of lunch, a sleepless night were all bad signs, so Leonard would insist on bed rest and regular meals, and Virginia would reluctantly concur.

Once she had persuaded Leonard to move back to Bloomsbury with their press, and they had found a new, permanent vacation home in Sussex, Virginia felt able to relax for a few years into an alternating routine of bed rest and vigorous social activity that was familiar and acceptable. In bed or comfortably settled on the couch, her writing board propped up on her knees, her books around her, Nelly bustling in with tea and biscuits from time to time, and hearing the rapid *tap-tap-tap* of Leonard's typewriter in the next room, she could work even if she could not have visitors or venture abroad. Life as an invalid was dull and a little demeaning, but it was productive, and so much better than being locked up, on a diet of milk, laxatives, and opiates, in some select clinic for deranged gentlewomen.

ও

In the interwar years, as her social and professional world expanded and she became well known, Virginia attracted a stimulating and supportive group of women friends. Among these was the New Zealander writer Katherine Mansfield, who was one of the first writers published by the Hogarth Press. Woolf and Mansfield were rivals in the world of literary journalism, and the relationship they developed was brief and rather prickly. Mansfield was young, attractive, and confident in her sexuality — Mansfield made no secret of the affairs she had had with both men and women — none of which endeared her to Woolf. Though of a socially prominent family in her native country, Mansfield was a colonial, her accent perhaps not quite cut-glass pure, and in company she came across to Virginia as tacky and shallow. Katherine managed to conceal from Virginia how very ill she was (she died of tuberculosis in January 1923), and so, when Katharine failed to reply to a friendly letter, Virginia was hurt and offended.

But for all her feelings of professional rivalry and puritanical distaste, the literary editor in Woolf had seized upon "the living power, the detached existence of a work of art" in Mansfield's story "The Prelude," so she published it. On the few occasions when the two women were alone together, they talked avidly and found they could cover much more ground than was ever possible with condescending men like Tom Eliot or Lytton Strachey. Woolf confided to her diary that

> I find, with Katherine, what I don't find with the other clever women, a sense of ease & interest, which is, I suppose, due to her caring so genuinely if so differently from the way I care, about our precious art. Though Katherine [as the wife of John Middleton Murry, the editor of the *Athenaeum* magazine] is now in the very heart of the professional world — 4 books on her table to review — she is, & will always be I fancy, not the least of a hack. I don't feel as I feel with Molly Hamilton, that is to say, ashamed of the inkpot.

Katherine Mansfield was only one of the women in Virginia Woolf's acquaintance who desired women as well as men — Alix Strachey, Carrington, Mary Hutchinson, Dorothy Wellesley, and Dorothy Strachey Bussy were others. But as she journeyed through her thirties and forties, Virginia found herself more and more in the company of interesting and creative people who did not marry and identified themselves quite openly as gay and lesbian. The lesbian and gay communities were distinct and not especially friendly to each other, but they did come together in certain places — London, of course, but also in Sussex and the adjacent county of Kent. Knole and Sissinghurst in Sussex were the country estates of Edward Sackville-West and Vita Sackville-West, the best-selling author E. F. Benson had taken on the lease and the patrician ways of Henry James at Lamb House in Rye on the Kentish coast, and Dame Ellen Terry and her daughter, Edy Craig, presided over a group of lesbians at Smallhythe, some ten miles inland.

Of course, Virginia Woolf had been in the company of homosexual men since Bloomsbury began, but she was never as intimately involved in gay men's lives as her sister was. Maynard Keynes was never really a friend of Virginia's, and so, though she found Lydia Lopokova infuriating, the marriage of Maynard and Lydia was not the personal betrayal for her that it was for Vanessa. Lytton's willing submission to the sadistic tastes of his new young Oxford lover Roger Senhouse was kept from her, but Lytton's companion Carrington didn't know of it either. Of all the Newnham and Slade School "Cropheads," Virginia liked Carrington best, and she worried to see Carrington neglecting her art and her self-interest to care for Lytton.

With Morgan Forster (known to the world as E. M. Forster), a novelist who had achieved earlier and greater success than she, Virginia enjoyed an affectionate and mutually admiring but intermittent relationship. Morgan, known as "the Mole" in Bloomsbury, was by the 1920s engaged in a series of passionate love affairs with working-class men and came under the influence of a misogynistic gay theorist. Fearing to feed the Bloomsbury gossip mill, he was careful not to air his new views or confide personal details to the increasingly feminist Virginia Woolf.

When she found herself at gay parties, Virginia Woolf felt like an anthropologist gathering information on an alien tribe. The new generation of gay men fascinated and appalled her because they were so very much "not in the style of our day in Cambridge," Woolf wrote to Ethel Smyth, the notable composer and lesbian activist. Woolf means, I think, that the new generation were not tall and gangly like Lytton and Maynard (six foot seven) or broad and brawny like Duncan or her brother Adrian (six foot five). Two of these confidently gay young men, however, became friends and colleagues of the Woolfs

— John Lehmann, who for several years was an editor and then a partner in the Hogarth Press, and Eddy Sackville-West, an artist and music critic.

One evening over dinner, John Lehmann recalls in *Thrown to the Woolfs,* Virginia opened the conversation by asking, like an affectionate aunt trying to be tolerant and *à la page,* "Now, John, tell us about your bugger-boys." Unwilling to enter into a discussion of his complicated personal life, Lehmann offered an amusing anecdote about Fred, a young guardsman he had once known, noting that brief sexual encounters between upper-class men like himself and working-class men like Fred were quite common. "But does this really go on all the time in London?" Virginia exclaimed. "Leo, have you ever heard of it?" And Leo of course had.

Eddy Sackville-West and his coterie of musicians and artists were a lot harder for Virginia to take seriously than Lehmann and his rugged, scruffy socialist writers. Sackville wore makeup, spoke in a high voice, had ruffles at throat and wrists in the evening, and lolled in Japanese silk pajamas at home. He struck Virginia as a lap dog, and her reaction to him led Virginia to write an extraordinarily revealing letter to Ethel Smyth, in which she analyzes her feelings toward men, gay and straight:

When I go to what we call a "Buggery Poke" party, I feel as if I had strayed into the male urinal; a wet, smelly, trivial kind of place. I fought with Eddy Sackville over this, I often fight with my friends. How silly, how pretty you sodomites are I said; whereat he flared up and accused me of having a red-nosed grandfather. For myself, why did I tell you that I had only once felt physical feeling for a man [presumably Lytton Strachey] when he felt nothing for me? I suppose in some opium trance of inaccuracy. No — had I felt physical feeling for him, then, no doubt, we would have married, or had a shot at something. But my feelings were all of the spiritual, intellectual, emotional kind. And when 2 or 3 times in all, I felt physically for a man, then he was so obtuse, gallant, foxhunting and dull that I — diverse as I am — could only wheel around and gallop the other way. Perhaps this shows why Clive who had his reasons, always called me a fish. Vita also calls me a fish. And I reply (I think often while holding their hands and getting exquisite pleasure from contact with either male or female body) "But what I want of you is illusion — to make the world dance."

Ethel Smyth was an older woman who fell in love with Woolf and became a close friend in Woolf's last years. Smyth made little effort to conceal her lesbian identity, and she was an ardent suffragist. Smyth's "Women's March" became the anthem of the women's suffrage movement and was played not only on the streets of England but in the exclusive Paris salon of Natalie Clifford Barney, where Smyth was often a welcome guest. The younger artist Ethel Sands, who shared two elegant homes with her female partner, Nan Hudson, also became a confidante and supportive friend to Virginia Woolf by the early 1930s. It was to Sands, as we have seen, that Woolf felt able to confide her regrets about not having children, and Woolf's trust in Smyth allowed her to explore emotional depths that she could never broach with Vanessa. These women were deeply attracted to Woolf — as Woolf once remarked, "these Sapphists *love* women," and their friendships were never "untinged with amorosity" — but with neither of them was Woolf tempted to have a physical relationship. The great love affair of Virginia Woolf's adult life was with another member of the English lesbian community — though one who carefully kept her membership secret from the public — Vita Sackville-West.

Vita Sackville-West, to use her maiden name and the name under which she published, was already a successful author when she met Virginia Woolf, and the two came together first because of a commonality of professional interests. The Woolfs had a publishing house, and Sackville-West made overtures to them about publishing her next book or books. The Woolfs and the Nicolsons (Vita in private life was Mrs. Harold Nicolson) met over dinner at the Bells' home at Gordon Square, and then exchanged Sussex visits, and were at first not much impressed with one another. The Nicolsons were accustomed to cold and dog hair but not to a chaos of books and manuscripts and a dearth of finger bowls and Limoges china. The Omega Workshops designs of Bell and Grant made the Nicolsons wince. For their part, the Bell-Woolfs were bored by the Nicolsons' references to sitting next to Winston Churchill at dinner or lunching at Woburn Abbey and unimpressed by their attempts at repartee. Virginia was quickly of the opinion that Vita's mind lacked depth.

But despite a hint of dark mustache Virginia noticed on her new friend's lip, Vita was a blazing physical presence, wearing a pink sweater and pearls even in the Sevenoaks fishmonger's shop. Virginia soon fell in love with Vita's voluptuous body and the romantic mix of feudal aristocracy and Spanish gypsy in her lineage, and, as Hermione Lee puts it, Virginia began to "make Vita up," in the sense of creating a persona for her — rather in the way she had "made up" her sister.

For a time Vita was more than happy to play her assigned role, and she entranced Virginia by driving her over to visit Knole, the ancient and immense "calendar" castle with, supposedly, 7 courtyards, 52 staircases, and 365 rooms where she had spent her youth. Vita Sackville-West was the only child of a mother and father who were Sackville-West first cousins, but she could not inherit Knole because she was born female, and Knole was subject to an entail on a male heir. When Vita and Virginia lay down on the bed that Elizabeth I had once slept in, in the royal bedroom at Knole, Woolf felt she was next to a romantic hero as well as an exciting woman. That scented, silk-cravated Eddy, not Vita — the very image of aristocratic vigor as she strode around the Sussex countryside in jodhpurs and boots — was heir to Knole, filled Virginia's feminist heart with sympathy and rage.

In her correspondence with Violet Dickinson as a young woman, Virginia had been a furry wombat or a fragile sparrow. Now, in her letters to Vita, Virginia split herself into two. The first Virginia was the renowned wit and brilliant intellect who looked down on Vita and called her a donkey. The second Virginia was a furry animal, a squirrel, a little dog, and finally a "potto," a small exotic creature wistfully eager to nestle in her lover's capacious bosom. Virginia ends a 1930 letter to Vita "With a soft, wet warm kiss from poor Potto." After spending a night alone with Vita, Virginia was so excited, she had to tell her sister about it. The two sisters were waiting to check out in a pharmacy, and, to the fascination no doubt of the others in line, Vanessa, taking her change and "talking as loud as a parrot," responded to her sister's news of Vita with "but do you really like going to bed with women? . . . and how do you do it?"

For a while, Vita was fascinated by Virginia, and Harold began to fear that this time his wife had finally found her great love and would leave him in a scandal that would make Vita's affair with Violet Trefusis seem pale. But amorous dalliance was never enough for Vita, and Virginia's mixture of fragile neediness and intellectual scorn wore thin. Vita Sackville-West was an eager and experienced lover who had gotten her first orgasms at the hands of a boy on her relatives' Scottish farm, and she was falling madly in love with girls when she was still in school. Virginia, as we have seen, had always felt more desire for women than for men, so one would expect her affair to be a glorious revelation to her. As it turned out, however, Virginia was no more homosexual than heterosexual, and Vita was no more able to make her relax and feel comfortable in her body than awkward, inexperienced Leonard had been. Vita confessed to her husband, Harold, who liked to be kept up to date on her amours, that she was afraid that if, as it were, she turned up the heat when she took Virginia Woolf in her arms, Virginia would go mad.

Within a year or so, Vita was taking long trips abroad with her rich old friend Dorothy Wellesley, and then, to her husband's relief and Mrs. Wellesley's chagrin, Vita went blithely and unapologetically on to her next conquest, Hilda Matheson of the BBC. Virginia was jealous and hurt and clingy for some time, but she took counsel and amusement from the in-depth analysis of the complications of lesbian society provided by Ethel Smyth, a doyenne of the "Sapphic" scene both in England and in France.

And if Vita Sackville-West had failed to give Virginia Woolf orgasms, she did something more important — she sparked Woolf's period of greatest creativity. It was in the course of her intimate friendship with Vita that Woolf produced what many consider her masterpieces — *To the Lighthouse, Orlando,* and *A Room of One's Own. Orlando,* with a protagonist who ranges through history and across continents and changes from man to woman in different historical eras, has become a classic of queer literature, especially since Sally Potter's extraordinary 1992 movie starring Tilda Swinton. For the first Hogarth Press edition of the novel, Vita Sackville-West posed for photographs in costume, and when she finally received her inscribed copy, she was both furious at what her friend Virginia had dared to "make up" of her and cognizant that this was a supreme love letter.

Professionally, Vita Sackville-West came through for the Woolfs. She was a prize-winning poet and a novelist who sold far more copies than Virginia, and publishing some of her prose work with the Hogarth Press was a coup for Virginia and Leonard. Vita's novel *The Edwardians,* published by the Hogarth Press in 1930, was a bestseller and put Leonard's account book solidly in the black for the first time.

ə❧

Beloved within the English lesbian community was Ellen Terry, the famous actress whose unconventional yet thoroughly Victorian career included a succession of wildly acclaimed theatrical performances, a couple of undistinguished husbands, two flamboyant male lovers, two illegitimate children, and a damehood. Ellen Terry fascinated Virginia Woolf, since, as we know from Woolf's skit "Freshwater" (discussed in Chapter 2), Terry was part of the Pattle family lore of Virginia's mother. Woolf wrote a kind review of Terry's rather disjointed autobiography when it came out, and decades later, as she notes in a letter to Ethel Smyth on January 24, 1934, she enjoyed the edition of Terry's correspondence with George Bernard Shaw prepared by Edy Craig and Christopher St. John. She was less enthusiastic about the 1932 *Memoirs of Ellen Terry* put out by the same team. Woolf could easily have met Terry, who died in 1928. It was not until 1933, however, that Woolf visited Smallhythe Place, the rambling collection of Tudor buildings that Terry had managed to buy and where she lived her last years, surrounded by a loving, protective, creative, fiercely feminist group of women.

Chief among those women was Terry's daughter "Edy" — Edith Ailsa Geraldine Craig (1869–1947) — a director, playwright, and costumier to whom Woolf was introduced socially by Vita Sackville-West. Vita's Sissinghurst home was just eight miles from Smallhythe. Edy and her two closest companions, Christopher St. John (born Cristabel Marshall) and Clare (Tony) Atwell, were leaders of the radical, bohemian wing of the English lesbian community between the wars. Unlike aristocratic "Sapphists" (to use Woolf's preferred term) such as Vita Sackville-West, Dorothy Wellesley, Violet Keppel Trefusis, and Una Troubridge, the Smallhythe group inherited no trust funds;

took no husbands; dressed for comfort, not fashion, often in the sturdy garb associated with men; and struggled to support themselves with their writing, their art, and their theatrical projects.

Edy Craig and Virginia Woolf were never friends, though both were good friends of Ethel Smyth, whose operas brought her into Craig's theatrical world. As early as 1922 Woolf was attending the rehearsal of a play by her friend Beatrice Mayor, which was being put on in London by Craig's pioneering women's theater group, the Playwrights Theatre, and directed by Craig herself. In the diary entry of March 30, Woolf describes "Miss Craig," "a rosy, ruddy personage in white waistcoat, with black bow tie and gold chain loosely knotted," and she savors "the supple, candid, free and easy good sense of the theatrical manners" as interpreted by Edy Craig.

This rehearsal was to bear fruit many years later. In *Between the Acts,* the novel left in draft when she died, Woolf imagines a musical pageant celebrating English history staged in the garden of a big house in southern England. The play is written and directed by Miss Latrobe, and, as she is the first to realize, it is less than a success, even by local village standards. After the audience and the players have departed, Miss Latrobe (Virginia Woolf never gives her a first name) emerges from behind the tree where she has watched the whole shambolic performance. Shouldering the heavy case of records used in the performance, unable to face the evening alone in her cottage (her actress partner, Woolf tells us, has left her), Miss Latrobe repairs to the local pub to drown her theatrical sorrows alongside men who have only contempt for her and her kind. If only the actors "had known their parts," she muses over a glass of beer, if only the audience "had understood her meaning," if only "the pearls had been real and the funds illimitable," perhaps "her gift" might have been recognized.

But live theater is essentially a transitory art, its glory fleeting, its failures forgotten, and in her fatigue and disappointment Miss Latrobe is already thinking of her next production. "She put down her case and stood looking at the land. Then something rose to the surface. 'I should group them here,' she murmured, 'here.' It would be midnight; there would be two figures, half concealed by a rock. The curtain would rise. What would the first words be?" By the last pages of the novel, she has found those first words.

Miss Latrobe is not a portrait of Edy Craig. Craig lived in the shadow of her extraordinary mother, but she inherited no small measure of the love, respect, and admiration that Dame Ellen earned, and she was never alone. After the death of her mother, Craig lived in a community of like-minded women. Equally, the pageant that Woolf evokes in the novel is not *A Pageant of Great Women,* Edith Craig's most successful work, in which Woman is pitted against Prejudice. That said, in its urgency as much as in its arguments, Craig's modern morality play was clearly an influential text for Woolf as she came to write her own feminist polemic, *A Room of One's Own.*

But in choosing to end her last novel with a woman theater director who is quietly but clearly identified as lesbian, Woolf was not only paying tribute to Edith Craig and the pioneer theater group she led, which is only now receiving the attention it deserves. Woolf was also suggesting that Miss Latrobe and her pageant could be symbolic of England in the early years of World War II. The cultured, leisured county society that Woolf conjured up in her novel was, she knew, a lighthearted farce between two great tragedies, and by 1940 it was as much a thing of the past as Alfred and the cakes and good Queen Bess. Hitler, with his blitzkrieg and his concentration camps, had put an end to the Sussex world where Virginia and Leonard had created their haven of peace and contentment and collaboration, and the vast sadistic insanity of the real world was not only bombing Virginia's London home but breaking through her fragile mental defenses.

Soon she would be overrun, but while she could still think and write Woolf imagined a pageant in which a small, unremarkable English village community comes together to reenact great moments of its national past and does it very badly — just as Prime Minister Neville Chamberlain had done with the "Peace for Our Time" he negotiated in 1939 with Adolf Hitler. But square, bossy, pragmatic, visionary, unappreciated Miss Latrobe recognizes failure with a sigh as Britain did after the disaster and triumph of Dunkirk, and she quickly moves on to her next production, irrationally sure that she has a gift and the world, in some small way, will be the better for it. And though Woolf did not live to see it, Britain did not give up hope and did in the end struggle through to victory.

જ

Virginia Woolf and Vita Sackville-West remained friends and professional colleagues to the end, meeting occasionally for delectable lunches and exchanging affectionate letters. But just as Virginia knew quite well that Vita would
never leave Harold, for her or any other woman, so Vita knew that Virginia
would never leave Leonard. Even at the height of their love affair, when the
two women went on vacation together in France, after a couple of weeks of
writing to Leonard every day, Virginia could not wait to get back home. Vita
was fascinating, exciting, wondrous, and in *Orlando,* Woolf celebrated her
lover and friend in a way that the twenty-first century has found inspirational.
But her attraction to people, men and women, was always, in Woolf's own
words, "spiritual, intellectual, emotional," and once she drilled down into Vita's mind, she was disappointed, even bored. Vita simply did not stand comparison with Leonard.

Virginia Woolf knew that, in her husband, she had by rare good fortune
come upon a friend, a partner, an intellectual equal, the best companion, the
person in the world who most shared her values and who most valued her
ideas. The Woolfs had what the Greeks called *homophrosyne,* a sharing of
mind, and they worked as a team. When they started the Hogarth Press with
a cheap, dysfunctional little printing machine, she set the type and he pulled
the handle. When their publishing enterprise took off, they ran it together and
shared in the profits.

Leonard Woolf was certainly not a perfect man. He was a workaholic, and
at times, the pace of the treadmill Leonard had strapped himself to brought
him close to nervous collapse. Never an easy man, he would become irrationally stingy, dogmatic, pettifogging, and demanding. People at the Hogarth
Press like John Lehmann knew to keep clear of the boss when he fiddled obsessively with stray bits of string to conceal the quickening tremor in his hands. If
Virginia was a manic-depressive with regular suicidal impulses, Leonard was a
chronic functional depressive. *Downhill All the Way,* his title for the final volume of his autobiography, is shorthand for the way he saw life. But, as he said
many times, Leonard's love with Virginia was the beacon that lit up the darkness of his life. In his proposal letter Leonard had sworn to love and protect

Virginia always, and he was as good as his word. Keeping his wife alive was in part how he avoided suicide himself.

In her marriage, as in so many other ways, Virginia Woolf broke ground and achieved success. Given the obstacles that stood in the way, the happiness she felt and gave is remarkable. As she says over and over again in her letters and diaries, she loved Leonard, cared for him, relied on him, missed him when he went away, was happy when he came back, knew that to him she was incomparable. Over the Woolfs' thirty-year marriage, trust, affection, commitment, physical intimacy, and shared values proved more important than desire and orgasm — to both of them. That such things could not in the end prevail against her mental illness was their tragedy.

When Virginia Woolf was fifty-nine, her disease, whatever we label it, got the better of her. Diseases do that in the end, for all of us. At a time of national catastrophe, her London home blown to pieces by a German bomb, facing the very real prospect that, if the Nazis invaded, she and her Jewish husband would be consigned to an English Auschwitz, Woolf was overtaxed, physically as well as mentally. She knew she was once more descending into madness and felt that, in such perilous times, caring for her was a burden her husband, family, and friends should not have to bear. So she kept hold of sanity while it was hers and chose death.

She put on her old coat, went out to the cold little lodge where she did her writing, and wrote her last letter to Leonard. It begins: "Dearest, I want to tell you that you have given me complete happiness. No one could have done more than you have done. Please believe that. But I know I am wasting your life. It is this madness."

Then she walked out the back gate, past the church, and down to the river Ouse, which was running high. She put a large stone in her pocket and walked into the icy, swift-flowing water.

EPILOGUE:
THE BELL CHILDREN AND THEIR AUNT

TO HER lasting sorrow, Virginia Woolf had no children, but she had books that have stood the test of time, a husband who guarded her estate, and heirs to carry her legacy forward. Woolf was a marvelous aunt. These excerpts from her letters illustrate the exuberant love, the intelligent sympathy, and the zany humor she lavished on them when she got the chance. To nineteen-year-old Quentin, who had written to her from Cassis and whose literary flair she presciently diagnosed, she wrote on May 11, 1929, "Dearest Quentin — oh, but you're Claudian . . . How you have seduced me by the charm of your language. I have thrown to the floor the last page of my most hated book, it is as dry as a captains biscuit . . . and turned to this succulent sheet . . . How could I write to you when you were at Cassis and every page was left in the drawing room to be read by Clive Angelica Duncan Sabine Miss Campbell and Colonel Teed?"

To twelve-year-old Angelica, who had written to inquire about the new litter of puppies the Woolfs' dog Pinka was expecting, Virginia wrote in June a year later, "Darling Angelica, What a treat to get your letter! . . . How I wish I could sew like you and Mummy . . . When you come and stay at Rodmell will you give me lessons? Pinka sat on one of the puppies so there are only five — four daughters and one son, all coal black . . . we are going to call one Sheba. The son will be called Othello . . . Oh dear how I wish you would run in now and then we could have some pranks with the sugar ... Love from Pinka, Sheba, Othello, Leonardo."

She signed herself to Angelica simply "Jinny."

For her Bell nephews and niece, Woolf loved to play the crazy aunt, but they knew they had a national treasure in her, and after her death they set out to repay all her kindnesses and offered paeans to her complicated character. In their writings about Bloomsbury — notably *Virginia Woolf, Bloomsbury Recalled,* and *Deceived with Kindness* — Quentin Bell and Angelica Bell Garnett do something quite remarkable. They write books their publisher aunt would have been proud to put into print and paragraphs that their writer aunt would have been happy to pen. And let us not forget that Anne Olivier Bell, Quentin's wife, devoted decades of her life to editing Virginia Woolf's diary, displaying a scholarly precision and a delicacy of taste Woolf the reviewer would have praised. It is not fanciful to date the reemergence of Virginia Woolf as a major literary and intellectual figure to the 1972 publication of Quentin Bell's carefully researched and documented, finely reasoned, deeply personal biography. Clear, witty, observant, cultured, masters of the art of telling a good story while getting the facts, Quentin and Angelica reveal themselves the worthy heirs of Virginia Woolf.

Of Bloomsbury as a group, Quentin and Angelica have much to say, much of it charming, but of their parents — Vanessa and Clive and Duncan — they use humorous and whimsical anecdotes to offer an unacknowledged indictment. Virginia Woolf in her diary had gone out of her way to protect her sister, to present Vanessa in as flattering a light as possible. Angelica Bell Garnett especially does the opposite. She tells a compelling story of how her mother, watched by both her fathers, ruined her childhood and then stood back and let her husband ruin her adulthood. *Deceived with Kindness: A Bloomsbury Childhood* is not an exercise in scholarly biography like her brother's *Virginia Woolf.* It is an anguished cri de coeur, and it does not have the last word, but no one has taken an ax to the legend of Bloomsbury as Angelica Garnett did.

As I was reading for this book, I became aware of a little vein of sadism running through the history of Bloomsbury. I don't mean adult, negotiated sadomasochism as practiced by Lytton Strachey and Roger Senhouse, but casual, unacknowledged acts of cruelty, which only Virginia and Leonard

Woolf appeared to notice. Not by chance was it to Virginia Woolf that Roger Fry talked about the everyday bloody beatings he had been forced to assist in at his prep school, to Virginia that an anguished Rupert Brooke wrote about the hideous affair of a small choirboy being gang-raped by older boys during evensong. Not by chance was it Leonard Woolf, in his comical party costume, who, as we saw in the last chapter, spoke up to the policeman in defense of a prostitute.

In his final meditation on Bloomsbury as an old man, Quentin Bell details, without judgment, the casual sadism to which he was introduced as a very young man. He tells of the ghastly night when George Bergen, Duncan's latest lover, took him out on a wild toot with a group of homosexual prostitutes he found repulsive — and then tried to proposition him within Duncan's hearing. Worse yet, Quentin tells the story of how, as a special treat when he was a teenager, he was taken by his father, Clive Bell, to lunch at a villa at St. Cloud. There Quentin was offered his first cocktail, and when their host, a little man with lovely brown eyes, played a record of "Chinese music," Quentin and his father sat and listened. "The music consisted," writes Quentin Bell, "of a Chinese woman uttering fearful shrieks; the little man explained that the woman's long fingers were stretched between two tables; as someone broke them with a mallet, each finger produced a shriek." The "little man" was Pablo Picasso, and such was Quentin's pleasure in being treated as a sophisticated adult by his father and such his awe at being in the company of a giant of the art world that, he tells us, he found horror "an inappropriate emotion."

While I was researching this book on Virginia Woolf, I had an emotion that I refused to dismiss as inappropriate, and it too related to Clive Bell, the husband Vanessa Bell never found it useful to divorce, the biological father of Julian and Quentin, and the man Angelica for eighteen years believed was her father.

Sitting in the library at Trinity College, Cambridge, one day in 2017 and waiting for my host to come and collect me, I idly started to flip through a collection of dirty postcards belonging to Clive Bell. Apparently no rich American collectors had found the postcards interesting enough to purchase, so Bell's heirs had given them to his old college. I myself was ready to dismiss the collection as icky but harmless (topless young women being fondled by mustachioed Edwardian blokes) until I came upon a sequence of three commercially produced postcards with photographs of a very small girl preparing to take a bath. The cards feature rhymed captions full of sexual double-entendres.

These postcards had been sent to Clive under the cover of an envelope by a good friend signing himself "Gerry." This, I managed to work out, was the diplomat Gerald Wellesley, then "our man in Buenos Aires," and, as he makes clear, an appreciative patron of Miss Kitty Beldan, the waning star of an Argentine brothel. Kitty, one gathers from Gerry's comments on the back of the postcards, had been brought into the oldest profession at a very young age and intended her small daughter Dulcie to follow in her footsteps. Gerry regretfully reports to Clive that Kitty has just embarked with a touring company in order to give maximum exposure to her fetching little Dulcie. "There is a considerable demand for a child her age among the Elder Statesmen," Gerry chortles to Clive.

Gerald Wellesley was one of Clive Bell's most prestigious friends. Wikipedia tells us he had a distinguished diplomatic career, served creditably as an officer in World War II (nicknamed, according to Wikipedia, "the Iron Duchess" by his men), and, following the deaths in close succession of his brother and his childless nephew in the early 1940s, became 7th Duke of Wellington, Prince of Waterloo, Duke of Ciudad Rodrigo.

How seriously you take the future duke's choice of postcards for his friend Clive's collection or his written remarks praising the charms of "Mademoiselle Dulcie" will depend on your view of how private morality maps onto public probity and how pornography maps onto sexual practice. To me, small-child pornography, all by itself, is an abomination, and to sit in the Wren Library at my alma mater, Cambridge University, and be suddenly confronted with proof that Clive Bell and Gerald Wellesley found sex between a man and a child at the very least a titillating joke was a shock. Another apparently innocuous and unwritten postcard sent to Bell for his collection, showing a bowler-hatted man in close-up against a street scene, with a couple of young girls and their attendant, suddenly took on a new meaning.

Virginia Woolf loved children, cared about them, saw, with a clarity rare in her generation, how often both boys and girls were seen as sexual objects and abused. She always distrusted and disliked Clive Bell, and it was not by chance that it was to Clive Bell, already notorious in Bloomsbury circles for his "poppets," that she wrote the following. "Yes, I saw Christabel [Aberconway] and she was a good deal perplexed about a matter of conscience. That is to say she was kissed last June on the top of a Welsh hill by Canon Bowlby [who] has just been acquitted of improperly behaving to schoolgirls in a train. 'Now what is my duty', says Christa. 'Ought I to have given evidence of his behavior to me? Because not a soul in England will believe those wretched little girls.'"

I owe Virginia Woolf an incalculable debt. Over my long lifetime, she has taught me many things. I thought I knew her work well. But when, in the final days of writing this book, I came upon the letter I have just quoted, I was so surprised, I wept. What she said was so relevant to our world today.

She and Christabel Aberconway were right. We must in conscience listen to what wretched little girls and wretched little boys have to say.

ACKNOWLEDGMENTS

I could not have written this book without the support of three key people — my husband, Stuart Esten; my agent, Jill Kneerim; and my editor, Deanne Urmy. Stuart is my tech guru as well as my loving partner, there every day to haul me out of some word-processing ditch I have fallen into. Jill Kneerim is my savviest critic and most ardent promoter. Our friendship is one of the pleasures of my life. My thanks also to Lucy Cleland, Jill's associate at Kneerim and Williams, whose enthusiasm for the book and breadth of information have been invaluable. Deanne Urmy has the uncanny knack of knowing where you are going as a writer before you know yourself. She has guided me with rare critical acumen and ready sympathy, and the shape the book has taken owes much to her vision.

Deanne has been supported by a superb team at Houghton Mifflin Harcourt, notably Jennifer Freilach who shepherded the book expertly through production. Jenny Xu and Leah Petrakis both did sterling work on my behalf, especially during my arduous pursuit of permission to use images and quotations. Copyeditor Susanna Brougham brought to my book the precision, the breadth of culture, and the sympathetic involvement that every writer dreams of. Finally, I was the beneficiary of the laserlike focus of proofreader Ellen Fast.

On my two research trips to England, in 2015 and 2017, I emerged from my cocoon and reveled in the active assistance and enthusiastic support of my network of relatives and friends in England. My brother-in-law Adrian Gill and his wife, Kim, providentially live in Sussex, near Virginia Woolf's beloved South Downs, and they not only put me up but drove me expertly to Monk's House and Charleston. The Cliftonville home of my brother Harry Scobie and his wife, Sue, also proved superbly placed. While staying with the Scobies, piloted by Harry, I was able to explore Henry James's house in Rye, Ellen Terry and Edy Craig's home in Smallhythe, and Vita Sackville-West's homes at Knole and Sissinghurst. In London, I made forays into Bloomsbury and Kensington from the home of my friend Elizabeth Blunt, who cooked me delicious dinners and gave invaluable information on bus routes. In Cambridge, I stayed with my old friends Stella and Alan Weeds, and Alan, a fellow and former bursar of Trinity College, used his clout, at very short notice, to get me into the archive of both Trinity and King's College. My thanks to all these relatives and friends for organizing my visits and taking such great care of me.

As a writer, I am never lonely, with endless books to read and the internet to offer instant answers. As a woman, I am neither alone nor lonely as I am lucky enough to be surrounded by family and friends. My children, Christopher and Catherine Gill, my daughter-in-law, Jennifer Litzow Gill, and my son-in-law, Tobias McElheny, all live within a twenty-mile radius of me. Of my seven grandchildren, Bronwyn Mako Wada Gill has strayed as far as Worcester, Massachusetts, but the other six — Fiona Amane Wada Gill, Delia Kotone Wada Gill, Eyob Gill, Kalkidan Gill, James McElheny, and Susannah McElheny — are all in the Boston area and likely to remain so for a while. My coeval boosters — my sister-in-law Linda Crosskey and her husband, John Crosskey, along with Fran and Kenneth McElheny and Joan and Merv Litzow (whom Ken memorably named "the Outlaws") cheer me on and offer bibliographic suggestions.

Writing in 2019 I feel the need to end this list of debts by saying how happy and privileged I am to be an American.

In the United States, everyone I meet recognizes me as British because of my accent, while in the United Kingdom, people have long identified me as an American. That sense of deracination used to bother me. How weird is it to be asked which part of the United States you come from when you are back on a visit to your Welsh hometown, admiring the ducks on a small lake about a mile from where you were born? But today I take pride in floating somewhere mid-Atlantic, neither fish nor fowl nor good red herring, as the old British saying goes. Despite my funny accent, I can be 100 percent American without losing my membership in a thriving, achieving, contributing international tribe that stretches from Great Britain, France, and the Netherlands to Japan, Ethiopia, and Australia. I and mine are swirling around in the melting pot, doing what we can to keep the United States of America great.

SELECTED BIBLIOGRAPHY

Annan, Noel — *Leslie Stephen: The Godless Victorian* (1951/1984)

———. *The Dons* (1999)

Anscombe, Isabella — *Omega and After: Bloomsbury and the Decorative Arts* (1981)

Aplin, John — *A Thackeray Family Biography, Volume 1: The Inheritance of Genius, 1798–1875* (2010)

———. *A Thackeray Family Biography, Volume 2: Memory and Legacy, 1876–1919* (2011)

Bell, Quentin — *Virginia Woolf,* 2 vols. (1972)

———. *Charleston: A Bloomsbury House and Garden* (with Angelica Bell Garnett and Henrietta Garnett) (1987)

———. *Bloomsbury Recalled* (1995)

Bell, Quentin, and Angelica Garnett — *Vanessa Bell's Family Album,* with an introduction by Quentin Bell (1981)

Bell, Vanessa — *Selected Letters of Vanessa Bell,* ed. Regina Marler (1998)

Black, Ros — *A Talent for Humanity: The Life and Work of Lady Henry Somerset* (2010)

Bussy, Dorothy Strachey — *Olivia* (1949)

Butler, Samuel — *The Way of All Flesh* (1912)

Cameron, Julia Margaret — *Victorian Photographs of Famous Men and Fair Women, with Introductions by Virginia Woolf and Roger Fry* (1926/1973)

Carrington, (Dora) — *Carrington: Letters and Extracts from Her Diaries,* ed. David Garnett (1970)

Dalrymple, William — *White Mughals: Love and Betrayal in Eighteenth-Century India* (2002)

DeSalvo, Louise — *Virginia Woolf: The Impact of Childhood Abuse on Her Life and Work* (1989)

Dunn, Jane — *A Very Close Conspiracy: Vanessa Bell and Virginia Woolf* (1990)

Forster, E. M. — *The Longest Journey* (1907)

———. *Maurice* (1913–14/1971)

———. *A Passage to India* (1924)

———. *Goldsworthy Lowes Dickinson* (1934)

———. *Marianne Thornton: A Domestic Biography* (1976)

Gadd, David — *The Loving Friends: A Portrait of Bloomsbury* (1974)

Garnett, Angelica — *Deceived with Kindness* (1984)

Garnett, David — *Lady into Fox* (1922)

———. *Aspects of Love* (1955/1990)

Garnett, Henrietta — *Family Skeleton* (1987)

———. *Anny: A Life of Anne Thackeray Ritchie* (2005)

———. *Wives and Stunners: The Pre-Raphaelites and Their Muses* (2012)

Gérin, Winifred — *Anne Thackeray Ritchie* (1981)

Glendinning, Victoria — *Vita: A Biography of Vita Sackville-West* (1973)

———. *Leonard Woolf: A Biography* (2006)

Goldhill, Simon — *A Very Queer Family Indeed: Sex, Religion, and the Bensons in Victorian England* (2016)

Holroyd, Michael — *Lytton Strachey and the Bloomsbury Group: His Work, Their Influence* (1967)

———. *Lytton Strachey: The New Biography* (1994)

———. *A Strange Eventful History: The Dramatic Lives of Ellen Terry, Henry Irving, and Their Remarkable Families* (2008)

Houlbrook, Matt — *Queer London: Perils and Pleasures in the Sexual Metropolis, 1918–1957* (2005)

Hughes, Thomas — *Tom Brown's Schooldays* (1857)

Jamison, Kay Redfield — *Robert Lowell: Setting the River on Fire — A Study of Genius, Mania, and Character* (2017)

Knights, Sarah — *Bloomsbury's Outsider: A Life of David Garnett* (2015)

Leavis, F. R. — "After 'To the Lighthouse,'" (1942), in *A Selection from "Scrutiny"* compiled by F. R. Leavis, pp. 97–100 (1968)

Lee, Hermione — *Virginia Woolf* (1997)

Lehmann, John — *Thrown to the Woolfs* (1978)

Levy, Paul — *G. E. Moore and the Cambridge Apostles* (1981)

———. "The Painter and the Novelist," *New York Review of Books,* May 11, 2017

Marcus, Steven — *The Other Victorians* (1966)

Moffat, Wendy — *A Great Unrecorded History: A New Life of E. M. Forster* (2010)

Nicolson, Nigel — *Portrait of a Marriage* (1973)

Olsen, Victoria — *Julia Margaret Cameron and Victorian Photography* (2003)

Parmar, Priya — *Vanessa and Her Sister* (2015)

Partridge, Frances — *Love in Bloomsbury* (1981/2014)

Rachlin, Ann — *Edy Was a Lady, Featuring the "Lost" Memoirs of Ellen Terry's Daughter Edith Craig* (2011)

Raverat, Gwen — *Period Piece* (1952)

Ray, Gordon N. — *Thackeray: The Uses of Adversity, 1811–1846* (1955)
——. *Thackeray: The Age of Wisdom, 1847–1863* (1958)
Ritchie, Anne Thackeray — *The Fairy Tale Fiction of Anne Thackeray Ritchie* (1868/1874/2010)
——. *Five Old Friends* (1875)
——. *From an Island* (1877)
——. *A Book of Sibyls: Miss Barbauld, Mrs. Opie, Miss Austen* (1883/Kindle)
Robb, Graham — *Strangers: Homosexual Love in the Nineteenth Century* (2003)
Rose, Phyllis — *Parallel Lives* (1983)
Russell, Bertrand — *The Autobiography of Bertrand Russell, 1914–1944* (1951)
Sackville-West, Vita — *The Land* (1927)
——. *The Edwardians* (1930)
Sellers, Susan — *Vanessa and Virginia* (2009)
Seymour, Miranda — *Ottoline Morrell: Life on the Grand Scale* (1994)
Shone, Richard — *The Art of Bloomsbury: Roger Fry, Vanessa Bell, and Duncan Grant* (1999)
Skidelsky, Robert — *John Maynard Keynes, 1883–1946: Economist, Philosopher, Statesman* (2003)
Spalding, Frances — *Roger Fry* (1980)
——. *Vanessa Bell* (1983)
——. *Duncan Grant* (1997)
Stephen, Leslie — *The Life of Sir James Fitzjames Stephen, Bart. K., C.S.I, a Judge of the High Court* (1895)
——. *Sir Leslie Stephen's Mausoleum Book,* ed. Alan Bell (1896/1977)
Stoppard, Tom — *The Invention of Love* (1997)
Strachey, Lytton — *The Letters of Lytton Strachey,* ed. Paul Levy (2005)
——. *Eminent Victorians* (1918)
Tennyson, Alfred — *In Memoriam* (1850)
Terry, Ellen — *The Story of My Life* (1908)
Thackeray, William Makepeace — *Vanity Fair* (1848)
——. *Pendennis* (1850)
Tomalin, Claire — *The Invisible Woman: The Story of Nelly Ternan and Charles Dickens* (1990)
Trefusis, Violet — *Echo* (1931)
——. *Broderie anglaise* (1935)
——.*Violet to Vita: The Letters of Violet Trefusis to Vita Sackville-West,* ed. Mitchell A. Leaska and John Phillips (1991)
Turnbaugh, Douglas Blair — *Duncan Grant and the Bloomsbury Group* (1987)
Vanderbilt, Consuelo — *The Glitter and the Gold* (1953)
Woolf, Leonard — *The Village in the Jungle* (1913)
——. *The Wise Virgins* (1914/2017)
——. *Sowing* (1960)
——. *Growing* (1961)
——. *Beginning Again* (1963)
——. *Downhill All the Way* (1967)

Woolf, Virginia — *The Voyage Out* (1915)

———. *Night and Day* (1919)

———. *Jacob's Room* (1922)

———. *The Common Reader,* 2 vols. (1922 and 1932)

———. *Mrs. Dalloway* (1925)

———. *To the Lighthouse* (1927)

———. *Orlando* (1928)

———. *A Room of One's Own* (1929)

———. *The Waves* (1932)

———. *Flush* (1933)

———. "Freshwater, a Comedy" (1935)

———. *The Years* (1937)

———. *Three Guineas* (1938)

———. *Roger Fry: A Biography* (1939)

———. *Between the Acts* (1941)

———. *The Death of the Moth and Other Essays,* ed. Leonard Woolf (1942)

———. *The Diary of Virginia Woolf,* 5 vols., ed. Anne Olivier Bell and Andrew McNeillie (1977–1984)

———. *The Letters of Virginia Woolf,* 6 vols., ed. Nigel Nicolson and Joanne Trautmann (1977–1979)

———. *Virginia Woolf: Women and Writing,* ed. Michèle Barrett (1979)

———. *Virginia Woolf: Moments of Being,* ed. Jeanne Schulkind (1985)

———. *The Essays of Virginia Woolf,* 6 vols., ed. Andrew McNeillie and Stuart N. Clarke (1986–2010)

———. *Virginia Woolf, a Passionate Apprentice: The Early Journals, 1897–1909,* ed. Mitchell A. Leaska (1990)

———. *Carlyle's House and Other Sketches,* ed. David Bradshaw, with a foreword by Doris Lessing (2005)

Woolf, Virginia, and Julia Stephen — *On Being Ill* (2012)

NOTES

Introduction

PAGE

xiii   *Despite the best efforts:* In the United States a key example in twentieth-century literary history of the denigration of the Victorian woman writer is Harriet Beecher Stowe. Even Rodgers and Hammerstein with *The King and I* could not persuade Americans that *Uncle Tom's Cabin* was not only a civil rights milestone that could leap international boundaries but a great read. Virginia Woolf wrote review essays on Christina Rossetti's poetry and on Elizabeth Barrett Browning's great poem *Aurora Leigh,* both of them included in Michèle Barrett's invaluable collection *Virginia Woolf: Women and Writing* (New York: Harcourt Brace Jovanovich, 1979).

xv   *"noble character than learn":* Noel Annan, in the 1984 revised version of his 1951 biography *Leslie Stephen: The Godless Victorian* (New York: Random House), p. 119. The courtship correspondence of Leslie and Julia Stephen is now held in the Berg Collection of the New York Public Library.

fiercely anti-feminist: Ibid., p. 110. Both Leslie and Julia Stephen were against giving women the right to vote. In 1889, Julia Stephen, along with her social reformer friend Octavia Hill and the future Fabian Beatrice Potter (later Webb) signed An Appeal Against Female Suffrage.

   Beatrice Potter changed her political views when she married Sidney Webb. Prominent in the Fabian Society and the new political ranks of the Labour Party during World War I, the Webbs became close allies of Leonard Woolf.

xvi   *"I don't know if I ever":* Mary Kingsley, quoted by Woolf in *Three Guineas* (New York: Harcourt Brace & World, 1938), p. 4.

"It is a voracious receptacle": Ibid. The "Arthur" to whom Woolf refers is Arthur Pendennis, the eponymous hero of a novel by William Makepeace Thackeray.

xvii *Virginia Woolf's education:* The same argument has been made for Agatha Christie, who, though born eighteen years after Woolf, was also self-educated. Christie's crippling shyness was partly the result of her having been designated as too dumb, in both senses of the word, to benefit from formal education. She had an exaggerated respect for Oxford-educated men like her second husband, Max Mallowan. See my book *Agatha Christie: The Woman and Her Mysteries* (New York: The Free Press, 1990).

xviii *rare achievement for a woman:* In Dwight Garner's profile of the new editor of the *Times Literary Supplement,* Stig Abell, in the *New York Times* of May 26, 2018, Garner cites the fact that, between its founding in 1902 and 1921, of the 1,036 contributors to the *TLS,* 81 were clergymen, 67 came out of the (then) all-male Oxford college Balliol, and 76 were women.

xix *"for everybody, for nobody":* Virginia Woolf, *The Common Reader,* First Series (New York: Harvest Books, 1925/1955), p. 119.

xx *reference to or quotation from:* In just the first three months of 2017, three such citations appeared in the *New York Times Book Review.* Monica Ali's review of a novel by Rachel Cusk, on January 29, is called "A Room of Her Own"; Stacy Schiff, on March 26, mentions that each essay by Richard Holmes "can be read as a riff on Virginia Woolf's sly observation that the actual length of a person's life is open to dispute"; in a "By the Book" interview with Phillip Meyer on April 2, Meyer states, "I'll usually start the day with Virginia Woolf." More recently, on October 28, 2018, Carina Chocano opened her "First Words" essay in the *New York Times Magazine* with these words: "In 1931, Virginia Woolf spoke to members of the London and National Society for Women's Service on the subject of her professional experiences as a woman." Chocano goes on to note that Woolf acknowledged that her path as a woman writer had been "smoothed by Fanny Burney, by Aphra Behn, by Harriet Martineau, by Jane Austen, by George Eliot," and that she bitterly commented on the way the culture at large minimizes and scorns the physical experience of women. This essay was written in the aftermath of the furor over Brett Kavanaugh's confirmation as an associate justice of the Supreme Court. In her "By the Book" interview of January 13, 2019, Dani Shapiro says she always has Woolf's *Writer's Diary* within reach "as part of the conversation I've been having with Woolf since I began reading her in my 20s." Later in the interview, Shapiro notes that her ideal literary dinner party would consist of Woolf and Freud arguing, with Leonard Woolf as referee.

xxiii *"a chain of women who":* Angelica Garnett, prologue to *Deceived with Kindness: A Bloomsbury Childhood* (New York: Harcourt Brace Jovanovich, 1984), p. 12.

1. Virginia Woolf's Indian Ancestresses

3 *"If you want to know where":* The Letters of Virginia Woolf: Volume Six, 1936–1941, edited by Nigel Nicolson and Joanne Trautmann (New York and London: Harcourt Brace Jovanovich, 1980), p. 461.

"Antoine de l'Etang was one": Julia Margaret Cameron, *Victorian Photographs of Famous Men and Fair Women, with Introductions by Virginia Woolf and Roger Fry* (London: Hogarth Press, 1926; London: A & W Visual Library, 1973, with a preface, corrections, and notes by Tristram Powell), p. 13. Citations refer to the 1973 edition, which was also published by David R. Godine, in Boston.

4 *"His person was pleasing"*: Quentin Bell, *Virginia Woolf* (New York: Harcourt, 1972), vol. 1, p. 14.

"The Chevalier de l'Etang was": Cameron, *Victorian Photographs*, p. 21.

5 *"This was something I"*: William Dalrymple, *White Mughals: Love and Betrayal in Eighteenth-Century India* (New York: Penguin Books, 2002), p. xlv. Virginia Woolf's maternal grandmother, Maria Pattle Jackson, was the older sister of Sophia Pattle Dalrymple, William Dalrymple's great-great-grandmother.

the bustling Franco-Indian port: The opening sequences of the movie *The Life of Pi* are set in the charming old Franco-Indian quarter in Pondicherry.

6 *This paucity of portraits:* Thanks in no small measure to the Pattle descendants William Dalrymple and Deborah Spooner, there has in the last few years been a small explosion of information about the de l'Etangs and the Pattles on the internet. Just in 2018–19, interest in Thérèse has increased, and two sketches of her have turned up on the web — the work, as far as I can determine, of her fifth great-granddaughter Deborah Spooner. Wikitree now offers a very much more accurate family tree, and the extensive professional career of Antoine de l'Etang in the military and in various equestrian centers in northern India has been researched.

7 *the queen's final months:* I started to feel for Marie Antoinette when I read about her final year of imprisonment. Her young son was torn away from her and placed in the hands of cruel men. She was forced to watch as the severed head of her best friend, the Duchess de Polignac, was paraded back and forth in front of her window. At the end Marie Antoinette suffered from constant vaginal bleeding, was obliged to change her clothing in front of her guards, and had no secret place to hide her blood-stained rags. Wearing a pure white dress on the tumbrel and as she knelt before the guillotine was an act of valor that any woman who has blushed from menstrual stains will salute.

a miniature by a French artist: In 1930, Virginia Woolf's stepbrother Sir George Duckworth gave her a miniature that a cousin of his had left him, of "old Pattle surrounded by wife and daughters done in France." *The Letters of Virginia Woolf: Volume Four, 1929–1931,* edited by Nigel Nicolson and Joanne Trautmann (New York: Harcourt Brace Jovanovich, 1978), pp. 144 and 214. Scholars at Smith College, which owns a copy of the Pattle family group portrait, believe that James Pattle had remained in India and was painted in later.

9 *"Isabel reveled in the freedom"*: Ros Black, *A Talent for Humanity: The Life and Work of Lady Henry Somerset* (Chippenham and Eastbourne, UK: Antony Rowe Publishing, 2010), p. 8.

10 *"Dr Jackson's half-French wife"*: "A Sketch of the Past," in *Virginia Woolf: Moments of Being,* edited with an introduction and notes by Jeanne Schulkind, 2nd ed. (New York: Harcourt Brace Jovanovich, 1985), p. 85. Hereafter cited as Woolf, *Moments of Being.*

"this [late-eighteenth-century] promiscuous": Dalrymple, *White Mughals,* p. xlv.

Lytton Strachey's astonished protest: Lytton Strachey's friend and fellow Cambridge Apostle E. M. Forster, through his war service in Egypt, his visits to India, and his interracial friendships and loves, made the leap out of racial prejudice into connection, as did Leonard Woolf. Forster's acknowledged masterpiece *A Passage to India* was another novel that Lytton Strachey, whose literary taste was usually unerring, found it hard to praise and harder to like. See Wendy Moffat's superb *A Great Unrecorded History: A New Life of E. M. Forster* (New York: Farrar, Straus & Giroux, 2010).

11 *Virginia Woolf sardonically noted:* Virginia Woolf to Violet Dickinson, *The Letters of Virginia Woolf: Volume One, 1888–1912,* edited by Nigel Nicolson and Joanne Trautmann (New York: Harcourt Brace Jovanovich, 1975), p. 202.

12 *"[Florence] said that my diamond":* Ibid., p. 164.

13 *Julie, Antoinette, and Virginie:* The name Julie became popular following the publication in 1761 of Jean-Jacques Rousseau's horrendously long, nauseatingly sentimental, and inexplicably popular epistolary novel *Julie, ou la nouvelle Héloïse. Paul et Virginie* (1787), by Jacques-Henri Bernardin de Saint-Pierre, was another massive bestseller in Europe but at least mercifully short. As I remember, Virginie dies in a shipwreck at the end of the novel because she is too virginal to take off her clothes. I mention this since the way that her name seemed to define her as a sexual being will, as we shall see, haunt Virginia Woolf.

names passed down in: As my reader can see from the family tree that opens this chapter, Adeline the second was Adeline Pattle Mackenzie (1814–1838), Adeline de l'Etang Pattle's eldest daughter. Adeline Pattle Mackenzie's younger sister Maria Pattle Jackson (Virginia Woolf's maternal grandmother) named her first child Adeline, so Adeline Maria Jackson Vaughan (1837–1881) is Adeline the third. Virginia Somers, the sixth Pattle sister, named her elder daughter (the future Duchess of Bedford) Adeline Marie, so she was Adeline the fourth. Finally — according to the limited family tree we have — Julia Stephen named her third daughter Adeline Virginia Stephen after her sister Adeline Vaughan and her aunt Virginia, Countess Somers. Thus, our Virginia Woolf was, according to official records, Adeline the fifth. The name Julie, or Julia in English, was passed down from Julie-Antoinette-Adeline de l'Etang Pattle to her second daughter, Julia Margaret Pattle Cameron, on to Julia Cameron's daughter Julia Cameron Norman, and to her niece Julia Jackson Stephen, Virginia Woolf's mother.

14 *Woolf got this salacious:* Quentin Bell, in his biography of Virginia Woolf, goes one better by writing that "James Pattle was, we are told, an extravagantly wicked man . . . known as the greatest liar in India" who also drank himself to death. Bell, *Virginia Woolf,* vol. 1, p. 14.

15 *He and Adeline were married:* A very battered portrait of James and Adeline Pattle hung in the servants' hall in the dark basement at 22 Hyde Park Gate, where Virginia Woolf grew up. Annan, *Leslie Stephen,* p. 105. That picture seems not to have survived.

16 *as much of the rum:* When I visited Quebec City recently, a guide recounted how

early French colonists in Canada often wished to be buried in their native France, and that the corpses were preserved in barrels of rum. When the funeral barrels from Canada were offloaded upon arrival in Europe, they were often suspiciously light — the rum had been drunk en route.

"beautiful dead Pattles": Entry for January 19, 1918, in *The Diary of Virginia Woolf: Volume One, 1915–1919,* edited by Anne Olivier Bell with an introduction by Quentin Bell (New York: Harcourt Brace, 1977), p. 107.

2. Pattledom

18 *stories of "Pattledom"*: Sir Henry Taylor, a distinguished scientist and devoted friend of Julia Cameron, is said to have coined the name Pattledom. Virginia Woolf seized on the term.

19 *"Once when we were children"*: Woolf, "A Sketch of the Past," in *Moments of Being,* p. 87.
    the East India Company: The English East India Company (EIC) began in 1600 as a trading company with a monopoly on trade with the then vaguely mapped and understood East Indies. It remained a privately held shareholding enterprise, with its own army and its own board of governors, and by the late eighteenth century its profits were almost too huge to grasp. For example, in 1783, eager to ensure its trading privileges, the EIC was able to loan the British government one million MORE pounds to finance the wars with the French in North America. By 1820 the EIC had not only a huge slice of all the trade with the subcontinent but had also taken over the tax collection system of larger and larger areas of India, thus offering even humble tax collectors unrivaled opportunities to line their own pockets at the expense of rural communities. For several centuries India was the source of unlimited funds for the English mercantile class. William Makepeace Thackeray's family had deep roots in Anglo-India, and in *Vanity Fair* he gives a devastating portrait of the returning "Nabob" in Jos Sedgwick — fat, idle, stupid, and rich.

21 *"He was the fool"*: Virginia Woolf, *Night and Day* (Bristol, UK: CuriousPages, 2016), p. 86.
    Indian homonym Patel: Michael Holroyd, *A Strange Eventful History: The Dramatic Lives of Ellen Terry, Henry Irving, and Their Remarkable Families* (New York: Farrar, Straus & Giroux, 2008). Holroyd notices that Pattle might once have been Patel: "It was inconvenient for the family having a name that approximated so closely with the indigenous Indian surname Patel since that gave rise to dark stories (that an ancestor had married the daughter of a high-class Bengali)" (p. 32). As we have seen, the "dark stories" were confirmed by the Indian historian and Pattle descendant William Dalrymple in 2003, even though a Bengali woman who married a European colonist could not pass on her family name.
    Little Holland House: By the 1870s, with London putting out its tentacles, and with cow pastures in Kensington becoming densely packed streets like Hyde Park Gate, where the Stephen family lived, the Hollands decided to develop their Little Holland House property.

24 *Josiah Wedgwood, the scion:* Jenny Uglow gives a stirring account of the intellectual brilliance as well as the commercial acumen of the Wedgwoods in her book *The Lunar Men* (2002).

his poet sister Christina: While preparing her Rossetti review, Woolf wrote in her diary that "Christina has the great distinction of being a born poet ... but if I were bringing a case against God, she is one of the first witnesses I would call. First she starved herself of love, which also meant life; then of poetry in deference to what she thought her religion demanded." Entry for August 4, 1918, in *The Diary of Virginia Woolf,* vol. 1, p. 178.

25 *Barbara's first cousin Florence:* From the age of Victoria till after World War I, in England everyone who was anyone seems to have known everyone else, even if they did not choose to invite them all to tea or dinner. An astonishing number of them were related by blood and marriage. Thus, to take a random sample, Florence Nightingale was first cousin to the pioneering feminist and artist Barbara Leigh Smith Bodichon — though Barbara's illegitimate birth made it impossible for the two cousins ever in their lives to be in the same room. For more on this see my book *Nightingales* (New York: Ballantine Books, 2005). Another of Florence's cousins, Blanche Smith, married Arthur Clough, a poet educated at the Rugby School under Dr. Thomas Arnold, whose poems are devoutly quoted in *Tom Brown's Schooldays,* the famous novel by Thomas Hughes, who was a close friend of Leslie Stephen and another guest at Dimbola Lodge and Little Holland House. To continue with the Arnold connection, the successful and fiercely anti-feminist novelist Mrs. Humphry Ward, whose literary example would terrify Virginia Woolf, was one of Dr. Arnold's granddaughters. Sarah Pattle Prinsep's granddaughter Laura Gurney married Sir Thomas Troubridge, and their son Ernest married Una Taylor. Una Troubridge was the lover (not the wife! as the editor Tristram Powell mistakenly believed) of Radclyffe Hall, who was born a woman and wrote *The Well of Loneliness* — and Una Troubridge was one of the first translators of Colette. I could go on. It was a very small world. One of the key texts here is Noel Annan's essay "The Intellectual Aristocracy," reprinted in *The Dons* (Chicago: University of Chicago Press, 1999), pp. 304–41. Alas, the essay contains not a single reference to the sources that inform it!

George du Maurier: One of the minor characters in George du Maurier's famous play *Trilby* is supposedly based on Val Prinsep, and Ellen Terry may have been an inspiration for Trilby herself.

the Pattle descendant Henrietta: Henrietta Garnett, *Wives and Stunners: The Pre-Raphaelites and Their Muses* (New York: Macmillan, 2012).

"the tactical hypocrisy": Graham Robb, *Strangers: Homosexual Love in the Nineteenth Century* (New York: Norton, 2003), p. 120.

26 *the Prinseps' resident artist:* This story has recently been retold, on the basis of extensive research, by the renowned English biographer Michael Holroyd. For the following account of Ellen Terry and Pattledom I am indebted to his book *A Strange Eventful History.* Holroyd became very seriously ill when researching this book and lost his research notes. Thus, as he explains in his graceful introduction, he offers

none of the extensive notes and scholarly apparatus of his earlier work. I thus quote Holroyd's book and assume his quotations and paraphrases are reliable.

hands-on management: In Woolf's essay on Julia Cameron, Sarah's older sister, Woolf gleefully recounts how, when confronted with a clergyman wearing filthy neck linen in her local parish, Mrs. Prinsep collected the linen of all the parish clergy and had it washed, starched, and ironed to her exacting standards in her own laundry. Cameron, *Victorian Photographs,* p. 14.

27 *Ellen Ternan, the woman:* Ternan and her mother and sisters were all professional actors, and, like the Terrys, fiercely set on respectability. For over forty years they managed to conceal or deny the fact that Ellen had been Dickens's mistress. Now we know that Charles Dickens and Nelly were lovers and that the respectable Mrs. Ternan was not only cognizant of but complicit in her daughter's lucrative extramarital relationship. See Claire Tomalin, *The Invisible Woman: The Story of Nelly Ternan and Charles Dickens* (New York: Viking, 1990).

"emotionally unstable, sexually": Holroyd, *A Strange Eventful History,* p. 32. Watts married again, and his second wife, who was devoted to him, once admitted that her husband "couldn't do very much but he liked to fumble around."

28 *"It makes your nose swell":* Here I adhere closely to the account given by Michael Holroyd, based, as far as I can tell, on various biographies of Watts, including Wilfrid Blunt's *England's Michelangelo: A Biography of George F. Watts* (London: Hamilton, 1975).

30 *greatest woman actor:* The charming, if rather run-down, Ellen Terry Museum at Smallhythe Place in Tenterden, Kent, charts the theatrical career of this great Victorian actor. The museum's most valuable and astonishing piece on display is the dress encrusted in iridescent shells that Terry wore as Lady Macbeth. A famous portrait of Terry, by John Singer Sargent, shows her in this dress. A couple of the Watts portraits of the young Ellen, either originals or copies, are also part of the Smallhythe collection.

This museum, one of the more modest properties under the National Trust, suffers for lack of money. When we were having tea in the barn, my brother and I had to avoid the shower of bird droppings coming down from a hole in the roof. On the other hand, the picturesque, rambling Tudor house and its charming gardens at the back remain largely the same as they were when Ellen and her daughter, Edy Craig, lived there, an advantage for a literary historian like myself.

31 *cool, form-fitting garments:* The Honourable Mrs. Edward Twistleton-Wickham-Fiennes, "observing the flowing uncorseted garb of the Pattle ladies and the general *laisser-aller* of the social life, began to suspect 'grave moral defect,'" but she was American by birth, so she didn't really count. Holroyd, *A Strange Eventful History,* p. 32.

32 *the Pattle paisley shawls:* Frances Spalding, *Vanessa Bell* (New York: Ticknor and Fields, 1983), p. 46.

"I longed to arrest all": Cameron, *Victorian Photographs,* p. 9.

33 *Charles Hay Cameron:* Charles Hay Cameron enjoys a rather longer entry in the early *Dictionary of National Biography,* near his wife's. He was another remarkable

Victorian and often referred to as a Benthamite, someone who subscribed to a system of nonreligious ethics and financial principles designed to ensure the best possible life for the greatest number of people. Bentham advocated freedom of expression, equal rights for women, abolition of slavery, abolition of the death penalty, animal rights, and the decriminalization of homosexual acts.

34 *"is there nobody commonplace?":* Cameron, *Victorian Photographs,* p. 18.

"in poetry and fiction and": Ibid. I gather from this volume that Julia Cameron had shown an interest in photography before she began to take pictures, having corresponded on the subject with her close friend Sir J.F.W. Herschel, the English astronomer who originated the terms "positive" and "negative."

"The gift from those I loved": Ibid., p. 10.

35 *Catharine Beecher and Isabella Beeton:* The hugely successful *Mrs Beeton's Book of Household Management* was published in London in 1861. In the United States, Catharine Beecher (the older half-sister of Harriet Beecher Stowe) published many books, including *A Treatise on Domestic Economy for the Use of Young Ladies at Home and at School* (1841), *Miss Beecher's Domestic Receipts Book* (1846), and *Principles of Domestic Science* (1870).

"became truly artistic, instead": Entry for Julia Margaret Cameron, *Dictionary of National Biography,* 8th ed. (London: Smith & Elder, 1886).

Magda Kearney, an Australian: The monograph "Julia Margaret Cameron Biography: The Victoria and Albert Museum," by Magda Kearney, curator of the National Portrait Gallery of Australia, can be found on the internet.

her artfully ill-focused lens: Julia Cameron explained, in "Annals of My Glasshouse," how her early untutored efforts at photography developed into artistry: "I began with no knowledge of the art. I did not know where to place my dark box, how to focus my sitter, and my first successes in my out-of-focus pictures were flukes. That is to say that when focusing and coming to something which was, to my eyes, very beautiful, I stopped there instead of screwing in the lens to the more definite focus which all other photographers insist on." Cameron, *Victorian Photographs,* p. 10.

36 *Another was May Hillier:* May Hillier became Julia Cameron's parlor maid, and then, according to Virginia Woolf's account, "was sought in marriage by a rich man's son, filled the position with dignity and competence, and in 1878 enjoyed an income of two thousand four hundred pounds a year." Woolf, introduction to Cameron, *Victorian Photographs,* p. 17.

When in a recent exhibition: In the summer of 2014, I managed to catch the small, overcrowded exhibit on Virginia Woolf at the National Portrait Gallery in London, superbly curated by Frances Spalding. The reproduction in Cameron, *Victorian Photographs,* does not do justice to the image of the widowed Julia Duckworth.

Hemileia vastatrix: This is the same fungus that in the twenty-first century wiped out so many coffee plantations in South America and Central America. I am grateful to my daughter, Catherine Gill, for this information.

"Julia is slicing up Ceylon": Woolf, in Cameron, *Victorian Photographs,* p. 18.

"There was peace": Ibid.

37 *"A rather strange-looking lady"*: Henrietta Garnett, *Anny: A Life of Anne Thackeray Ritchie* (London: Chatto and Windus, 2005), p. 229.
    "birds fluttering in": Woolf, in Cameron, *Victorian Photographs*, p. 19.

38 *skit called "Freshwater"*: *Freshwater: A Comedy by Virginia Woolf* (New York: Harvest, 1976) includes drawings by Edward Gorey and an excellent introduction by the editor, Lucio B. Ruotolo. The inspiration for publishing the little book seems to have come from Quentin Bell and was part of the family's efforts to save Charleston and rehabilitate the Bloomsbury image.

3. High Society

42 *"Aunt Virginia, it is plain"*: Woolf, "Sketch of the Past," in *Moments of Being*, p. 88.
    the duchess had come: Woolf, "22 Hyde Park Gate," in *Moments of Being*, p. 164.
    Adeline's sister, Isabella: The cover of Ros Black's biography shows the portrait by G. F. Watts of Isabella Caroline Somers-Cocks, whose long oval face, dark hair, large dark eyes, and thick black eyebrows suggest her Bengali ancestry.

43 *Plantagenet John of Gaunt*: John of Gaunt had several children by his mistress Katherine Swynford. John and Katherine were finally able to marry, and their Beaufort children were legitimized and permitted to marry into royal families. Perhaps some of my readers will recall the 1954 bestselling novel *Katherine,* by Anya Seton, and several recent novels based on Katherine's life by Alison Weir.

44 *officially anathema*: The 1886 Labouchere Amendment, making homosexual acts, even between consenting adults and in private, illegal in the United Kingdom, is notorious in gay historiography. However, as Graham Robb points out in his important book *Strangers: Homosexual Love in the Nineteenth Century,* p. 20, it was a parliamentary reaction to a sensational press campaign that aroused public ire and merely made explicit what had long been on the books. As Robb shows, there were very few prosecutions under the sodomy laws in England — Paris was far more dangerous for gay men. Following the Labouchere Amendment, the prosecutions ticked up only a small notch, according to Robb and also Matt Houlbrook, in *Queer London: Perils and Pleasures in the Sexual Metropolis, 1918–1957* (Chicago: University of Chicago Press, 2005).

45 *"horrible and foul crime"*: Black, *A Talent for Humanity*, pp. 30–31.
    "the land of Michelangelesque": Bell, *Virginia Woolf,* vol. 1, p. 15. Following the police raid on the male brothel on Cleveland Street in 1890, Lord Henry was joined in exile in Italy by his younger brother Lord Arthur Somerset, who, unlike the unfortunate Rev. Veck and a poor clerk called (!) Newlove, who both got prison sentences after the raid, was allowed by the police to escape to the Continent. There, according to Robb, Lord Arthur lived for some thirty-seven years with his male lover.
    Encouraged by middle-class: The Wikipedia entry on Lady Isabella Caroline Somerset includes a 1904 photograph of her with the religious writer Hannah Whitall Smith, Mary Berenson (wife of the art historian Bernard Berenson), Karin Costelloe Stephen (wife of the psychoanalyst Adrian Stephen, Virginia Woolf's brother), and Ray Strachey (wife of Oliver Strachey, Lytton Strachey's brother).

47   *The Bedford-Beaufort connection: Sir Leslie Stephen's Mausoleum Book,* edited with an
      introduction by Alan Bell (Oxford: Clarendon Press, 1977), p. 75.
      "The children of Sir Leslie": Leonard Woolf, *Beginning Again: An Autobiography of
      the Years 1911 to 1918* (New York: Harcourt Brace Jovanovich, 1963; published also in
      London, 1964), p. 74.

49   *"my first appearance as":* The Diary of Virginia Woolf, vol. 1, p. 316. In an August 1901
      letter to her cousin Emma Vaughan, Virginia Woolf describes meeting their aunt
      — her namesake Virginia Somers. "One night we [that is, she and her siblings and
      their father while on holiday] gave a small dinner party to which Bea Cameron [Julia
      Cameron's grandson] came, and when we came up for dinner we saw a large white
      form artistically grouped on the sofa — it was Aunt Virginia! . . . I can never quite see
      Aunt V's surpassing charm or beauty. The charm at any rate need not have vanished
      though the beauty has almost entirely. Save her great eyes, which *are* beautiful — and
      her enthusiasms and loud whispers and French manners, I think she was rather disap-
      pointing." *The Letters of Virginia Woolf,* vol. 1, p. 44.
      "Am I a Snob?": "Am I a Snob?" is included in Woolf, *Moments of Being,* pp. 203–20.
      The Bloomsbury Memoir Club had inherited from the meetings of the Cambridge
      Apostles the custom of asking a speaker to give a talk on a specific, often frothy, and
      apparently inconsequential topic. Woolf acknowledges this tradition and the influ-
      ence of G. E. Moore when she remarks, "Dominated, I suspect, by the iron rod of old
      Cambridge, dominated too by that moral sense which grows stronger in Maynard the
      older he gets, that stern desire to preserve our generation in its integrity, and to pro-
      tect the younger generation from its folly, Maynard never boasts" (p. 206).

50   *Beatrice Thynne:* The rather pathetic Beatrice Thynne crops up quite often in
      Virginia Woolf's letters and diary. Woolf remarks of her in May 1919: "Beatrice
      Thynne has inherited a quarter of a million; two large properties & one of the finest
      libraries in England. She has no idea what to make of them; visits them in a distracted
      way to see which she'd like to live in; can't make up her mind to settle in either & fi-
      nally spends most of her time in Gray's Inn, looked after by a charwoman. Her only
      acknowledgement of her balance is that now & then she pulls out strings of pearls
      & parades the squares of the Inn, with such effect that Lady H. Somerset has to beg
      her to remove them." *The Diary of Virginia Woolf,* vol. 1, p. 274. I quote this passage
      in full, both because this is Woolf practicing her character sketches but also showing
      that, despite the sharp disagreement over the Stephens' removal to Bloomsbury from
      Kensington, Woolf was still bumping into people from her parents' world, like her
      mother's first cousin Lady Henry Somerset.

4. Finders Keepers

56   *No one, it seemed, was keen:* In her diary entry for December 28, 1919, Woolf notes
      that the family is negotiating the sale of 22 Hyde Park Gate, fifteen years after the
      death of Sir Leslie Stephen. *The Diary of Virginia Woolf,* vol. 1, p. 317.
      "Thoby made £1000": The Letters of Virginia Woolf, vol. 1, p. 232. In 1930, Vanessa Bell

was seeking to sell another drawing by Thackeray, which was in her studio, to the Pierpont Morgan Library for five hundred pounds. *The Letters of Virginia Woolf,* vol. 4, pp. 155 and 156.

57 *as a "fine fellow":* Here I am closely following what Virginia Woolf writes about Jacob. Flanders, the central character in her novel *Jacob's Room,* is based on her brother Thoby. The phrase "stumble through a play" is Woolf's.

pretty, vivacious Irene Noel: Irene Noel was "the heir to her father Frank Noel of Achmetaga. Thoby Stephen was competing with his Cambridge friend Desmond MacCarthy for Irene's hand but she married Philip Baker, who thenceforth was known as Philip Noel Baker." *The Diary of Virginia Woolf,* vol. 1, note, p. 115.

58 *Smith allowed Anne and Harriet:* Gordon N. Ray, *Thackeray: The Age of Wisdom, 1847–1863* (Oxford, UK: Oxford University Press, 1958), p. 423.

"a dowry for Laura": Annan, *Leslie Stephen,* p. 72.

61 *That was a salary to make:* "*Cornhill* paid its contributors handsomely, and the salary of five hundred pounds a year, which George Smith offered Stephen, not only exceeded what Longman (publisher of *Fraser's Magazine* and also in search of an editor) could pay, but it enabled him to give up some of his journalism so that he could settle to the task of writing . . . *The History of English Thought in the Eighteenth Century.*" Annan, *Leslie Stephen,* p. 66.

62 *"Stephen's most important":* Ibid., pp. 86 and 87.

63 *"I feel as if we owed more":* John Aplin, *A Thackeray Family Biography: Volume 2, Memory and Legacy, 1876–1919* (Cambridge, UK: Lutterworth Press, 2011), p. 189.

64 *"When I read Dickens":* Spalding, *Vanessa Bell,* p. 13.

"What is it to be a gentleman?": Woolf, "A Sketch of the Past," in *Moments of Being,* p. 116.

5. William and Isabella

67 *Prince Albert was at:* For a careful look at the origins and development of Prince Albert's sexual obsessions and their effects on his wife, his children, and English society in general, see my book *We Two: Victoria and Albert — Rulers, Partners, Rivals* (New York: Ballantine Books, 2009).

they were largely taboo: Writing for a preponderantly male readership, novelists in the Great Tradition of French fiction — Stendhal, Balzac, Maupassant, Flaubert, Zola — had far greater freedom to explore the sexual mores of all classes of society. A cultural abyss separates the two nineteenth-century masterpieces *David Copperfield* (1850) and *Madame Bovary* (1856).

68 *William Makepeace Thackeray:* This discussion of the Thackeray family is based on the following works: Gordon N. Ray, *Thackeray: The Uses of Adversity, 1811–1846* (New York: McGraw-Hill, 1955) and *Thackeray: The Age of Wisdom, 1847–1863;* John Aplin, *A Thackeray Family Biography, Volume 1: The Inheritance of Genius, 1798–1875* (Cambridge, UK: Lutterworth Press, 2010) and *Volume 2: Memory and Legacy, 1876–1919;* Winifred Gérin, *Anne Thackeray Ritchie: A Biography* (Oxford, UK: Oxford

University Press, 1981); and Henrietta Garnett, *Anny: A Life of Anne Thackeray Ritchie*.

70 *Sophia and Virginia Pattle:* Garnett says that the Pattle sisters were in France, staying with their grandmother in Versailles. *Anny,* p. 22.

72 *former French mistress:* Ibid., p. 17. Garnett states matter-of-factly (p. 44) that Thackeray always had mistresses, a fact that standard biographies of the writer, using the same archival material, were careful to omit.

73 *Madness, Thackeray was discovering:* In middle age, Jane Shawe, Isabella's sister, also became insane. Anny Thackeray Ritchie did what she could to help her aunt, who was poor as well as mad.

75 *Cowan Bridge School:* Cowan Bridge appears as Lowood School in *Jane Eyre,* and in the person of Helen Burns, Charlotte Brontë gives us her memory of the life and death of her brilliant eldest sister, Maria.

77 *his mistress Ellen Ternan:* See, notably, Claire Tomalin, *The Invisible Woman* (1990) and *Charles Dickens: A Life* (1999).

   also had a secret life: Even his extremely guarded biographer Gordon Ray, writing in the 1950s, establishes that, as a young man, Thackeray explored the highly erotic world of French cabarets and masked balls. Henrietta Garnett discovered in the Thackeray private papers that, after leaving Cambridge, Thackeray had a longstanding affair with a French governess. Ray notes circumspectly that, when on vacation in Europe with his extended family, Thackeray would occasionally disappear for weeks, giving no explanation. Furthermore, not all of Thackeray's secret life may have involved women. At Cambridge, he moved comfortably in the territory between homosociality and homosexuality, forming lifelong friendships with two men, Edward Fitzgerald and Richard Monckton Milnes, who today are confidently listed by queer historians in the column of notable gay writers. When Thackeray came into the public eye after *Vanity Fair,* Fitzgerald wrote to reassure him that he need not worry for his reputation. Fitzgerald had destroyed all the letters Thackeray had sent him when they were young students. Thackeray himself, according to the biographer John Aplin, burned all his youthful correspondence.

78 *renegade royal historians:* On the issue of the prince consort's possible homosexual relationships, see my book *We Two,* pp. 409–10, note 135.
   "She had been her father's": Woolf, *Night and Day,* p. 58.

79 *Historians, novelists, and playwrights:* To name but a few, see Steven Marcus, *The Other Victorians* (1966); Phyllis Rose, *Parallel Lives* (1983); Colm Tóibín, *The Master* (2004); the five volumes of Peter Gay, *The Bourgeois Experience: From Victoria to Freud* (1984–98); and Tom Stoppard, *The Invention of Love* (1997).

6. Anny and Minny

81 *Adelaide Kemble Sartoris:* Again, it is useful to see how important it was for Virginia and Vanessa Stephen to have in Anne Thackeray Ritchie a living link to the high Victorian period in all its complexity. Adelaide and Fanny Kemble not only had outstanding

careers in the performing arts as young women but also managed the tricky transformation into respectable society matrons.

82 *Margaret Thackeray:* Victorian family life is odd in all sorts of ways. Margie Thackeray at age twenty married one of Sir Richmond Ritchie's brothers — in fact, his older brother Gerald. Thus, Margie was the distant cousin, adoptive daughter, and sister-in-law of Anne Thackeray Ritchie.

83 *modern versions:* Thackeray Ritchie's updating of fairy stories makes her a forerunner of Angela Carter, Stephen Sondheim, and the Disney Company. I recommend her *Five Old Friends* (1875), available on Kindle.

Leslie Stephen never went: Annan, *Leslie Stephen,* p. 99.

84 *the Yorkshire Sodom:* On the sadomasochistic tastes of Richard Monckton Milnes, see my book *Nightingales,* pp. 223–32.

87 *"rode round to offer":* H. Garnett, *Anny,* p. 31.

89 *companionship and respect:* See Annan, *Leslie Stephen,* p. 29.

91 *"absolutely faultless":* Sir Leslie Stephen's *Mausoleum Book,* pp. 31–34. The praise is effusive: "I must dwell a little more upon her beauty: for beauty . . . was of the very essence of her nature. I have never seen — I have no expectation that I shall ever see — anyone whose outward appearance might be described as so absolutely faultless . . . Her beauty was of the kind that seems to imply . . . equal beauty of soul, refinement, nobility and tenderness of character; and which yet did not imply as some beauty called 'spiritual' may seem to do, any lack of 'material' beauty" . . . and so on.

100 *"a shade out of control":* L. Woolf, *Beginning Again,* pp. 70–71.

101 *"[Mrs. Hilbery's] large blue eyes":* Woolf, *Night and Day,* p. 9. Woolf's novel was published very soon after Thackeray Ritchie's death, and the Ritchie "cousins" Hester and William were, according to the biographer Henrietta Garnett, deeply offended by Woolf's portrayal of their mother. See Garnett, *Anny,* p. 266. They had a point: their mother had been meeting literary deadlines since the age of sixteen, had a long list of published books to her name, and had successfully edited and written the biographical introduction to *The Complete Works of William Makepeace Thackeray.*

102 *character based on Leonard:* I read the relationship of Ralph Denham and Katharine Hilbery that Virginia Woolf develops in *Night and Day* as based closely on her own courtship with Leonard. Denham's confession of his love to Katharine — "I've made you my standard since I saw you. I've dreamt about you, I've thought of nothing but you, you represent to me the only reality in the world" (p. 169) — is based on things Leonard actually said to Virginia during their courtship. No wonder she married him. And whereas men have often said such things to women in the height of passion, few live up to them in marriage, as Leonard did.

she is basing Katharine: See especially the page-long letter Woolf composes for Mrs. Hilbery, relaying to Mrs. Mulvain, her sister-in-law, the news that Katharine is engaged to William Rodney, a man both eminently suitable and somehow not quite up to snuff. *Night and Day,* p. 81. When Mrs. Hilbery writes of her daughter "Of course Katharine has what he [William, her fiancé] does not. She does command, she isn't nervous: it comes naturally to her to rule and control," Virginia is definitely thinking of her sister Vanessa.

7. Virginia Woolf's Mad, Bad Sister

107 *"I was so surprised at":* H. Garnett, *Anny,* pp. 167–68.
"It is true that my baby": Ibid., p. 156.
a natural mimic: Ibid., p. 167.

108 *forty-one hundred pounds:* Aplin, *A Thackeray Family Biography,* vol. 2, p. 10.

110 *removed from the bench:* Fitzjames was removed from the bench when he told the jury, in the famous trial of Florence Maybrick, accused of murdering her husband, that "an adulteress by nature was likely to commit murder" — a step too far even at that time.

112 *"the receptacle of Leslie":* Lee, *Virginia Woolf,* p. 93.

115 *"explore [her] body":* Woolf, "A Sketch of the Past," in *Moments of Being,* p. 69.
Bell is discounting: Quentin Bell, *Bloomsbury Recalled* (New York: Columbia University Press, 1995), p. 46. Bell says Gerald's inspecting of Virginia was "horrid," but a "schoolboy's misdemeanor" of which many are probably guilty. "There was nothing else at all against Gerald."

116 *lifelong consequences:* In *The Years,* one of her last and less admired novels, Woolf breaks important ground in the history of sexual abuse by showing how one small girl is affected by one apparently trivial incident. Rose Pargiter is the youngest child in a family of seven, her whole family is nervously awaiting the death of Mrs. Pargiter, and Rose is bored and neglected. She lives largely in an imaginary world, in which she is an intrepid soldier engaged on a special mission.

One evening, Rose is eager to have a real adventure — to go to a local shop on her own to buy a toy. This is strictly forbidden, but she steals her nurse's key and slips out of the house unnoticed in the growing dusk. A man on a street corner sees her go by, and his appearance frightens her. Upon her return with her purchase, he exposes himself to her. Rose gets home safely but she is no longer a brave soldier, and she has nightmares. When her older sister begs to know what Rose has seen that has so upset her, Rose will not say. She is never able to tell anyone about this incident, but as Rose Pargiter grows up into a warrior for social justice, her whole life will become an attempt to deal with her fears.

117 *She had her own room:* In her reconstruction of the complex six-story house at 22 Hyde Park Gate in "A Sketch of the Past," collected in *Moments of Being,* Virginia Woolf places the kitchen and the servants' "lounge" in the sub-basement; the dining room in the basement; the hallway leading to the street, the two drawing rooms, and the conservatory where she and Vanessa worked on what is known in the United States as the first floor; her parents' rooms on the second floor; the Duckworths, on the third floor; the nurseries, later bedrooms for herself and her three full siblings, on the fourth floor; and finally Leslie's big study and, presumably, the servants' bedrooms on the fifth floor. In her final years, Grandmother Jackson had rooms on the second

floor, near her daughter's bedroom. There was one full bathroom plus three flush toilets in the house. It is not clear from this plan where Laura was accommodated — on the Duckworths' floor, on her father's floor, or in one of the nurseries.

119 *DeSalvo, who bothered:* Louise DeSalvo, *Virginia Woolf: The Impact of Childhood Abuse on Her Life and Work* (New York: Ballantine Books, 1989). DeSalvo has a long section (pp. 45–51) on the sexual attitudes of both J. K. "Jem" Stephen and his father, Fitzjames Stephen. Jem excelled both socially and academically at Eton and then at Cambridge and was famous in his set for his clever, licentious verse. DeSalvo offers quotes to illustrate how deeply Jem hated women and imagined committing violence against them. After coming down from the university, Jem became tutor to the Duke of Clarence, then third in line to the English throne, but was dismissed by the Prince of Wales when rumors circulated that he was introducing the young prince to a "dissipated and unstable life" — that is, open homosexuality. It has been suggested that Jem Stephen or the Duke of Clarence could have been Jack the Ripper.

120 *"an idiot asylum":* Lee, *Virginia Woolf,* p. 101.

121 *"She was perfectly all right":* H. Garnett, *Anny,* note on p. 256.
Laura's "dowry": Aplin's second volume on the Thackeray family is full of new information about Laura. There is no doubt that Leslie Stephen knew about the arrangements that William Makepeace Thackeray had made for his wife, Isabella, which his daughter Anne continued. After Minny's death, Leslie used part of the money he inherited from her to buy a small house for her mother that was nearer to London and thus easier for his sister-in-law, Anne, to visit. Stephen's biographers cite this as an example of his affectionate generosity, but according to John Aplin, Isabella did not live in that house for very long since her caretakers preferred to be near the sea. The house then reverted to Leslie to sell or rent, so his generosity cost him little.

122 *"Leonard says Laura is":* Lee, *Virginia Woolf,* p. 103.
"there was Thackeray's": Woolf, "Old Bloomsbury," in *Moments of Being,* p. 182.

8. Julia Prinsep Jackson Duckworth Stephen

128 *"Can I remember ever":* Woolf, "A Sketch from the Past, in *Moments of Being,* p. 83.
130 *"What a jumble of things":* Ibid., pp. 83 and 84.
133 *the* Mausoleum Book: In 1977, the Clarendon Press published *Sir Leslie Stephen's Mausoleum Book,* edited and with an excellent introduction by Alan Bell.
"drape and arrange": Virginia Woolf's introduction to Cameron, *Victorian Photographs,* p. 12.
"Somehow Jackson did not": Sir Leslie Stephen's *Mausoleum Book,* p. 26.
136 *"dropped like a stone into":* H. Garnett, *Anny,* p. 82. Garnett is summarizing a section from the Thackeray family's correspondence.
perfection in spats: Virginia Woolf seems to have questioned her aunt Mary Fisher about Herbert Duckworth, and the response may have surprised her. "Oh darling," Aunt Mary replied, "a beam of light, like no one I have ever met . . . when Herbert

Duckworth came into the room . . . when Herbert Duckworth smiled . . ." Woolf, "A Sketch of the Past," in *Moments of Being,* p. 89. Julia Stephen's sister, it would seem, was also a little in love with Herbert.

never talked about Herbert: Julia's close friend Kitty Maxse told Virginia Woolf that on only one occasion did Julia Stephen refer to Herbert, remarking that her first marriage had been the time she "was as unhappy and as happy as it is possible for a human being." Ibid.

137 *"the perfect type":* Sir Leslie Stephen's *Mausoleum Book,* p. 35.

140 *write letters of farewell:* The character Christina Pontifex pens such a letter in the novel *The Way of all Flesh* (1903) as she approaches her fourth confinement. Mrs. Pontifex in fact survives, though the baby dies. The book's author, Samuel Butler, says writing such letters was a custom among women of his parents' generation.

141 *the chubby little blond:* I am not simply being mean about George Duckworth. In one of the Cameron group pictures, the widowed Julia Duckworth is shown with her son George on her knee, a rather sullen and quite chunky three- or four-year-old. Cameron, *Victorian Photographs,* plate 30.

heavily veiled in black: H. Garnett, *Anny,* p. 223.

142 *"I was only 24 when":* Sir Leslie Stephen's *Mausoleum Book,* p. 40.

a man of means: A good measure of the affluence of the Duckworths is to be found in "Aunt Minna," that is, Sarah Duckworth, Herbert's sister, who inhabited a house in Hyde Park Gate near the Stephens. She lived a life of considerable luxury and no labor, traveling abroad regularly, with some grateful young woman relation in tow.

143 *"clothed in drab":* Sir Leslie Stephen's *Mausoleum Book,* p. 41. Stephen is quoting from one of Julia's letters to him.

144 *"I have so long felt that":* Lee, *Virginia Woolf,* p. 193.

"My hope is for Leslie and Julia's": Aplin, *A Thackeray Family Biography,* vol. 2, p. 28. It is this phrase from Thackeray Ritchie, a close friend writing at the time of the wedding about Julia's situation — "to give up her liberty and her *prestige* and her money" — that leads me to conclude that, when she married, Julia may have lost her dower rights from Herbert Duckworth or her allowance from his family.

145 *what her parents' marriage:* The Oxford World Classics edition of *The Voyage Out* details the several versions of the novel and presents the 1915 version. This volume, first issued in 1992 and updated in 2000, has an insightful biographical preface by Frank Kermode plus a good critical bibliography, and it is superbly edited and introduced by Lorna Sage.

149 Notes from Sickrooms: This pamphlet was reproduced, along with and under the title of Virginia Woolf's essay "On Being Ill," in a new edition, introduced by Hermione Lee and published by Paris Press, Ashfield, Massachusetts, in 2012.

150 *self-involved phony:* One of the things Leslie Stephen achieved in the *Mausoleum Book* was to settle the score with his despised brother-in-law Vaughan. See *Sir Leslie Stephen's Mausoleum Book,* pp. 68–70.

152 *"I do not think that either":* Ibid., pp. 74–75.

a little house at Chenies: Ibid., p. 75.

158 *"Professions for Women":* "Professions for Women" was published in *The Death of the Moth and Other Essays* in June 1942, a year or so after Woolf's death. The essay is included in Michèle Barrett's *Virginia Woolf: Women and Writing.*

159 *Patient Griselda Redux:* Chaucer's Griselda, my readers may remember, was "tested" by her husband, who first rescued her out of extreme poverty, then systematically took away everything he had given her — her children, her home, her clothes, her status. Griselda was "patient" — that is, she endured suffering — and in the end got her husband and children and position back. Moral?

Nightingale's marvelous aunt: For more on Florence Nightingale's remarkable feminist aunts Patty Smith and Julia Smith, and her first cousin Barbara Leigh Smith Bodichon, see my book *Nightingales.*

160 *"It was like meeting her":* Lee, *Virginia Woolf,* p. 81.

"I ceased to be obsessed": Ibid., p. 80.

9. Stella Duckworth Hills

161 *the autobiographical pieces:* Both these essays, along with other shorter autobiographical essays are collected in the invaluable small volume *Virginia Woolf: Moments of Being,* beautifully edited with an introduction and notes by Jeanne Schulkind.

162 *"in the shade of":* Woolf, "A Sketch of the Past," in *Moments of Being,* p. 96.

"was not clever, she seldom read": Ibid., pp. 41–42.

165 *"How proud, priggishly, I was":* Ibid., p. 112.

170 *"Stella's coming out":* Ibid., p. 43.

171 *"It was very natural":* Ibid., p. 102.

even he never thought: After Stella's death, Jack separated off part at least of the fortune that Stella had brought into the marriage and divided the income from it between his wife's sisters Vanessa and Virginia. Hills became a successful and affluent lawyer, and despite his speech defect was for a short time a member of Parliament.

172 *"What her mother felt":* Woolf, "A Sketch of the Past," in *Moments of Being,* p. 44.

173 *he already treated Julia:* Kitty Maxse, talking with Virginia Woolf about Jack and how mean his mother had been to him, once remarked that Mrs. Hills probably resented the way her son treated Julia Stephen as a mother.

174 *"Next to the war memorial":* L. Woolf, *Beginning Again,* p. 66.

181 *"The marriage would have":* Woolf, "A Sketch of the Past," in *Moments of Being,* p. 105.

183 *"My darling Thoby, I want":* King's College Library Collection, CHA/1/79.

"Stella went to Laura": *Virginia Woolf, a Passionate Apprentice: The Early Journals, 1897–1909,* edited by Mitchell A. Leaska (New York: Harcourt Brace Jovanovich, 1990), pp. 11–12 and 13.

185 *"a pendant gold watch":* Spalding, *Vanessa Bell,* p. 21. Spalding notes that Vanessa made the pendant into a wristwatch and wore it all her life.

a very dark reading: DeSalvo, *Virginia Woolf: The Impact of Sexual Abuse,* p. 60.

10. A Close Conspiracy

188 *"I do not want to go":* Woolf, "A Sketch of the Past," in *Moments of Being*, p. 107. The quotations in this chapter, unless otherwise indicated, are from this unfinished essay written between 1939 and 1940. I give some page numbers in the text to help my readers make their way around this extraordinary document.

189 *"Sometimes," remarks Nigel:* Nigel Nicolson's introduction to *The Letters of Virginia Woolf*, vol. 1, p. xvii.

197 *"Eros came with a commotion":* Bell, *Virginia Woolf*, vol. 1, p. 44.
"There is no way of knowing": Lee, *Virginia Woolf*, p. 156.

200 *"My dear old Bar . . .":* Woolf to George Duckworth, April 22, 1900, *The Letters of Virginia Woolf*, vol. 1, p. 31.

201 *"recording a love that had":* Ibid., p. xviii. Nicolson is surely accurate in saying that "in her early letters, Virginia barely conceals the passion she had conceived" for Violet, and that their relationship may "have gone further than childish endearments."
some stray little postcard: Random letters from famous people have a tendency to turn up when someone starts looking for them. For example, after the death of "Sido," Colette's mother, all of Colette's hundreds of letters to Sido vanished, probably destroyed by Colette's older brother. Even so, odd postcards from Colette to Sido were eventually found by a zealous collector. See my novel-biography *Becoming Colette* (Amazon, 2015).

203 *"I am glad that I shall":* *Selected Letters of Vanessa Bell*, edited by Regina Marler (Mt. Kisco, NY: Moyer Bell, 1998), p. 23.

204 *if she picked up the phone:* In *Bloomsbury Recalled*, Quentin Bell uses this incident of Sir George calling his sister Vanessa as the introduction to his essay on his mother, titled "Ludendorff Bell."

11. From Cambridge to Bloomsbury

209 *"Oh how thankful I shall":* Woolf to Violet Dickinson, [October 1904], *The Letters of Virginia Woolf*, vol. 1, p. 147.

210 *B.A. M.A. (Cantab):* One of the perks of going up to Cambridge, as I recall, was that a few years after graduating you got mysteriously promoted from B.A. to M.A. without your needing to take a single course.
Cambridge Conversazione Society: The Cambridge Conversazione Society around the turn of the twentieth century had a strong showing of philosophers, including Alfred North Whitehead, Bertrand Russell, G. E. Moore, and, briefly, Ludwig Wittgenstein. As one looks at the various men who figure in the biography of Virginia Woolf, it is interesting to note which of them were Apostles — and which were not. Sir Leslie Stephen was not an Apostle, but his more successful and affluent elder brother, James Fitzjames Stephen, was. The loyal disciple and discreet biographer of Leslie Stephen, Frederic Maitland, was an Apostle. Leslie Stephen's eldest grandson, Julian Bell, was an Apostle, but by his time the prestige of the group was in decline. See Paul

Levy's brilliant book *G. E. Moore and the Cambridge Apostles* (Oxford, UK: Oxford University Press, 1981). This is the same Paul Levy to whom we owe the erudite and enlightening 2003 edition of the letters of Lytton Strachey.

"By far the most valuable": G. E. Moore, *Principia Ethica*, pp. 188–89. Quoted as preface to Part I of Robert Skidelsky, *John Maynard Keynes, 1883–1946: Economist, Philosopher, Statesman* (New York: Penguin Books, 2003).

211 *"Old Bloomsbury" was obsessed*: See Woolf, "Old Bloomsbury," in *Moments of Being*, pp. 179–201.

group of elite young men: The generation at Trinity College, circa 1810, of Tennyson and Hallam, Thackeray and Monckton Milnes, was already "Cambridge." Byron, whose statue in stone graces the Wren Library at Trinity College, was a little too early and over the top to be "Cambridge." There was also, of course, an "Oxford," which to outside observers looked remarkably like "Cambridge" but to insiders was as different as chalk from cheese. A "Cambridge" visitor to "Oxford" might be compared to Marco Polo, journeying far to encounter an ancient but alien civilization crumbling into picturesque decline. That was certainly the reaction of Virginia Woolf, who wrote to Violet Dickinson in December 1907: "I have been staying in Oxford, and stretching my brains with trained Arabs, with not an ounce of flesh on them. The atmosphere at Oxford is quite the chilliest and least human known to me; you see brains floating like so many sea anemones." *The Letters of Virginia Woolf*, vol. 1, pp. 319–320.

Downing and Selwyn: When considering the hostile attacks launched at the Bloomsbury group by the critic F. R. Leavis, it is not irrelevant to note that Leavis was a fellow of Downing.

when the Newnhamites: These Newnhamites had affairs with and/or married men on the fringes of Bloomsbury, such as Adrian Stephen, Rupert Brooke, James Strachey, Ralph Partridge, Harry Norton, and Gerald Shove. Virginia Woolf knew these women, liked them, criticized them, and feared them. They made her feel old-fashioned and fuddy-duddy, and she nicknamed them, along with students of the Slade School of Art such as Carrington and Barbara Hiles, the "Cropheads" because they had dared to cut their hair to cheek length. Quentin Bell says that his mother, Vanessa Bell, came up with the name "neo-pagans" for this group of young women and men who loved to camp out and go swimming in the nude together. Once, staying with Rupert Brooke at Grantchester, Virginia shocked herself, more than the world, by going skinny-dipping with her host.

212 *it was not until 1947*: Skidelsky, *John Maynard Keynes*, p. 12.

"We were anarchical": A draft of this paper is now held in the Wren Library at Trinity College.

their supervision essays: "Supervisions" is what Cambridge calls tutorials. Oddly, from our point of view today, both Vanessa and Virginia Stephen learned to type as teenagers not because it might be useful to them personally but because it might be useful to a male writer to have a sister or daughter willing to type for free. Lytton Strachey's brilliant and highly educated sisters — one of them became Mistress of Newnham

College — typed his work for him until he could afford to employ young male secretaries.

213 *his gyp would have cleaned:* Both Cambridge and Oxford Universities had a specific lexicon. In Cambridgese, the college servant who looked after your room or suite as an undergraduate was the "gyp." A student at Trinity or King's who hosted a party for his friends could expect his gyp to clear up, wash and put away the plates, and clean the floor of ash, crumbs, spit, and vomit. The gyps also cleaned the shared bathrooms. College service offered regular and not badly paid employment for local men in Cambridge, and many treasured the opportunity to be a gyp for a noble, affluent, or handsome undergraduate.

"body and spirit, reason and emotion": E. M. Forster and Ronald Edward Balfour, *Goldsworthy Lowes Dickinson* (London: E. Arnold, 1934), p. 29.

214 *"One would think that life":* Euphrosyne was a collection of poems by Lytton Strachey, Clive Bell, Saxon Sydney-Turner, and Walter Lamb. Woolf's typescript is reproduced as Appendix C at the end of vol. 1 of Quentin Bell's biography, pp. 205–6 in the 1972 edition.

"chanting the better-known": In his autobiography, Leonard Woolf gives a similarly fond account of the Midnight Society chanting "Atalanta in Calydon." Swinburne was at one point in his late teens the protégé of Richard Monckton Milnes, another alumnus of Trinity College, Cambridge, and reputedly the most famous late-nineteenth-century British collector of sadomasochistic literature and artifacts, as well as the work of the Marquis de Sade. See my book *Nightingales* for a full account of Richard Monckton Milnes, later Lord Houghton. My readers may remember that Monckton Milnes was at Trinity with William Makepeace Thackeray and that Thackeray took his two daughters to visit his old friend at Fryston in Yorkshire, where the young poet Swinburne regaled the company with one of his — for the time — shockingly sexual poems. In his letters, Lytton Strachey says that one of his aunts had described to him a similar session at Fryston that she had attended. "This was before the publication of Atalanta. What a remote past! Shall we ever have such memories? Well, well, perhaps ours will be more exciting," wrote Lytton nostalgically to Leonard Woolf on April 3, 1906. *The Letters of Lytton Strachey,* edited by Paul Levy (New York: Farrar, Straus and Giroux, 2005), p. 104.

215 *Wyndham Lewis led:* Wyndham Lewis fell out with Roger Fry and Duncan Grant in 1912 over commissions for the Omega Workshops and was thereafter one of Bloomsbury's most vociferous critics.

The novelist D. H. Lawrence: See Skidelsky, *John Maynard Keynes,* p. 184.

they elected "embryos": In a letter to Leonard Woolf in October 1905, Lytton Strachey writes that Keynes was "pushing the candidacy [for the Society] of a 17-and-a-half-year-old Austrian, Ernst Goldschmidt, head prostitute of Vienna . . . who has fled to Cambridge to avoid the ceaseless buggery to which he finds himself exposed." Lytton comments to Leonard, "Isn't it a little comic to choose Cambridge as a refuge?" *The Letters of Lytton Strachey,* p. 83. Arthur Hobhouse was a "Greek god," recalled Duncan Grant. Douglas Blair Turnbaugh, *Duncan Grant and the Bloomsbury*

Group (Secaucus, NJ: Lyle Stuart, 1987), p. 37. When Maynard failed to get "Hobby" into bed, Lytton wrote on August 3, 1905, "Why didn't you — it would have been the only thing — rape him before you left? And then abandon him?" *The Letters of Lytton Strachey,* p. 74. "Catamite" is a very old English word for a young male lover. The kings Edward II, James I, and William III of England were rumored to have had catamites.

increasingly homophobic: Graham Robb, in *Strangers: Homosexual Love in the Nineteenth Century,* and Matt Houlbrook, in *Queer London: Perils and Pleasures in the Sexual Metropolis 1918–1957,* both insist that the nineteenth century was a kind of paradise for gay Englishmen. It was a time when the English establishment (the Court of St. James, the judiciary, Parliament, the cabinet, the church, Oxbridge, the armed forces) included a large percentage of men who were gay all their lives or who had enjoyed homosexual relationships as boys and young men. Among working-class men — sailors, policemen, guardsmen, messengers, hall porters — it was both common and acceptable in their families and communities to earn money by sodomizing and fellating affluent men. As historians of gay life, Robb and Houlbrook offer statistics to show that, even after the Oscar Wilde scandal and the passage of the Labouchere Amendment, the highly punitive laws against homosexual acts in private or public were almost never enforced. Apart from the odd raid for PR purposes, the police were not interested in apprehending the men meeting in the bathhouses or lying in the bushes in Hyde Park, in part because the men apprehended might be personal friends of the chief constable. On the other hand, the Metropolitan Police were not averse to picking up working-class "dolly-boys" parading around Piccadilly. Of the handful of "respectable" men prosecuted, several were let off by sympathetic juries of their peers. Robb states flatly that, for gay men in England, "it was in the 20th century that the Dark Ages began" (p. 37).

Thus Lytton Strachey was right in seeing homosexuality written all over nineteenth-century English culture and exposing the hypocrisy of men like Thomas Arnold of the Rugby School and the tragedy of closeted religious homosexuals like General Charles George Gordon. What he failed to see was that the hypocrisy and the secrecy were protective — the lives of most Victorian gay men were anything but barren and despairing.

recorded in his diary: Graham Robb includes the following extract from Keynes's diary: "Stable boy of Park Lane/ Auburn haired of Marble Arch/ Lift boy of Vauxhall/ Jew boy/ The Swede of the National Gallery/ The young American of Victoria Sta[tion]/ The young American near the British Museum/ The chemist boy of Paris/ David Erskine M.P./ The blackmailer of Bordeaux." Robb, *Strangers,* p. 172.

the higher sodomy: According to the playwright Tom Stoppard, Oxford was the university where the Platonic theory of sodomy really held sway around the turn of the twentieth century. In his play *The Invention of Love,* Stoppard has Benjamin Jowett, the provost of Balliol College and the foremost Victorian translator of Plato, discuss with the famous literary critic Walter Pater the unfortunate case of the "Balliol Bugger" and his tutor, William Hardinge. Pater insists that the personal letters that had gotten Hardinge thrown out of Balliol were merely an expression of an older man's affectionate regard for a younger student, and quite in the tradition of Plato and the *Phaedrus*. The *Phaedrus* is the Platonic dialogue in which Socrates argues that the love between an older male lover for his young male beloved is the closest mankind can come to the divine. Jowett demurs, while not exactly disagreeing: "A Platonic enthusiasm as far as Plato was concerned meant an enthusiasm of the kind that would empty the public schools and fill the prisons were it not nipped in the bud. In my translation of the *Phaedrus* it required all my ingenuity to rephrase his depiction of *paederastia* into the affectionate regard as exists between an Englishman and his wife. Plato would have made the transposition himself if he had had the good fortune to be a Balliol man." Stoppard, *The Invention of Love,* p. 21.

216 *only one disgruntled lover:* Gay men in the early twentieth century went less in fear of prosecution under the law than of blackmail by sex partners unsatisfied with financial arrangements, and the exposure in the press that might result. One don at King's College did commit suicide, apparently in fear of a scandal, and, to the alarm of Lytton and Maynard, the dead man's brother, furious with grief, threatened to sue the college. Maynard reassured Lytton that he need not be afraid as long as he did not troll the streets of London looking for rough trade.

Sebastian Sprott: Painting a happy picture of the Charleston of his youth and describing how in the 1920s his mother cheerfully welcomed all the many lovers of her husband, Clive, and her gay friends Lytton, Duncan, and Maynard, Quentin Bell writes: "Maynard [Keynes] brought catamites who ranged from the absolutely charming to the perfectly appalling." Foreword to *Selected Letters of Vanessa Bell,* p. xii. For more on Sprott, who for a time was Lytton Strachey's lover and secretary and introduced Strachey to Roger Senhouse, see Holroyd, *Lytton Strachey;* Skidelsky, *John Maynard Keynes;* and Moffat, *A Great Unrecorded History.*

Don Juan of Bloomsbury: Clive Bell was still vigorously defending the reputations of his gay friends in the 1960s. In the introduction to the revised edition of his biography of Lytton Strachey, which openly admitted Strachey's homosexuality for the first time in print, Michael Holroyd notes that Clive Bell was one of the men who pressed hardest to stop his book's publication.

"obsession with buggery": "The word bugger was never far from our lips . . . we [she and Vanessa] listened with rapt interest to the love affairs of the buggers. We followed the ups and downs of their chequered histories; Vanessa sympathetically; I . . . frivolously, laughingly." Woolf, "Old Bloomsbury," in *Moments of Being,* p. 196.

"The Goth [Thoby Stephen]": The letters of Thoby Stephen to Clive Bell that are held in the King's College Library confirm the accuracy of Bell's assertion that their relationship was as impersonal as it was affectionate.

217 *recent television chronicles:* I refer to the recent Netflix series *The Crown* — which was frank about the swinging bisexual life of Princess Margaret's husband, Lord Snowdon — and Amazon's *A Very British Scandal,* about the leader of the Liberal Party in the 1960s and 1970s, Jeremy Thorpe. If Alan Hollinghurst, a novelist and chronicler of gay life in the United Kingdom, is to be believed, the illustrious public school

Winchester and Oxford University still formed a protected space for gay men in the 1950s, when the anti-homosexual ferment was at its peak. See Alan Hollinghurst, *The Swimming Pool Library* (1988) and *The Sparsholt Affair* (2018).

218 *women of Girton and Newnham:* In her superb biography of E. M. Forster, Wendy Moffat records the astonishing fact that, until the 1890s, any woman found on the streets of Cambridge at night could be apprehended by the university police as a prostitute and locked up in "a private prison called 'the Spinning House.'" This prison was closed when two young women, falsely accused of prostitution, sued the university, and lost; nonetheless, the case forced the university to revise its code of proctorial authority. Moffat, *A Great Unrecorded History*, p. 48.

219 *"a big mild mastiff":* Holroyd, *Lytton Strachey*, p. 195. Holroyd is paraphrasing a letter from Henry James, offers a few direct quotes including this one, but does not say to whom the letter was written, or when.

220 *wearing a bathing suit:* Upper-middle-class men before World War I still preferred to bathe nude, even in mixed company and public places. My readers may remember the scene in the Merchant Ivory Productions movie *A Room with a View,* when a group of decorously clad women come upon their male companions, including Mr. Beebe the vicar, cavorting naked in a small pond.

221 *result of the social chasm:* Similar plots are not uncommon in the adventure stories of the period by men like Erskine Calder and John Buchan and, of course, in the comic adventures of P. G. Wodehouse's Drone Club members. An upper-middle-class man mysteriously, without words, conveys to friends an interest in a certain woman, and thus, according to the rules of chivalry, puts that woman off limits. He may or may not, at the end of the book, marry the woman with whom he has exchanged barely two words. Is it any wonder that so many English women fell for bounders who actually talked to them?

222 *"Have you read the Lysistrata":* King's College Library, JTS/191. I am quoting the translation that Stephen quotes for Bell and doing the best I can to read Stephen's difficult handwriting.

223 *the Darwin sisters:* Among the Darwin sisters was Gwen Darwin Raverat, who became a renowned artist and author of the beloved Cambridge memoir *Period Piece*. The Darwin home at the end of Silver Street, enlarged and renovated, is now the home of Darwin College. I have happy memories of the place since, when I was an undergraduate in the early 1960s, it was the main building and administrative center of the new third women's college, then called New Hall, now Murray Edwards College. I had many of my supervisions at Silver Street, and all of us New Hall undergraduates and tutors could then cram into the dining room, with its dark-green walls, for hall at night. My Cambridge experience was, in fact, much closer to that of the Girtonians described by Virginia Woolf, in her feminist essays, than to that of women undergraduates of King's and Trinity today.

"The three young men": Virginia Woolf, *Carlyle's House and Other Sketches,* edited by David Bradshaw, with a foreword by Doris Lessing (London: Hesperus Press, 2003),

p. 8. This real-life scene echoes the scene in E. M. Forster's novel *The Longest Journey* in which Agnes Pembroke bursts uninvited into the college rooms of her cousin Rickie, to the consternation of Rickie's friends and the active hostility of his intimate chum Stewart Ansell. It will take Rickie many painful years to understand what Stewart grasps immediately — women are incompatible with undergraduate life at colleges like Trinity.

224 *"When I first knew [Sydney-Turner]":* Strachey to Bernard Swithinbank, July 1, 1905, *The Letters of Lytton Strachey,* p. 71. Bernard Swithinbank was a very handsome young man who had known Maynard Keynes at Eton. For a brief time, Lytton was madly in love, but Swithinbank rejected him and, to Lytton's great distress, took up instead for a time with Duncan Grant in Paris. Saxon Sydney-Turner, like Leonard Woolf, was obliged to get a job in the civil service when he left Cambridge because he had no unearned income and his widowed mother and younger siblings needed his help. In 1910 Virginia Woolf visited Saxon, as she then called him, at his family home in Hove, and in her letter she sympathetically describes the dingy and depressing boarding house kept by Saxon's mother. *The Letters of Virginia Woolf,* [December 27, 1910], vol. 1, p. 443.

225 *"Those Thursday evening parties":* Woolf, "Old Bloomsbury," in *Moments of Being,* p. 186. This paper presented to the Memoir Club is dated by editors to 1921 or early 1922.

226 *"Later on MacCarthy and I":* *The Letters of Lytton Strachey,* p. 69.
"a great power of romanticizing": Woolf, "Old Bloomsbury," in *Moments of Being,* pp. 187–88.
"grubby poodles": Henry James was even harsher in his appraisal of Clive Bell. He warned Lady Ottoline Morrell to beware of Bell, calling him "that sullied little piece of humanity." Miranda Seymour, *Ottoline Morrell: Life on the Grand Scale* (London: Hodder & Stoughton, Sceptre Books edition, 1994), p. 374. From everything I can ascertain, Henry James was right.
"It was some abstract question": Woolf, "Old Bloomsbury," in *Moments of Being,* p. 190.

228 *"I knew theoretically":* Ibid., p. 194.

229 *women were the alien:* See especially *Speculum of the Other Woman* (Ithaca, NY: Cornell University Press, 1985), Luce Irigaray's groundbreaking work on the canon of Western philosophy, from Plato to Freud. I got nothing but trouble for undertaking the English translation of that book, but it has informed my thought and I cannot, quite, regret it.

12. The Landmark Year

230 *his next practical joke:* The remarkable Dreadnought Hoax of 1910, a scandal that made the national papers, was hatched by Adrian Stephen, with the participation of his sister Virginia and his friend Duncan Grant, another man who adored practical jokes. With long robes and cork-blackened faces, speaking in some kind of linguistic

hodgepodge, they posed as Arab royalty and were given the full royal treatment by the crew and captain of HMS *Dreadnought*. See Lee, *Virginia Woolf,* pp. 278–83.

231 *or indeed in 1956:* Perhaps my readers remember the happy homemaker persona that Doris Day, a woman who had been working in the entertainment industry since her teens and became the most successful female vocalist of all time, adopted in so many of her highly successful movies.

"extraordinary beauty": L. Woolf, *Beginning Again,* pp. 26–27.

232 *Gerald Kelly:* Gerald Kelly, Eton and Trinity Hall, Cambridge, was to become a very important figure in British art circles over the next decades, knighted by the king, whose portrait he was chosen to paint, and serving as the president of the Royal Academy during World War II.

234 *On her honeymoon with Max:* For the full story of Agatha and Max, see my book *Agatha Christie: The Woman and Her Mysteries.*

238 *disease of virgin women:* Hysteria is closely related to shell shock, as army psychologists in World War I came to realize, and both men and women can suffer from it. Many years ago, I was researching Freud and Charcot and was thrilled when my dentist recounted to me a hysterical moment in his own life. He and his first wife were having serious marital problems and he was wretched from constant colds and sinus infections. One day, after another argument with his wife, he suddenly said to himself, "My God, she is always getting up my nose," whereafter he got a divorce and his nasal problems cleared up.

241 *Prince Albert forty years:* Queen Victoria had typhoid as a teenager, and one reason she was so shocked by the death of her husband was that she was confident that Albert would fight off the disease as she had done. For a full discussion of the death of Prince Albert from typhoid, see Chapter 27 of my book *We Two.*

"sew up the ulcer": The Letters of Virginia Woolf, vol. 1, p. 246.

242 *"I do feel that Thoby's life":* Vanessa Stephen to Madge Vaughan, December 11, 1906, *Selected Letters of Vanessa Bell,* pp. 45–46.

243 *"Dearest Madge, Nessa":* The Letters of Virginia Woolf, vol. 1, p. 250.

"That does not mean that": Ibid., pp. 250 and 265. Madge was at this time a very close friend to Virginia, who in a letter of February 1907 feels able to give a truer expression to her state of mind following Thoby's death: "You and your children [in a photograph] are just by my inkstand. They give me great pleasure — so does their mother. Thoby used to say that you were the most beautiful person he had ever seen. It is very hard not to have him here — I cant get reconciled — but we have to go on. Adrian is well — but I cant be a brother to him!" (p. 283).

"Nessa became engaged": Ibid., p. 268.

244 *a visit to Clive's family:* According to Quentin Bell, Virginia Woolf visited the Bells of Cleeve House on only this one occasion. The nightmare of that visit was summed up for her by the fact that the inkpot in which she dipped her pen was formed from a horse's hoof.

"I shall want all my sweetness": The Letters of Virginia Woolf, vol. 1, p. 273.

13. The Great Betrayal

245 *"I see he [George] is much"*: Ibid., p. 299. Evidently Violet had been trying to mend bridges between the Bells and the Duckworths.

246 *29 Fitzroy Square:* Interior scenes of the 2017 movie *Phantom Threads,* starring Daniel Day Lewis and Vicky Krieps, were reportedly filmed in a house on Fitzroy Square. The house in the movie, elegantly restored and maintained, is very different from the rundown rental at number 29 in 1907, but the long sequence of narrowing staircases and lowering ceilings give a sense of what life must have been like when the Stephens and their friends lived in the square.

247 *"supremely happy and fulfilled":* A. Garnett, *Deceived with Kindness,* pp. 25–26.

249 *"It contains all the beauty":* Woolf to Clive Bell, [February 1907], *The Letters of Virginia Woolf,* vol. 1, p. 282.
   "Give my love to my sister": Ibid., March 22, 1907, p. 290.
   "Nessa is like a great": Ibid., p. 30.
   "Nessa and Clive came": Ibid., p. 316.

250 *"'Of course,'" Vanessa imagines:* Vanessa Bell to Virginia Woolf, [May 4, 1908], *Selected Letters of Vanessa Bell,* p. 64.

251 *"Mrs Raven-Hill, Mrs Armour":* Clive Bell's letter to Virginia Woolf is quoted by Frances Spalding in her biography of Vanessa Bell, p. 71. For Vanessa's letter to Virginia, see *Selected Letters of Vanessa Bell,* p. 61.

252 *"I have been writing Nessa's":* Woolf to Clive Bell, April 15, 1908, *The Letters of Virginia Woolf,* vol. 1, p. 325.
   "Talk about freedom of talk": Vanessa Bell to Virginia Woolf, April 19, 1908, *Selected Letters of Vanessa Bell,* p. 61. I find it interesting that six women associated with the Bloomsbury group — Anne Raven-Hill, Molly MacCarthy, Nelly Cecil, Karin Stephen, Ethel Smyth, and Dorothy Brett — became profoundly deaf as young women.
   "renew his gallantries": Bell, *Virginia Woolf,* vol. 1, p. 142.

253 *"no less . . . and not much":* Ibid., p. 138.

254 *salacious little essays:* I have no proof, but I am ready to bet that, in some of his leisure hours in Paris, Clive Bell read some of the semi-pornographic novels put out by "Willy's" team of ghost writers, including notably his wife, Colette, the actual author of the best-selling series of Claudine novels. For the whole fascinating story of the Colette-Willy marriage, see my novel-biography *Becoming Colette.*

255 *rumors had been floating:* Bell, *Virginia Woolf,* vol. 1, p. 119. Stella Duckworth, September 1893: "Mr. Headlam went at 10.30. I cannot think of him without a shudder & yet he is much to be pitied." It is Quentin Bell, not I, who makes the inference that Headlam desired young girls.
   "Vanessa icy, cynical, artistic": Lee, *Virginia Woolf,* p. 243.

256 *to a private clinic:* The director of this clinic, a Miss Jean Thomas, was infatuated with Virginia Woolf. Vanessa, in a letter to Virginia, teases her about the raging lesbian

passions she has ignited during her stay at the clinic. By 1911, Clive and Vanessa had reached an agreement that Virginia was a lesbian.

"We have been your humble": Quoted in *Selected Letters of Vanessa Bell*, p. 49, with the reference "VWL VI, 493."

258 *"despite her belief in honesty"*: Spalding, *Vanessa Bell*, p. 171. Spalding continues in the same passage: "[Vanessa Bell's] letters reveal a great many details about her daily life, but when it comes to what she was feeling or suffering as a result of those dearest to her it is as if she disappears into another room and firmly closes the door."

"our more or less high": Ibid., p. 172.

"Yes I will tell you": *The Letters of Virginia Woolf: Volume Three, 1923–1928*, edited by Nigel Nicolson and Joanne Trautmann (New York and London: Harcourt Brace Jovanovich, 1977), p. 172.

260 *"seeing them together"*: A. Garnett, *Deceived with Kindness*, p. 28.

"a cuckoo who lays eggs": Bell, *Virginia Woolf*, vol. 1, p. 133.

14. Vanessa's Way, Part 1

265 *"I almost wrote you"*: *The Letters of Virginia Woolf*, vol. 4, pp. 40 and 68.

when Carrington became: As woman and as artist, Carrington (she hated her given name, Dora) is one of the most interesting women associated with, though never really a member of, the Bloomsbury group. To discover her and her art, I urge my readers to find the 1995 movie *Carrington*, with Emma Thompson giving an incandescent performance in the title role. It was through the movie and its footage showing the interiors Carrington painted in the homes she shared with Lytton Strachey that I was able to discover just how fine an artist Carrington was.

266 *"Do you miss your Dolph"*: *Selected Letters of Vanessa Bell*, p. 108.

267 *Lady Ottoline Morrell:* For more about the fascinating Lady Ottoline Morrell, I recommend Miranda Seymour's wonderful biography *Ottoline Morrell: Life on the Grand Scale*. Seymour goes into detail on the way the Bells and Lytton Strachey, together with their mutual friends, exploited Lady Ottoline and undermined her. Virginia Woolf, as her letters and diaries make clear, liked and admired and marveled at Lady Ottoline. A caricature of Lady Ottoline appears in D. H. Lawrence's novel *Women in Love*. In the 1969 movie *Women in Love*, which is important watching for anyone interested in Bloomsbury, the Lady Ottoline character is played by Eleanor Bron.

268 *"I sometimes feel"*: Lytton Strachey to Leonard Woolf, September 9, 1904, *The Letters of Lytton Strachey*, p. 32.

269 *"Only those just getting"*: Spalding, *Vanessa Bell*, p. 65, quoting from Bell's unpublished memoir.

270 *This was the doctrine preached:* In his biography of Lytton Strachey, Michael Holroyd calls the relationship of Lytton and Carrington one of the great love stories of the twentieth century. For my part, any love that leads a young, talented, and beautiful woman to, first, prostitute herself to men like Partridge and Penrose whom Lytton lusted for, and finally commit suicide after his death, is not an idyll.

I have long admired the narrative verve and elegant prose style of Lytton Strachey in *Eminent Victorians,* but my sympathy for the man declined after I read Frances Marshall Partridge's account of an interview that she once had in London with Lytton, in 1924. Ralph Partridge, whose marriage to Carrington had foundered, had fallen deeply in love with Frances (Fanny) Marshall, and he wanted to live with her in London on weekdays and on weekends stay together at Ham Spray, the house that Ralph and Carrington ran for Lytton Strachey. Lytton became very upset that his comfort and pleasure when in the country was about to be disrupted by young Fanny Marshall, so he summoned her to the Ladies Lounge of the Oriental Club. I quote Marshall; apparently Lytton's words were engraved on her memory: "You see, I rely very much on Ralph's practical support, sound sense and strength of character. Fond as I am of Carrington, I fear she loses her head sometimes. So that I think I ought to warn you that if you and Ralph set up house together, I can't promise to stay at Ham House with Carrington, and I think you know what this would mean to her. What would become of her?" Frances Partridge, *Love in Bloomsbury* (London: Taurus Park Paperbacks, 2014), electronic edition, Loc. 1585. So, to preserve his own comfort, Lytton Strachey is willing to threaten Frances, the woman he knows his loyal friend Ralph loves, and to consider abandoning Carrington, the woman who adores him, knowing this may well cause Carrington's suicide. In my book, this is not sexual freedom but rather male privilege and moral turpitude. This record of the conversation with Lytton Strachey in 1924 is all the more striking because Frances Marshall Partridge's memoir is, by and large, a bright, breezy, and bowdlerized account of life in Bloomsbury. She says nothing about the cruel way her employer David Garnett treated his wife, Rachel Marshall Garnett, who was her older sister. She jokes about Clive Bell's determined attempts to seduce her, before she and Ralph were finally able to marry.

"entered the smoking room": Spalding, *Vanessa Bell,* p. 64. Another part of Lytton's influence on the culture of Bloomsbury was his voice, a variant of the peculiar speech patterns of the Strachey family, which modulated erratically, piano and forte, across octaves and was copied by, reportedly, generations of young men in London seeking to be trendy. Michael Holroyd, in his various books on Strachey, writes literally pages about Lytton's voice.

"The word bugger was never": Woolf, "Old Bloomsbury," in *Moments of Being,* p. 196. The conversations at Cambridge led by G. E. Moore famously revolved around the nature of good.

"Vanessa by her behavior": Spalding, *Vanessa Bell,* p. 64.

271 *"From the opening gut"*: Michael Holroyd, *Lytton Strachey and the Bloomsbury Group: His Work, Their Influence* (New York: Penguin Books, 1967), pp. 377–78. Woolf was among the first to praise *Eminent Victorians,* but she was privately dismissive of Strachey's later work and scathing about his pretentions as a poet. This may be why Holroyd, in his celebration of Lytton Strachey's literary genius, is so scathing in turn in his estimation of Woolf, as both a woman and a writer. Holroyd opines that Woolf is a writer of no importance and calls her "anaemic," "a nature clogged with self-

obsession," radiating an "ascetic, sexless charm" (note on p. 242 and pp. 222–23). In the second chapter of his memoir *Basil Street Blues,* first published in 1999, however, Holroyd cites Woolf favorably for the views on biography she expressed in her 1937 essay "Reflections on Sheffield Place," which prefigure his own.
"has some awful females": Selected Letters of Vanessa Bell, pp. 82–83.

272 *their mutual friends:* Raymond Mortimer was a celebrated writer of the 1920s and 1930s, now perhaps best known as one of the lovers of Harold Nicholson, Vita Sackville-West's husband. "Dadie" Rylands was a don at Cambridge University, a notable theater critic, and, as Wendy Moffat documents in her biography of E. M. Forster, a man notable even in gay circles for his sexploits.
"Dearest dearest creature": The Letters of Lytton Strachey, p. 641.

273 *Dillwyn Knox:* In Dillwyn Knox, John Maynard Keynes found a mind of a brilliance comparable to his own. Those interested in code breaking will recognize Knox's name as one of the great code breakers of his generation, instrumental in cracking German military codes in both world wars. Lovers of the post-1945 English novel will know that "Dilly" Knox was one of the uncles of the great novelist and biographer Penelope Fitzgerald. Dilly and his brothers and brother-in-law, all affluent men and pillars of the English educational and religious establishment, lifted not a finger to help Fitzgerald when, through no fault of her own, she and her small children were on the edge of destitution.
"Vanessa explained how interesting": Spalding, *Vanessa Bell,* p. 79.

274 *"Dear Maynard, it is plainly": Selected Letters of Vanessa Bell,* p. 163. For some years Vanessa and Virginia co-rented Asheham, a property that both the Woolfs and the Bells liked a lot. However, when their lease ended, they were forced to find other properties in Sussex.

275 *paid Duncan and Vanessa:* On a flying visit to Cambridge to read some papers, I was entranced to spot two of Keynes's Bell-Grant pieces installed in the archive room of King's College. In the corner of the room was a wooden chest that turned out to be the "Ark" in which the Apostles stored their papers for the Cambridge Conversazione Society. In the King's archivist's inner sanctum I saw on the wall Simon Bussy's devastating profile portrait of Lady Ottoline Morrell, which, I was assured, was the original. Fun!

276 *"a vast success":* Bell, *Bloomsbury Recalled,* p. 96.

277 *"I had a sort of inkling":* With the acid sophistication she had learned her husband preferred, Vanessa wrote to Clive, "I hope you'll see your whore [Anne Raven-Hill] soon and get some amusing gossip out of her." Spalding, *Vanessa Bell,* p. 90.

278 *an illustrious Quaker family:* The three big English chocolate companies of the early twentieth century were Cadbury, Rowntree, and Fry, all founded by Quakers.

279 *"Did you hear of our adventures": The Letters of Virginia Woolf,* vol. 1, p. 465.

280 *the enthusiastic collaboration:* Desmond MacCarthy was enrolled to manage the first exhibition and Leonard Woolf the second. Fry, assisted by Vanessa and in 1912 by Duncan, hung the paintings himself. Virginia Woolf and Lytton Strachey, neither of

whom pretended to be art experts, went around the exhibitions and recorded remarkably fresh and insightful comments.

281 *"Roger is the greatest fun":* Quoted in John Lehmann, *Thrown to the Woolfs* (New
York: Holt, Rinehart and Winston, 1978), p. 32.

282 *"[Duncan] and I have decided":* Selected Letters of Vanessa Bell, p. 100. Sadly for
Vanessa Bell, her joking wish to "emulate Gill" will bring anyone up short who is con-
versant with early-twentieth-century British art. Eric Gill (no relation to me!) was
one of the most successful and renowned English artists of the early twentieth century. He was also a sexual pervert and child abuser. According to the secret diary Gill
kept, he began his incestuous career with his own sister and went on to have sex for
many years with his two eldest daughters as well. Even his dog was not spared. Gill
hid his sexual activities well, converting to Roman Catholicism in his forties, founding a lay religious order, wearing a monk's robe and a chastity belt. His work became
increasingly religious and his commissions were often ecclesiastical. Such was Gill's
fame in England that when Fiona MacCarthy in 1989 revealed the contents of Gill's
diary, she was criticized for injuring Gill's surviving daughter. It is possible that Gill's
male contemporaries, in the overwhelmingly male society of English artists, got a
whiff of what Eric Gill was up to in his isolated homes, but in 1911, Vanessa Bell certainly did not and could not. She would have seen only Gill's early, mildly erotic
woodcuts.

"And then — what": Vanessa Bell to Roger Fry, November 23, 1911, *Selected Letters of
Vanessa Bell,* p. 112.

"Dearest," wrote Vanessa: Vanessa Bell to Clive Bell, *Selected Letters of Vanessa Bell,* p.
164.

284 *"Discretion is not the better":* Holroyd, *Lytton Strachey,* p. xvi.

friend and collaborator: Quentin Bell and Frances Spalding, both experts in British
art criticism, make it clear that the most successful book published by Clive Bell —
Art (1914) — was an extension and popularization of Fry's theories.

15. Virginia's Way, Part 1

286 *he fell in love with Virginia:* Virginia Woolf told Ethel Smyth that she had been joking if she ever said Leonard had waited seven years for her as Jacob waited for Rachel.
"He saw me it is true and thought me an odd fish and went off next day to Ceylon,
with a vague romance about us both [her and Vanessa]. And I heard stories of him . . .
and Lytton said he was like Swift and would murder his wife, and someone else said
Woolf had married a black woman. That was my romance — Woolf in the jungle."
Woolf to Ethel Smyth, June 22, 1930, *The Letters of Virginia Woolf,* vol. 4, p. 180.

287 *"I feel all my heart drawn":* See Nigel Nicolson's introduction to the first volume of
The Letters of Virginia Woolf, p. xviii.

"I want everything": The Letters of Virginia Woolf, vol. 1, p. 496.

289 *"after your awful description":* Selected Letters of Vanessa Bell, p. 127.

Thrown to the Woolfs: The author, the very distinguished English editor and publisher John Lehmann, was for a time a member of the group of gay men in Berlin in the 1930s chronicled by Christopher Isherwood in *Berlin Stories*. One of these stories, centered on the character Sally Bowles, became the basis for the musical *Cabaret*.

290 *"are evidently both a little"*: *Selected Letters of Vanessa Bell*, p. 132.

291 *more serious mental breakdown*: Various attempts have been made to diagnose the exact nature of Virginia Woolf's mental illness. Kay Redfield Jamison, one of the foremost American medical experts on "mood disorders," confidently refers to Virginia Woolf as bipolar in her detailed analysis of the relationship between Robert Lowell's poetry and his bipolar disease. *Robert Lowell: Setting the River on Fire — A Study of Genius, Mania, and Character* (New York: Knopf, 2017).

"I am obsessed at night": *The Letters of Virginia Woolf*, vol. 4, p. 80. In *Beginning Again,* the third volume of his autobiography, Leonard Woolf offers a detailed and moving account of his wife when mental illness overcame her.

"In the lava of my madness": Ibid., p. 180.

"After being ill": Ibid., p. 231.

292 *"Can't you imagine us"*: Vanessa Bell to Virginia Woolf, August 11, 1908, *Selected Letters of Vanessa Bell*, p. 67.

293 *"I'm always angry with"*: Lee, *Virginia Woolf*, p. 537.

"How any woman with": *The Letters of Virginia Woolf*, vol. 4, p. 176.

294 *"Think — not one moment's"*: Ibid., p. 180.

"if this young man had": Woolf, *Mrs. Dalloway*, various editions. I quote from the Martino Publishing edition, 2012, p. 203.

295 *"unmitigated, pure, often"*: L. Woolf, *Beginning Again*, p. 26.

"My Darling Goose M": *The Letters of Virginia Woolf: Volume Two, 1912–1922*, edited by Nigel Nicolson and Joanne Trautmann (New York and London: Harcourt Brace Jovanovich, 1976), p. 191.

296 *"five-finger exercises"*: Woolf, *Carlyle's House and Other Sketches,* p. vii.

after an eighteen-month gap: To recapitulate the notes of Woolf's brilliant and dedicated editor Anne Olivier Bell, *The Diary of Virginia Woolf* as we have it today begins in January 1915, continues until February 15, 1915, and then takes up again on August 3, 1917. As Woolf's anchor to reality, the diary would then continue, with odd gaps, until 1941, when it gave way to the hurricane of Hitler's war.

"loose drifting material": Entry for April 20, 1919, *The Diary of Virginia Woolf*, vol. 1, p. 266.

297 *Clive's mistress Mary*: In the photos of Mary Hutchinson in the Bell Collection at Trinity College, Cambridge, one can see what a beautiful and elegant woman she was. Her wide smile and beautiful teeth mark her off from the Stephen sisters Vanessa and Virginia, who keep their mouths closed in their portraits and photos.

298 *dreamy fantasy*: Leonard Woolf gives some examples of his wife's inspired whimsy through the character Camilla Lawrence in his 1914 novel *The Wise Virgins,* reissued in 2007 with an introduction by Woolf's biographer Victoria Glendinning, by Yale University Press.

her outworn bloomers: Both Virginia Woolf and Vanessa Bell preferred not to spend money on underclothes, so, when elastic failed, they apparently relied on safety pins to keep their bloomers and petticoats in place. One reason why Virginia liked to have her sister shop for dresses on her behalf was that she hated to reveal to shop assistants the inadequacy of her underwear.

299 *"When one sees Clive":* The Diary of Virginia Woolf: Volume Two, 1920–1924, edited by Anne Olivier Bell, assisted by Andrew McNeillie (New York and London: Harcourt Brace Jovanovich, 1978), p. 105. In the same diary entry Woolf writes: "We talked chiefly about the hypnotism exerted by Bloomsbury over the younger generation." So, there we have it, straight from the horse's mouth. By January 1918, Bloomsbury was in full swing.

16. Vanessa's Way, Part 2

301 *the very kind of man:* The 1987 biography of Duncan Grant by Douglas Blair Turnbaugh *(Duncan Grant and the Bloomsbury Group: An Illustrated Biography)* features a large number of reproductions of Grant's nude studies of men, as well as a nude study of himself as a young man.

actually had all that sex: Unlike his friend, patron, and one-time lover Maynard Keynes, Duncan Grant did not keep a list of his amours and his conquests. But as Turnbaugh's biography makes clear, his life was one very long (he lived to be ninety-three) succession of lovers — relatives like Lytton, fellow artists like George Bergen, beautiful young bisexuals like David Garnett and Paul Roche, criminal types picked up on the street, and boys solicited on the train between London and Lewes, the railway station nearest to Charleston. Grant preferred sleeping with young, beautiful men who could serve as models.

it was men he desired: Reportedly Grant was once taken to a heterosexual brothel as a very young man, and managed to perform well. He also had a brief fling with an actress. Apart from these experiences, and his affair with Vanessa Bell, all his sexual partners were male.

303 *"I am so uncertain of":* Spalding, *Vanessa Bell,* pp. 172–73.

304 *David Garnett:* For my account of David Garnett I am indebted to Sarah Knights's carefully researched and fair-minded biography *Bloomsbury's Outsider: A Life of David Garnett* (London: Bloomsbury Reader, 2015).

tall, blond, athletic: The arresting cover of Knights's book shows Garnett from the back, naked, climbing up to a second-story window.

305 *at Wissett Lodge:* Here I am simplifying the series of country places occupied by the Bell-Grant-Garnett threesome in the first years of the war. For the full account, see Spalding, *Vanessa Bell.*

306 *"no little Grant has yet":* Spalding, *Vanessa Bell,* p. 139, quoting a letter from Vanessa to Clive tentatively dated to March 25, 1915.

conscientious objectors: Bloomsbury is somewhat famous for its antiwar stance during World War I, but in fact the group was divided. Maynard was far too valuable to the Treasury to be sent to the trenches. His formidable efforts to make the British war machine as economical as possible was one of the reasons why he was so disliked by his fellow Apostle Bertrand Russell, the most cogent exponent of the antiwar cause and a man willing to go to jail for his arguments. Morgan Forster was sent to Egypt with the Red Cross, did diligent work there, and met an Egyptian taxi driver who changed his life. Desmond MacCarthy had, as they say, a good war, as part of naval intelligence. Saxon Sydney-Turner continued in the civil service. Leonard was willing to fight alongside his two brothers, one of whom was killed in the war, the other seriously wounded in the same battle, but the severe tremor in Leonard's hand made him a poor choice to bear arms.

could not imagine hefting: It is well established that Lytton Strachey suffered from Marfan syndrome, a degenerative disease of the connective tissue.

308 *"My visit to Charleston": The Diary of Virginia Woolf,* vol. 1, p. 182.

"caked with earth, stiff": Ibid., p. 189.

309 *dalliances with Barbara Hiles:* Barbara Hiles was one of the Slade School "Cropheads" who invaded Bloomsbury, rather to the indignation of Virginia Woolf and Vanessa Bell. Saxon Sydney-Turner was very much in love with Barbara, and David Garnett had sex with her, but she married Nicholas Bagenal, a lower-class Irish man who also worshiped at the Bloomsbury altar. After the death of her husband, according to Quentin Bell in *Bloomsbury Recalled,* Barbara Bagenal hooked up with Clive Bell, serving as his social secretary and travel companion. Though they did not at all care for her, Clive's children and his friends were grateful to Barbara for keeping their libidinous father more or less on the straight and narrow.

Alix Sargant-Florence: Michael Holroyd, who knew her through his research on Lytton Strachey, intriguingly describes Alix Sargant-Florence Strachey as "author of 'The Unconscious Motives of War,' a once brilliant cricket player and dancer at night clubs." Sarah Knights, the biographer of David Garnett, says that Alix, "six feet tall and stick thin," was possessed of "a Red Indian profile . . . and a first-class mind" and notes that she proved unexpectedly resistant to David Garnett's virile allure. Reportedly, Alix tried to cure her analysand Harry Norton's homosexuality by having sex with him — an interesting twist on therapy abuse, and quite unsuccessful.

Alix Strachey has long been assumed by historians of psychoanalysis to be merely an assistant to her husband, James, in translating into English and editing the landmark *Complete Works of Sigmund Freud.* But it was Alix, not James, who studied modern languages at Cambridge, and the contemporary letters and memoirs prove that James Strachey put his formidable intellect in gear only after he finally agreed to marry Alix. It was she who decided they should go to Vienna for analysis with Freud, and, if I interpret a remark by Lytton correctly, it may have been Alix who first came up with the idea of translating Freud into English. "The story of the Prof's [that is, Sigmund Freud's] treachery to Alix over her translation was very shocking," wrote Lytton to his brother James in Vienna, on April 14, 1921, "but if yours holds good I suppose she can now devote herself to that." *The Letters of Lytton Strachey,* p. 484.

"that he had for a long time": Spalding, *Vanessa Bell*, p. 169.

"I copulated on Saturday": Ibid., p. 172.

310 *younger women like Fredegond:* Virginia Woolf had given the nicknames "the Turnip," "the Owl," and "the Bat" to Carrington, Alix, and Fredegond, respectively. Upon learning this, they indignantly launched a concerted attack on Woolf at the 1917 Club. Lee, *Virginia Woolf*, p. 380.

311 *"A fortnight ago all"*: *The Diary of Virginia Woolf*, vol. 1, p. 208.

312 *D. H. Lawrence:* Following the death of D. H. Lawrence, Virginia Woolf said that she was shocked and grieved, especially as Lawrence was younger than she was, but confessed she had never been able to get through any of his novels.

forty or fifty pounds: In the 1920s, Vanessa Bell had a successful solo exhibition in London and sold a number of paintings, but neither she nor Grant could compare with Augustus John, who was getting several hundred pounds for every canvas, at sold-out exhibitions. Vanessa was also commissioned to decorate rooms and design fabrics and furniture for family and friends, and Virginia was scrupulous in her insistence on paying Vanessa for her work. On April 29, 1929, she sent Vanessa a check for 39 pounds, 6 shillings, 8 pence. *The Diary of Virginia Woolf*, vol. 4, p. 45, note 4. And she had much of the furniture from the house in Cassis, which Vanessa and Duncan had decorated for her, shipped back, at some expense, to Monk's House. Vanessa Bell also, of course, did the cover designs for all of Virginia's published works.

313 *"You've wrecked one"*: Entry for Saturday, July 27, 1918, *The Diary of Virginia Woolf*, vol. 1, p. 172. Throughout the diary, Clive Bell features as a fat, balding blowhard, absurdly small in accomplishments compared with Virginia's husband, Leonard, and relentlessly engaged in self-promotion. By the late 1920s, he is recorded by Virginia as an aging Lothario, a laughingstock in London, and an embarrassment to his family.

314 *"chained in a kitchen"*: Ibid., p. 314.

315 *"Mary produced chocolates"*: Ibid., p. 197.

"I see that it is after": *Selected Letters of Vanessa Bell*, p. 223.

be known as Angelica: Angelica Garnett's names at birth were registered as Helen Vanessa. The name Angelica, by which she was thereafter always known, was reportedly added at the suggestion of Virginia Woolf.

316 *The agreement reached:* Priya Parmar, in her novel *Vanessa and Her Sister* (New York: Ballantine Books, 2014), says that Virginia Woolf was of no help when Vanessa was giving birth to Angelica. The published correspondence indicates that this is inaccurate.

the 1st Lord Melbourne: I offer a sketch of the social background of Queen Victoria's beloved Lord Melbourne in my book *We Two*.

suited him very well: Both Maynard Keynes and Duncan Grant, unlike Leonard Woolf and Clive Bell, were close to their mothers as boys and men, and Grant's mother, a skillful needlewoman, worked a number of her son's designs for chair seats and cushions. Mrs. Grant and Vanessa Bell maintained polite relations, but on one occasion, when Vanessa, with her daughter and the nanny in tow, arrived in France, where Duncan had fallen ill with typhoid, Mrs. Grant and her sister made it clear that Duncan's health was their concern, not Vanessa's.

Infidelities and illegitimate children: Douglas Blair Turnbaugh's biography, among others, is informative about the unconventional lives of members of Duncan Grant's family.

317 *left-wing intellectuals:* David Garnett's mother, Constance Garnett, famous in the annals of literature for bringing Tolstoy and Dostoyevsky to the English reading public, was paid a pittance for her immense labors of translation. As a very young man David was even more radical than his family, risking imprisonment in his support of Indian anarchist groups. One reason why David Garnett became a friend of Julian Bell's when Julian was at Cambridge is that Garnett, unlike the men at Charleston, understood and sympathized with Bell's left-wing views, having held them himself at about the same age.

318 *"She is a wistful, patient":* Entry for Wednesday, March 5, 1919, *The Diary of Virginia Woolf,* vol. 1, p. 250.

319 *"Its beauty is the remarkable":* Widely quoted, including in Spalding, *Vanessa Bell,* p. 177.

321 *"They recognised in":* A. Garnett, *Deceived with Kindness,* pp. 28–29.

323 *By narrative magic:* David Garnett, *Aspects of Love* (London: Chatto & Windus, 1955; New York: Knopf, 1990). First put on in the West End, then on Broadway, the show *Aspects of Love* was made into a movie and is still being licensed to amateur musical groups. Rights to the novel have proved a gold mine for Garnett's surviving children.

324 *"all kinds of people besides":* A. Garnett, *Deceived with Kindness,* pp. 41 and 42.

325 *she finally learned:* This claim by Bell Garnett is contested by Sarah Knights, who cites a diary entry by David Garnett in which he says that he told Angelica, then his lover but not his wife, of his relationship with Grant during World War I.

326 *a magical grandmother:* This is the testimony of Henrietta Garnett in "Visits to Charleston: Vanessa," her contribution to the collection *Charleston, Past and Present* (New York: Harcourt Brace Jovanovich, 1987).

327 *Then, as if Quentin:* Quentin Bell, in the chapter on his early years in his 1995 *Bloomsbury Recalled,* calls himself "piggy in the middle." He was the child both his parents loved least, noticed least, praised least. In his essay on his mother, Quentin Bell is calm and judicious, but his very even-handedness makes it all the more devastating when he does judge. "Of the three of us I was the least precious," he wrote, "but in saying this I would not suggest that I did not have as much maternal affection as any one person could cope with" (p. 96). He does not say so, but he is surely suggesting that his older brother, Julian, who rushed off to his death in the Spanish Civil War in 1935, and his sister, who in 1984 revealed how unhappy and self-destructive she had been in her life, may have had more maternal affection than they could cope with.

". . . but Angelica being of": Selected Letters of Vanessa Bell, pp. 278–79.
329 *"came in conflict with the police":* The Letters of Virginia Woolf, vol. 4, p. 129.
"[Virginia] tried to probe": A. Garnett, *Deceived with Kindness*, p. 114.

17. Virginia's Way, Part 2

331 *Together, they glued the pages:* An early imprint of the Hogarth Press, a narrative poem about Paris by Hope Mirrlees, has been acquired by the Smith College Library. It is very slender, very amateurish, and very moving.
"She says she will not": Entry for June 9, 1919, *The Diary of Virginia Woolf,* vol. 1, p. 279.
334 *"I can't tell you how":* The Letters of Virginia Woolf, vol. 4, p. 40.
335 *"How I hated marrying":* Ibid., pp. 195–96.
337 *"I find, with Katherine":* Entries for April 17 and May 16, 1919, *The Diary of Virginia Woolf,* vol. 1, pp. 265 and 273.
Dorothy Strachey Bussy: Dorothy Strachey Bussy was a fascinating woman, and I tend to think of Lytton as her little brother. In her thirties, Dorothy astonished her family by announcing her marriage to the French painter Simon Bussy and moving to France to live with him. In the eyes of the Strachey clan, Bussy was an uneducated peasant and his house in France was a hovel, but the Bussy marriage succeeded and they had a wonderful daughter, Janie. She became a friend and instructor in left-wing ideology to Quentin Bell and died tragically young, of gas poisoning, in her bath. Dorothy was an excellent writer and linguist, and she was formerly best known as the English translator of André Gide, whom she passionately loved and admired. Today Strachey Bussy is best known as the author of the anonymously published 1949 novel *Olivia* (now reissued by Amazon Books), which has become a classic in lesbian literature.
The lesbian and gay communities: When in late summer 2017 I was visiting Lamb House and Smallhythe, along with Knole and Sissinghurst, all within a short distance of one another, the National Trust guides told me of the ongoing effort in England to explore the gay and lesbian cultures of the interwar period and find out how they interacted. When I went to the British Museum, posters were proclaiming this research project.
338 *Lytton's willing submission:* While preparing an edition of Lytton Strachey's letters, Paul Levy, one of the trustees of Strachey's estate, discovered just how far the sadomasochistic practices of Strachey and Senhouse had gone in the last years of Strachey's life. He discovered a letter — apparently not found or possibly neglected by Michael Holroyd in his research — in which Strachey lovingly assures Senhouse that the wound to his abdomen sustained during a ritual crucifixion was healing well. See the introduction and the 1930 letters in *The Letters of Lytton Strachey,* edited by Paul Levy.

misogynistic gay theorist: For more on this, see Moffat, *A Great Unrecorded History.*

339 *"When I go to what":* Woolf to Ethel Smyth, August 15, 1930, *The Letters of Virginia Woolf,* vol. 4, p. 200.

340 *Vita Sackville-West:* Many books of letters and memoirs and commentary, plus a number of novels, have been published about Vita Sackville-West. The most important work probably is still her younger son Nigel Nicolson's *Portrait of a Marriage* (New York: Atheneum, 1973). In his introduction Nicolson divulged for the first time to the general public what had been well known to the world of London letters and the diplomatic corps — namely, that his parents were happy in their marriage while each engaged in a long series of same-sex affairs. Nicolson was painfully honest in discussing how his parents' marital arrangements affected the lives of himself and his elder brother. The rest of the book consists of the secret account his mother had written about her passionate love affair with Violet Trefusis. Nicolson found this document among Vita's papers after her death and decided to make it public. In my research I was interested to read several books by Trefusis, who mainly published in French, including her 1935 novel *Broderie anglaise,* which offers a transposed version of her love triangle with Vita and Virginia; in it, Vita appears as a male. For a careful and truthful account of the relationship between Virginia Woolf and Vita Sackville-West, I refer my reader to Hermione Lee's biography of Woolf, notably Chapter 28, "Vita."

341 *Eddy, not Vita:* Edward Sackville-West, as a visit to the castle makes clear, had no love for Knole and no desire to live there. He took one turret of the great place for himself and decorated it to his taste, and, at least to me, his apartments and the marvelous deer park are the star attractions at Knole. Vita may have mourned Knole, but the home she and Harold created at the equally ancient ruin at Sissinghurst, now set in the extraordinary garden Vita created with Harold's assistance, is far more beautiful. At Sissinghurst, Vita chose to live separate from her family and her servants in an extremely inconvenient tower, which, unlike cousin Eddy's, seems made for one person, not for parties. In France, Violet Trefusis had a tower too.

"With a soft, wet warm": *The Letters of Virginia Woolf,* vol. 4, p. 248.

"talking as loud as": Ibid., p. 36.

343 Memoirs of Ellen Terry: Ibid., p. 271.

344 *their theatrical projects:* The best account of Ellen Terry and her daughter, Edy Craig, is still that given by Michael Holroyd in *A Strange Eventful History.* More recently, his book has been fleshed out and vividly illustrated by Anne Rachlin, in *Edy Was a Lady: Featuring the "Lost" Memoirs of Ellen Terry's Daughter Edith Craig,* with a foreword by Sir Michael Holroyd and with a message from Sir Donald Sinden, CBE (Leicester, UK: Matador, 2011).

"Miss Craig," "a rosy": Entry for March 30, 1922, *The Diary of Virginia Woolf,* vol. 2, p. 174.

"She put down her case": Virginia Woolf, *Between the Acts* (New York: Harcourt, 1941), p. 210.

346 *called* homophrosyne: I am grateful to Daniel Mendelsohn and his book *An Odyssey: A Father, a Son, and an Epic* (London: William Collins, 2017) for this word.

347 *"Dearest, I want to tell"*: Hermione Lee, in *Virginia Woolf*, gives a full and deeply moving account of the last days of Virginia Woolf. The final letter to Leonard is quoted in full on p. 747.

Epilogue: The Bell Children and Their Aunt

348 *"Darling Angelica"*: *The Letters of Virginia Woolf*, vol. 4, pp. 55 and 173.

350 *gang-raped by older boys*: See Lee, *Virginia Woolf*, p. 292.
"The music consisted": Bell, *Bloomsbury Recalled*, p. 34.

351 *"There is a considerable"*: Trinity College Library, Cambridge, Bell Archive, Box 6.
Gerald Wellesley: Gerald Wellesley was the husband of Dorothy Wellesley, who was a patron of the Hogarth Press and a close friend of Vita Sackville-West.

352 *relevant to our world today;* I wrote these last pages in the days following the testimony of Christine Blaney Ford before the Senate Judiciary Committee, charged with determining whether Judge Brett Kavanaugh should be seated on the Supreme Court of the United States. Professor Blaney Ford claimed that Kavanaugh had attempted to rape her during a party when they were teenagers. Kavanaugh passionately denied the accusation and was duly confirmed.

PHOTO CREDITS

INDEX

Aberconway, Christabel, 269, 352

Albert, Prince, and Queen Victoria, 67, 75, 78, 85, 133, 141–42, 241, 370n67, 384n241

"Am I a Snob?" (Woolf), 49–51, 369n49

Annan, Noel, 58, 62, 83–84, 91, 110, 219

Aplin, John, 64, 371n77, 374n121

Armstrong-Jones, Antony (Lord Snowdon), 217, 381n217

"Atalanta in Calydon," 214–15, 222–23, 379n214

Atkinson, G. B., 137–38

Bagenal, Barbara Hiles, 309, 378n211, 392n309

Bagenal, Nicholas, 392n309

Beadle, Virginia de l'Etang, 13

Beecher, Catharine, 35, 367n35

Beeton, Isabella, xiii, 35, 367n35

Bell, Anne Olivier, 349

Bell, Clive, 269, 351–52, 387n270, 392n309
  Art, 389n284
  Bloomsbury group and, 210, 212–20, 222–23, 225–26, 229, 232–34, 263,

268, 275, 287, 379n214, 381n216, 383n226
  children's reflections on, 349–50
  marriage to Vanessa (*See under* Bell, Vanessa Stephen)
  Mary Hutchinson and, 303, 310–11, 313, 315
  Virginia's flirtation with, 248–54, 257–60, 265
  Woolfs' relationship with, 298–99, 313, 334–35, 384n244, 393n313
  World War I and, 306–7, 310

Bell, Julian Heward, 250, 257, 263, 272, 277, 305–6, 315–16, 319–21, 325–28, 377n210, 394n317, 394n327

Bell, Quentin, 132, 247, 320
  Bloomsbury group and, 255, 349–50, 384n255
  Bloomsbury Recalled, 115, 274, 283, 349, 373n115, 392n309, 394n327
  childhood of, 305–6, 315–16, 394n327
  father Clive and, 252–53, 263, 389n284
  Freshwater and, 368n38
  "Ludendorff Bell," 377n204
  Maynard Keynes and, 276, 381n216
  mother Vanessa and, 204, 277, 327, 378n211

Bell, Quentin (*cont.*)
  Vanessa Bell's Family Album and, 305, 327
  Virginia and, 293, 348, 384n244
  Virginia Woolf, 4, 6–7, 12, 45, 196–97, 349,
    363n14
Bell, Vanessa Stephen, 32, 48, 56, 59. *See also*
    Vanessa and Virginia's relationship
  Anne Thackeray Ritchie and, 80–81, 99,
    371n81
  as artist, 88, 165–66, 189, 191, 200, 231, 264,
    275, 303, 308, 376n185, 393n312
  Bloomsbury and Bloomsbury group and,
    210, 218, 223, 225–26, 229–34, 246,
    257, 263–66, 381n216
  brothers George and Gerald and, 114–15,
    195–201, 204, 377n204
  childhood of, 32, 38, 80–81, 83–84, 112,
    116, 118, 127, 151, 163
  daughter Angelica and, 320–21, 323–29,
    349
  Duncan Grant and, 263–64, 274–76,
    281–83, 300–311, 316–19, 393–94n316
  father Leslie and, 88, 102
  illness of, 234–41
  Jack Hills and, 198–200
  Laura Stephen and, 122
  letters of, 3, 191, 200–204, 318, 326
  Lytton Strachey and, 267–72, 282
  marriage to Clive, 59, 193, 239–54, 256–60,
    266–68, 271, 274–78, 281–83, 290,
    306, 310–13, 316–17, 324–25, 329, 340,
    350, 386n256, 388n277
  Maynard Keynes and, 268, 273–76
  mental illness of, 110, 237–38, 279–80
  mother Julia and, 145, 150, 158, 160, 173,
    176, 179, 187, 268
  move to Bloomsbury and, 202–3, 207–8
  Newnhamites and, 378n211
  photography of, 305, 327–28
  portrait of Thérèse de l'Etang and, 5, 12
  Roger Fry and, 276–85
  sister Stella and, 165–67, 182, 184–91
  Thackeray's estate and, 369–70n56
  Thoby's death and, 241–43
  Virginia compared to, 255, 264–65, 333,
    338

Bergen, George, 291n301, 350
Between the Acts (Woolf), 321–22, 344–46
Black, Ros, 9, 42–43
Bloomsbury and Bloomsbury group,
  207–60
  Bunny and Angelica and, 320–21
  "Cambridge" men and, 211–12, 214–19,
    223–26
  "Cropheads" and, 338, 378n211, 392n309
  George Duckworth and, 48
  homosexuality and, 46, 211, 215–18,
    220–21, 228
  misogyny and, 218–19, 221–24, 229,
    383n229
  move to, 56, 59, 202–3, 207–8
  Pattledom and, 22, 31, 38–39
  sadism and, 349–50
  sex and sexual morality and, 67, 79,
    263–65, 269–70, 301, 324
  Thoby's death and, 241–44
  Vanessa and Clive's marriage and, 241–54,
    256–60
  Victorian era and, 64–65
  Virginia and Vanessa's roles in,
    264–65
  Virginia's flirtation with Clive and,
    248–54, 257–60
  women associated with, 211, 378n211,
    385n252, 386n265
  World War I and, 306–7, 391–92n306
Bloomsbury Memoir Club, 49–51, 114–16,
    122, 161, 194, 197, 209, 211–12, 214,
    216, 218, 226–27, 270, 286, 369n49
Bodichon, Barbara Leigh Smith, 25, 159,
    365n25
Brontë, Charlotte, and family, 24–25, 63, 66,
    75, 143, 287
  Jane Eyre, 76, 81, 117, 371n75
Brooke, Rupert, 223–24, 273, 295, 304, 350,
    378n211
Browning, Elizabeth Barrett, xii–xiv, 25, 63,
    69, 82–84, 135, 287, 360n xiii
Browning, Robert, 25, 63
Burne-Jones, Edward, 25
Bussy, Dorothy Strachey, 337–38, 395n338
Butler, Belinda Norman, 121

Butler, Fanny Kemble, 81, 371–72n81
Butler, Samuel, *The Way of all Flesh,* 375n140

Cambridge Conversazione Society, 210,
    214–15, 227, 268, 377n210, 388n275
Cambridge University, 11, 47, 49, 56, 59–60,
    83–84, 377n210
    "Cambridge" men, 210–14, 216, 218,
        222–26, 228–29, 378n211
    King's College, 211–12, 216, 273, 379n213,
        381n216, 388n275
    Trinity College, 69–70, 88–89, 97, 137,
        162, 211–12, 214, 219, 223, 228, 273,
        378n211
    Trinity Hall, 89–91, 193, 211
Cameron, Charles Hay, 22–23, 33–34, 36–39,
    133, 366–67n33
Cameron, Julia Margaret Pattle
    "Annals of My Glasshouse," 34, 367n35
    childhood of, 7–8, 15
    high society and, 40, 87, 142
    Hogarth Press's volume of photographs,
        xxii, 3–4, 31
    Julia Stephen and, 141, 144, 156, 160
    Pattledom and, 18, 22, 24–25, 32–39,
        131–33
    photography of, 34–36, 38, 135, 141, 246,
        367nn34–35
    Thackerays and, 87
    Victorian Photographs of Famous Men and
        Women, 14, 38, 367n36
Carmichael-Smyth, Anne Becher Thackeray,
    68–71, 85, 87
Carmichael-Smyth, Henry, 68–70
Carnarvon, Lady, 195–96
Carrington, Dora, 246, 263, 265–66, 270,
    272–73, 287, 337–38, 378n211,
    386–87n270, 386n265, 393n310
catamites, 215–16, 380–81nn215–216
Cecil, Nelly (Lady Robert), 48–49, 209, 255,
    385n252
Charcot, Jean-Martin, 238, 294
Christie, Agatha, 20, 34, 234–35, 361n xvii
Colefax, Sybil, 50–51
Colette, 251, 254, 385n254
Collins, William Wilkie, 66, 76, 85

The Common Reader (Woolf), 331
The Complete Works of Sigmund Freud, 332,
    392n309
Cornhill, 61–62, 85–86, 95, 370n61
Cox, Katherine "Ka," 211, 279
Craig, Edy, xxii, 30, 338, 343–45, 366n30
Crowe, Amy and Eyre, 81–82
Cunningham, Michael, *The Hours,* 336

Dalrymple, John, 41
Dalrymple, Sophia Pattle, 5, 15–16, 22, 24,
    40–41, 70, 371n70
Dalrymple, Walter, 43
Dalrymple, William, 4–5, 10–11, 25, 41,
    362nn5–6, 364n21
Darwin, Charles, 22, 24, 35, 81
Darwin sisters, 223, 382n223
de l'Etang, Ambroise-Pierre-Antoine, 3–7,
    11–12, 40, 141, 362n6
de l'Etang, Thérèse Blin de Grincourt, xxi,
    xxiii, 3–13, 131, 362n6
DeSalvo, Louise, 119, 185, 196, 374n119
The Diary of Virginia Woolf (Woolf),
    296–99, 313, 369n50, 390n296,
    391n299
Dickens, Charles, 27, 63–64, 66–69, 77–78,
    83, 85, 366n27
Dickinson, Goldsworthy Lowes, 210, 284
Dickinson, Violet, 12, 48, 56–57, 168, 185, 189,
    193, 201, 208–9, 231, 234, 236–37, 239,
    241–44, 249–50, 254–55, 279, 284,
    287, 291–92, 341, 377n201, 378n211
Dictionary of National Biography, 37–38,
    62–64, 77, 82, 147, 284, 366n33
Disraeli, Benjamin, 24
Dodgson, Charles (Lewis Carroll), 29–30
Dreadnought Hoax, 383–84n230
Duckworth, George, 48, 208, 362n7
    after Stella's death, 189–90, 194–201,
        208
    childhood of, 139, 145, 375n141
    education and career of, 109, 162–63
    Laura Stephen and, 116–20, 122
    marriage of, 11, 230
    mother Julia and, 112, 176–77
    sister Stella and, 170, 175–77, 180, 186

Duckworth, George (*cont.*)
  Vanessa's relationship with, 195, 237, 242,
    245–46, 267, 302
  Virginia and Vanessa sexually abused by,
    114–16, 195–97
Duckworth, Gerald
  Bloomsbury group and, 226
  childhood of, 11, 141–42, 145
  education and career of, 109, 162–63,
    331
  Laura Stephen and, 116–19, 122
  mother Julia and, 112, 176–77
  move to Bloomsbury and, 208
  sister Stella and, 170, 175–77, 190
  Virginia sexually abused by, 114–16, 120,
    196–97, 322, 373n115
Duckworth, Herbert, 18, 48, 61, 112,
    136–43, 148–51, 154, 162–63, 178,
    374–75n136, 375n144
Duckworth, Margaret Herbert, 11, 48, 195,
    208, 230, 245–46
Duckworth, Sarah "Aunt Minna," 163,
    375n142

East India Company, 5–6, 13, 19–21, 32–33,
    68, 131, 364n19
Eliot, George, 25, 30, 63–64, 66–69, 82,
    85–86, 90, 92, 287
Eliot, T. S., 331–32
Euphrosyne, 214, 379n214

feminism and feminist theory, xv, xviii–xx,
    32, 158, 229, 270, 343
Fisher, Mary Jackson, and Herbert, 3, 80, 131,
    150, 153, 374–75n136
Fitzgerald, Edward, 371n77
Flush (Woolf), 83, 331
Forster, E. M., 210, 213, 263, 306, 338, 363n10,
    382n218, 388n272, 392n306
  The Longest Journey, 383n223
Freshwater (Woolf), 38–39, 343, 368n38
Fry, Helen Coombe, 277–78, 281,
    284
Fry, Roger, 207, 210, 212–13, 246, 274,

276–86, 300–303, 306, 324, 350,
    379n215, 389n284

Garnett, Angelica Bell
  Bloomsbury group and, 324–25, 349
  Bunny Garnett and, 263–64, 317, 319–25,
    394n325
  childhood of, 39, 315–19, 326, 349,
    393nn315–16
  Deceived with Kindness, 319, 328–29, 349
  mother Vanessa and, 201, 247–48, 266,
    321, 323–29, 394n327
  Vanessa Bell's Family Album and, 305
  Virginia and, 39, 248, 259–60, 327–29,
    348–49
Garnett, David "Bunny," 258, 263–64, 274,
    303–9, 317–23, 325, 387n270, 391n301,
    391n304, 392n309, 394n317, 394n325
  Aspects of Love (D. Garnett), 322–23,
    394n323
Garnett, Henrietta, 64, 72, 87, 111, 136,
    371nn70–72, 371n77, 372n101
  Wives and Stunners, 25
Garnett, Rachel Marshall, 320–21, 387n270
Gaskell, Elizabeth, xii–xiv, 24, 66, 69, 143
Gauthier-Villars, Henry, 254
Gill, Eric, 282, 389n282
Gladstone, William, 22, 24
Grant, Duncan, 334, 393–94n316
  Adrian's relationship with, 301–2, 304,
    383–84n230
  Angelica and Quentin and, 324–26,
    349–50
  biography of, 391n301, 394n316
  Bloomsbury group and, 210, 216, 246, 253,
    255–56, 263, 269, 271, 273–75, 280,
    300–302, 379nn214–15, 381n216,
    383n224
  Bunny Garnett and, 258, 303–9, 317–23,
    325
  Vanessa's relationship with, 39, 193, 258,
    263–64, 274–76, 281–83, 300–311,
    316–19, 324–25
  World War I and, 306–7

Hardinge, William, 380–81n215
Headlam, Walter, 249, 255, 385n255
Hill, Octavia, 174–76, 183, 360n xv
Hillier, May, 36, 367n36
Hills, Jack
 Julia Stephen and, 172–73, 376n173
 Laura Stephen and, 105, 121
 Maitland's biography of Leslie and, 105,
   203
 Stella Duckworth and, 171–72, 180–82,
   184, 190, 233–34, 240, 376n171
 Vanessa's relationship with, 198–200, 231,
   257, 302
 Virginia's relationship with, 104–5,
   184–85, 194
Hills, Stella Duckworth, 161–87
 childhood of, 109, 116, 118–19, 145, 153,
   161–68
 death of, 48, 185–86, 188–91, 198, 239–40,
   247
 engagement and marriage of, 104, 180–85,
   198–99, 239–40
 Laura Stephen and, 120, 123,
   183–84
 Leslie Stephen and, 162–64, 167–68, 171,
   173, 176, 179–82, 199–200
 mother Julia and, 139, 141–43, 156, 158,
   161–66, 170–78, 198, 327
 Virginia's relationship with, 165–68, 175,
   177–78, 182, 184–87, 203
Hobhouse, Arthur, 215, 379–80n215
Hogarth Press, 3–4, 31, 284, 289, 314, 331–32,
   336, 339, 342–43, 346, 395n331
Holmes, Oliver Wendell, 90, 107, 153
Holroyd, Michael, 27, 29, 271, 364n21,
   365–66n26, 381n216, 382n219,
   387–88nn270–271, 392n309
homosexuality, male, 43–46, 67, 79, 253, 273,
   284, 289, 311, 322, 350, 368nn44–45,
   371n77, 374n119, 379–82nn215–217,
   390n289, 392n309,
   395n338
 Bloomsbury and Bloomsbury group and,
   46, 211, 215–18, 220–21, 228

Labouchere Amendment, 368n44,
   380n215
Houlbrook, Matt, 217, 380n215
Hunt, William Holman, 25, 28, 41, 135,
   195
Hutchinson, Mary, 260, 269, 297, 303,
   310–13, 315, 337–38, 390n297
hysteria, 238–39, 384n238

Jackson, John, 131–34, 151
Jackson, Maria Pattle, 7, 9–12, 15, 23, 38, 47,
   120, 131–32, 135–36, 150–52, 154,
   159
Jacob's Room (Woolf), 57, 127, 203, 220–22,
   242, 331, 370n57
James, Henry, 51, 112, 195, 219, 226, 258, 338,
   382n219, 383n226
John of Gaunt, 43, 368n43
Jowett, Benjamin, 34, 222, 380–81n215

Kearney, Magda, 35
Kelly, Gerald, 232, 253, 384n232
Kew Gardens (Woolf), 331
Keynes, John Maynard, 89, 255, 393n316
 Angelica and, 320–21, 324–25
 biography of, 274, 305
 Bloomsbury group and, 210–11, 214–16,
   218, 246, 263, 265, 269, 271–76, 300,
   335, 379–81nn215–216, 383n224
 Dillwyn Knox and, 273, 388n273
 "The Economic Consequences of the
   Peace," 276
 as economist, 214, 216, 276, 334
 Essays in Biography, 214
 marriage of, 266, 311, 338
 Vanessa's relationship with, 268, 273–76,
   301, 304–5, 307, 311–12
 Virginia and, 49, 369n49
 World War I and, 295, 307, 391–92n306
Keynes, Lydia Lopokova, 216, 266, 276, 338
Kingsley, Mary, xvi
Knights, Sarah, 319, 391n304, 392n309,
   394n325
Knox, Dillwyn, 273, 388n273

Lamb, Walter, 252, 255, 379n214
Lawrence, D. H., 215, 312, 393n312
Lee, Hermione, 41, 111, 152, 196–97, 237, 290, 341
    Virginia Woolf, 397n347
Lehmann, John, 281, 289, 339, 346, 390n289
lesbianism, 79, 189, 253, 264, 287, 337–45, 385–86n256, 395n338
Lewes, George Henry, 25, 30
Lewis, Wyndham, 215, 379n215
Lowell, Robert, 291, 390n291
Lysistrata, 222

MacCarthy, Desmond, 49, 57, 210, 225–26, 269, 302–3, 370n57, 388n280, 392n306
MacCarthy, Mary Warre-Cornish (Molly), 269, 385n252
Maitland, Florence Fisher, 12, 104, 170
Maitland, Frederic, 104–6, 170, 195, 203, 377n210
Mallowan, Max, 234–35, 361n xvii
Mansfield, Katherine, 336–37
Marie Antoinette, 3–4, 7, 12, 40, 362n7
Marler, Regina, 318
Maurier, George du, 25, 365n25
Maxse, Kitty Lushington, 170, 375n136, 376n173
Melymbrosia (Woolf), 250
Midnight Society, 214, 218, 268, 379n214
Mill, John Stuart, xv, 90
Millais, John Everett, 25, 77
misogyny, 218–19, 221–24, 229, 382n221, 383n229
Mitchell, Silas Weir, 294
Moffat, Wendy, 382n218, 388n272
Monckton Milnes, Richard, 70, 84, 371n77, 378n211, 379n214
Moore, G. E., 210–14, 377n210, 387n270
Morrell, Lady Ottoline, 49, 267, 273, 277, 279, 305, 310, 383n226, 386n267, 388n275
Mortimer, Raymond, 272, 388n272
Mrs. Dalloway (Woolf), xxii, 294, 331

Murry, J. Middleton, *The Critic in Judgement,* 331

Nicolson, Harold, 340–42, 346, 396n341
Nicolson, Nigel, 189, 201, 377n201, 396n340
Night and Day (Woolf), 21, 49, 78, 101–3, 175, 331, 372–73nn101–102
Nightingale, Florence, 25, 82, 133, 135, 140, 159, 365n25
    Notes on Nursing, 149
Noel, Irene, 57, 222, 234, 370n57
Norton, Harry, 210, 212–13, 223–24, 265, 273, 277–78, 311, 378n211, 392n309

"Old Bloomsbury" (Woolf), 211, 226–27, 270, 286
Olivier sisters, 211, 312–13, 317
Orlando (Woolf), 12, 293, 331, 342–43, 346

Partridge, Frances Marshall, 211, 269, 387n270
Partridge, Ralph, 263, 378n211, 386–87n270
"The Pastons and Chaucer" (Woolf), xix
Pater, Walter, 380–81n215
Patmore, Coventry, 159
Pattle, Adeline de l'Etang, 7–8, 10, 13–17, 22, 131, 363n15
Pattle, James, 7, 13–15, 362n7, 363nn14–15
Pattle, Thomas, 13
Pattledom, 18–39, 364n18
    Bloomsbury and, 22, 31, 38–39, 246
    Julia Cameron and, 18, 22, 24–25, 32–39
    Julia Stephen and, 18–19, 25, 28–29, 31, 36–38, 114, 131–35, 140, 367n36
    Leslie Stephen and, 91, 130–35
    Sarah Prinsep and, 18, 21–23, 25–26, 28–29, 131–32, 366n26
Pattle family portrait (1818), 7, *8,* 362n7
Plato, *Phaedrus,* 215, 272, 381n215
Powell, Tristram, 4
Pre-Raphaelite Brotherhood, 25
Prinsep, Henry Thoby, 21–22, 26, 132–33, 143, 149–50
Prinsep, Sarah Pattle, 7–8, 15, 18, 21–23, 25–26, 28–29, 40, 131–33, 366n26

Prinsep, Valentine, 25, 28, 136, 365n25
"Professions for Women" (Woolf), 158

Raven-Hill, Anne, 233, 251–53, 257, 268–69, 385n252, 388n277
Raverat, Gwen Darwin and Jacques, 258
Ray, Gordon, 371n77
"Reflections on Sheffield Place" (Woolf), 388n271
"Reminiscences" (Woolf), 161–62, 169, 376n161
Ritchie, Anne Thackeray
  childhood of, 71–77, 81–87, 109
  Jane Shawe and, 371n73
  Julia Stephen and, 63, 80–81, 94, 96–99, 124, 144, 160, 375n144
  Leslie Stephen and, 63, 80, 91–94, 96–99, 179
  marriage of, 97–100, 108, 141
  mother Isabella and, 62, 71–73, 94, 109, 124, 374n121
  Pattledom and, 18, 24, 31, 37
  Stephen family and, 63, 80–81, 96–99, 107–9, 111–12, 114, 119, 121, 151, 371n81
  Thackeray's estate and, 57–58, 60–61
  William's death and, 79
  Woolf and, 63, 65, 78–81, 99–103, 189, 372n101
  as writer, 63–64, 69, 79, 83, 85–86, 96, 100, 372n83
Ritchie, Hester, 37, 57, 121, 372n101
Ritchie, Richmond, 97–100, 108, 141, 245
Ritchie, William, 57, 372n101
Robb, Graham, 25, 217, 368n44, 380n215
Roche, Paul, 326, 391n301
Roger Fry (Woolf), 284–85
A Room of One's Own (Woolf), xix–xx, xxiii, 60, 159, 296, 331, 342, 345
Rossetti, Christina, xii–xiv, 24, 360n xiii, 365n24
Rossetti, Dante Gabriel, 24–25, 30, 135
Rousseau, Jean-Jacques, *Julie, ou la nouvelle Héloïse,* 363n13
Ruskin, John, 27, 111–12, 165

Russell, Adeline Somers (Duchess of Bedford), 42, 45–48, 152
Russell, Bertrand, 42, 215, 272–73, 295, 377n210, 392n306
Russell, George (Duke of Bedford), 42
Rylands, George "Dadie," 272, 388n272

Sackville-West, Edward, 338–39, 341, 396n341
Sackville-West, Vita, 49, 338, 340–44, 346, 388n272, 396n340
  The Edwardians, 343
Saint-Pierre, Bernardin de, *Paul et Virginie,* 363n13
Sands, Ethel, 293, 328, 340
Sartoris, Adelaide Kemble, 81, 87, 371–72n81
Savage, Charles, 11, 104, 184, 190, 196, 208, 292, 294
Senhouse, Roger, 272, 338, 395n338
Shawe, Jane, 70, 94, 109, 371n73
Shove, Fredegond Fisher, 211, 298, 393n310
Shove, Gerald, 210, 225, 298, 378n211
"A Sketch of the Past" (Woolf), 42, 115, 161, 163, 165–66, 169, 171, 189, 203–4, 219, 373n117, 376n161, 377n188
Skidelsky, Robert, 274, 305
Smith, George, 58, 61–62, 87, 95, 370n61
Smith, Julia, 159
Smyth, Ethel, 3, 14, 31, 291, 294, 328, 335, 338–40, 342–44, 385n252, 389n286
Snowden, Margery, 168, 201, 231, 233, 238–39
Somers, Virginia Pattle (Countess), 9, 11, 15–16, 22, 24, 40–44, 47, 70, 131, 208, 369n49, 371n70
Somers-Cocks, Charles (Earl Somers), 9, 41–44
Somerset, Arthur (Lord), 368n45
Somerset, David, 46
Somerset, Henry (Lord), 42–46, 368n45
Somerset, Isabella Somers (Lady), xxi, 9, 42–46, 48, 368n42, 368n45, 369n50
Somerset, "Somey," 43–46
Spalding, Frances, 198, 258, 270, 281, 285, 290, 386n258, 389n284
Spooner, Deborah, 14–15, 362n6
Sprott, Sebastian, 216, 381n216

Stephen, Adrian, 59, 322
  Bloomsbury and, 56, 202, 208, 210, 230,
      243–44, 246–48, 252, 263, 275,
      278n211
  childhood of, 110–12, 116, 150–51, 163, 165,
      179, 184
  Dreadnought Hoax, 383–84n230
  Duncan Grant and, 301–2
  Laura Stephen and, 122
  trip to Greece and Turkey, 234–36
  Virginia and, 203
  World War I and, 306–7
Stephen, Caroline Amelia, 34, 80, 87, 208–9
Stephen, Fitzjames (Leslie's brother), 56, 80,
      88, 90, 110, 134, 137, 373n110, 374n119,
      377n210
Stephen, Harriet (Minny) Thackeray
  childhood of, 71–77, 81–87
  daughter Laura and, 98–99, 106–9, 111,
      114, 124
  death of, 96, 149
  marriage of, 60–63, 92–96, 107, 134–35,
      144, 374n121
  Pattledom and, 24
  Thackeray's estate and, 57–58, 60–61
  William's death and, 79
Stephen, James (Leslie's father), 88, 110
Stephen, J. K. "Jem," 110–11, 118–20, 123, 199,
      374n119
Stephen, Julia Jackson Duckworth, 127–60
  Anne Ritchie and, 63, 80–81, 94, 96–99,
      124, 375n144
  anti-feminism of, xv, 360n xv
  beauty of, 135–36, 139, 141, 155–57, 168–69
  daughter Stella and (*See under* Hills, Stella
      Duckworth)
  death of, 177–79, 186
  family home and, 59
  Herbert Duckworth's marriage to, 136–43,
      148, 150–51, 154, 375n136
  high society and, 45–48
  Laura Stephen and, 105, 109, 112–14,
      116–20, 144–45
  Leslie Stephen and death of, 179–80, 189,
      199–200

  Leslie Stephen's admiration for, 61, 91,
      131–32, 135
  Leslie Stephen's marriage to, 62, 98, 116,
      134, 144–55, 159–60, 239
  Leslie Stephen's relationship with, 60, 96,
      104–5, 108–9, 112, 142–44, 372n91
  Notes from Sickrooms, 149, 157
  nursing relatives and friends, 148–51, 164
  Pattledom and, 18–19, 25, 28–29, 31, 36–38,
      131–35, 140, 367n36
  Thérèse de l'Etang and, 9–11
  Virginia's childhood and memories of,
      127–30, 154–60, 169–70, 173, 177,
      187, 203
Stephen, Karin Costelloe, 211, 246, 301–2,
      385n252
Stephen, Katharine, 121–22
Stephen, Laura Makepeace, 104–24
  Anne Ritchie and, 64, 81
  childhood of, 96, 98–99, 105–9, 111–14,
      116–20, 145
  death of, 121–22
  father Leslie and, 104–12, 120–22
  institutionalization of, 105–6, 120–21, 152,
      161, 183
  Jack Hills and, 203
  Julia Stephen and, 105, 109, 112–14,
      116–20, 144–45, 152
  mental illness of, 64, 95, 109–11, 124
  mother Minny and, 98–99, 106–9, 111,
      114, 124
  possible sexual abuse of, 114, 116–19, 204
  Stella Duckworth and, 120, 123, 183–84
  Thackeray's estate and, 57–59
  Virginia and, 122–23, 183–84
Stephen, Leslie, 47–48, 66, 83–84, 87–88,
      90–91
  after deaths of Julia and Stella, 190–94
  Anne Ritchie and, 63, 80, 91–94, 96–99,
      179
  anti-feminism of, 360n xv
  biography of, 104–6, 203
  childhood and early life of, 88–90
  daughter Laura and, 104–12, 120–22
  death of, 202, 207–8

Herbert Duckworth and, 136–38, 140,
144, 154, 162–63
Julia Stephen and (*See under* Stephen, Julia Jackson Duckworth)
marriage to Minny, 92–96, 107, 134–35,
144, 374n121
Mausoleum Book, 92, 130, 132–33, 137,
151–52, 158–60, 170, 203, 375n150
Pattledom and, 22, 26, 31, 38, 91, 130–35
Stella Duckworth and (*See under* Hills,
Stella Duckworth)
Thackeray's estate and, 58–62
Virginia's childhood and memories of,
128–29, 184, 203, 227
writing and editorial work, 61–64, 77, 82,
90, 95, 370n61
Stephen, Thoby
Bloomsbury group and, 48, 202, 208–10,
213–14, 216–23, 225–33, 248, 268–69,
381n216
childhood of, 114, 116, 132, 150–51, 163,
165, 179
illness and death of, 241–44
Irene Noel and, 57, 370n57
Laura Stephen and, 114, 120–21
Leonard Woolf and, 286, 289
Leslie Stephen and, 193
mental illness of, 110
Stella Duckworth and, 182–83
Thackeray's estate and, 56–59
trip to Greece and Turkey, 57, 234–37
Vanessa and, 200, 232
Virginia and, 190, 200, 203
Stoppard, Tom, 380n215
Strachey, Alix Sargant-Florence, 211, 246,
309, 332, 337–38, 392–93nn309–310
Strachey, James, 210, 223–25, 246, 273, 332,
378n211, 392n309
Strachey, Lady, 16, 31, 41, 131
Strachey, Lytton, 27, 57, 78, 363n10, 392n309
Bloomsbury group and, 207, 210–19,
221–22, 224–26, 228–29, 233,
246–48, 311, 383n224
Bunny Garnett and, 319–20
"The Death of Milo," 271

Dora Carrington and, 246, 263,
265–66, 270, 272–73, 338,
386–87n270, 386n265, 386n270
Duncan Grant and, 300–301, 391n301
Eminent Victorians, 31, 273, 284,
387nn270–71
family of, 131, 378–79n212
homosexuality and, 379–81nn215–216
Leonard Woolf and, 10–11, 234,
379nn214–15
Roger Senhouse and, 272, 395n338
Vanessa's relationship with, 267–72, 282,
300–301, 304, 311
Virginia's relationship with, 103, 252–53,
255–57, 286–87, 292, 329, 387n271,
388–89n280, 389n286
voice of, 387n270
World War I and, 306, 392n306
Swinburne, Algernon, 84, 215, 222–23,
379n214
Swithinbank, Bernard, 224, 383n224
Sydney-Turner, Saxon, 210, 212–14,
218–19, 222, 224–27, 230, 252, 277,
296, 379n214, 383n224, 392n306,
392n309

Tennyson, Alfred, 22, 24, 34–35, 38–39, 63,
70, 101, 197, 241, 378n211
Ternan, Ellen, 27, 77–78, 85, 366n27
Terry, Ellen, 26–30, 36, 39, 338, 343, 345,
365n26, 366n30
Terry, Kate, 27–29
Thackeray, Anne (Edward's daughter), 82,
107–8
Thackeray, Edward, and family, 82, 92, 98,
108
Thackeray, Isabella Shawe, 63–65, 70–74, 85,
92, 94, 109, 119, 121, 124, 374n121
Thackeray, Margaret, 82, 107–8, 372n82
Thackeray, Richmond, 20, 68–69, 74
Thackeray, William Makepeace
birth and early life of, 68–71, 85
estate of, 57–60, 87
high society and, 51, 378n211
"Lord Bateman," 56–57

Thackeray, William Makepeace (*cont.*)
    marriage and family life of, 70–79,
        81–87, 94–95, 109, 124, 371n72,
        371n77, 374n121
    Pattledom and, 24–25, 364n19
    Pendennis, xvi, 361n xvi
    Vanity Fair, 58, 67, 69, 82, 364n19, 371n77
    Virginia Pattle's beauty and, 40
    Virginia Woolf and, 64–65, 101
    as writer, 66–69, 74–77, 100
Thomas, Jean, 279, 385n256
Thorpe, Jeremy, 217, 318n217
Three Guineas (Woolf), xvi, xix–xx, 159, 295, 331
Thynne, Beatrice, 50, 189, 255, 369n50
Thynne, Katherine, 50, 255
To the Lighthouse (Woolf), 32, 127, 130, 147,
    155, 160, 169–71, 177, 192, 203, 247,
    293, 296, 331, 333, 342
Trefusis, Violet, 342–44, 396n340
Turnbaugh, Douglas Blair, 391n301, 394n316
22 Hyde Park Gate, 38, 55–56, 64, 122–23,
    146, 153, 363n15, 369n56, 373–74n117
"22 Hyde Park Gate" (Woolf), 129

Vanessa and Virginia's relationship, 297,
    333–34, 341–42, 391n298
    Charleston situation and, 308–11, 313–16,
        318–19
    Vanessa as mother of Angelica and,
        327–28, 393n316
    Virginia's flirtation with Clive and,
        248–53, 257–58, 265, 386n258
    Virginia's marriage and, 287–92, 334–35
    Virginia's protectiveness, 349
    work for each other, 331–32, 393n312
Vanessa Bell's Family Album, 305, 327–28
Vaughan, Adeline Jackson, 80, 131, 141, 150, 154
Vaughan, Henry, 80, 150, 153, 375n150
Vaughan, Madge Symonds, 200–201, 208–9,
    242–43, 291, 384n243
Vaughan cousins, 168, 193, 200, 369n49
The Voyage Out (Woolf), 127, 145–47, 160,
    375n145

Waterlow, Sydney, 255, 259
Watts, George Frederick, 26–30, 32, 36, 39,
    240, 366n27, 368n42
The Waves (Woolf), xvii, 185, 331, 333
Webb, Sidney and Beatrice Potter, 360n xv
Webber, Andrew Lloyd, 323
Wedgwood, Josiah, 22, 24
Wellesley, Dorothy, 337–38, 342–44,
    397n351
Wellesley, Gerald, 351, 397n351
Woolf, Leonard, 12, 19–20, 360n xv
    Angelica and, 320–21, 328–29
    Anne Thackeray Ritchie and, 100–101
    autobiography of, 47–48, 174, 347
    Bloomsbury group and, 39, 210, 212–14,
        217–19, 225–26, 228–29, 246–47,
        253, 256, 268, 274, 334–35, 349–50,
        379nn214–15, 388n280
    Clive Bell compared to, 334, 393n313
    Downhill All the Way, 346
    as Jew, 10–11, 130, 290, 295, 334–35, 347
    Laura Stephen and, 122
    Night and Day and, 102, 372n102
    Vanessa described by, 231–32, 237–38
    The Village in the Jungle, 10–11
    Virginia's marriage to, 59, 99–100, 130,
        181, 189, 259, 265–66, 284, 286–98,
        313–14, 318, 322, 330–36, 346–47,
        389n286
    The Wise Virgins, 335–36, 390n298
    World War I and, 295, 306–7, 392n306
Woolf, Virginia
    childhood of, 19, 26, 32, 38, 80–81, 83–84,
        112, 116, 127–30, 132, 151, 163, 165–66
    death of, 322, 347
    maternal lineage of, 2, 7–8
    mental illness of, 95, 99, 104–5, 110–11, 123,
        184, 186, 190, 196–97, 201, 208–9,
        291–98, 336, 347, 390n291
    seven siblings of, 54
    sexual abuse of, 114–16, 119–20, 196–97,
        204, 322, 373nn115–16
Writer's Diary (Woolf), 361n xx

The Years (Woolf), 167, 175, 203, 331, 373n116